ReORIENT

Global Economy in the Asian Age

Andre Gunder Frank

UNIVERSITY OF CALIFORNIA PRESS

Berkeley / Los Angeles / London

University of California Press
Berkeley and Los Angeles, California

University of California Press, Ltd.
London, England

Library of Congress Cataloging-in-Publication Data

Frank, Andre Gunder, 1929-
    ReORIENT: global economy in the Asian Age / Andre Gunder
Frank.
        p.   cm.
    Includes bibliographic references and index.
    ISBN 0-520-21129-4 (alk. paper)
    ISBN 0-520-21474-9 (pbk. : alk. paper)
    1. International economic relations—History.   2. Capitalism—
History.   3. Competition, International—History.   4. Economic his-
tory.   I. Title.   HF1359.F697   1998
    337—dc 21   97-24106

Printed in the United States of America
9 8 7 6 5 4 3 2 1

There is no history but universal history—as it really was.

Leopold von Ranke

Il n'y a pas d'histoire de l'Europe, il y a une histoire du monde!

Marc Bloc

History is marked by alternating movements across the imaginary line that separates East from West in Eurasia.

Herodotus

History is all things to all men. . . . Perhaps the most important methodological problem in the writing of history is to discover why different historians, on the basis of the same or similar evidence, often have markedly different interpretations of a particular historical event.

R. M. Hartwell

The great enemy of truth is very often not the lie—deliberate, contrived and dishonest—but the myth—persistent, persuasive and unrealistic.

John F. Kennedy

orient: The East; lustrous, sparkling, precious; radiant, rising, nascent; place or exactly determine position, settle or find bearings; bring into clearly understood relations; direct towards; determine how one stands in relation to one's surroundings. Turn eastward.
reorient: Give new orientation to; readjust, change outlook.

from *The Concise Oxford Dictionary*

Contents

Preface

*I think authors ought to look back and give us some record of how their works
developed, not because their works are important (they may turn out to be
unimportant) but because we need to know more of the process of history-writing. . . .
Writers of history are not just observers. They are themselves part of the act and need
to observe themselves in action.*

John King Fairbank (1969: vii)

In this book I turn received Eurocentric historiography and social theory upside down by using a "globological" perspective (the term is
taken from Albert Bergesen's 1982 article). Early modern economic history is viewed from a world-encompassing global perspective. I seek to
analyze the structure and dynamic of the whole world economic system
itself and not only the European (part of the) world economic system.
For my argument is that we must analyze the whole, which is more
than the sum of its parts, to account for the development even of any
of its parts, including that of Europe. That is all the more so the case
for "the Rise of the West," since it turns out that from a global perspective Asia and not Europe held center stage for most of early modern
history. Therefore the most important question is less what happened
in Europe than what happened in the world as a whole and particularly
in its leading Asian parts. I render historical events from this much
more global perspective and propose to account for "the Decline of the
East" and the concomitant "Rise of the West" within the world as a
whole. This procedure pulls the historical rug out from under the *anti*-
historical/scientific—really ideological—Eurocentrism of Marx, Weber,

Toynbee, Polanyi, Braudel, Wallerstein, and most other contemporary social theorists.

Since as Fairbank observes, writing history is part of history itself, I will follow his counsel to give the reader some record of how my work developed. I will signal only the most significant intellectual way stations and avoid wasting the reader's time with nonessential personalisms. Yet I cannot avoid reference to at least some persons who—often unintentionally—have lighted the way to me and to whom I wish to express my thanks in this preface.

My anthropologist friend Sid Mintz and I have been debating without end since the mid-1950s. He has said, "Culture matters"; and I have always retorted, "Structure matters." My thesis was first impressed on me in the seminar with the eminent cultural anthropologist Robert Redfield, audited on the second floor of the social science building at the University of Chicago. That is where I was introduced to holism and the importance of its pursuit in social science. In the parallel graduate-student coffee-time "seminar," I argued that what Redfield was missing was structure. Perhaps I had gotten the idea the previous semesters, when I had audited the visiting structural functionalist anthropologists Raymond Firth and Meyer Fortes. I say "audited," because I was supposed to be up on the fourth floor of the social science building, where I was getting my Ph.D. in the Department of Economics. Since then, the members and products of this department and their brethren outliers in the University of Chicago's business and law schools (some of them my then fellow economics graduate students) have gotten about half the Nobel prizes in economics granted in this world, among them five in the last six years. I, on the other hand, flunked my Ph.D. exam three times in a row in inter-*national* economics, which was my strongest field on the fourth floor; the significance of the hyphen and the italic typeface in the adjective preceding "economics" above should become evident in the present book. The previous sentence may also offer clues to why I felt more comfortable on the second floor. However, much of the "the personal is political" and theoretical intellectual account is already related in my autobiographical "Underdevelopment of Development" (Frank 1991c, 1996). So here I will stick only to what seems most germane for the history behind this book, which pretends to rewrite history.

In 1962 I went to Latin America, armed with the names of some friends given to me by Eric Wolf, also an anthropologist—and with his early writings on how world capitalism had intervened to form (or underdevelop) parts of Mesoamerica. In 1963 in Rio de Janeiro I wrote *On Capitalist Underdevelopment* (Frank 1975); and in 1965 in Mexico I debated in a national newspaper with Rodolfo Puiggros, who defended the then received wisdom that Latin America had been feudal (reprinted in Frank 1969). The 1963 manuscript had opened with a critique of received theory (it was published in revised form in 1967 as "The Sociology of Development and the Underdevelopment of Sociology" and was reprinted in Frank 1969). It was a scathing critique of all the theory I had received on both floors of the social science building as well as from the library at the University of Chicago. In particular relevance to the present book, my critique was directed most of all against Weberian sociology, transmitted to my generation by Talcott Parsons in his mistitled *The Structure of Social Action* ([1937] 1949) and *The Social System* (1951). It was applied to the "Third World modernization theory" by my still good friend and former mentor Bert Hoselitz, as well as by my friend Manning Nash and others there and elsewhere. After reading my draft, Nancy Howell advised me to keep only the theoretical references to them and to take out all the many personal ones, which I then did. Now she again asks me to do the same in the present work, especially with regard to herself; but this time I am more reluctant to do so.

In all these and other works, I sustained that "not feudalism, but capitalism" had generated "the development of underdevelopment" in Latin America and elsewhere in the "Third" World. The crucial factors in this underdevelopment, I argued, were not so much "internal" to any of its regions, let alone due to its peoples, but were generated by the *structure and function* of the "world system" itself, of which all were integral parts. However, I then wrote and continued to think that the "capitalist world system" was born when Columbus "discovered" America. That is why in the early 1970s in Chile I entitled a book analyzing the development of that system *World Accumulation 1492–1789* (Frank 1978a). My account had reached only as far as the latter date when the 1973 military coup in Chile sent my family and me back to my birthplace in Berlin.

Events in Chile before the coup already had obliged me to jump a couple of centuries ahead to concern myself with the present world economic crisis of accumulation, an expression of which I regarded the Chilean coup itself. So that is what I then did in several books and countless articles for the next two decades. Nonetheless in the back of my mind, I kept harboring the sneaking suspicion that if "the system" had been born in 1492, or had emerged since 1450 as Wallerstein announced, it could not have just done so suddenly like Pallas Athene out of the head of Zeus. *Something* before, maybe even also systemic, must have led up to the voyages of Columbus and Vasco da Gama and to the rise of the "world capitalist system."

While still in Chile, I wrote a blurb for the dust jacket of the first edition of the first volume of Immanuel Wallerstein's *The Modern World-System* (1974). I said that it is a rendition of "the early development of a world economy, the understanding of which is essential for the proper appreciation of all subsequent development. This book should become a classic immediately upon publication." (It did.) The other two dust-jacket blurbs were by Fernand Braudel and Eric Wolf. Braudel said that historians already knew that "Europe had formed a world economy around itself. What they had never thought of . . . [and] which characterizes I. Wallerstein's thought is that this entity [the world-system] provides a new framework for the subject of European history, that . . . is compelling." Eric Wolf's blurb said that the book would become indispensable for understanding the development of the world system and that "it is a book that people will have to deal with, argue with, cite, learn by *in order to* make their own points, take their own departures." I cite these blurbs here because of how revealing they are for subsequent developments related below.

Some of these developments ran in several parallel strands but need not be related here, because they were already signaled in the preface to my *World System: Five Hundred Years or Five Thousand?* (Frank and Gills 1993). Nonetheless, I wish to bring at least the following developments together in this preface, because they are also essential to an understanding of the genesis and purpose of the present book.

Eric Wolf wrote *Europe and the People Without History* (1982) to show how they had been incorporated into the modern world-system at the cost of much of their own welfare and culture. Since his thesis is that they *do* have a history, he placed a question mark after the title; but the publishers didn't like it and took it off again. Publishers never like question marks: the same thing happened to Michael Barratt Brown with his *After Imperialism* (1963), or so both authors told me. Eric Wolf's editor, Stanley Holwitz, had invited me to referee the book for publication, but alas for family reasons I had to decline. I much appreciated the book, and not only because its introduction singled out Wallerstein's and my above cited books as the forerunners of his own. At a public tribute to Eric at the 1990 meetings of the American Anthropo-

logical Association, I tried to set the record straight after a student had
said that my work had been a major influence on Wolf's. On the contrary I pointed out, Eric and his work had been the most important
early influence on mine in showing me my way to and around Latin
America: it was Eric who had signaled that all this was about the world
capitalist system, already in colonial times.

It turned out for two reasons to be a good thing that I had been
obliged to decline to referee Wolf's book. One day at my dinner table
in Amsterdam, I told him privately that I was appalled at what then
seemed to me a "giant step backward" in his book, which said that
"capitalism" began in 1800 and not in 1492 as he had previously led me
to believe. The second reason is that since that dinner-table conversa-
tion I have found more reason to agree with his book's thesis after
all, as my present book demonstrates. For, if there is such a thing as
"capitalism" at all, which I now doubt, it would seem better to date it
from the industrial revolution in Europe since 1800, as Wolf claims. But
now I also see that the "world system" to which he and I referred in
our blurbs for Wallerstein's book began much earlier than any of us
three imagined. However that also opens the question of what it means,
if anything, to call the world economy or system "capitalist."

Then Janet Abu-Lughod (1989) wrote *Before European Hegemony:
The World System A.D. 1250–1350*. Some years before the publication of
the book itself, a special issue of a journal was devoted to the discussion
of an article-length version of her thesis. The editor asked me to contribute a comment, which I did (Frank 1987). That led me back to my
"sneaking suspicion" about the possible earlier roots of the "modern"
world system. Abu-Lughod confirmed them by laying them bare for
the "thirteenth-century world system," as she called it. But she said that
it was only a forerunner of the different modern one, for which she
accepted Wallerstein's thesis of its independent (re)invention after 1450.
The main point of my critique was extended in my review of her book
(Frank 1990b): the "modern capitalist world-system" was not the rein-
vention, but the *continuation* of Abu-Lughod's version of the *same*
world system already in existence since at least 1250. However, if this
world system already existed two hundred years before Wallerstein's
starting date of 1450, then why not still earlier?

In the preface to my *World Accumulation 1492–1789*, I had quoted and
followed another admonition, which I called Fairbank's (1969: ix) Rule
No. 2: "*Never* try to begin at the beginning. Historical research prog-
resses backward, not forward. . . . Let the problems lead you back." The

"problem" was the origin—and therewith the nature—of the "world system," and my time had finally come to let it lead my historical research backward as far as the evidence could take me. If the beginnings of "the system" were not in 1800, nor in 1492 or 1450, nor in 1250, then perhaps around A.D. 1000. Of course, Wallerstein did not and still does not want to admit any of this, even though he would write that it is clearly laid out and widely accepted that "the long swing was crucial." According to him, this swing was upward after 1450, but downward from 1250 to 1450, and previously upward from 1050 to 1250 (Wallerstein 1992, circulated in manuscript in 1989). As editor of *Review,* he graciously published my first article, which argued that we probably can and should trace the origins of the world system back much farther still, among other reasons because of this long cycle cited by Wallerstein himself (Frank 1990a).

Barry Gills had already written (but never published) something similar on his own several years before. When he read the draft of my 1989 article, we made the initially obvious connection and then started to work it out. The results were our joint articles on "The Cumulation of Accumulation," on long cycles from 1700 B.C. to A.D. 1700, on an interdisciplinary introduction to the five-thousand-year world system, and the book *The World System: Five Hundred Years or Five Thousand?* of which we are contributing editors (Gills and Frank 1990/91, 1992; Frank and Gills, 1992, 1993). Gills generously shared his erudition with me, both of his historical lore and of his theoretical sophistication. He also loaned me much of his well-selected library and his own early manuscripts. Therein, he was of enormous help to push or allow me to go much further much faster than I otherwise might have. However, he also drew me into some directions about "international relations" and "hegemony" that I liked less and pursued mostly for the sake of our collaboration.

At the same time, Christopher Chase-Dunn had begun to collaborate with Thomas D. Hall. Chris had been a number-cruncher who had, among many other things, "tested" and found support for my and others' dependency theory. Simultaneously, but mostly separately, we were also pioneers in incorporating the analysis of the Soviet Union and other socialist countries into that of the "capitalist world system." Tom Hall's work on tribal and nomad societies in the American Southwest expanded to include nomads elsewhere and with Chase-Dunn also included "marcher states" on the "borders" of or temporarily outside the world system. Together, they embarked on constructing more world system theory on the basis of their comparative analysis of several little and big "world-systems." These include several small ones but also the major one Gills and I were researching and David Wilkinson's "central civilization," the combination of which Chase-Dunn and Hall rebaptized as the "central world system."

Chase-Dunn also encouraged me to go to the 1989 meeting of the International Society for the Comparative Study of Civilizations (ISCSC), where I met Wilkinson and Stephen Sanderson. From there, I went on to the 1989 meeting of the World History Association (WHA), where I met William McNeill, who has encouraged my work on history ever since. Jerry Bentley, the editor of the just-launched WHA *Journal of World History* also attended both meetings and subsequently published my review of Abu-Lughod and my "Plea for World System History" (Frank 1990b, 1991a). Stephen Sanderson has also been working on parallel strands in his *Social Transformations* (1995). The book includes a study of Japanese development as parallel to that of Britain, which I also use in the present book. Sanderson subsequently edited a special issue of the ISCSC journal *Comparative Civilizations Review,* which led to his edited book of comparative studies, *Civilizations and World Systems* (1995). It contains contributions by most of the above-named authors and also includes my "Modern World System Revisited: Re-reading Braudel and Wallerstein" (Frank 1995). Simultaneously, George Modelski and William R. Thompson (1992, 1996) have expanded their long-standing collaboration from their earlier focus on post-1494 political hegemony and war in the European world to the study of innovation and Kondratieff waves starting in A.D. 930 in China and also to prehistoric world system evolution. The collaboration, help, and encouragement of these colleagues and now also friends was already acknowledged in greater detail in the preface to *The World System: Five Hundred Years or Five Thousand?* (Frank and Gills 1993) and is gladly reaffirmed here.

The thesis of this Frank and Gills book is that the same features that characterize Wallerstein's "modern" five-hundred-year-old world system can also be found in the *same* system going back at least five thousand years. David Wilkinson and Jonathan Friedman and Kaisa Ekholm joined us with their similar theses (which were worked out separately long ago but by now were mutually influential). My friends (and co-authors of two other books on more recent times) Immanuel Wallerstein and Samir Amin contributed chapters, which demur from the pre-1500 thesis. Wallerstein (1991, 1993) answered, defending his world-system with a hyphen against my world system without a hyphen and still insists that we should "hold the tiller firm" (Wallerstein 1995). Both he and Amin continue to stand their ground in their contributions to a festschrift in my honor (Chew and Denemark, 1996). Abu-Lughod declined to take a stand on this issue and argued that we can't tell if we are now dealing with the same or a new world system in modern times (Frank and Gills, 1993).

The modern "father" of world history, William McNeill, was kind enough to write a foreword (and also to contribute it to my festschrift in "representation of historians"). He now agrees that his own *The Rise of the West* (1963) devoted insufficient attention to world systemic connections and that we must now increasingly map them through all networks of communication. I agree. McNeill's University of Chicago colleague Marshall Hodgson and I shared an apartment in 1954. Marshall talked to me about his own writings, some of which are only now collected in Hodgson's posthumously published *Rethinking World History* (1993). Alas at the time, I was quite unable to understand what he was talking about. If I had understood, it would have saved me about forty years of wandering near-blindly through the historical woods. Only now do I profusely cite and studiously follow Hodgson's guides to rethinking world history.

One way to answer Abu-Lughod's question about whether we are dealing now with the same or a new world system and also to do as McNeill and Hodgson counsel would seem to be to attempt two related things: One is to trace the roots of Abu-Lughod's thirteenth-century world system backward, which she said she was not interested in doing. But I was and did (Frank and Gills 1993). The other task is to look for the possible continuation of Abu-Lughod's system or Frank and Gills's five-thousand-year one into early modern times, which she also declined to do. Therefore, that is the task I undertake in the present book. However, doing so also poses many questions about what the implications of our reading of history before 1500 are for the reinterpretation of the early modern (and eventually contemporary and future) history of the world system since 1500.

In 1993 I read the third volume of Braudel's (1992) trilogy, *The Perspective of the World*, and I re-read some Wallerstein to do an internal critique of their writings (Frank 1995). I confined myself to showing how their own data and especially Braudel's observations about them flatly contradict their own thesis on the European-centered world-economy/system. An earlier version of the same critique had been published as "The World Economic System in Asia before European Hegemony" (Frank 1994). This title combined elements of Wallerstein's and Abu-Lughod's titles with that of the then recently published *Asia before Europe* by K. N. Chaudhuri (1990a). Both authors had shown that Asia was far more important, if not hegemonic, in the world economy before Europe. Re-reading Braudel and Wallerstein showed that, despite themselves and contrary to their own thesis, there were *not several* world economies in the early modern era. Instead there was *only one* world economy and system in which Europe was not and could not have been hegemonic, as they mistakenly claimed. Thus, also contrary to their claims, this world economy and system also could not have started in Europe.

Here the significance of the three dust-jacket blurbs for Wallerstein's first edition of *The Modern World-System* will have become apparent. Braudel said that Wallerstein provided a new framework for the subject of European history so that they could better reinterpret what historians already knew, that is that *Europe had formed a world around itself*. I had written in my blurb that the book would be an instant classic, because we needed it *for the proper appreciation of all subsequent development*. And Eric Wolf added that Wallerstein's was a book that people would have to argue with and learn by *in order to take their own departures*.

Yes indeed, for my critiques of Braudel and Wallerstein do learn from and argue with Wallerstein to suggest that Braudel is both right and wrong: Wallerstein provides a better framework for the subject of European history, but not for world history, Wallerstein's title notwithstanding. And Braudel and other historians are wrong to have "known" all along that Europe had formed a world "around itself." My above-cited critiques show on their own evidence that Europe did not expand to "incorporate" the rest of the world into its "European world-economy/ system." Instead, Europe belatedly joined, or at least cemented its previously looser ties with, an already existing world economy and system. To combine Abu-Lughod's and Chaudhuri's titles, pride of place belonged to *Asia Before European Hegemony*. Or to add Braudel's and Wallerstein's own titles as well, we need a new *Perspective of the Modern World System of Asia Before European Hegemony*.

In this regard, I have related before (in Frank 1991c, 1996) what my then about fifteen-year-old sons told me almost two decades ago. Their remarks turn out to be even more relevant to the thesis of the present book than I or they could have realized at the time: Paulo said that if Latin America was colonial, it *could not* have been feudal; Miguel said that England is an *underdeveloping* country. The significance of these observations to the present book is several-fold. If Latin America was colonial, it was so because it was part and parcel of the world system. Therefore, not only can it make no sense to call it "feudal," but it also makes questionable sense to categorize it at all—even as "capitalist"—other than as a dependent part of the world economy or system. What do we gain by any such definition, if we can even "define" it at all? Really nothing: indeed this focus on "modes of production" only diverts our attention from the much more importantly defining world system of which everything is a part, as I have already argued elsewhere (Frank 1991a, b, 1996; Frank and Gills 1993).

In that world economy/system, we can observe "the development of underdevelopment" here and there, then and now. Much of Latin America and Africa are still underdeveloping. However, now we can also observe that "Great" Britain is also underdeveloping, as my son Miguel had observed in 1978, before Margaret Thatcher took over as prime minister. Miguel (and maybe Mrs. Thatcher) lacked sufficient world systemic hindsight to make the following observation, but in fact we can see that Britain has been *under*developing since the beginning of the Great Depression in 1873. How so? Even with the benefit of Wallerstein's modern-world-system perspective, we can now see that some sectors, regions, countries, and their "economies" not only move up, but also *move down* in their relative and even absolute positions within the world economy and system as a whole. Britain began its decline over a century ago, when its pride of place began to be taken by Germany and North America. They fought two world wars—or one long war from 1914 to 1945—to dispute who would take Britain's place. Alas for some, today their place in the sun is also being displaced by the "Rising Sun" in East Asia. One of the theses of this book is that these developments should come as no surprise, because parts of East Asia already were at the center of the world economy/system until about 1800. In historical terms, "the Rise of the West" came late and was brief.

So one of my early purposes in the present book is to show first that there already was an ongoing *world* economy before the Europeans had much to do and say in it. There are two naturally derivative points: One is to show that Asia, and especially China and India, but also Southeast Asia and West Asia, were more active and the first three also more important to this world economy than Europe was until about 1800. The other derivative point is that therefore it is completely counterfactual and antihistorical to claim that "historians already knew that Europe built a world around itself." It did not; it used its American money to buy itself a ticket on the Asian train. However, this historical fact has still other far-reaching implications, both for history and for social theory based on historical understanding.

Under the title "Let's Be Frank about World History," my friend Albert Bergesen (1995) points out that the proposition "the world economy/system did not begin in Europe" also pulls the rug out from *all* Eurocentric social theory. It is based on the temporal precedence and structural priority of a Europe around which the remainder of the world was allegedly built. If Europe did not have this place and function, then the derived Eurocentric social theory also does not rest on the firm historical foundation that it claims to have in what historians "knew." Thus, the very scaffolding of Western social theory threatens to come tumbling down around us. It now does so through its own undoing or at least through the wrongdoing of its principal architects and all the "master" builders who constructed their theoretical scaffolding and built on unstable historical foundations. As I show in chapter 1, these architects of our social theory include Marx, Weber, Werner Sombart, Karl Polanyi, and others, as well as Braudel and Wallerstein (and indeed Frank 1978a, b). All of them (mis)-attributed a central place in their theories to Europe, which it never had in the real world economy. How and where does that leave us? Well, just about like the proverbial (European/American/Western) Emperor Who Had No Clothes. Naked!

More or less well-known critiques of this Eurocentrism have already been made at the ideological level by Edward Said (1978) in his discussion of the idea of *Orientalism,* Martin Bernal (1987) when he argued for the African origins of Western culture in *Black Athena,* and Samir Amin (1989) when he inveighed against *Eurocentrism,* as well as others cited in chapter 1. I mention these three here mostly as other precursory strands for the critical part of this book. Another major one is J. M. Blaut (1993a), who literally demolishes all the myths of European "exceptionalism" in *The Colonizer's Model of the World.* All these writers have done yeomen work to point out the now naked Eurocentric Emperor. So what is to be done, as Lenin might have said? Bergesen insists that we do something "globological" about it, even if it is not yet quite clear just how to do it.

It is not my purpose to fashion a new set of clothes for the same old Eurocentric Emperor, although others who are too embarrassed by his new-found nakedness may wish to try. I frankly prefer no emperor at all. However, I am not naive enough to think that we can just think him away. Nor will it do simply to "deconstruct" him and his garb, postmodernist fashion. I do believe that we are in dire need of an alternative *Perspective of the World* for the new world (dis)order in the making.

The World System: Five Hundred Years or Five Thousand? (with a question mark!) was my first attempt to fashion an alternative "perspective of the world" and analytical tool to grapple with its own structure and function. Marta Fuentes used to say that I was still a "functionalist," because I asked her all the time what the sense was of this, that, or the other. She said that by "sense" I really meant "function" within the structure of the system. She thought it was all only in my head. I think the system is really out there in the real world, and it is about time that we fashion ourselves at least a rudimentary mental picture of this system, its structure, and its dynamic. My friend Robert Denemark agrees. He co-edited the festschrift for me, which was nice of him. However, he is also very demanding of both of us. He insists that we must, and helps me to, study the *whole* (system), which is more than the sum or its parts. That is, we need a more holistic theory and analysis of the whole world, and not of just the part that centers around Europe.

Alas, we lack even an adequate terminology, not to mention the analytic constructs and overarching theory, to replace "international" trade and other relations. To say instead "world trade" in the "global system" (or vice versa) is only a small step in the right direction, if that. The point is to elucidate how the flow of trade and money through the "body" of the world's economy is analogous to the oxygen-carrying blood that pulses through the circulatory system (or to the other information carried by the nervous system). The world economy also has a skeleton and other structures; it has organs that are vital to its survival but whose "function" is also bodily determined; it has cells that live and die and are replaced by others; it has daily, monthly, and other short and long cycles (indeed, a life cycle); and it seems to be part of an evolutionary (albeit not predestined) scheme of things. Last but by no means least, our world economy and "system" is not independent of the ecology or the cosmos, with both of which it can and does have mutual interactions, which also bear more and more systematic attention. The other co-editor of the festschrift for me, Sing Chew, insists that my attempts at "humanocentric" analysis are not enough. What we need, he says, is "ecocentric" theory *and praxis*. Alas, we or at least I lack even the conceptual wherewithal adequately to address either of these problematiques, let alone their combination.

This book is my first more holistic attempt at extending Denemark's and my "perspective of the (whole) world" onward to early modern world economic history. The task is to attempt to see how the structure/function/dynamic of the world economy/system itself influences, if not determines, what happened—and still happens-in its various parts. The whole is not only greater than the sum of its parts. It also shapes the parts and their relations to each other, which in turn transform the whole.

So this is the record of how the beginnings of the present work developed out of partly parallel and partly already intermingled strands. This book now seeks to go beyond these roots in order to make my own points and take my own departures, as Eric Wolf correctly predicted. That means to take and make a departure, indeed a radical break, also from him and all the others—including myself—cited above. Nonetheless, I gratefully acknowledge much help from *all* of them and others.

I gladly accepted the invitation in March 1994 from my often co-author Barry Gills and his University of Newcastle to begin the joint construction there of such an alternative perspective. Its twenty-page first draft was entitled "The Modern World System under Asian Hegemony: The Silver Standard World Economy 1450–1750" (Gills and Frank 1994). This work was interrupted, largely due to illness on my part. Only in late 1995 did it become possible again for me to pursue and now to expand this work, but now, after my retirement from the University of Amsterdam, on my own here in Toronto.

Not really on my own! For Nancy Howell and I were married in Toronto in 1995, and she has given me untold emotional and moral support to resume this project and carry it further as the present book. It would and could not ever have been undertaken, let alone completed, without Nancy. Moreover, she also provided me with the physical facilities to do so in a beautiful study in our home and access as her spouse (a compensation for my lack of any other institutional support) to the library facilities of the University of Toronto.

That access also allows me the use of e-mail to communicate about issues in and sources for this book with colleagues all over the world. There have been so many, in addition to those already acknowledged elsewhere in this preface, that I can here only name and thank a few of the many whom I have consulted (some still by snail-mail) who have helped me most: Bob Adams in California, Jim Blaut in Chicago, Greg Blue in British Columbia, Terry Boswell in Georgia, Tim Brook in Toronto, Linda Darling in Arizona, Richard Eaton in Arizona, Dennis Flynn in California, Steve Fuller in England, Paulo Frank in Geneva, Jack Goldstone in California, Takeshi Hamashita in Tokyo, Satoshi Ikeda in Binghamton, N.Y., Huricihan Islamoglu in Ankara, Martin Lewis in North Carolina, Victor Lieberman in Michigan, Angus Maddison in Holland, Pat Manning in Boston, Bob Marks in California, Joya Misra in Georgia, Brian Molougheney in New Zealand, John Munro in Toronto, Rila Mukherjee in Calcutta, Jack Owens in Idaho, Frank Perlin in France, Ken Pomeranz in California, Anthony Reid in Australia, John Richards in North Carolina, Morris Rossabi in New York, Mark Selden in Ithaca, N.Y., David Smith in California, Graeme Snooks in Australia, Dorothy and Burton Stein in London, Sun Laichen in Michigan, and Richard von Glahn, John Wills, and Bin Wong all in California.

The attentive reader will find that most of these names reappear in the text in connection with my use of their work or the work used or recommended by them. Before proceeding to publish especially my disputes with them (for example, about estimates and other issues regarding population, trade, production, income, money, cycles and institutions in China, Europe, India, Central Asia, Southeast Asia, and West Asia, as well as Africa), I submitted my relevant text for their personal review and acceptance. I then amended my text in accordance with their collegial comments, for which I wish to express my gratitude here. Unfortunately, communication was not possible or was interrupted about my disputes with some colleagues in India.

Last but not least, I am thankful to David Wilkinson for his suggestion of how to entitle this book; to Paul DeGrace, cartographer at the Department of Geography of Simon Fraser University, for converting my hand-sketched designs into his computer-generated maps and to the World Society Foundation in Zurich, Switzerland, for financial support to pay for them and other expenses; to my longtime friend Stan Holwitz and now also my editor at the University of California Press in Los Angeles for humoring me through the travails of the book's production in Berkeley; and to the ever active production editor there, Juliane Brand. My special and greatest thanks in this department go to Kathleen MacDougall. Her good substantive suggestions far beyond the call of duty as copy editor helped me strengthen this book's content and argument, while her professional expertise combined with endless patience and good cheer much improved its form and communicability to the reader, in whose name I therefore thank her as well.

To conclude, I hope I may be excused if I repeat something from the preface of my previous book on world accumulation:

> The very *attempt* to examine and relate the simultaneity of different events in the whole historical process or in the transformation of the whole system—even if for want of empirical information or theoretical adequacy it may be full of holes in its factual coverage of space and time—is a significant step in the right direction (particularly at a time in which this generation must "rewrite history" to meet its need for historical perspective and understanding of the single historical process in the one world of today). (Frank 1978a: 21)

To end this already too long preface, I would like to continue my quotation from and agreement still with John King Fairbank:

> The result can only be an imperfect approximation. Fortunately, no one has to regard it as the last word. Once an author looks back at what he thought he was trying to do, many perspectives emerge. Foremost is that of ignorance, at least in my case. A book that to its author is a mere antechamber to a whole unwritten library, bursting with problems awaiting exploration, may seem to his readers to have a solidity which shunts their research elsewhere. It is useless to assure them that the book is really full of holes. (Fairbank 1969: xii)

Unlike Fairbank, at least I need not fear that any of *my* readers may be fooled into seeing a nonexistent solidity here. Surely, they will note that this book *is* full of holes. I do hope, however, not to shunt all of their research elsewhere, and I invite them to use at least some of it to help fill these holes—and to dig up new ones of their own.

Andre Gunder Frank
Toronto, January 26, August 8, and December 25, 1996

CHAPTER I

Introduction to Real World History vs. Eurocentric Social Theory

The really important lesson to be learned from Marx and Weber is the importance of history for the understanding of society. Though they were certainly interested in grasping the general and universal, they concerned themselves with the concrete circumstances of specific periods, and the similarities and contrasts of diverse geographical areas. They clearly recognized that an adequate explanation of social facts requires a historical account of how the facts came to be; they recognized that comparative-historical analysis is indispensable for the study of stability and change. In a word, it is these two extraordinary thinkers in particular, who stand out as the architects of a historical sociology well worth emulating; for both of them subscribed to an open, historically grounded theory and method.

Irving Zeitlin (1994: 220)

The expectation of universality, however sincerely pursued, has not been fulfilled thus far in the historical development of the social sciences. . . . It is hardly surprising that the social sciences that were constructed in Europe and North America in the nineteenth century were Eurocentric. The European world of the time felt itself culturally triumphant. . . . Every universalism sets off responses to itself, and these responses are in some sense determined by the nature of the reigning universalism(s). . . . Submitting our theoretical premises to inspection for hidden unjustified a priori assumptions is a priority for the social sciences today.

Immanuel Wallerstein (1996b: 49, 51, 60, 56)

Holistic Methodology and Objectives

My thesis is that there is "unity in diversity." However, we can neither understand not appreciate the world's diversity without perceiving how unity itself generates and continually changes diversity.

We all have to live in this one world in which diversity must be tolerated and could be appreciated in unity. Of course, I refer to toleration and appreciation of diversity in ethnicity, gender, culture, taste, politics, and color or "race." I do not advocate acceptance of inequality in gender, wealth, income, and power without struggle. Therefore, we could all benefit from a world perspective that illuminates not only the subjective immorality but also the objective absurdity of "ethnic cleansing" and "clash of civilizations," which once again have become popular in some circles today. This book proposes to offer at least some basis in early modern world economic history for a more "humanocentric" perspective and understanding.

The European but exceptionally worldly historian Fernand Braudel remarked that "Europe invented historians and then made good use of them" to promote their own interests at home and elsewhere in the world (Braudel 1992: 134). This statement is revealing in several important ways. First, it is not really true that the writing of history was invented by Europeans, not even by Herodotus and Thucydides. History had also been written by the Chinese, Persians, and others. Moreover, Herodotus himself insisted that "Europe" has no independent existence, since it is only a part of Eurasia, which has no real internal boundaries of its own. Perhaps Braudel had in mind a generation of historians who wrote long after Herodotus. Yet even they invented Eurocentric history long after Arab historians, chroniclers, and world travelers of such fame as Ibn Batuta, Ibn Khaldun, and Rashid-al-Din, who had already written Afro-Eurasian world history which was much less Arab- or Islamocentric.

Indeed, Europeans seem to have invented geography as well, for "Eurasia" itself is a Eurocentric denomination, albeit one invented on a distant marginal peninsula of that land mass. Before his untimely death in 1968, Marshall Hodgson (1993) denounced maps drawn according to the Mercator projection, which makes little Britain appear about as large as India; and J. M. Blaut (1993b) has shown how Eurocentric the mapping of the "march of history" has been. Martin Lewis and Karen Wigen (1997) refer to *The Myth of Continents*. One example is that against all geographical reality Europeans insist on elevating their peninsula to a "continent" while the much more numerous Indians have but a "subcontinent" and the Chinese at best a "country." The relevant geographical and historical unit is really Afro-Eurasia. However, that could more appropriately be called "Afrasia," as Arnold Toynbee suggested and the former president of the World History Association Ross

Dunn recently recalled. Even this syllabic order still fails to reflect the real orders of geographical and demographic magnitude and historical importance of these two continents. Europe, of course, is none of the above.

Latter-day historians, it is true, have preponderantly gazed at their own European navel. That might be excused or at least explained by the social, cultural, political, and economic support they have received to do so. After all, historians received much support to write "national" histories in ideological support of European and American "nation-states" and to serve the ideological, political, and economic interests of their ruling classes. However, these historians also went beyond the confines of their own "nations," to claim that "Europe" or "the West" was and is the "navel" (indeed also the heart and soul) of the rest of the world. If they gave any credit to anyone else, it was only grudgingly with a "history" that, like the Orient Express on the westward bound track only, ran through a sort of tunnel of time from the ancient Egyptians and Mesopotamians, to the classical Greeks and Romans, through medieval (western) Europe, to modern times. Persians, Turks, Arabs, Indians, and Chinese received at best polite, and often not so polite, bows. Other peoples like Africans, Japanese, Southeast Asians, and Central Asians received no mention as contributors to or even participants in history at all, except as "barbarian" nomadic hordes who periodically emerged out of Central Asia to make war on "civilized" settled peoples. From among literally countless examples, I will cite the preface of one: "*The Foundations of the West* is an historical study of the West from its beginnings in the ancient Near East to the world [*sic!*] of the mid-seventeenth century" (Fishwick, Wilkinson, and Cairns 1963: ix).

Modern history, both early and late, was made by Europeans, who "built a world around Europe," as historians "know," according to Braudel. That is indeed the "knowledge" of the European historians who themselves "invented" history and then put it to good use. There is not even an inkling of suspicion that it may have been the other way around, that maybe it was the world that made Europe. Yet that is what I propose to demonstrate, or at least to begin to show, in this book.

This book sets itself a number of tasks. They are at once far-reaching and still very limited. The tasks are far-reaching in that I seek to challenge the Eurocentric historiography on which much of received "classical" and "modern" social theory is based. The intentionally set limits are even greater: I—and I hope the reader—will be satisfied with the bare outlines of an alternative rendition of the world economy between

1400 and 1800. It offers a basis for a now only very preliminary—but later hopefully deeper and wider—structural, functional, dynamic, and transformational global analysis and theory of the single world political economy and social system in which we all (have to) live together.

Quite possibly the limitations of this book are even greater than the ones I have set intentionally and so will prevent me from reaching even this limited goal. However, it is already exceptional even to attempt a review of the early modern global world economy and its structural characteristics in order to inquire how they impinge on its sectoral and regional parts. Most of the historical development of this world economy and its parts may receive shorter shrift than it requires and deserves. The attempt is not so much to write a world history of this period, nor even an economic history, which is beyond my present capabilities, as to offer a global perspective on early modern economic history. Although historical evidence is important, I seek less to challenge received evidence with new evidence than to confront the received Eurocentric paradigms with a more humanocentric global paradigm.

The principal intent is to show why we *need* a global perspective and approach, which we require not only on the history of the world economy itself, but also so that we can locate its subordinate and participant sectors, regions, countries, or whatever segments and processes within the global whole of which they are only parts. Concretely, we need a global perspective to appreciate, understand, account for, explain—in a word, perceive—"the Rise of the West," "the development of capitalism," "the hegemony of Europe," "the rise and fall of great powers," including formerly "Great" Britain, the United States, and the former Soviet Union, "the Third-worldization of Los Angeles," "the East Asian miracle," and any other such process and event. None of these were caused only or even primarily through the structure or interaction of forces "internal" to any of the above. All of them were part and parcel of the structure and development of a single world economic system.

A derivative observation is that Europe did not pull itself up by its own economic bootstraps, and certainly not thanks to any kind of European "exceptionalism" of rationality, institutions, entrepreneurship, technology, geniality, in a word—of race. We will see that Europe also did not do so primarily through its participation and use of the Atlantic economy per se, not even through the direct exploitation of its American and Caribbean colonies and its African slave trade. This book shows how instead Europe used its American money to muscle in on and benefit from Asian production, markets, trade—in a word, to profit from the predominant position of Asia in the world economy. Europe climbed up on the back of Asia, then stood on Asian shoulders—temporarily. This book also tries to explain in world economic terms how "the West" got there—and by implication, why and how it is likely soon again to lose that position.

Another derivative thesis is that early modern Europe was neither more important in the world economy nor more advanced in any way than other regions of the world. This was not the case even counting all of its Atlantic outliers. Nor was Europe in any way "central" to or a "core" of any world-embracing economy or system. The "world-economy and system" of which Europe was the "core" in the sense of Braudel (1992), Wallerstein (1974), and others including Frank (1967, 1978a, b), was itself only a minor and for a long time still quite marginal part of the real world economy as a whole. We will see that the only real means that Europe had for participating in this world economy was its American money. If any regions were predominant in the world economy before 1800, they were in Asia. If any economy had a "central" position and role in the world economy and its possible hierarchy of "centers," it was China.

However, the very search for "hegemony" in the early modern world economy or system is misplaced. Europe was certainly not central to the world economy before 1800. Europe was not hegemonic structurally, nor functionally, nor in terms of economic weight, or of production, technology or productivity, nor in per capita consumption, nor in any way in its development of allegedly more "advanced" "capitalist" institutions. In no way were sixteenth-century Portugal, the seventeenth-century Netherlands, or eighteenth-century Britain "hegemonic" in world economic terms. Nor in political ones. None of the above! In all these respects, the economies of Asia were far more "advanced," and its Chinese Ming/Qing, Indian Mughal, and even Persian Safavid and Turkish Ottoman empires carried much greater political and even military weight than any or all of Europe.

This observation also has relevance to the contemporary and future world development problematique. The recent economic "development" of East Asia is receiving much attention around the world these days, but it generates equally much bewilderment about how to fit the observed developments into the Western scheme of things. The problem is easily illustrated by considering the absurdity of reclassifying Japan as part of "the West" or of having called the Japanese "honorary whites" in South Africa during apartheid. Beyond Japan, the focus shifted especially to the Four Tigers or Dragons of South Korea, Taiwan, Hong Kong, and Singapore. However, increasing notice is now also being taken of the other little dragons countries in Southeast Asia and of the big Chinese dragon looming on the horizon. Even the press sees that

> in large ways and small, subtle and heavy-handed . . . China is making itself felt across Asia with a weight not seen since the 18th century. . . . Now that the dragon has stirred, it is altering issues from regional trade patterns to manufacturing, from the decisions Asian governments make. . . . [which] confirms a shift in the geopolitics of a region stretching from Japan and South Korea to the Southeast Asian belt. (Keith B. Richburg of the Washington Post Service in the *International Herald Tribune,* 18 March 1996)

To drive still further home the relevance of this point to the present argument, it may be apt to quote from the same paper on two successive days. Under the headline "America Must Learn to Respect Asia's Way of Doing Things," we learn that

> Westerners have been accustomed to telling Asians what to do. That period is now coming to an end. Asian countries are becoming strong enough to assert their autonomy and maintain it. . . . Any further attempt to remake Asian countries on Western lines is not likely to succeed. It would carry the risk of bringing about another in the long series of conflicts between Asians and the West. . . . Westerners need to accept the equality of Asians, and their right to do things their own way . . . and asserting the validity of "Asian" values. (Bryce Harland, *International Herald Tribune,* 3 May 1996)

Under the subtitle "At Issue Is the Nature of the International System," this same newspaper reported on the following day that

> The conflict over China is a conflict about the nature of the international system, and its political, financial and trade agencies. By design or otherwise, China is aggressively pushing to shape an alternative international system friendlier to Beijing's aims [which is] evident in the Chinese struggle to remake the WTO [World Trade Organization] rules for admission. (Jim Hoagland, *International Herald Tribune,* 4–5 May 1996)

Why is this so? Hill Gates (1996: 6) argues that it is because in the world only China has been exceptional in successfully resisting being

"reshaped by the pressures of capitalism originating in western Europe
... [and] to have survived the Western imperialist remaking of the
world in the past few centuries." Others have sought and offered all
manner of "explanations" for this Asian awakening, from "Confucianism" to "the magic of the market without state intervention." Alas, the
contemporary East Asian experience does not seem to fit very well into
any received Western theoretical or ideological scheme of things. On
the contrary, what is happening in East Asia seems to violate all sorts
of Western canons of how things "should" be done, which is to copy
how "we" did it the "Western way." Too bad!

The implications of this book are that the "Rise" of East Asia need
come as no surprise just because it does not fit into the Western scheme
of things. This book suggests a rather different scheme of things instead, into which the contemporary and possible future events in East
Asia, and maybe also elsewhere in Asia, can and do fit. This is a global
economic development scheme of things, in which Asia, and especially
East Asia, was already dominant and remained so until—in historical
terms—very recently, that is less than two centuries ago. Only then, for
reasons to be explored below, did Asian economies lose their positions
of predominance in the world economy, while that position came to be
occupied by the West—apparently only temporarily.

The Western interpretation of its own "Rise of the West" has suffered
from a case of "misplaced concreteness." What should become increasingly apparent is that "development" was not so much "of the West" as
it was of and in the world economy. "Leadership" of the world system—more than "hegemony"—has been temporarily "centered" in one
sector and region (or a few), only to shift again to one or more others.
That happened in the nineteenth century, and it appears to be happening again at the beginning of the twenty-first, as the "center" of the
world economy seems to be shifting back to the "East."

This idea is also cropping up elsewhere, but in rather dubious form.
The book *Coming Full Circle: An Economic History of the Pacific Rim*
(Jones, Frost, and White 1993) begins a millennium ago with a description of the economic growth in Song China. Yet Ming and Qing China
and Japan are described as essentially isolated and largely stagnant,
while the Pacific becomes first "a Spanish lake," and then subject to "Pax
Britannica" and "the American Century"; only after an alleged interval
of five to seven hundred years and substantial intervening Western
incursions are the Pacific Rim and its eastern shores rising again. On
the other hand, Western incursions in Asia remain only superficial and
marginal until the past two centuries, and the ascendancy of the West

is termed brief and fleeting in Felipe Fernandez-Armesto's 1995 study of the last millennium of world history. Nonetheless in his account, the present and possible future rise to dominance of China and other parts of Asia in the world only resurrects the Chinese economic and cultural predominance of the Song dynasty from nearly a thousand years ago. In my book, in contrast, I argue that that lapse in dominance lasted less than two centuries. Moreover, I seek to show how these shifts have also been part and parcel of a long cyclical process of global "development." This introductory chapter—and the concluding one—explore the implications of these historical observations for social theory.

Globalism, not Eurocentrism

"The West" has for some time now perceived much of the rest of the world under the title "Orientalism" (the pairing of the terms "West" and "Rest" comes from Huntington 1993, 1994). The Western world is replete with "Oriental" studies, institutes, and what not. This Western ideological stance was magnificently analyzed and denounced by the Palestinian American Edward Said in his 1978 book, *Orientalism*. He shows how Orientalism operates in the Western attempt to mark off the rest of the world in order to distinguish the West's own alleged exceptionalism. This procedure has also been denounced by Samir Amin in his 1989 work, *Eurocentrism*. Martin Bernal, in *Black Athena* (1987), has shown how, as part and parcel of European colonialism in the nineteenth century, Europeans invented a historical myth about their allegedly purely European roots in "democratic" but also slave-holding and sexist Greece. The Bernal thesis, apparently against the original intentions of its author, has been used in turn to support the idea of Afrocentrism (Asante 1987). In fact, the roots of Athens were much more in Asia Minor, Persia, Central Asia, and other parts of Asia than in Egypt and Nubia. To compromise and conciliate, we could say that they were and are primarily Afro-Asian. However, European "roots" were of course by no means confined to Greece and Rome (nor to Egypt and Mesopotamia before them). The roots of Europe extended into all of Afro-Eurasia since time immemorial. Moreover, as will be shown in this book, Europe was still dependent on Asia during early modern times, before the nineteenth-century invention and propagation of the "Eurocentric idea."

This Eurocentric idea consists of several strands, some of which are privileged by political economists like Karl Marx and Werner Sombart, and others by sociologists like Émile Durkheim, Georg Simmel, and Max Weber. The last named did the most deliberately to assemble, combine, and embellish these features of Eurocentrism. All of them allegedly serve to explain *The European Miracle,* which is the telling title of the book by Eric L. Jones (1981). However, Jones's book is only a particularly visible tip of the iceberg of almost all Western social science and history from Marx and Weber, through Oswald Spengler and Arnold Toynbee, to the spate of defenses of supposed Western exceptionalism since World War II, particularly in the United States.

The use and abuse of this kind of Eurocentric "theory" has been critically summarized with regard to Islam, although the same applies equally to other parts of "the Orient":

> The syndrome consists of a number of basic arguments: (i) social development is caused by characteristics which are internal to society; (ii) the historical development of society is either an evolutionary process or a gradual decline. These arguments allow Orientalists to establish their dichotomous ideal types of Western society whose inner essence unfolds in a dynamic process towards democratic industrialism. . . . (Turner 1986: 81)

However, as the Islamicist and world historian Marshall Hodgson wrote,

> All attempts that I have yet seen to invoke pre-Modern seminal traits in the Occident can be shown to fail under close historical analysis, once other societies begin to be known as intimately as the Occident. This also applies to the great master, Max Weber, who tried to show that the Occident inherited a unique combination of rationality and activism. (Hodgson 1993: 86)

Hodgson (1993) and Blaut (1992, 1993a, 1997) derisorally call this a "tunnel history," derived from a tunnel vision, which sees only "exceptional" intra-European causes and consequences and is blind to all extra-European contributions to modern European and world history. Yet as Blaut points out, in 1492 or 1500 Europe still had no advantages of any kind over Asia and Africa, nor did they have any distinctively different "modes of production." In 1500 and even later, there would have been no reason to anticipate the triumph of Europe or its "capitalism" three and more centuries later. The sixteenth- and seventeenth-century

development of economic, scientific, rational "technicalism" that Hodgson regards as the basis of the subsequent major "transmutation" occurred, as he insists, on a worldwide basis and not exclusively or even
especially in Europe.

Europeans and Arabs at least had a much more global perspective
before it was suppressed by the rise of Eurocentric historiography and
social theory in the nineteenth century. For instance, the Tunisian
statesman and historian Ibn Khaldun (1332–1406) evaluated and compared the "wealth of nations" before and during his time:

> This may be exemplified by the eastern regions, such as Egypt,
> Syria, India, China, and the whole northern regions, beyond the
> Mediterranean. When their civilization increased, the property of
> the inhabitants increased, and their dynasties became great. Their
> towns and settlements became numerous, and their commerce
> and conditions improved. At this time, we can observe the condi-
> tion of the merchants of the Christian nations who come to the
> Muslims in the Maghreb. Their prosperity and affluence cannot
> be fully described because it is so great. The same applies to the
> merchants from the East and what we hear about their conditions,
> and even more so to the far eastern merchants from the countries
> of the non-Arab Iraq, India, and China. We hear remarkable sto-
> ries reported by travellers about their wealth and prosperity.
> These stories are usually received with skepticism. (Ibn Khaldun
> 1967: 279)

Even in the eighteenth century Father Du Halde, the most learned
French publicist of matters Chinese (who never left Paris and used Jesuit
and other travelers and translators as sources) wrote that in China

> the particular riches of every province, and the ability of trans-
> porting merchandise by means of rivers and canals, have rendered
> the empire always very flourishing. . . . The trade carried on
> within China is so great, that all of Europe is not to be compared
> therewith. (quoted by Chaudhuri 1991: 430; for a longer version
> also see Ho Ping-ti 1959:199)

In a discussion of Du Halde's work, Theodore Foss (1986: 91) insists
that not only philosophical but also technological and other practical
texts from China were translated and studied in the West with utilitarian
interest. Indeed, Donald Lach and Edwin van Kley (1965–) have written volumes under the title, *Asia in the Making of Europe* (seven volumes
so far have been published, with others promised). For a summary of
this work, see the review article by M. N. Pearson (1996) or the "Com-

posite Picture" at the end of Lach and van Kley (1993: vol. 3, book 4). They observe for instance that "sixteenth-century Europeans had considered Japan and China to be the great hopes of the future"; by the end of the seventeenth century, they continue, "few literate Europeans could have been completely untouched [by the image of Asia], and it would have been surprising indeed if its effects could not be seen in contemporary European literature, art, learning, and culture." Lach and van Kley support this observation with the fact that hundreds of books about Asia had been written, reprinted, and translated in the these two centuries in all major European languages by European missionaries, merchants, sea captains, physicians, sailors, soldiers, and other travelers. These included at least twenty-five major works about South Asia, fifteen about Southeast Asia, twenty on the archipelagoes, and sixty about East Asia, not to mention countless shorter works (Lach and van Kley 1993: 1890). The Indian empire was considered to be among the world's richest and most powerful, but China remained its most impressive and the Europeans' ultimate goal (Lach and van Kley 1993: 1897, 1904). Asian philosophy was admired, but arts and sciences less so; medicine, crafts and industry, and their respective practitioners were highly respected and oft imitated (Lach and van Kley 1993: 1914, 1593 ff.).

A revealing historical sidelight is that the seventeenth-century German philosopher Leibniz was retained by a West German ruler who was rightly suspicious of the ambitions of his neighbor Louis XIV. So Leibniz wrote Louis to offer a piece of advice: rather than pursuing any possible ambitions across the Rhine, it would be much more politically economic for France to turn southeastward to challenge the Ottomans:

> In fact, everything exquisite and admirable comes from the East Indies. . . . Learned people have remarked that in the whole world there is no commerce comparable to that of China. (Leibniz 1969: vol. 5, 206; the quotation was kindly supplied by Gregory Blue)

The French did not pursue this advice until the time of Napoleon, who probably not by accident also took the trouble to recover a copy of Leibniz's letter when he invaded Germany. As observers like Lach and Said have noted, this European high regard for Asia did not really change until the nineteenth century, after the inception of European industrialization and colonialism, which then profoundly altered European perceptions and pronouncements, including their historiography and social science. Even today, Paul Bairoch acknowledges the greater economic and cultural development in early modern times of many parts of Asia compared to Europe. This testimony is all the more significant because along with Patrick O'Brien (1982, 1990, 1997), Bairoch (1974) is one of the principal explicit disputants of the Wallerstein/Frank thesis that the relations of Europe with the rest of the world had an important impact on European development itself. Although this denial continues today—like O'Brien's (1997)—Bairoch (1997: vol. 2, 528, his dots) nonetheless acknowledges that "Riches and power . . . in fact we can consider that around the beginning of the sixteenth century the principal civilizations of Asia had attained a level of technical and economic development superior to that of Europe."

Indeed, Bairoch also points to the superiority specifically of China, India, Japan, Korea, Burma, Cambodia, Laos, Thailand, Vietnam, Indonesia, and the Ottomans; he calls Istanbul, at 700,000 inhabitants, the largest city in the world, with Beijing the second largest at only slightly fewer inhabitants. He also notes that Muslim North Africa was more urbanized than Europe: Paris had 125,000 inhabitants around 1500, whereas Cairo had 450,000 inhabitants and Fez had already declined from 250,000. Moreover, Calicut in India had 500,000 and even Pegu in Burma and Angkor in Cambodia had already declined from 180,000 and 150,000 inhabitants respectively (Bairoch 1997: vol. 2, 517–37). Curiously, Bairoch also asserts (on p. 509 of the same volume) that "with the sixteenth century began the European domination over other continents." That of course is the European gospel, which really began in the mid-nineteenth century as per Marx and company. This worldview is still so pervasive that when *LIFE* magazine employed two dozen editors, consulted scores of experts, and devoted months of stormy meetings to the compilation of a list of the 100 most important people and events of the millennium for its September 1997 issue, it came up with the following results:

> Westerners . . . have done a disproportionate amount of the global moving and shaking. . . . All but 17 [of the 100] are of European extraction; only 10 are women. This reflects not the biases of LIFE's editors and expert advisers but the sociopolitical realities of the past thousand years. (p. 135)

SMITH, MARX, AND WEBER

So it is not surprising that, among European observers of special interest for us, Adam Smith and Karl Marx also regarded these matters of great importance and interest. However, they did so from the differing perspectives of their respective times. Smith and Marx both agreed and disagreed about early modern history and the place of Asia in it. Smith wrote in *The Wealth of Nations* in 1776:

> The discovery of America, and that of the passage to the East Indies by the Cape of Good Hope, are the two greatest events recorded in the history of mankind. (Smith [1776] 1937: 557)

Marx and Engels' *Communist Manifesto* follows with this observation:

> The discovery of America, the rounding of the Cape, opened up fresh ground for the rising bourgeoisie. The East-Indian and Chinese markets, the colonization of America, trade with the colonies, the increase in the means of exchange and in commodities generally, gave to commerce, to navigation, to industry, an impulse never before known, and thereby to the revolutionary element in the tottering feudal society, a rapid development. . . . (Marx and Engels 1848)

Smith however—writing before the industrial revolution in Europe but echoing the philosopher David Hume, who wrote a quarter century earlier—was the last major (Western) social theorist to appreciate that Europe was a johnny-come-lately in the development of the wealth of nations: "China is a much richer country than any part of Europe," Smith remarked in 1776. Smith did not anticipate any change in this comparison and showed no awareness that he was writing at the beginning of what has come to be called the "industrial revolution." Moreover, as E. A. Wrigley (1994: 27 ff.) notes, neither did the English economists Thomas Malthus or David Ricardo one and two generations later, and even John Stuart Mill writing in the mid-nineteenth century still had his doubts.

However, Smith also did not regard the "greatest events in the history" to have been a European gift to mankind—of civilization, capitalism, or anything else. On the contrary, he noted with alarm that

> to the natives, however, both of the East and the West Indies, all the commercial benefits which can have resulted from those events have been sunk and lost in the dreadful misfortunes which they have occasioned. . . . What benefits, or what misfortunes to mankind may hereafter result from these great events, no human wisdom can foresee. (Smith [1776] 1937: 189)

But by the mid-nineteenth century, European views of Asia and China in particular had changed drastically. Raymond Dawson (1967) documents and analyzes this change under the revealing title *The Chinese Chameleon: An Analysis of European Conceptions of Chinese Civilization*. Europeans changed from regarding China as "an example and model" to calling the Chinese "a people of eternal standstill." Why this rather abrupt change? The coming of the industrial revolution and the beginnings of European colonialism in Asia had intervened to reshape European minds, and if not to "invent" all history, then at least to invent a false universalism under European initiation and guidance. Then in the second half of the nineteenth century, not only was world history rewritten wholesale, but "universal" social "science" was (new)born, not just as a European discipline, but as a *Eurocentric* invention.

In so doing, "classical" historians and social theorists of the nineteenth and twentieth centuries took a huge step backward even from European, not to mention Islamic, perspectives that had been much more realistically world embracing up through the eighteenth century. Among those who saw things from this narrower (Eurocentric) new perspective were Marx and Weber. According to them and all of their many disciples to this day, the essentials of the "capitalist mode of production" that allegedly developed in and out of Europe were missing in the rest of the world and could be and were supplied only through European help and diffusion. That is where the "Orientalist" assumptions by Marx, and many more studies by Weber, and the fallacious assertions of both about the rest of the world come in. To briefly review them, we may here follow not only my own reading but also, to pick one among many, that of so authoritative a reader as Irving Zeitlin (1994).

Marx seems to have been selective in the sources he drew on to characterize "Asia," not to mention Africa. Among the classical political economists that influenced Marx, Smith ([1776] 1937: 348) had given "credit to the wonderful accounts of the wealth and cultivation of China, of those of antient [ancient] Egypt and . . . Indostan." In this regard however, Marx preferred to follow Montesquieu and the Philosophes such as Jean-Jacques Rousseau as well as James Mill, who had instead "discovered" "despotism" as the "natural" condition and "model of government" in Asia and "the Orient." Marx also remarked on "the cruellest form of state, Oriental despotism, from India to Russia." He also attributed this form of state to the Ottomans, Persia, and China, indeed to the whole "Orient." In all of these, Marx alleged the existence of an age-old "Asiatic Mode of Production." He alleged that in all of Asia the forces of production remained "traditional, backward, and stagnant" until the incursion of "the West" and its capitalism woke it out of its otherwise eternal slumber.

Although Marx noted that the Indian and Chinese purchasing power gave impulse to European markets, England was allegedly showing India the mirror of its future and the United States was bringing progress to Mexico thanks to its 1846 war against that country. Furthermore, Marx alleged that the "transition from feudalism to capitalism" and the "rising bourgeoisie" in Europe had transformed the world, supposedly since the genesis of capital (if not capitalism) in the sixteenth century—also in Europe.

For Marx, Asia remained even more backward than Europe, where "feudalism" at least had the seeds of a "transition to capitalism" within itself. In alleged contrast, "the Asiatic Mode of Production" would require the progressive benefits of this "transition" in Europe to jolt and pull it out of its built-in stagnation—even though he said that it was the Asian markets that gave impetus to those of Europe. The supposed reason for this alleged stagnation was the imagined lack of "capitalist relations of production," which kept all of Asia "divided into villages, each of which possessed a completely separate organization and formed a little world to itself."

But this division of Asia into separate little worlds had already been contradicted by Marx's simultaneous claims, as well as those of other European writers, that Asia was also characterized by "Oriental despotism." That was regarded as a form of sociopolitical organization necessary for managing these societies' large-scale irrigation projects, which were of course themselves incompatible with the allegedly isolated villages. Karl Wittfogel (1957) would later popularize this "theory," but then ironically as a cold-war ideological weapon against communism and Marxism. But never mind all these internal contradictions! As we will see throughout this book, all of these characterizations by Marx were no more than a figment of his and other Eurocentric thinkers' imagination anyway, and had no foundation in historical reality whatsoever. This fallacy also extends to the obverse—the "capitalist mode of production"—which was allegedly invented by Europeans and has ever since been held to be responsible for European, Western, and then global development.

Indeed, in his excellent critique of Marxists such as Perry Anderson and others, Teshale Tibebu (1990: 83–85) argues persuasively that much of their analysis of feudalism, absolutism and the bourgeois revolution and "their obsession with the specificity . . . [and] supposed superiority of Europe" is Western "civilizational arrogance," "ideology dressed up as history," and "Orientalism painted red," that is, the "continuation of orientalism by other means."

Other social theorists may have risen to dispute Marx (and supposedly to agree with Smith), but they all agreed with each other *and with Marx* that 1492 and 1498 were the two greatest events in the history of mankind, because that is when Europe discovered the world. Never mind that the world had been there all along and that at least the Afro-Asiatic part of it had long since shaped Europe itself. Indeed, the eminent historian of medieval Europe Henri Pirenne (1992) stressed Europe's external dependence when he pointed out in 1935 that there could have been "no Charlemagne without Mohammed." Nevertheless, history and social theory have been marked ever since by the alleged uniqueness of (Western) Europeans, which supposedly generated "the Rise of the West." What is worse, they allegedly also had to assume the civilizing mission of the white man's burden, bestowing "the development and spread of capitalism" on the world as Europe's and the West's gift to mankind. (Lately, some feminists have denied that this process has been a gift also to womankind).

Weber of course agreed with Marx about all these European origins and characteristics of "capitalism," and with Sombart too. Weber only wanted to go them one better. Sombart had already singled out European rationality, and its alleged roots in Judaism, as the sine qua non of "capitalism" and its "birth" in Europe. Weber accepted that too. He further embellished the argument about irrigation-based "Oriental despotism" to allege that Asia had an inherent inability to generate economic, not to mention "capitalist," development on its own. However, Weber actually went to a lot of trouble to study "the city," "religion," and other aspects of different civilizations in Asia. The great student of bureaucracies, Weber had to recognize that the Chinese knew how to manage them and the country at large. Moreover, he had more time than Marx to observe how Western money made its way to and around various parts of Asia.

That additional acquaintance of Weber with Asian realities also complicated his argument and made it more sophisticated than the crude Marxian version. For instance, Weber recognized that Asia had big cities. So they had to be somehow "fundamentally different" from European ones, both in structure and in function. Weber's mistake in this regard emerges clearly from William Rowe's (1984, 1989) careful examination of this argument in his study of the Chinese city Hankow.

To continue the critique of the Eurocentric idea and the use and abuse of Weberian theory, I return to Turner's argument: that

> Islamic society is either timelessly stagnant or declines from its inception. The societies are consequently defined by reference to a cluster of absences [that allegedly] define the West—the missing middle class, the missing city, the absence of political rights, the absence of revolutions. These missing features . . . serve to explain why Islamic civilization failed to produce capitalism. (Turner 1986: 81)

So what was the essential difference, the missing ingredient that "the West" allegedly had and "the Rest" did not have if Weber himself could not find all these factors to be missing in the Oriental societies he studied? For Marx, what was missing was "the capitalist mode of production"; Weber added also as a missing element the proper religion and how it interfaces with the other factors to generate that "capitalist mode." Weber went to the trouble to study various major world religions and concluded that all of them had an essential mythical, mystic, magical, in a word antirational component, which "necessarily" handicapped all their true believers in coming to grip with reality rationally, unlike the Europeans. Only the latter were beneficiaries of "the Protestant ethic and the spirit of capitalism." No more than Marx did Weber argue that this ethic and spirit were the be all and end all of capitalism, and the Weberian argument has been even harder to understand than the Marxian one.

This rational spirit is supposedly the missing secret yeast that, when combined with all the others, makes "the West" rise, but not "the Rest." Without it, the Asians could not possibly develop capitalism and therefore could not really "develop" at all, or even use their cities, production, and commerce. Never mind that Catholics in Venice and other Italian cities had already managed quite well, thank you, without this special gift of yeast long before Calvin and others gave it to Northern Europeans. Also never mind that not all those gifted with the Protestant ethic manage so well either, whether in Eastern Europe or in the European colonies early on in the South of the United States and still in the Caribbean, and elsewhere—as I have already argued (Frank 1978b). Nonetheless, David Landes explicitly claims empirical support for the Weberian thesis in his *The Unbound Prometheus* (1969) and categorically denies that Muslim "culture" can permit any technological initiative.

Yet, the Japanese took up "the Chrysanthemum and the Sword"

(Benedict 1954) and produced and prospered without Western colonialism or foreign investment, not to mention the Protestant ethic, even after their defeat in World War II. So James Abbeglen (1958) and Robert Bellah (1957) sought to explain these developments by arguing that the Japanese have the "functional equivalent of the Protestant ethic," while, too bad for them, the Confucian Chinese do not. Now that both are surging ahead economically, the argument has been turned around again: it is East Asian "Confucianism" that is now spurring them onward and upward. In the real world economy of course, none of this is neither here nor there.

This Eurocentrism had nineteenth-century sociological great-grandfathers in the "father of sociology" Auguste Comte and in Sir Henry Maine, who distinguished between supposedly new forms of thinking and of social organization based on "science" and "contract," which allegedly replaced age-old "traditional" ones. One grandfather was Émile Durkheim, who idealized "organic" vs. "mechanical" forms of social organization; another was Ferdinand Toennis, who alleged a transition from traditional "Gemeinschaft" to modern "Gesellschaft." In a later generation, Talcott Parsons idealized "universalist" vs. "particularist" social forms, and Robert Redfield claimed to have found a contrast and transition or at least a "continuum" between traditional "folk" and modern "urban" society and a certain symbiosis between "low" and "high civilization." Even Toynbee (1946), although he studied twenty other civilizations, heralded the uniqueness of the "Western" one; and Spengler warned of its "decline."

Critics of Western capitalist development who wanted to reform or replace it nonetheless also subscribed to the same fundamental thesis. The Marxist and contemporary neo-Marxist version is the alleged fundamental difference between "Asiatic," "feudal" or other forms of "tributary modes of production" and the "capitalist mode of production" (Wolf 1982, Amin 1991, 1993, 1996). Lenin alleged that "imperialism as the highest stage of capitalism" also was an outgrowth of a development that was initiated in and spread by Europe. More recently, Karl Polanyi alleged that there were no market relations, to say nothing of trade and a division of labor over long distances, anywhere in the world before what he called the "Great Transformation" took place in Europe during the nineteenth century. Archaeological findings have time and again disconfirmed Polanyi's (1957) denial of trade and markets in early empires, and I have already added my own theoretical and empirical critiques elsewhere (Gills and Frank 1990/91, Frank and Gills 1992, 1993,

Frank 1993a). At issue here is that the spread and dominance of the market allegedly started only recently in (Western) Europe and spread out over the world from there. Robert McIver opens his foreword to the first Polanyi book with the claim that it makes most other books in its field obsolete or outworn. If so, it does so only inasmuch as it renders "obsolete" the many previous acknowledgments of the real importance of market, including the world market, relations, and influences. Polanyi replaces this age-old reality by myths about the alleged primacy of noneconomic social relations of "reciprocity" and "redistribution." My book will show that, on the evidence, such "great transformation" as there was began long before the eighteenth century and certainly was not initiated in or by Europe.

All of these "ideal type" dyadic and other distinctions have in common that first they posit essentialist sociocultural features and differences that are far more imaginary than real, and then they allege that the differences distinguish "us" from "them." In the terminology of Samuel Huntington (1993, 1996), they separate "the West" from "the Rest." Indeed, allegedly these features also distinguish modern (Western) society from its own past as well as from other societies' often still lingering present. Moreover, these "ideal" types attribute some kind of pristine self-development to some peoples—mostly to "us"—but not to others, and their subsequent diffusion (when positive) or imposition (if negative) from here to there. The quintessential culmination of this "tradition" was Daniel Lerner's (1958) *The Passing of Traditional Society*. In the real world, the only practical holistic choice has been "none of the above." This "underdevelopment of sociology" was challenged by me thirty years ago (Frank 1967). However successful, that challenge was nonetheless insufficiently holistic. The present book is my attempt to do better.

Here, the evidence and argument is that almost all of the above cited received social science theory is vitiated by Eurocentric bias and arrogance. We will observe that the historical evidence effectively negates the alleged European origin, let alone superior exceptionalism, of modern social development—and thereby pulls the historical rug out from under social science theory as we know it. I will readily agree that we should try to salvage as much of it as we can still use; but all of this received wisdom is nonetheless in serious need of review and questioning.

Witness that even a world historian and social theorist with the erudition of Braudel (1993) still claims that

China's economic achievements were modest and, to be frank, backward compared with those of the West. . . . Her inferiority lay in her economic structure [which was] less developed than that of Islam or the West. . . . Nor were their entrepreneurs eager to make profits. . . . They only half-heartedly shared the capitalist mentality of the West. . . . The Chinese economy was not yet mature. . . . Nor was there any credit system until the eighteenth (and in some places) until the nineteenth century. . . . The Tokugawa revolution isolated Japan from the rest of the world, and tightened the grip of feudal habits and institutions. (Braudel 1993: 194–5, 285)

We will observe throughout this book how historically inaccurate—and also contradicted by his own observations elsewhere—is this estimation by the master historian and critical student of capitalism.

CONTEMPORARY EUROCENTRISM AND ITS CRITICS

Now we are all—knowingly or not—disciples of this completely Eurocentric social science and history, all the more so since Parsons enshrined Weberianism in sociology and political science when the United States became economically and culturally dominant in the world after World War II. His mistitled *Structure of Social Action* and *The Social System,* as well as the derived "modernization theory," and the economist W. W. Rostow's (1962) *Stages of Economic Growth* are all cut from the same Eurocentric cloth and follow the same theoretical pattern. Well may we ask, what was the point? Rostow's "stages" are little more than a "bourgeois" version of Marx's stage-by-stage development from feudalism to capitalism to socialism—all starting in Europe. Like Marx, Rostow claims that the United States, following England, would show the rest of the world the mirror of its future. Rostow (1975), also explains the "origins of the modern economy" in *How It All Began,* by the scientific revolution that allegedly distinguished modern Europe. In his *Unbound Prometheus,* Landes (1969) finds the cultural conditions for "technological change and industrial development" during the last two centuries only in Western Europe itself. Cipolla (1976: 276) observes "that the Industrial Revolution was essentially and primarily a socio-cultural phenomenon and not a purely technical one, [which] becomes patently obvious when one notices that the first countries to industrialize were those which had the greatest cultural and social similarities to England."

Other authors also have offered only "internal" explanations to account for the alleged superiority and ascendance of the West over the rest of the world. For these writers, the rise of Europe was also a "miracle," which was due to allegedly unique qualities that Europeans had and all others lacked. Thus, Lynn White Jr. (1962), John Hall (1985), and Jean Baechler, Hall and Michael Mann (1988) find the rest of the world deficient or defective in some crucial historical, economic, social, political, ideological, or cultural respect in comparison to the West. The claim is that the presence in "the West" of what was allegedly lacking in "the Rest" gave "us" an initial internal developmental advantage, which "we" then diffused outward over the rest of the world as the "civilizing mission" of "the white man's burden."

This myth has been well examined by Blaut (1993a) under the apt title *The Colonizer's Model of the World: Geographical Diffusionism and Eurocentric History*. Blaut microscopically examines, exposes, and demolishes the myth of "the European miracle" in its myriad forms of biology (racial superiority and demographic continence); environment (nasty, tropical Africa; arid, despotic Asia; temperate Europe); exceptional rationality and freedom (as against "Oriental despotism," the centerpiece of the Weberian doctrine and part of the Marxian one); alleged European historical superiority in technology (despite its borrowings from and dependence on earlier Chinese, Indian, and Islamic advances); and society (development of the state, significance of the Church and "the Protestant ethic," the role of the bourgeoisie in class formation, the nuclear family, etc.).

Blaut (1997) goes over these arguments in even greater detail in his line-by-line dissection of the writings of eight Eurocentric historians, among them the usual suspects: Weber, White (1962), Jones (1981), Robert Brenner in Aston and Philpin (1985), Mann (1986), Hall (1985) and Baechler, Hall and Mann (1988), who therefore require much less examination here. Blaut effectively establishes the theoretical, intellectual, and ideological Eurocentric family relations among all of these writers; and his examination of their arguments against the canons of scientific evidence and elementary logic literally demolishes each and every one of them.

Thus, Blaut effectively demonstrates what Hodgson already said, that each of the alleged European exceptionalisms and the whole European miracle are no more than myths firmly based only in Eurocentric ideology. Therefore, its derived social "science" is empirically and theoretically untenable as well. Blaut also compares feudalism and protocapitalism in Europe, Asia, and Africa before 1492 to argue that in the late

Middle Ages and early modern times Europe had no advantage over Asia and Africa on any of these fronts. Therefore, Blaut correctly argues, it is wrong to attribute the subsequent development of Europe and the West to any of these supposedly internal European exceptionalisms. The same and especially the Weberian allegations of "specific and peculiar achievements of Western rationalism" have more recently also been disputed by the anthropologist Jack Goody (1996), who surveys analogous ones in West, South, and East Asia. Alas, even Molefi Kete Asante's (1987: 4) stinging critique of Eurocentric critical theorists is all too apt:

> They are, in essence, captives of a peculiar arrogance of not knowing that they do not know what it is that they do not know, yet they speak as if they know what all of us need to know. . . . [So] my work has increasingly constituted a radical critique of Eurocentric ideology that masquerades as a universal view. (Asante 1987: 4)

Another recent lonely critic, Frank Perlin, observes:

> The creation of the "scientific fact" frequently, and even systematically, turns out to have been its opposite, the establishment of myth, marking "our" general complicity in the very facts beyond science that "we" "scientists" and "intellectuals" alike (justly) abhor. . . . How can it be that the sciences of society have permitted so little of contrary substance to be said to the peddlers of myth that, instead, so much that we purvey has simply reenforced, even fed their industry, mostly in spite of ourselves? (Perlin 1994: xi, 15)

Indeed! The present book is my attempt to confront the peddlers of myth with contrary evidence, including much assembled by Perlin. The importance of giving Afro-Eurasian peoples and regions outside of Europe their historical due is further underscored by the recent compilation of some scattered articles and unpublished manuscripts by Hodgson in *Rethinking World History:*

> A Westernist image of world history, if not disciplined by a more adequate perspective, can do untold harm; in fact it is now doing untold harm. That is why I lay so much stress on not assuming "decadence" in Islamic society before the eighteenth century unless one has really good evidence. . . . One of the most important tasks of world history, as I see it, is to give people a sense of the pattern of time periods and geographical areas which is free of the multifarious Westernist presuppositions. . . . We must force

ourselves to realize what it means to say that the West is not the modern world, gradually assimilating backward areas to itself; but rather a catalyst, creating new conditions for other forces to work under. . . . The great modern Transmutation presupposed numerous inventions and discoveries originating in all the several citied people of the Eastern Hemisphere, discoveries of which many of the earlier basic ones were not made in Europe. . . . At least as important was the very existence of the vast world market, constituted by the Afro-Eurasian commercial network, which had cumulatively come into being, largely under Muslim auspices, by the middle of the second millennium. . . . Without the cumulative history of the whole Afro-Eurasian Oikoumene, of which the Occident had been an integral part, the Western Transmutation would be almost unthinkable . . . [for only therein] European fortunes could be made and European imaginations exercised. (Hodgson 1993: 94, 290, 68,47)

I entirely agree with Blaut, Perlin, and Hodgson, whose theses are amply confirmed by the evidence in the chapters that follow. Moreover, I want to give credit where credit is due. In a more recent book than the one cited above, Jones (1988) himself expresses doubts about his former book (1981): he quotes another author to the effect that "possibly the most exiting thing to do next would be to prove the theory wrong," and then goes on himself to say that "as a title *The European Miracle* was just a little too seductive":

> *Growth Recurring* is a doubling back too, but more from the implications of the title of *The European Miracle* than from its account of Europe's performance. . . . On the other hand, I no longer see it as miraculous in the sense of "the natural law of a unique event". . . . I began to ponder whether I had been right to hunt for special positive features that may have enabled Europe to become the first continent to achieve sustained growth. The trap seemed to lie in assuming that because Europe is different, the difference must tell us about the inception of growth. . . .
> (Jones 1988: 5, 6)

Jones makes two further revealing confessions: One is that he read and was influenced by the same Marshall Hodgson as I, but too late for Jones's previous book. The other is that nonetheless even in his later book his main "disadvantage . . . relates to ingrained point of view, and not to political or religious attitudes, but something deeper. I was born and brought up an Englishman . . . " (Jones 1988: 183–4). So his new attempt to be "non-racist, non-sexist, and so forth . . . ought to be heartwarming" (Jones 1988: 186). That it is. Yet Jones still labors under so many self-confessed disadvantages that after again reviewing China and adding Japan he is still hard put to "prove the theory wrong," and his "summary and conclusion" is that "formulated this way, Japanese and European history seem to be matters of accidentally contrived balances of forces. Indeed, why not?" (Jones 1988: 190) In this book, I try to do more to prove his theory wrong and hope to do better than to appeal only to accident as an alternative explanation.

ECONOMIC HISTORIANS

One might naively think that for the study of economic history as it really was, the place to turn is to economic historians. Yet they have been the worst offenders of all. The vast majority of self-styled "economic historians" totally neglect the history of most of the world, and the remaining minority distort it altogether. Most economic historians seem to have no perspective—not even a European one—of the world at all. Instead, their "economic history" is almost altogether confined to the West. *The Study of Economic History: Collected Inaugural Lectures 1893–1970,* edited by N. B. Harte (1971), is a collection of twenty-one such lectures by the most eminent English-speaking economic historians. They in turn review and comment on the "economic history" written by their colleagues in the profession over most of the preceding century: almost every word is about Europe and the United States and their "Atlantic economy," which hardly includes even Africa. The rest of the world does not exist for them.

Going through the International Congress of Economic History's recent conference proceedings reveals that some 90 percent of the "international" contributions are about the West. Lately, a couple of the congresses and/or volumes of proceedings have had titles like *The Emergence of the World Economy 1500–1914* (Fisher, McInnis, and Schneider 1986). Yet the preponderance of the contributions are still about the West.

The author of one of the most noteworthy examples of this kind of Eurocentric economic history recently won the Nobel Prize for economics. *The Rise of the Western World: A New Economic History* was written by the 1993 Nobel laureate in economics Douglass C. North with Robert Paul Thomas (1973). It merits special note not only for the recognition given to one of its authors, but also because of the explicitness of its title, its emphasis on "new," and the revision of received theory. Yet under their subtitles "Theory and Overview: 1. The Issue" and on the very first page, they clearly state "the development of an efficient economic organization *in Western Europe* accounts for the rise of the West" (North and Thomas 1973:1; my emphasis). They then trace this institutional change, and especially the development of property rights, to increased economic scarcity, which was generated in turn by a demographic upturn in Western Europe. The rest of the world and its demographic upturn as well was not there for them. Moreover, as North and Thomas (1973: vii) emphasize in their preface, their economic history is also "consistent with and complementary to standard neo-classical economic theory," which we may suppose influenced the awarding of the Nobel Prize.

North and Thomas's book illustrates at least three related problems and my objections: First, Eurocentrists refuse to make and are reluctant even to accept comparison with other parts of the world, which reveal similarities not only in institutions and technological but also in the structural and demographic forces that generated them. Second as we will see in chapter 4, these comparisons show that the alleged European exceptionalism was not exceptional at all. Third, the real issue is not so much what happened here or there, but what the global structure and forces were that occasioned these happenings anywhere, which are analyzed in chapter 6.

What is even more serious is that the small minority of economic historians who do refer to "the Rest" very seriously distort both "the East" and its economic relations with "the West." Their perspective on the "world economy" is that it emerged out of Europe and that Europe built a world economy around itself, as Braudel said that historians "knew" had happened. Take for instance a recent review article on "Maritime Asia, 1500–1800" written by John Wills (1993) for the *American Historical Review*. Wills revealingly subtitles it "The Interactive Emergence of European Domination." He reviews over a dozen books and cites perhaps a hundred others that deal with some "interaction" between East and West. However, most of the action reviewed remains directed from Europe toward Asia, and almost none the other way around. Moreover, the claim in the review's title that European "domination emerged" from 1500 onward to 1800 is not at all substantiated. Indeed, it is disconfirmed even by the evidence supplied by the authors that Wills himself reviews and cites. So the very title of his article still reflects Eurocentric bias far more than it describes reality.

Another current example of Eurocentrism is the series by the innovative publisher Variorum reprinting many of the best but otherwise much less accessible articles on economic history, especially about and from outside the West; its newest series is being published under the umbrella title "An Expanding World: The European Impact on World History, 1450–1800." To promote the series the publisher cites endorsements by the "dean" of world historians, William McNeill, and by the former professor of Economic History at Oxford University, Peter Mathias, who promises that "this series will widen and deepen our understanding of the world stage." On the contrary, it deepens our misunderstanding of the world stage, for even this series carries no hint of what really happened on the world stage from 1450 to 1800: true, the world economy expanded, but primarily in Asia; and the world economic expansion impacted on Europe much more than Europe had any "impact" on "world history" before 1800. Although the title of one of the books is *The European Opportunity,* the series concentrates on what Europe did, rather than on its opportunities in the world economy and especially in Asia, of which Europe only took advantage.

Marxist economic history may seem different, but it is equally, indeed even more, Eurocentric. Thus, Marxist economic historians also look for the sources of "the Rise of the West" and "the development of capitalism" within Europe. Examples are the famous debate in the 1950s on "the transition from feudalism to capitalism" among Maurice Dobb, Paul Sweezy, Kohachiro Takahashi, Rodney Hilton and others (reprinted in Hilton 1976) and the Brenner debate on "European feudalism" (Aston and Philpin 1985). G. E. M. de Ste. Croix (1981) on the class struggles in the ancient "Greco-Roman" civilization and Perry Anderson (1974) on "Japanese feudalism" also considered each of these as a particular "society." Marxists may claim to devote more attention to how the economic "infrastructure" shapes society; but they show no awareness of how one "society" is shaped by its relations with another "society" and still less of how all societies were shaped by their common participation in a single world economy. The very existence of a world economic system was explicitly denied by Marx and only belatedly acknowledged by Lenin. However, Lenin's "imperialism" also was of recent European origin. In Rosa Luxemburg's version, the "world" capitalist economy had to rely on "external non-capitalist" space and markets outside of the capitalist system into which to expand.

LIMITATIONS OF RECENT SOCIAL THEORY

The issue may be rephrased in terms of how deep in time and how wide in space to search for the roots of "the Rise of the West."

For instance, Christopher Chase-Dunn and Thomas Hall (1997) write that the roots of the rise of the West and the emergence of the modern world-system go back at least two millennia. But the question comes, where and how widespread were these roots? The entire body of Euro-centric historiography and social theory looks for these roots only un-der the European street light. For some it shines as far back in time as the Renaissance; for others longer, perhaps through the entire Christian era back to Judaism. Prominent among theorists of the latter viewpoint is Michael Mann (1986,1993), who searches for the "sources of social power" and finds them in ideological, economic, military, and political power (in that order). He observes that "Europe has been an ideologi-cal [Christian] community for a millennium" (Mann 1993: 35). There is the rub: however deep in time, the roots are still allegedly European! In Blaut's (1997: 51) apt characterization, Mann and others visualize no more than a technological Orient Express traveling on the westbound track from the ancient Middle East, through ancient Greece, to medi-eval and modern Western Europe.

However, McNeill (1963), who entitled his pathbreaking book *The Rise of the West: A History of the Human Community,* showed that its roots extend far beyond Europe through the entire Afro-Eurasian ecu-mene. That was of course also the message of Hodgson's (1993) *Re-thinking World History* (written at the same time as McNeill's book). Afro-Eurasia also is the basis of Chase-Dunn and Hall's (1997) analysis of the "rise and demise" of the "modern world-system," as it was of Frank and Gills's (1993) *The World System: Five Hundred Years or Five Thousand?* The question remains, however. What are the implications of this temporally deeper and spatially wider perspective for the (re)in-terpretation of early modern world history? The remainder of this book is written to begin to answer this question from a more global perspec-tive.

The theoretical, analytical, empirical, and—in a word—"perspective" limitations of contemporary received theory are the heritage and re-flection of our "classical" social theory and the equally (or even more so) Eurocentric historiography on which it is based. This social theory was vitiated by its colonialist Eurocentrism when it was conceived in the nineteenth century. The same theory itself became even more vitiat-ing while being further developed in the West and propagated around the world in the twentieth century. Now at the end of this century, this theory and the entire Eurocentric historiography on which it is based is wholly inadequate to address the coming twenty-first century in which Asia promises to rise—again.

Apart from the absurdity of much of the alleged historical basis of received social theory, it still has another theoretical flaw, which is indeed the major theoretical shortcoming of all this theory. That flaw is that, however "universalist" its pretensions, none of this social theory is globally holistic.

To find the really germane factors in economic, social, and cultural "development," we must look holistically at the whole global sociocultural, ecological-economic, and cultural system, which itself both offers and limits the "possibilities" of all of us. Since the whole is more than the sum of its parts and itself shapes its constituent parts, no amount of study and/or assemblage of the parts can ever lay bare the structure, functioning, and transformation of the whole world economy/system.

My argument is that we now need an entirely differently based world history and global political economy. Received classical social theory from "Marx Weber" and their disciples is vitiated by its ingrained Eurocentrism, a bias that is not usually admitted or, perhaps, self-perceived. That bias distorts all perception of, indeed even blinds us from seeing, the reality of the world outside the West. Moreover, the same Eurocentrism also prevents or distorts any realistic perception even of Europe and the West itself. Eurocentric social theory is innately incapable of coming to any terms with the (economic/systemic) reality of one single world, which itself has shaped the very different but not separate "realities" of both the "East" and the "West," the "South" and the "North," and all other parts of the one whole world. So the real issue is not really whether Marx or Weber or anybody else, are right or wrong about this or that part of the of the world system. The real theoretical issue is that none of them have so far even sought holistically to address the systemic global whole, and the real theoretical challenge is to do so.

The reader may well question this affirmation and challenge by reference to what historiography and social theory have already done or claimed. For instance, William McNeill has fathered world history. Not only did he entitle his major work *The Rise of the West* (1963). He also criticized Toynbee for treating world history in terms of twenty-one different civilizations, when McNeill suggested that there were only three major contributory "civilizational" streams to world history and to the rise of the West. So far so good. However, looking back twenty-five years after the publication of his book, McNeill (1990: 9) recognized that "the central methodological weakness of my book is that while it emphasizes interactions across civilizational boundaries, it pays inadequate attention to the emergence of the ecumenical world system within which we live today"; he now sees that his "three regions and their people remained in close and uninterrupted contact throughout the classical era" since 1500 B.C., and therefore a fortiori since A.D. 1500!

For this good reason, my book will show that we live in one world, and have done so for a long time. Therefore, we need a holistic global world perspective to grasp the past, present, and future history of the world—and of any part of it. The difficulties in adopting a world perspective and in overcoming a Eurocentric perspective of, or on, the world seem, nonetheless, still to be considerable. For instance, they were insuperable for Braudel and still are so for Wallerstein. Both of their books were written from a European perspective of the world, as I have argued elsewhere (Frank 1994, 1995) and propose to demonstrate even more so in the present book.

Braudel's "perspective of the world" since 1500 is broader than most. Yet he too divided the world into a "European world-economy" and several other and separate external "world-economies" outside the same. Braudel did, of course, also study and describe at least parts of these "other" world economies, especially in vol. 3 of his trilogy on civilization and capitalism. Indeed, so did Marx in his own vol. 3 of *Capital*. Yet both neglected to incorporate the findings of their third volumes into the model and theory of their first volumes. Moreover, their neglect was quite conscious, intentional, and deliberate: their Eurocentrism convinced both that any and all historical model and social theory, be it universal or not, must be based on the experience of Europe alone. Their only concession was that Europe and its model did have consequences for the rest of the world.

It was Wallerstein's (1974) *The Modern World-System*—and if I may say so also my own contemporaneously written (vide the Preface) *World Accumulation* and the companion *Dependent Accumulation* (Frank 1978a, b)—that sought to systematize these consequences of European expansion and "capitalist" development for both Europe and the rest of the world. Both writers emphasized the negative "underdeveloping" impact of European expansion in many other parts of the world and their contribution in turn to capital accumulation and development in Europe and then also in North America. Wallerstein focused more on the core-periphery structure of the system, which of course I also recognized under the term "metropolis-satellite"; and I focused more than he on the structurally related cyclical dynamic in the system.

Both of us however, Wallerstein (1974, 1980, 1989) and Frank (1978a,b), limited our modeling and theoretical analysis to the structure and process in the modern "world" economy/system. I saw and Wallerstein still sees this system as centered in Europe and expanding from there to incorporate more and more of the rest of the world in its own European-based "world" economy. That is the limitation of this Wallersteinian/Frankian theory: it cannot adequately encompass the whole world economy/system, as long as it remains still Eurocentrically confined to only a part, and not even the major part, of the whole world economy. It may be of some empirical or historical use to show how "our" system incorporated the Americas and parts of Africa into itself "early" on in the sixteenth century and other parts of the world only after 1750.

However, this European-based model of a "world" system is theoretically not only insufficient but downright contrary to the whole real world economic/systemic theory that we really need. Alas, that does not yet exist, and one of the reasons it does not is precisely because we have all, Marx, Weber, Polanyi, and still Braudel, Wallerstein, and Frank, looked under the European street light. However worldly we sought to be, our own still latent if not recognized Eurocentrism made us think that that is where we ought to look for evidence with which to construct our theory. Many other students may not have thought about it at all and only look there because—thanks to us, as well as others— the (European and North American) theoretical and empirical light shines brighter there.

In my view, little is gained, and much better opportunities at reformulation are needlessly squandered, by inventing new latter-day variations on this old theme, which are little more than euphemistic. Thus Eric Wolf (1982) and Samir Amin (1991) stand by a so-called "tributary mode of production," which supposedly characterized the whole world before 1500, according to the former, and much of it until 1800 according to the latter. Or take the case of Gates (1996), who builds her analysis of a thousand years of "China's motor" on "the tributary and petty-capitalist modes of production" and is hard put to show, though she tries, how and why they support and promote patriarchy in China. In contrast, my book will show that, regardless of the variety of their domestic relations—never mind "mode" or "modes"—of production, far more important is participation in a single world economy, which is only obscured by this undue or even misplaced emphasis on "modes of production."

The latest misplaced and therefore irrelevantly misleading discussion by van Zanden (1997) is summarized by its very title: "Do We Need a Theory of Merchant Capitalism?" The entire Spring 1997 issue of *Review* is devoted to this "issue," to which the editor, Wallerstein, also contributes. On the basis of his analysis of labor markets in the Dutch seventeenth-century "Golden Age," van Zanden argues for the affirmative: "merchant capitalism is in a sense 'capitalism in the process of construction' . . . for this growing world market . . . concentrated in relatively small urbanized commercial islands in a noncapitalist sea." Therefore also it is an heretofore insufficiently recognized but necessary "stage" between pre- or protocapitalism and industrial capitalism. To his credit, Wallerstein (1997) denies this thesis by showing that merchant and Dutch capitalism then and now were no more than part and parcel of "historical capitalism." Thus, "entrepreneurs or companies who make large profits do so . . . by being simultaneously producers, merchants, and financiers, or moving back and forth between these roles as economic circumstances make one or another of them more lucrative" (Wallerstein 1997: 252). Of course, but Wallerstein and the others fail to observe that the same was and is equally true throughout the world economy and not only in the small European "capitalist" part.

Several other authors (Ad Knotter, Catharina Lis and Hugo Soly) draw on recent works about "industrialization before industrialization" in the Netherlands, Flanders, and elsewhere in Europe. It is enough to make only these comparisons to show that "van Zanden's terms do not enable analysis of the process: the articulation of merchant capitalism and precapitalist modes of production was not at issue, and the protoindustry was not the most dynamic element in the transition to industrial capitalism" (Lis and Soly 1997: 237). All the more so would these "modes of production" cease to be the issue if, instead of limiting their purview only to parts of the marginal peninsular Europe, the examination is extended to the rest of the world—let alone analyzing them as part and parcel of the whole global economy, as this book does.

A (very) few other students, perhaps not surprisingly especially from Afro-Asian backgrounds, have decided that we must expand or change our theoretical perspective and orientation. Among them are Janet Abu-Lughod (1989), who inquired into what happened "before European hegemony," and K. N. Chaudhuri (1990a), who looked at "Asia before Europe." Of course, they are also handicapped by having to place so much reliance on the already existing European and other Western light posts, which cast very dim light if any on the more distant evidence.

Fortunately, these more world-visionary scholars are increasingly joined by mostly non-"Western" (if often still Western-trained or influenced) researchers, who dig up their own regional and local archival and archaeological pasts with little more than a torchlight or a candle to help them. The evidence they uncover is a treasure—some literally so thanks to underwater archaeology that brings to the surface the contents of long-sunk merchant ships and treasure. These findings can and should offer a wider and deeper basis for inductive synthesis by more far-reaching historiography and the construction of a truly holistic world economic/systemic model and theory.

However, evidence alone is still not enough and no substitute for a holistic whole world-encompassing theoretical model. That is what we need but still lack to help organize and interpret the existing evidence—and guide the search for more and better evidence from the farthest reaches of the world, well beyond the reach of the old Western theoretical street light. This book can take no more than a few hesitating initial steps in that direction. My hope is however that my very shortcomings will encourage others who are far more capable than I am to take giant new steps in that direction.

It would seem to be much easier to do so for the early modern world economy and system that is under investigation here than for earlier times. Indeed, when I was researching the extent of the Bronze Age world economy and system by pursuing the range of its long cycles, I used the analogy of a jigsaw puzzle. I noted that the difference from assembling such an ordinary puzzle is that it is not possible to follow the easy course of starting at the already given straight outer edges and work inward. Instead, I had to start from the presumed center and work outward to search out the boundary edges of the world system jigsaw puzzle. Moreover these boundaries were not even stable but were themselves moving outward over time as well. The task was to establish where and when that was happening.

Assembling the jigsaw puzzle of the early modern world economy would seem to be much easier. The need to establish its outer edges would seem to be obviated by the hard evidence itself, first of its Afro-Eurasian dimensions and then of the only belated incorporation of the Americas after 1492 and of Oceania after 1760. Once we look at this whole world economy, it is easy to start at the "outward" edges of the jigsaw puzzle, even though they are not straight but round. Indeed, an early title of this book was "The World Is Round." All we need to do is to go around it, pick up the pieces, and fit them in where they belong in relation to their neighbors. Then, the picture should emerge almost by itself, unless we get the relationships among the pieces wrong. But then, the historical, geographical, and sociopolitical economic evidence itself permits us to check out our placement of each piece in its relation to the next. All we really need, is a (little more?) holistic vision of the whole. Yet most historians and social theorists accept and do none of the above. Not only do they have no holistic perspective, but they do not even miss it. Even worse, they remain adamant in rejecting the whole altogether.

Nonetheless without looking at the global jigsaw puzzle map, we cannot find the rightful place or comprehend the real functional relations of any of its pieces. What was the place and role of that red piece over there whose shape resembles the outlines of the British Isles? We also cannot know what to make of the many other pieces that are also colored red, one of which is shaped like a big vertical terrestrial wedge and another like a big horizontal kidney surrounded by water. And near the first red piece, we have to place some blue, yellow, and green pieces, each of which in turn has is own same-colored outliers. We need the whole global context to place these other colored jigsaw pieces in their rightful places on the map, especially those with several straight edges that look like someone had drawn them as lines on a table(as in fact the European colonial powers did carve up Africa in 1884 in Berlin). Indeed without holistically analyzing the whole jigsaw puzzle and its creation, we will never comprehend why and how its "designers" assigned which colors, shapes, and places to what pieces, let alone what relation they have to each other and to the whole.

What is still most amiss among contemporary historians and social theorists is a holistic perspective. Historians mostly like to employ a microscope to look at and puzzle over only one piece of the whole at— and only over a short—time. My historian son inscribed a history book to me "from one who studies the trees to one who studies the forest." Even "world" historians, not to mention "civilizationists," are very wont to confine their attention to some big trees and only to compare some big pieces. Indeed, many like to focus particularly on their civilizational specificities or cultural similarities and differences. Some defend their procedure with the argument that "scientific" standards oblige us to study no more than partial pieces of the whole so that we can employ the comparative method to analyze their differences. They do not seem to realize that if the whole is more than the sum of its parts, that whole itself may also contribute to differentiating these parts and pieces of the whole jigsaw puzzle among each other. So they shy away from looking at the whole picture either because they will not see the whole, or because they just cannot see it. Therefore, they also fail to comprehend even some essentials of the piece at which they are looking or the two or more pieces that they wish to compare. Indeed, hardly any "world" historians even note that the real world out there is a whole global jigsaw puzzle, which they might assemble, not to mention seek to comprehend.

Outline of a Global Economic Perspective

Following is the outline of how chapters 2 through 7 begin assembling the jigsaw puzzle of the early modern world economy from 1400 to 1800.

Chapter 2 examines the structure and flow of trade, starting in the Americas and going eastward literally around the globe. It examines the pattern of trade imbalances, and their settlement through payment in money, which also flowed predominantly eastward. About a dozen regions and their relations with each other are examined, going from the Americas, via Africa and Europe, to and through West, South, and Southeast Asia, to Japan and China and from there both across the Pacific and also back across Central Asia and Russia. This review demonstrates the strength and growth of these "regional" economies and their trade and monetary relations with each other. It also shows, at least implicitly, what kind of a world economic division of labor existed, expanded, and changed in the early modern period from about 1400 to 1800. At the very least, this chapter shows that there was such a worldwide division of labor. It identifies many of the different products and services, sectors and regions, and of course enterprises and "countries" that effectively competed with each other in a single global economy. Thus, we will see that all received economic and social theory based on the neglect or outright denial of this worldwide division of labor is without historical foundation.

Chapter 3 examines the role of money in the world economy as a whole and in shaping the relations among its regional parts. There is a large literature on the flow of money from the silver mines in the Americas to Europe, and there has been some concern also with its onward remittance to Asia. However, insufficient attention has been devoted to macro- and microeconomic analysis of why the specie was produced, transported, minted, reminted, exchanged, etc. Beyond macro- and microeconomic analysis of this production and exchange of silver and other species as commodities, one section of this chapter examines the circulatory system through which the monetary blood flowed and how it connected, lubricated, and expanded the word economy.

Another section of chapter 3 examines why and how this capillary monetary system, as well as the oxygen-carrying monetary blood that flowed through it, penetrated and fueled the economic body of the world economy. We examine how some of these monetary veins and arteries were bigger than others, and how smaller ones reached farther into, and even served to extend and stimulate production on, the outward reaches of the world economic body at this and that, but not every, frontier. The hoary myth about Asiatic "hoarding" of money is shown to be without foundation, especially in the "sinks" of the world monetary supply in India, and even more so in China.

Chapter 4 examines some quantitative global economic dimensions. Although hard data are hard to come by, one section devotes some effort to assembling and comparing at least some worldwide and regional dimensions of population, production, trade, and consumption, as well as their respective rates of growth, especially in Asia and Europe. We will see that not only were various parts of Asia economically far more important in and to the world economy than all of Europe but also, as the historical evidence demonstrates unequivocally, that Asia grew faster and more than Europe and maintained its economic lead over Europe in all these respects until at least 1750. If several parts of Asia were richer and more productive than Europe and moreover their economies were expanding and growing during this early modern period, how is it possible that the "Asiatic mode of production" under any of its European designations could have been as traditional, stationary, stagnant, and generally uneconomic as Marx, Weber, Sombart and others alleged? It was not, and so this Eurocentric myth is simply absurd.

Other sections of chapter 4 bring evidence and the judgments of authorities to bear on comparisons of productivity and technology as well as of economic and financial institutions in Europe and Asia, especially with India and China. These comparisons show that the European put-down of Asia is unfounded in fact; for Asia was not only economically and in many ways technologically ahead of Europe at the beginning but also at the end of this period. However, this chapter also launches the argument that production, trade, and their institutions and technology should not only be internationally compared but must also be seen as being mutually related and generated on a world economic level.

Chapter 5 proposes and pursues a "horizontally integrative macrohistory" of the world, in which simultaneity of events and processes is no coincidence. Nor are simultaneous events here and there seen as differently caused by diverse local "internal" circumstances. Instead, one section after another inquires into common and connected causes of simultaneous occurrences around the world. Demographic/structural, monetary, Kondratieff, and longer-cycle analysis is brought to bear in different but complementary attempts to account for and explain what was happening here and there. Such cyclical and monetary analysis is used to help account in the 1640s for the simultaneous fall of the Ming in China and revolution in England, rebellion in Spain and Japan, and other problems in Manila and elsewhere. The French, Dutch Batavian, American, and industrial revolutions in the late eighteenth century are also briefly examined in cyclical and related terms. Another section of chapter 5 inquires whether the so-called "seventeenth-century crisis" of Europe was world wide and included Asia; and I explore the important significance of a negative answer for world economic history. Observation that the "long sixteenth century" expansion continued through the seventeenth and into part of the eighteenth century in much of Asia is used also to pose the question of whether there was an about five-hundred-year-long world economic and political cycle.

This question about the long cycle opens chapter 6 on how and why the West "won" in the nineteenth century, and whether this "victory" is likely to endure or to be only temporary. In previous works (Gills and Frank 1992, Frank and Gills 1993, Frank 1993a), I claim to have identified a half-millennium-long world economic system-wide cycle of alternate expansive "A" and contractive "B" phases, which were some two to three hundred years long each. I traced these back to 3000 B.C. and up to about A.D. 1450. Three separate test attempts by other scholars offer some confirmatory evidence of the existence and my dating of this alleged cycle and phases. Did this long-cycle pattern continue into early modern times? That is the first question posed in this section. The second one is that, if it did, does it reflect and help account for the continued dominance of Asia in the world economy through the seventeenth and into the eighteenth century, as well as for its decline and Europe's rise thereafter?

Chapter 6 also culminates the book's historical account and theoretical analysis of and argument for how "the Decline of the East" and "the Rise of the West" may have been systemically related and mutually promoted. To do so, one part examines the unequal regional and sectoral structure and the uneven temporal or cyclical dynamic that fueled the growth of production and of population in the single global economy. The argument is that it was not Asia's alleged weakness and Europe's alleged strength in the period of early modern world history but rather the effects of Asia's strength that led to its decline after 1750. Analogously, it was Europe's previously marginal position and weakness in the world economy that permitted its ascendance after 1800. This development also took advantage of "the Decline of Asia" after 1750, whose roots and timing are also examined in a separate section of the chapter. Moreover, I suggest that in this same continuing process of global development, the balance of economic, political, and cultural power may already have begun again to revert to Asia.

"The Rise of the West" is examined more concretely in the final part of chapter 6. My thesis—echoing but extending that of Blaut—is that the West first bought itself a third-class seat on the Asian economic train, then leased a whole railway carriage, and only in the nineteenth century managed to displace Asians from the locomotive. One section examines and cites the analysis of Adam Smith about how the Europeans managed to do so with the use of American money. They used it not only to expand their own economies, but also or even especially to buy themselves into the expanding market in Asia. Thus, the industrial revolution and its eventual use by the Europeans to achieve a position of dominance in the world economy cannot be adequately explained on the basis only of factors "internal" to Europe, not even supplemented by its accumulation of capital extracted from its colonies. We need a world economic accounting for and explanation of this global process. To do so, this section then proposes and examines a hypothesis based on worldwide and subsidiary regional demand-and-supply relations for labor-saving and power-producing technological innovation.

Since the whole is more than the sum of its parts, each part is not only influenced by other parts, but also by what happens in the whole world (system). There is no way we can understand and account for what happened in Europe or the Americas without taking account of what happened in Asia and Africa—and vice versa—nor what happened anywhere without identifying the influences that emanated from everywhere, that is from the structure and dynamic of the whole world (system) itself. In a word, we need a holistic analysis to explain any part of the system. The concluding chapter 7 reexamines the implications of this need for holistic analysis and our derivative findings and hypotheses for further research about historiography, received theory, and the possible and necessary reconstruction of both. The first part summarizes the historiographic conclusions of what not to do. The second part of this final chapter goes on to suggest better alternative theoretical directions.

Anticipating and Confronting Resistance and Obstacles

To begin with, we are badly equipped to confront our global reality when we are misguided into thinking that our world is only just now undergoing a belated process of "globalization." Our very language and its categories reflect and in turn misguide our thinking when they lead us to suppose that the parts came first and then only combined to make a whole: examples are our *society,* my *country,* the German word *Nationaloekonomie,* or *international* relations with or without *international* trade. They all sound as though we long lived— and some of us would still like to live—in some social, political, economic "units" which have had some allegedly pristine existence ever since (their) Creation. It is simply not true that they only became interrelated later or even now. That allegation and terminology is just about the most literally nonsensical "perspective of the world" and rendition of its reality imaginable. But short of inventing an entirely new vocabulary that would be unfamiliar to the reader, I am obliged to make do with received terminology and try to stretch it to encompass a more global reality. However, we need more than global terminology. We also need global analysis and theory.

Yet even proposing global analysis, let alone theory, of and for the world is a hazardous task. It meets with strong resistance and can evoke ferocious counterattacks. We may anticipate and address, if not remove, at least the iceberg tips of some of the obstacles that we may encounter in the stormy analytic seas ahead. Since the present proposal is only now being launched, I will base my anticipations on some of the previous experience of both Immanuel Wallerstein and myself. His experience is relevant because the scope of my present proposal is at the same time broader, if more superficial, than his was.

The most numerous obstacles are likely to be picayune nitpickings.

Other, more theoretical objections may be fewer, but larger. A particularly big obstacle is posed by Wallerstein himself.

One nitpicking objection is that I do not use (or even have the ability to use) primary sources. I reject that objection for several reasons. In 1966, I sent the manuscript of an innovative critique of received theses about Mexican history to one of the authors of the same. He kindly wrote back but said my manuscript was not worth publishing, because it was not based on primary sources. So I left it in my desk drawer until, thirteen years later, Wallerstein invited me to publish it in a series he was editing at Cambridge University Press (Frank 1979). Then the same author wrote a review, saying my book should not have been published because by now what I was saying was old hat, further research and analysis by others having converted my earlier, outlandish-seeming world economic thesis into accepted received theory.

This experience illustrates what kind of sources are necessary and legitimate to make a historical statement, particularly a paradigmatic one. One of the problems of using a microscope to do archival research is, of course, that it affords historians no wider view, unless they bring one with them from outside the archives. Moreover, if historians wish to exit from the received paradigm and/or even to challenge the one based on microscopic analysis, they all the more require a wider perspective. Of course if historians take too big a step back to examine the material with a telescope, they are bound to miss some of the details. That leads us on to the next objection.

It might be objected that, especially for lack of sufficient or even any primary sources, I do not know enough to tackle the whole world, or even several parts of it. Even Braudel (1992: 468) doubted that it is "wise for one historian to try to bring together in a single analysis fragments of a history still insufficiently explored by research." Others will say, "Oh, but what you suggest was not quite that way in my back yard in the one-, ten-, or hundred-year period to whose study I have devoted twenty years of my life." Yet as the world historian William McNeill pointed out in his foreword to a previous book of mine (Frank and Gills 1993), it is impossible to know everything, or even "enough," about anything, no matter how narrowly the topic may be defined. Elsewhere, he argues that

> macrohistorians ruthlessly by-pass most details of the available literary record. . . . This does not make macrohistory less exact or well attested. . . . Each scale of inquiry creates its own landscape

of significant meanings. Smaller is not closer to reality—as minutely specialized historians sometimes assume. It is just different.
. . . Good history results from a process of selection and criticism, picking out information from available sources that is relevant to whatever questions the historian asks—no more, no less. (McNeill 1996: 21)

Therefore, dearth of knowledge, to which I readily admit, is not really a function of the narrowness or breadth of the topic selected for study. On the contrary as chapter 5 will argue citing Joseph Fletcher, it is the all-too-common failure to do "horizontally integrative macrohistory" that results in the narrowness if not the very dearth of historical knowledge.

Some readers may object that I am looking at only one "economic" part or feature. At a combined 1996 meeting of the World History Association and the International Society for the Comparative Study of Civilizations, one member told me privately that "you are doing good economic history; that is why I am not interested"; another said publicly that "you are culturally blind." Advocates of political, social, cultural, religious, national, ethnic, and other kinds of analysis will complain that mine does not favor, appreciate, or kowtow to their particular/ist desires. Partisans will lament that this analysis is of little or no use to the struggle of "my people." They seek support instead from this or that ethnocentrism or from the new Afrocentrism, the old Islamocentrism, the even older Sinocentrism, Russian exceptionalism, and so on, none of which receive their oft-demanded support from the present analysis. My perspective also combats the Eurocentric Western exceptionalism now peddled in new garb by that old cold-warrior Samuel Huntington (1993,1996) as "The Clash of Civilizations?" (Credit where credit is due, the author also put a question mark behind the title of his 1993 Foreign Affairs article, but his all too eager public has already left it off. However by 1996, there was no more question mark in the title of his book.) Instead, as chapter 7 emphasizes, this book develops a perspective to support "unity in diversity."

Feminists may charge, and rightly so, that this perspective and analysis does not sufficiently rattle at the cage of the patriarchal gender structure of society, which disadvantages women to say the least. That is true, although this approach is no less amenable to genderization than received theory is; except that it does not deal with women per se, nor with men for that matter. Indeed, this structural analysis does not seem to deal with any people at all. Chapter 2 on the division of labor and trade, chapter 3 on how money goes around the world and makes the world go round, and chapters 5 and 6 on the world economic system's structure and dynamic just inquire into the political economic and social relations among people. In a sense in my book, history makes people more than people make history.

That will be enough to make many rail against some economic and/or other structural "determinism" that allegedly negates any and all voluntarist free-will political "agency." Of course, it is useless to point out to them that whatever constraints there are in the real world were not put there by any systematic observers. Moreover, no systematic observer I know has ever alleged that the objectively studied "system" leaves no room for individual, community, cultural, political, or other "bottom up" (indeed also "top down") subjective action and reactions. Yet good—or even bad—intentions are often not realized; and which intentions are and are not realized is subject to systemically generated opportunities and constraints, as examined in chapters 5 and 6.

However, there will also be more "concrete" complaints and demands by social theorists similar to the complaints Wallerstein has already encountered in response to his "modern world-system." A special Eurocentric charge is that the evidence does not support his, much less my, contention that Europeans benefited from something other than their own good efforts. Years ago, Paul Bairoch (1969, 1974), Patrick O'Brien (1982) and others explicitly countered the earlier theses of Frank (1967, 1978a, b) and Wallerstein (1974) that colonial and neocolonial trade contributed to European investment and development. Bairoch (1969) denied that commercial capital made any significant contribution thereto. O'Brien (1982, 1990) has on several occasions dismissed overseas trade and colonial exploitation as contributors to capital accumulation and industrialization in Europe, since by his calculations this trade, not to mention profits therefrom, amounted to no more than 2 percent of European gross national product (GNP) in the late eighteenth century. O'Brien (1982: 18) contends that "for the economic growth of the core, the periphery was peripheral." Now O'Brien goes even further and categorically contends, under the head "The Formation of a Global Economy, 1846–1914," that

> interconnections across continents and countries down to the middle of the nineteenth century seem limited. . . . Producers and traders the world over remained not merely insulated from foreign rivals but also protected . . . from competition even within national boundaries. . . . Integration occurred first on a local and

regional, then on a national, basis, and increasingly as the [nineteenth] century went on, it took place on a global scale. (O'Brien 1997: 76–77)

The present book demonstrates beyond the shadow of a doubt how wrong O'Brien is in fact, never mind in theory. Yet he has also argued that "neither quantification nor more historical scholarship will settle debates about the significance of oceanic trade for the Industrial Revolution" (O'Brien 1990: 177).

We must agree with O'Brien that the evidence will never settle this issue. Not that evidence is of no importance, but it does not bear so much on the real dispute between us, which is paradigmatic. O'Brien (1982, 1990) rejects even Wallerstein's only partially world-systemic perspective. Indeed, O'Brien (1997: 86–89) again alleges that "European dependence . . . remained negligible," that the "economic significance of Asia, Africa, and South America . . . remained at a low and stable level" (he cites Bairoch 1974 and 1993 in support); and that, though the "facts and gains" of colonialism and imperialism are beyond dispute "colonialism did not necessarily pay" and "imperialism turned out to be of limited benefit." Therefore, O'Brien (1997: 86) writes that the "suggestion" by Frank, Wallerstein, and Amin that European economic growth "occurred somehow at the expense" of others "remains contestable." Instead, O'Brien contends that for the history of European (and even British) industrialization "the 'perspective of the world' [the reference is to Braudel's title] for Europe emerges as less significant than the 'perspective of Europe' for the world"(O'Brien 1990: 177). To people with so ingrained and recalcitrant a Eurocentric perspective, no amount of evidence, such as that marshaled in chapters 4 and 6, can make any difference. They will simply persist in their Eurocentric claim that Europe's relations with the world made no difference to Europe but all the difference to the world.

Behind this denial of significance of world-economic/systemic factors lies a methodological postulate, which in this case is another aspect of the Eurocentric perspective: explanations should be sought "internal" to the explanandum. Yes, but "internal" to what? Thus, Cipolla (1976: 61) summarizes his own argument by saying "the idea of trade as an 'engine of growth' is a gross oversimplification." Marxists have their own version of this same contention. Robert Brenner (in Aston and Philpin 1985) contends that only internal class relations everywhere account for the development of capitalism anywhere. Mao Ze-dong generalized the same idea in his famous "On Contradiction" aphorism about eggs and stones. The application of external heat will produce a chicken only from "internal contradiction" within an egg and not from a stone. That may or may not be so for "any given society in question." The point is, however, that the real question is not about any "given society," but about the world economy and global system as a whole, and that everything is "internal" to that.

This debate about "internal vs. external" turns even the analysis of the European-based "modern world-economy/system" itself into yet another obstacle and resistance to be overcome. The argument is also that something "internal" to the European "modern world-system" generated the transition from feudalism to capitalism, which then spread to the rest of the world "outside." I contend that instead Europe and its "world-economy" were part and parcel of a long-preexisting Afro-Eurasian economy whose own systemic structure and dynamic became global—and itself generated many developments in Europe as well. Therefore, it is the "internal" operation of the global world economy—and not just of the European "world-economy"—that requires analysis.

What about class and class struggle? Bring the state back in! Allow more room for culture! My answers in short are that there is class in the world economy, but the class struggles between ruling and ruled classes have never had the motor force that Marx attributed to them—when he took off his historical materialist hat. The state and culture, and indeed class struggle itself, require much more analysis as being themselves dependent on the structure and dynamic of the world economy and system.

Others will argue that surely 99.99 percent of the people then living did not perceive what I attribute to the world economy/system, so it could not have made any impact on their consciousness. Yes and no. First of all, objective circumstances impact—indeed shape—subjective consciousness, especially in the absence of the subject's conscious awareness thereof. Second, consciousness is not everything; and one set of objective circumstances also affects other objective circumstances as well as the consciousness of the subject, as we will see in chapters 5 and 6.

Postmodernists will object as well. They may appreciate my "deconstruction" of manifest and latent terminological and conceptual Eurocentrism. Postcolonialists may also like the demonstration that the colonial idea is only recent and probably temporary in and about Asia. But those who think that there is no reality beyond its perception by the mind or its communication through language will dispute my insistence that it is the historical evidence itself which disconfirms received historiography and social theory. Moreover, they will themselves insist that only my imagination permits me to contend that there is a real global world economy and system out there and that its rendering here is no more than a figment of my imagination. They will be persuaded by no amount of argument or even evidence, unless they themselves drive their own rhetorical car into an imaginary tree and live to tell about it.

Here it will be more useful to confront those who admit the reality of the trees and even of a world economic and systemic forest. For instance, Wallerstein (1974, 1980, 1989), Frank (1978a,b), Braudel (1979, 1992), Wolf (1982), Blaut (1993a), Stephen Sanderson (1995), George Modelski and William Thompson (1996), and Chase-Dunn and Hall (1997) have offered a more helpful "perspective of the world" and its impact on local economic and social trees. Moreover, all of them have self-consciously already tried to offer broader perspectives to counter parochial Eurocentrism. Yet, although their scheme of things has not been sufficiently global and holistic to encompass the whole world economic forest, their analysis has nonetheless provoked strong resistance and counterattacks from the defenders of earlier social theory. How much more resistance and counterattack then will an even more holistically global analysis provoke, which turns the tables not only on most received theory but also on these theorists' own revisionism thereof?

Several instances of such resistance readily come to mind. Eric Wolf (1982) is rightly critical of others' neglect of the impact that Europe had on "the people without history." He shows that people outside Europe did have histories of their own and that the expansion of Europe impacted on them. However, he still underestimates their mutual impact on each other; and he does not ask how the one world in which all participate together impacts on each of them. Moreover he retains, indeed even resurrects, the primacy of "modes of production," from kinship, to tributary, to capitalist-based ones. That, I contend, still diverts attention from where it is most needed—on the world system as a whole.

Wallerstein (1974) did even more to incorporate the mutual relations of the European core and its periphery elsewhere in the world, in that he addressed the structure and transformation of a single political economic division of labor and its impact on core and periphery alike. However until 1750, most of the world still remains beyond his "modern world-system" and outside the Braudelian/Wallersteinian "European world-economy" on which it rests. In Wallerstein's perspective, Europe's expansion did incorporate parts of Africa, the Caribbean, and the Americas into the world-economy/system. However, he explicitly explains that this economy was only world-like and not at all world-encompassing. In his view, West, South, and East Asia, and indeed Russia, were only incorporated into this European world-economy/system after 1750. So Wallerstein's "world-system" perspective, theory, and analysis not only does not encompass most of the world before 1750; but he also claims explicitly that most of the world, including all of Eurasia east of the Mediterranean and of Eastern Europe, had played no significant part in the making and early history of his "modern world-system."

Therefore of course, Wallerstein's very limited history and theory of the modern "world" economy and system also precludes coming to grips with the global economy and real world system, which remained outside his purview until 1750. Nonetheless, what happened there was highly determinant of developments inside the Braudel/Wallerstein "European world-economy/system," as this book seeks to demonstrate especially in chapters 3, 4, and 6. To get even the remotest chance to study and understand any genesis, structure, and function, not to mention transformation and development, in this real world economy and system, we need an altogether more holistic theory and analysis, such as that presented in Chapter 6. However, Wallerstein (1991, 1992, 1993) has already several times demurred to any such amendment of world-system analysis; more recently, his "Hold the Tiller Firm" (1995) inveighs against any and all "nomothetic," "idiographic," and "reifying" revisionism, specifically including mine.

Even Blaut (1992, 1993a) resists holistic analysis of world economic development and its continuity despite debunking the myth of "the European miracle" and insisting that Europeans had no innate advantages over Asians in 1500. Others resist as well despite their long-term Eurasian historical perspectives, which include Sanderson's (1995) comparison between Japan and Britain, Modelski and Thompson's (1996) discovery of Kondratieff cycles going back to Song China (discussed in chapter 5), and Chase-Dunn and Hall's (1997) analysis of different "world system" modalities during the past ten thousand and more years. Nonetheless, all of them still insist that a sharp "break" occurred in world history around 1500, not only because Europeans found the Americas and a new way to the Orient in 1492 and 1498, but primarily because that initiated the development of capitalism in Europe and its dissemination from there. The abundant evidence in chapters 2 and 4 now questions the very basis of this position, which I used to share.

Other colleagues and friends in the social "sciences" also shy away from looking at the whole, even when they do avow holism. The most avowedly holistic are Samir Amin and Giovanni Arrighi, with whom Wallerstein and I have co-authored two books (Amin et al. 1982, 1990). Like Wallerstein, Amin and Arrighi also start to assemble their modern world jigsaw puzzles at the center and work outward; and they also continue to chose their "center" in Europe. They reject Eurocentrism; and Amin (1989) even entitled a book *Eurocentrism* to denounce it, while Arrighi is devoting increasing attention to East Asia. Yet both still start their own reviews of early modern history in Europe, because that is where "capitalism" started. Like Wallerstein (1991), Amin (1991, 1993, 1996) also wrote critiques of my thesis, defending instead the orthodox contention that a sharp break occurred in world history around the year 1500 — in Europe. Before that, "world-empires" (says Wallerstein) only produced and distributed on the basis of a "tributary mode of production" (says Amin, but also Wolf 1982). Then came the development in, and spread of, the "capitalist mode of production" from Europe. Arrighi does attribute more importance to China and East Asia (Arrighi 1996, Arrighi, Hamashita, and Selden 1996). Nonetheless, Arrighi's (1994) *Long Twentieth Century* still traces the development of the "capitalist world economy" and its innovation of financial institutions from their alleged beginnings in the Italian city states.

Thus Eurocentrism marks and limits even the severest critics of received Eurocentric social theory, including those who argue persuasively that the wider world played a much greater role in "the rise of the West" than this theory allows. Another vivid example comes from Alan Smith (1991). His *Creating a World Economy* begins with charges that Weber and the usual recent suspects from North and Thomas, Rostow, and Jones to Wolf, Wallerstein, and Frank ignore, truncate, or abuse the role of "the wider world" outside Europe. But Smith takes only a brief look at the history of this wider world in his second chapter and then immediately turns around in his third chapter to begin his own analysis, once again, with medieval Europe. He arrives at A.D. 1500 with "lineal trends" in society and polity that led to "steady progress," thanks to "technology that made continuing growth possible" (Smith 1991: 67, 5) — all in and from Europe. The entire remainder of the book is dedicated to Europe and its transition to capitalism, its overseas expansion, and the "peripheries and dependencies" in the world economy. Since Smith still seeks the "creation of the world economy" and the birth and spread of "capitalism" in and from Europe, he must also claim that many of the areas of the world still remained external to the new system. Eastern Africa, India, Ceylon, Indonesia, southeast Asia, China, Japan and the Middle East are all included in this category ... [because] participation in commercial relations was discretionary and ... seems to have had little lasting impact on the structures of the respective social formations. . . . One should not overestimate the role of international trade in forging linkages of substance between distant lands. . . . Only in Europe were ... [social processes of integration] carried to fruition. (Smith 1991: 7, 11)

With this same old Eurocentric litany of course, we will never find any of the structures, processes, or forces that were "creating a world economy" (to use Smith's apt title). Just as with all those he criticized for their shortcomings, Smith in 1991 still looks no further than what the dim European street light illuminates when it was put up in the nineteenth century. By contrast, Adam Smith in 1776 had taken his *Inquiry into the Nature and Causes of the Wealth of Nations* very much further afield and, as we will see especially in chapters 3 and 6, showed us vastly more of "wie es eigentlich gewesen ist"—"as it really was," as Leopold von Ranke put it.

Thus it seems this gospel about the European development of the modern world capitalist economy and system since 1500 or whenever forms a Maginot line of defense behind which one and all remain resistant to seeing the real world. My book proposes an end run around that line of defense. When I launched my thesis that the present world system began long before 1500, Wallerstein was gracious enough to publish it (Frank 1990a) and a follow-up article (Gills and Frank 1992) in the journal he edits, even though he himself always holds to the sacrosanct 1500 dividing line (Wallerstein 1993, 1995, 1996a). Yet according to Wolf (1982), the line is in 1800; to Marx and many others, sometime between 1600 and 1800; and according to Braudel (1992), all the time between 1100 and 1600. Chase-Dunn and Hall (1997) do insist that the rise of Europe and the West must be understood as part and parcel of more than two thousand years of Eurasian development; nonetheless, they too still regard the modern period since 1500 as a new departure into capitalism, which was initiated in and by Europe. The Gulbenkian Commission report *Open the Social Sciences,* written mostly by Wallerstein (1996b), denounces the Eurocentric, false "universalism" of nineteenth- and twentieth-century Western social science (see the second epigraph for this chapter). Yet even this urgent call to reconsider the bases of the social sciences in preparation for the twenty-first century also does not rattle the apparently sacrosanct cage of a European origin and center for capitalism and all that allegedly follows.

However, if we see that the world is round, Europe turns out to be the wrong place to locate the center; and the significance of the beginnings of "capitalism" there or anywhere appear increasingly dubious, to say the least. All the nineteenth- and twentieth-century social theorists reviewed above as well as many historians start their examination of early modern history in the wrong place. They only look under the European street light, whose illumination is ever dimmer as they work from Europe outward to examine its "expansion" as it "incorporated" the rest of the world. The farther they depart from their European lamppost, the less they can see. That is why for Wallerstein and many others Asia remained outside the "world-economy/system" until 1750 and was only "incorporated" after that.

This whole book and especially its chapters 4 and 7 insist that the reinterpretation by Frank and Gills (1993) of the period before 1500 also casts a long shadow over the received interpretations of the period since then. This modern world history is in dire need of reinterpretation. The Asian and world economic evidence, when examined under a non—or at least less—Eurocentric light, will reveal a wholly different picture. Chapter 4 will demonstrate that Asia already shone in the global economy long before 1750 and even then still continued to outshine Europe. In fact, Asia provided far more economic, not to mention cultural, illumination to Europe, than this then-still-marginal outpost (not lamppost!) brought to any part of Asia.

Beyond all these practical obstacles, theoretical resistance, and ideological counterattacks to any holistic analysis that encompasses more than just the European "world-economy" and the "modern world-system," we can also find outright theoretical principled rejection of any kind of holism. That is the position of John R. Hall, among others.

Hall rightly observes that "Frank consistently traces lines of determination in one direction only, from the whole to the part" and that "the modern world system, then, is to be understood via an assumption of holism, whereby the totality defines the nature of the parts as well as their relation to that totality" (Hall 1984: 46, 60).

In a later work, Hall applies his theoretical principles and his rejection of holism is praxis still more concretely. Hall first writes that

> my own critique has been that the assumption of holism promotes a misreading of the emergence of the capitalist world econ-

omy. . . . One alternative is to abandon the search for an encompassing theory of history in favor of a neo-Weberian approach
that encourages analytic historiography, but without privileging
any particular explanation in advance. . . . The neo-Weberian approach counters theories based in holism and necessitism, which
force events into the matrix of a universal history founded on
some prime mover—materialist, idealist, or otherwise. (Hall 1991:
58, 59, 60)

Then Hall falsely alleges that

the present analysis . . . shows that an assumption of holism
within the world-system perspective is inadequate to an explanation of historical change. . . . [The appeal of] world-system theory as a master theory of history . . . is unfounded for several
reasons. In the first place, universalist histories rarely are adequate. . . . Second, they unnecessarily narrow the agenda of historiography. Third, they fail to contend with the methodological
problems of historical inquiry. (Hall 1991: 83, 82)

While Hall's empirical observations about my holistic procedure do
me honor, none of his critiques of "world-system" have the slightest
foundation. In fact of course, universalism, holism, and real world system theory do contend with the methodological problems of broadening the agenda of historiography, as we must. That is because, as I
argued above in theory and will demonstrate below empirically through
historical analysis, received historiography and social theory have not
been nearly holistic enough in that they have largely evaded, not to
mention denied, the "totality" of the globe and its history. The only
thing in Hall's rejection of holism that we must assent to is that "once
holism is abandoned, the warrant of world-system theory as a master
theory of history no longer has force" (Hall 1991: 83). Herein Hall does
indeed put his finger on the de facto limits of the theory he critiques,
but that is no reason to throw out the historical baby along with the
theoretical bathwater. On the contrary, his in this respect correct observation is precisely the reason why we need to make our historiography
and social theory still more holistic and enough so in order to encompass the global whole, because as Hall himself rightly observed, "the
totality defines the nature of the parts as well as their relation to that
totality." So, it is the very neglect of this holism by so many others in
practice as well as its principled recalcitrant theoretical rejection by Hall
which show that holistic theory is as necessary as it is difficult in praxis.
That is so not the least because the opposition ranges from Bairoch's,

O'Brien's, and Hall's critiques of Wallerstein and Frank even to Wallerstein and his "world-system" followers themselves.

Some recent and current efforts by several other authors deserve special mention for addressing and illuminating this problematique. Though arrived at in partly different ways, our joint conclusions reinforce each other. Among these are several Asian authors including George Asiniero in the Philippines, who is working on the global place of Asia, and K. N. Chaudhuri, whose early work on India and the Indian Ocean (1978, 1985) is often cited below and is also used in his own *Asia Before Europe* (1990a). Bin Wong (1997) examines the industrial revolution through a new comparison of Europe and China. Takeshi Hamashita and Satoshi Ikeda in Japan see a China-centered regional economy in East Asia; both authors are extensively cited in chapter 2. Arrighi, Hamashita, and Selden (1996) propose to study this East Asian development during the past five hundred years. Nonetheless, none of them tackle the entire world economy. Dennis Flynn and his co-author Arturo Giraldez do make a world economic analysis, but they confine themselves to an analysis of the global market for silver (which I cite often in chapter 3); however, they also do signal the world economic significance of China.

A world economic perspective also marks the work of two other authors. Frank Perlin, on whose work I draw repeatedly in my chapter 2 on trade, chapter 3 on money, and chapter 4 on market institutions, applies his truly global perspective in his analysis of the economy of India. Nonetheless, he seems to shy away from bringing the same analytic perspective to bear on the world economy as a whole. Finally, Ken Pomeranz deserves special mention as the only other scholar who to my knowledge also brings a global perspective to bear on the development and industrial transformation of the world economy before 1800 and within it of the significance of China. After I had prepared this entire text, including this introductory chapter, he kindly supplied me his own manuscript in progress in which he makes technological, institutional, economic, and ecological comparisons that favor China over Europe, some of which I have belatedly also cited in my own manuscript. Pomeranz and I use parallel procedures and arrive at the same conclusions regarding the importance of examining developments in Europe within the global real world context in which they took place.

That also leads us to agree—as a minority of two standing against the conventional wisdom—that these developments were not the result of centuries of (intra-)European sociocultural or even economic preparation, but rather primarily the results of only belated and very sudden inflections and departures in European and world affairs. Among these, Pomeranz devotes much more and better analysis to the role of ecological/economic constraints, incentives, and possibilities. He shows how these were generated by Europe's coercive extraction not only of finance but also of real goods from its colonies in the Americas. Of course I also recognize these; but I place still greater emphasis on the benefits that Europe derived from its relations with Asia, to which he devotes less attention. Sing Chew (1997 and forthcoming) is also doing an ecological economic history with global scope, but like Pomeranz also, he nonetheless refrains from trying to analyze the world economy as a whole. Moreover, I devote more effort (in chapter 5) than they to what Joseph Fletcher (1985, 1995) called "horizontally integrative macrohistory" in which simultaneous events and processes in the world economy are examined and related on a global level.

In so doing, this book will argue, and I hope demonstrate, that the widespread failure to use a holistic global perspective not only confines us to parochial views, but that these also seriously distort all regional, sectoral, and indeed temporal findings because they fail to fit these findings into the global scheme of things. So do all attempts to escape from parochialism and get at structure and processes in the global whole by starting with a part, especially with one in the wrong place. That has been the original sin of received Eurocentric historiography and social theory, which started in Europe and worked from there outward. The same procedure and narrow parochialism have been even more characteristic of the "exceptionalism and . . . exaggerated sense of uniqueness" prevalent among historians of "American" history, as Gordon Wood (1997: 51) points out in *The New York Review of Books*. Even its recent "broadening" to "place the history of the United States within the setting of the entire Atlantic basin" is still limited to the concept of "Atlantic civilization." Moreover, Wood and the historians he reviews can think of no better remedies than "increasingly teaching joint comparative courses at various universities" and "publishing works that compare developments in the two continents of the Western Hemisphere."

This book turns this procedure around and instead works from the whole world inward. Or at least it begins by working our way around the globe, starting with trade, money, population, and production worldwide. Chapters 5 and 6 offer a more holistic conceptualization and an analysis of global processes, including European and American ones. Thereby, we arrive at conclusions and implications in chapter 7 that are very different from those of received Eurocentric social theory, which is thereby turned on its head, or rather head up!

CHAPTER 2

The Global Trade
Carousel 1400–1800

'World economic integration' is as significant a fact of organized life in earlier
centuries (despite all appearances to the contrary) as it more obviously is in the days of
instant computerized markets. . . . We must conclude that major changes involve
transitions in forms of integration and not, as is alleged, the emergence of
integration itself. . . . The history of the world should not be characterized as a
movement from locally constituted closures toward increasing world integration and
homogenization. . . . The conventional notion of 'diverse cultures' being 'penetrated'
by emergent universalist forces is misfounded. . . . Whether in the ninth and tenth
centuries, twelfth and thirteenth centuries, or seventeenth and eighteenth centuries,
the world has always been complex in its connectedness. . . . The continuum of
medieval and early-modern times has no single centre, not even a handful of
particular centres conceived as the sources affecting integration. Instead, its character
is prolific multicentredness.

Frank Perlin (1994: 98, 102, 104, 106)

An Introduction to the World Economy

The major thesis of this book is that, contrary to widespread doubts and denials, there was a single global world economy
with a worldwide division of labor and multilateral trade from 1500
onward. This world economy had what can be identified as its own
systemic character and dynamic, whose roots in Afro-Eurasia extended
back for millennia. It was this world political economic structure and

its dynamic that had motivated Europeans to seek greater access to the economically dominant Asia ever since the European Crusades. The same Asian magnet led to the "discovery" and incorporation of the Western Hemisphere "New" World into the Old World economy and system after the 1492 voyage of Columbus and to closer European-Asian relations after the 1498 circum-African voyage of Vasco da Gama. An alternate route to China via the Northwest Passage around and/or through North America—and also eastward through the Arctic Sea—continued to be eagerly sought for centuries thereafter.

The world economy continued to be dominated by Asians for at least three centuries more, until about 1800. Europe's relative and absolute marginality in the world economy continued, despite Europe's new relations with the Americas, which it used also to increase its relations with Asia. Indeed, it was little more than its new and continued access to American money that permitted Europe to broaden, though hardly to deepen, its participation in the world market. Productive and commercial economic activities, and population growth based on the same, also continued to expand faster and more in Asia until at least 1750, as this and the following two chapters document.

This chapter outlines the globe-encircling pattern of world trade relations and financial flows, region by region. The examination of the structure and operation of these global economic relations will demonstrate the existence of a world market in the early modern period beyond a reasonable doubt. My insistence on the same is intended to counter the widespread neglect and even frequent denial of the existence of this world economy by so many other students of that period. Indeed, it has recently become fashionable to claim that the world economy is only now undergoing "globalization." Moreover, the explicit denial, not to mention neglect, of the early modern world market and its underlying division of labor is still the mistaken basis of much historical research and social science theory about the "European world-economy" by Braudel and the "modern world-system" by Wallerstein and by their many disciples, not to mention their detractors like O'Brien, cited in chapter 1.

An "intercontinental model" of world trade between 1500 and 1800 on the basis of interregional competition in production and trade was proposed by Frederic Mauro (1961). However, its early existence was already observed by Dudley North in 1691: "The Whole World as to Trade, is but one Nation or People, and therein Nations are as Persons" (quoted in Cipolla 1974: 451). Moreover, this world market and the

flow of money through it permitted intra- and intersectoral and regional divisions of labor and generated competition, which also
spanned and interconnected the entire globe:

> The records show that there was competition . . . between alter-
> native products, such as East Indian and European textiles;
> between identical products from different regions enjoying simi-
> lar climates, e.g., sugar from Java and Bengal, sugar from Madeira
> and Sao Tome, and Brazilian and West Indian sugar; or between
> products grown in different climatic regions, as in the case of
> tobacco. . . . Chinese, Persian and Italian silk; Japanese, Hungar-
> ian, Swedish and West Indian copper; the spices of Asia, Africa
> and America; coffee from Mocha, Java and the West Indies: all of
> these competed. . . . The best barometer, however, is represented
> by the prices on the commodity exchange of Amsterdam. (Cipolla
> 1974: 451)

The Amsterdam that Cipolla singles out may have been the best market
price barometer for a time, but that should not be confused with the
climate itself and the ups and downs in its economic and financial
weather, which were worldwide. Of course, the global inter- and intraregional competitive and complementary or compensatory division of
labor went far beyond Cipolla's few examples. For instance, Rene Barendse observes regarding the Arabian Sea and the operation of the
Dutch East India Company (or VOC, from its commonly used Dutch
initials) there and elsewhere that

> The production was centralized on places where the costs of la-
> bour were lowest. This, not primarily low transport-costs, ex-
> plains [that] . . . comparative cost-advantages were pulling Asian
> and American markets together—no matter what mercantilist re-
> striction. Another case was the substitution of Indian, Arab and
> Persian products like indigo, silk, sugar, pearls, cotton, later on
> even coffee—the most profitable commodities traded in the Ara-
> bian seas in the late seventeenth century—by goods produced
> elsewhere; generally the American colonies. . . . Due to this global
> process of product-substitution, by 1680 the transit-trade of the
> Arabian seas with Europe had disappeared or was in decline; this
> was for a brief period cushioned by the rise of the coffee-trade.
> But it contributed to a prolonged depression in the commerce
> between the Gulf, the Red Sea and the Indian west coast. This
> decline of transit-trade was smoothed by internal trade within the
> Arabian seas. But the Middle East had to pay for imports from

India by selling bulk products in the Mediterranean, like grain or wool. A precarious balance . . . spawned an inflationary pull both on the Ottoman and the Safavid currency. (Barendse 1997: chap. 1)

These globe-encircling world market relations and their underlying division of labor and its resulting (im)balances of trade are outlined in this chapter and illustrated in the accompanying maps.

In the "regional" accounts of this chapter, we repeatedly see how the changing mix and selection of crops, or indeed the replacement of "virgin" forested land by crops, and the choice of manufactures and the commercialization of all of the above responded to local incentives and exigencies. We observe in both this and the following chapter how that resulted in the clearing of the jungle in Bengal and the deforesting of land in southern China. As a result, land, rice, sugar, silk, silver, and labor were exchanged for each other and timber or its products, which were then imported from Southeast Asia. However, we also see how many of these local and sectoral incentives were transmitted by regional and interregional market forces. Many of these in turn emanated from competitive or compensatory activities on the opposite side of the globe. Indeed, some of these pressures met, say in a village in India or China, after being simultaneously transmitted halfway around the globe in both eastward and westward directions, as well as in additional crisscross directions. Of course as chapter 6 stresses about Europe as well, the import of sugar from the Americas and of silk and cotton textiles from Asia supplemented the local production of food and wool and liberated forest and cropping land; thus the extent to which "sheep ate men" and men ate at all was also a function of the world market.

The wheels of this global market were oiled by the worldwide flow of silver. In chapters 3 and 6 we see how it was only their newfound access to silver in the Americas that allowed the Europeans even to participate in this expanding world market. More detailed attention to how the production and flow especially of silver money stimulated and extended production and trade around the globe is reserved for chapter 3, which demonstrates how the arbitraged interchange of different currencies and other instruments of payment among each other and with other commodities facilitated a world market for all goods. All this trade was of course made possible only by commonly acceptable forms of money and/or the arbitrage among gold, silver, copper, tin, shells, coins, paper money, bills of exchange, and other forms of credit. These had been in circulation across and around Afro-Eurasia for millennia (and according to some reports, also across the Pacific especially between China and the Western Hemisphere). Nonetheless, the incorporation into this Old World economy of the New World in the Americas and their contribution to the world's stocks and flows of money certainly gave economic activity and trade a new boost from the sixteenth century onward.

THIRTEENTH- AND FOURTEENTH-CENTURY ANTECEDENTS

Two recent books begin to offer a non-Eurocentric alternative reading of early modern world history. They are Janet Abu-Lughod's (1989) *Before European Hegemony: The World System A.D. 1250–1350* and N. K. Chaudhuri's (1990a) *Asia Before Europe,* which peruses its theme to 1750. Abu-Lughod offers an especially suitable point of departure for the analysis of the present book. She argues that eight interlinking city-centered regions were united in a single thirteenth-century Afro-Eurasian world system and division of labor. The eight interlinked regions are categorized as three related and interlocked subsystems: (1) the European subsystem, with the Champagne fairs, industrial Flanders, and the commercial regions of Genoa and Venice; (2) the mideastern heartland and its east-west routes across Mongol Asia, via Baghdad and the Persian Gulf, and through Cairo and the Red Sea; and (3) the Indian Ocean-East Asian subsystem of India, Southeast Asia, and China. Their major fortunes and misfortunes, as well as the mid-fourteenth-century crisis and the Black Death epidemic, were more or less common to all of them.

Europe was "an upstart, peripheral to an ongoing operation" in Asia, so that "the failure to begin the story early enough has resulted . . . in a truncated and distorted causal explanation for the rise of the west," rightly insists Abu-Lughod (1989: 9, 17). Indeed she sees Europe's own twelfth- and thirteenth-century development as at least in part dependent on trade with the eastern Mediterranean, which had been generated by the Crusades. These in turn would not even have taken place or would have been fruitless, had it not been for the riches of "the Orient." Indeed, the trade, industry, and wealth of Venice and Genoa were due primarily to their middlemen roles between Europe and the East, some of which the Italian cities had preserved even through the Dark Ages. During the periods of economic revival after A.D. 1000, both tried to reach into the trade and riches of Asia as far as they could. Indeed, Genoa attempted in 1291 to reach Asia by circumnavigating Africa.

Failing that, Europe had to make do with the three major routes to

Asia that departed from the eastern Mediterranean: the northern one through the Black Sea, dominated by the Genovese; the central one via the Persian Gulf, dominated by Baghdad; and as its replacement, the southern one through the Red Sea, which gave life to Cairo and its economic partner in Venice. The expansion of the Mongols under Genghis Khan and his successors cemented the decline of the middle route after the capture of Baghdad in 1258 and favored the southern one. The Mongols then controlled the northern route onward from the Black Sea and also promoted the trans-Central Asian routes through such cities as Samarkand, which prospered under Mongol protection. Yet all of these trade routes suffered from the long world economic depression between the mid-thirteenth-century and the end of the fourteenth century, of which the Black Death was more the consequence than the cause (Gills and Frank 1992; also in Frank and Gills 1993). The economic determinants of this growing and ebbing trade, production, and income, however, lay still farther eastward in South, Southeast, and East Asia. As we will observe below, a long cyclical economic revival began there again around 1400.

But before that, according to Abu-Lughod's (1989) reading, this world system experienced its apogee between 1250 and 1350 and declined to (virtual) extinction thereafter and was then reborn in southern and western Europe in the sixteenth century. In her words, "of crucial importance is the fact that the 'Fall of the East' preceded the 'Rise of the West' " (Abu-Lughod 1989: 388). We must agree with the latter statement but not with her timing nor with her claim that there was no continuity between the thirteenth and sixteenth centuries in a single world economy and system. I have criticized Abu-Lughod's interpretation of the "substitution" of one "system" by another, rather than the "restructuring" of the same system elsewhere (Frank 1987, 1991a, 1992, Frank and Gills 1993), and she has answered (Frank and Gills 1993). We may now take up our examination of the global world economy and system where Abu-Lughod's account ended around 1400.

The world economy was predominantly Asian-based and so were the economic enterprise and success of Venice and Genoa, both of which derived their wealth from their intermediary position between the riches of Asia and the demand for the same in Europe. Their trade with the western terminus of Asian trade in West Asia, from the Black Sea, via the Levant to Egypt was also the precursor of European expansion into the Atlantic Ocean and eventually down it around Africa to India and across it to the Americas, also in search of Asia. The reasons for the voyages of Columbus in 1492 and of Vasco da Gama in 1498 have been long debated. These events were not accidental. After all, Columbus "discovered" America because he went in search of markets and gold in East Asia. That happened when a growing bullion shortage and the consequent rise in the Afro-Eurasian world market price of gold made such an enterprise attractive and potentially profitable (which it turned out to be). As John Day, admittedly a monetarist, writes

> The problem [of specie shortages], in the long run, engendered its own solution. Rising bullion prices, the corollary of contracting stocks, largely account for the intensified prospecting for precious metal all over Europe, as well as the ultimately successful search for new techniques of extraction and refining. And it was the acute "gold fever" of the fifteenth century that was the driving force behind the Great Discoveries which would end by submerging the money-starved European economy with American treasure at the dawn of modern times. (Day 1987: 63)

Moreover, Iberian access to that treasure was blocked not so much by the oft-heralded Muslim expansion and the advance of the Ottomans and their capture of Constantinople in 1453, as has often been alleged. Probably more important were Venetian and Genovese competition on the trade routes through the eastern Mediterranean, Genovese interests in Iberia, and their attempts to circumvent the Venetian stranglehold on commerce through Egypt. That is the significance, Lynda Shaffer (1989) points out, of the oft-quoted observation by the Portuguese Tome Pires that "whoever is lord of Malacca has his hands on the throat of Venice." Recall that Columbus was Genovese, first offering his services to Portugal to open a new route to the Orient, and only later accepting Spanish patronage.

Moreover, whatever the immediate incentives for the voyages of Columbus, Vasco da Gama, and then Magellan and the others, they had a long-standing and widely shared European impulse. As K. M. Panikkar (1959: 21–22) insists, "the full significance of da Gama's arrival at Calicut can be recognized only if we appreciate that it was the realization of a 200-year-old dream and of seventy-five years of sustained effort. The dream was shared by all mercantile peoples of the Mediterranean, with the exception of the Venetians; the effort was mainly that of Portugal." However, C. R. Boxer (1990: ix) quotes an official 1534 Portuguese document which observed that "many people . . . say that it was India which discovered Portugal." We will have further occasion to reflect on this European enterprise regarding Asia in chapters that follow. Here we shall proceed to examine some of the results.

THE COLUMBIAN EXCHANGE
AND ITS CONSEQUENCES

Three major consequences of the 1492 and 1498 voyages and their subsequent migratory and trade relations merit more attention than the brief reference they can receive here. The first two are "the Columbian exchange" of germs and of genes and "ecological imperialism," as Alfred Crosby (1972, 1986) has termed them. The germs that the Europeans brought with them were by far their most powerful weapons of conquest. They were most devastating in the New World, whose population had no immunities to the disease germs the Europeans brought with them. This devastation is described by, among others, Crosby (1972, 1986) as well as by William McNeill in his *Plagues and People* (1977). In the Caribbean, almost the entire indigenous tribal population was wiped out in less than fifty years. On the continent, the germs of disease were carried faster, further, and far more devastatingly than the conquering troops of Cortez and Pizarro, who found that the smallpox they brought on shore preceded them inland. The new weeds and animals they also brought spread their damage more slowly.

In the New World of the Americas, the consequences were devastating. The populations of the Mesoamerican Aztec and Maya civilizations were reduced from about 25 million to 1.5 million by 1650. The Andean Inca civilization fared similarly, with a population decline from perhaps 9 million to 600,000 (Crosby 1994: 22). In North America also, the germs brought by the first European arrivals, probably in 1616–1617, cleared the land of many indigenous inhabitants even before the bulk of the settlers arrived. One estimate for the ultimate European impact in the United States is a decline of the indigenous population from 5 million to 60,000 before it began to rise again. Some estimates suggest a population decline in the New World as a whole from some 100 million to about 5 million (Livi-Bacci 1992: 51).

Even in nomadic Inner Asia, the Russian advance through Siberia would be spurred on by the germs of the soldiers and settlers as much as by their other arms. As Crosby (1994: 11) observes, "the advantage in bacteriological warfare was (and is) characteristically enjoyed by people from dense areas of settlement moving into sparser areas of settlement." On the other hand, the transfer of germs within Afro-Eurasia never caused population declines on a scale remotely comparable to the population decline in the Americas initiated by the new transatlantic contacts. The reason of course is the much greater immunity the peoples of Afro-Eurasia had already inherited from their many generations of mutual contacts through prior invasion and migration as well as long-standing trade. Similarly, the relatively greater impact of the Black Death on Europe had also been a reflection of the isolation and marginality of Europe within Eurasia.

The Columbian gene exchange involved not only humans but also animals and vegetables. Old World Europeans introduced not only themselves but also many new animal and vegetable species to the New World. The most important animals, but by no means the only ones, were horses (which had existed there previously but had died out), cattle, sheep, chickens, and bees. Among vegetables, Europeans brought wheat, barley, rice, turnips, cabbage, and lettuce. They also brought the bananas, coffee, and, for practical purposes if not genetically, the sugar that would later dominate so many of their economies.

Through the Columbian exchange, the New World in turn also contributed much to the Old World, such as animal species like turkeys as well as many vegetables, several of which would significantly extend cropping and alter consumption and survival in many parts of Europe, Africa, and Asia. Sweet potatoes, squash, beans, and especially potatoes and maize vastly increased cropping and survival possibilities in Europe and China, because they could survive harsher climates than other crops. The absolute and probably the relative impact was greatest on new crops in the more populated China where New World crops contributed to doubling agricultural land and tripling population (Shaffer 1989: 13). The growing of sweet potatoes is recorded in the 1560s in China, and maize became a staple food crop in the seventeenth century (Ho Ping-ti 1959: 186 ff.). White potatoes, tobacco, and other New World crops also became important. Indeed as we note below, the resultant population increase was far greater in China and throughout Asia than in Europe. Today 37 percent of the food the Chinese eat is of American origin (Crosby 1996: 5). After the United States, China today is the world's second largest producer of maize, and 94 percent of the root crops grown in the world today are of New World origin (Crosby 1994: 20). In Africa, subsistence was extended especially by cassava and maize, along with sunflowers, several nuts, and the ubiquitous tomato and chili pepper. Later Africa also became a major exporter of cacao, vanilla, peanuts, and pineapple, all of which were of American origin.

Of course, the third major consequence of the Columbian exchange was the New World's contribution of gold and silver to the world's stocks and flows of money, which certainly also gave a new boost to economic activity and trade in the Old World economy from the sixteenth century onward. These flows are examined in detail in chapter 3, but some of their consequences for trade flows and balances are reviewed in the present chapter.

SOME NEGLECTED FEATURES
IN THE WORLD ECONOMY

Several features of the interregional world trade network deserve special preliminary comment (though they cannot receive as much attention in this summary as they probably merit in reality). They are regionalism, trade diasporas, documentation, and ecology.

The identification of "regions" below—"the Americas," "Europe," "China"—is in part an arbitrary heuristic notational convenience and in part a reflection of reality, as Lewis and Wigen (1997) stress under the title *The Myth of Continents*. There have been and are regions in the world, within whose "boundaries" the division of labor and the density of trade relations is greater than across them. That greater "internal" than "external" density of trade relations may be due to geographic factors (mountains, deserts, or seas that divide and therefore also bound), political ones (the reach and cost of empires and their competition with each other), cultural factors (ethnic and/or religious affinity and language), and other factors, or any combination thereof. The bounding of the grouping depends on the purpose and changes from time to time, sometimes very suddenly. The regional "unit" or "group" may be an individual, a nuclear or an extended family, a village or town, a local "region," a "society," a "country," a "regional" region (the circum-Mediterranean), or a "world" region (the Americas, West Asia, Southeast Asia, the South Pacific). The very mention of these examples illustrates how ill-defined (indeed ill-definable) and fluid these "regional units" are and how arbitrary their identification is. The same exercise also serves to emphasize that the *intra*-regional ties, no matter what their density, are no obstacle to having *inter*-regional ones as well. Indeed, what is intra- or interregional is itself a function of how we identify the region or regions to begin with. If the world is a "region," then all are intrarelations. Similarly, the assertion that there is or was a *world* economy/system does not dispute that it is or was also composed of *regional* ones. Where, what, and when such regions existed, however, all depends.

So whether the Americas, or Europe, or Southeast Asia, or China were "regions" in our 1400–1800 period or not depends on our definitions. Intra-American trade, not to mention cultural affinity and contact or political relations, were surely less among most Western Hemisphere "subregions" than they were between each of them and one or another part of Europe. Some parts of Europe also had less relations among themselves than they did with peoples and areas in the Americas and Asia. On the other hand, perhaps most major regions (or, subregions?) on the Indian subcontinent or within "China" probably had denser intra-Indian or intra-Chinese interregional trade (also outside the changing confines of the Mughal and Qing empires) than they did with other parts of the world. (There are some observations about Indian intra- and interregional trade below and in the maps). However, parts of Southeast Asia, especially Manila and Malacca, and also Aden and Hormuz in West Asia, were entrepôts whose sixteenth- and seventeenth-century trade relations with many other parts of the world were greater than those with their own essentially nonexistent "regional" hinterlands.

Another notable but related feature of interregional trade in the world economy were the expatriate merchant and trade diasporas. They had already played important roles in the facilitation of trade in the Bronze Age and certainly did so in the early modern period. They also continue to do so today, as is testified by the "overseas" Chinese who now invest on the mainland and by expatriate Japanese and American "colonies" and even their "local" newspapers like the *International Herald Tribune,* a U.S. periodical originally published in Paris and now printed in a dozen cities around the world.

In the period under review, Malacca was peopled almost entirely by expatriate merchants, so much so that Pires counted eighty-four different languages spoken among them. Maharatshi merchants from Cambay and Surat were probably the most numerous in Malacca, but they were also residents—not to mention seasonal arrivals—in dozens of other port cities in Southeast, South, and West Asia. Manila counted up to 30,000 Chinese residents in the seventeenth century to oil the wheels of the transpacific-China silver and porcelain trade. Armenians from a landlocked country in western Central Asia established an also landlocked trade diaspora base in the Safavid Persian city of Isfahan, used it to trade all across Asia, and published an Armenian how-to-do-it handbook in Amsterdam. Arab and Jewish merchants continued to ply their worldwide trade as they had for at least a millennium and continue to do so today. New Englanders not only sought Moby Dick and other whales throughout the world oceans; they also plied the slave trade between Africa and the Caribbean, and they regularly buccaneered off the coast of Madagascar. Thousands if not millions of Chinese—not to mention Muslim trading expatriates, who "indianized" Southeast Asia—

migrated overseas. Central Asia also continued to be a crossroads for itinerant merchants and migrating peoples, as it had from time immemorial.

Ironically, most of the still-extant documentary evidence on Asian trade comes from private European companies, who of course only recorded what was of commercial or other interest to them, especially in regard to these trade diasporas. Therefore much of the evidence on Asian production and trade fell through the European cracks. This is particularly the case with the inland economies and the transcontinental caravan trade, which the Europeans hardly saw. However, there is reason to believe that they were fully as important as, and complementary to, the maritime trade throughout this entire period up to 1800.

All this "development" also had other far-reaching impacts, which recent studies call ecological or green imperialism. A major consequence has been widespread deforestation, both to make way for new cropland and to provide timber for shipping and other construction and even more wastefully for charcoal for smelting ores and refining metals and for other fuel (Chew 1997, and forthcoming). On the other hand, planting potatoes and maize presumably relieved pressure on land more suitable for other crops. And New World sugar supplied calories to Europe that it did not have to provide for itself. Later of course, imports of wheat and meat from the New World fed millions of Europeans and permitted them to put their scarce land to other uses, as did the import of cotton, replacing wool from sheep that had grazed enclosed land. We will return to the matter of ecological imperialism in some of the regional reviews below and again in chapter 6.

World Division of Labor and Balances of Trade

Of course, there were some abrupt and then secular changes in interregional relations, particularly because of the incorporation of the Americas by Europeans and the consequent growing participation of Europe in Afro-Eurasian and world trade from the sixteenth century onward. There were also—in other contexts important—cyclical changes, some of which are examined in Frank (1978a, 1994, 1995) and in chapter 5 below. Moreover, there was the rise to dominance of Europe beginning at the end of the eighteenth century, which we analyze in chapter 6. By and large however, the pattern of world trade and division of labor remained remarkably stable and displayed a substantially continuous, albeit cyclical, development over the centuries, if not millennia (as examined for the period before 1400 in Gills and Frank 1992; also in Frank and Gills 1993). There was certainly sufficient continuity in the period 1400–1800 to recognize the pattern outlined below.

MAPPING THE GLOBAL ECONOMY

A schematic and incomplete mapping and summary of the global division of labor, the network of world trade with its balances and imbalances, and how they were settled by flows of money in the opposite direction is set out in the maps and their legends below. It seems most efficient to use maps to identify some of the large variety of commodities—including many bulk commodities such as rice—that were exchanged in a complex network of trade in the world division of labor between about 1400 and 1800. The most schematic and least detailed world economic overview is in map 2.1. I have chosen a "Nordic/polar" global projection to permit a summary representation of circumglobal trade, including particularly the shipments of silver across the Pacific on the Manila Galleons. The reader should be aware however that to simplify and clarify their presentation, all trade routes on this and the following regional maps are only schematic. They do not pretend to be accurate, even if an effort was made to reflect global and regional geographical realities as well as the schematic representation permits. Moreover, contrary to the title and message of this book, the global Map 2.1, like map 3.1, is not oriented toward Asia as I wished. The reason is that my cartographer's university geography department in Western Canada did not have a less Eurocentric sample map to guide his computerized design, and even his cartographic software is not flexible enough to meet my request to spin this one just a little on its polar axis in order to *reorient* the map. So here we have yet another example of how difficult but therefore also how necessary it is to reorient. Related problems in the representation of land mass and distance appear on the regional maps; for instance, India appears smaller and regions to its north and south relatively larger than they are in reality.

The regional maps and their respective legends present in more detail the major regional and interregional trade routes. Map 2.2 represents the Atlantic region, including the Americas, Africa, and Europe,

Map 2.1
Major Circum-Global Trade Routes, 1400 – 1800

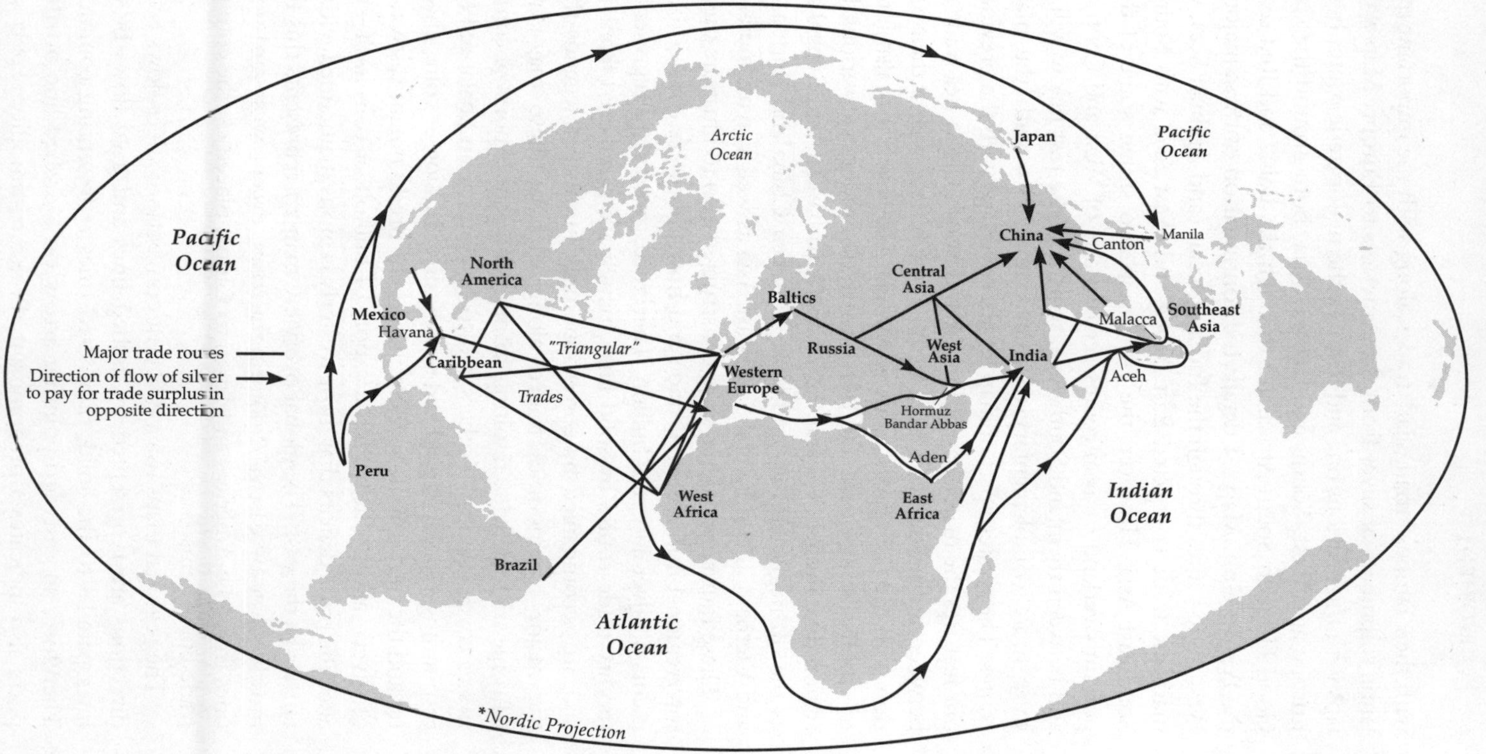

Pacific Ocean

Indian Ocean

Manila

Canton

Malacca

Southeast Asia

Aceh

Japan

China

India

West Asia

Central Asia

Hormuz
Bandar Abbas

Aden

East Africa

Russia

Baltics

Western Europe

West Africa

Arctic Ocean

North America

Mexico

Havana

Caribbean

"Triangular"

Trades

Peru

Brazil

Atlantic Ocean

Pacific Ocean

*Nordic Projection

Major trade routes

Direction of flow of silver to pay for trade surplus in opposite direction

with their famous "triangular" trades along with the important transatlantic shipments of silver from the Americas to Europe. Map 2.3 overlaps with the previous one and features the major trade routes between
Europe and West, South, and Central Asia, both around the Cape of
Good Hope in South Africa and through the Baltic and Red seas and
the Persian Gulf. Map 2.4 details the continuation of these major East-
West trade routes through the Indian Ocean (and Arabian Sea), whose
maritime trade connected East Africa and West Asia with South and
Southeast Asia. However, the same map also shows some of the important overland caravan routes across parts of West and Central Asia
and between them and South Asia, which, as the text below will insist,
were more complementary to than competitive with the maritime
routes. The western part of map 2.5 also overlaps with the previous one
but features the major Bay of Bengal and South China Sea trade routes
between India, Southeast Asia, Japan, and China as well as their connection with the transpacific trade at Manila. However, it is also intended
to emphasize maritime and overland trade among the various Indian
regions like Punjab, Gujarat, Malabar, Coromandel, and Bengal as well
as the oft-neglected overland trade between China and Burma, Siam,
and Vietnam in continental Southeast Asia as well as with India.

These four regional maps are constructed also to illustrate the major
interregional imbalances of trade and how they were covered by shipments of silver and gold bullion. Therefore, these maps represent commodity trade routes by solid lines, which are numbered from 1 to 13
and are accompanied by correspondingly numbered legends that list
the major commodities traded along each of these major routes.
Chronic trade deficits, resulting from insufficient exports of commodities to cover imports of others had to be paid for and balanced by corresponding exports of gold and mostly silver bullion or coin. This chapter and the next (on money) emphasize the predominant eastward flow
of silver—and profit from the export of bullion or coin itself—to balance the trade deficits that most westerly regions maintained with those
farther to the east. The global overview map 2.1 represents this flow of
mostly silver by eastward-pointing arrows, except westward-pointing
ones from the Americas and Japan to China, placed on the commodity
trade lines themselves.

The regional maps use a different convention: silver flows and their
directions are represented by dashed lines and gold flows by dotted
lines parallel to the solid, numbered ones representing commodities.
Therefore, an eastward-pointing arrow on a dashed line of silver exports also indicates a predominant reverse commodity export surplus

from east to west along the parallel solid line representing a commodity trade route. In particular, almost all European imports from the east were paid for by European exports of (American) silver. This is represented by the dashed lines with eastward-pointing arrows between Western Europe and the Baltics as well as West Asia, and from these regions onward successively to South, Southeast, and eventually East Asia, that is predominantly China. That was the "sink" for about half of the world's silver, as will be shown in chapter 3, which offers a separate map of major world silver production and flows.

Multilateral world trade around the globe is also discussed region by region in this chapter, beginning with the Americas and proceeding eastward around the globe. As we visit each major region in the world, we will note some of the specificities of each region and how these intervene in and help generate its relations with other regions, particularly those immediately to the west and east.

The net export of silver and/or gold bullion and coins is evidence of a negative, or deficitary balance of trade, except perhaps in some cases where the exporter is also a producer and commercial exporter of precious metals (for example, American and Japanese silver and African and Southeast Asian gold). Records of the shipment and remission of bullion and/or coin therefore offers the most readily available evidence of interregional trade deficits and surpluses, and of how these were settled and balanced. Unfortunately, we know less about the undoubtedly also very extensive use of bills of exchange and letters or other instruments of credit.

Europe, the Americas, and even Africa will receive relatively short shrift in this review for the following good reasons: First, as we have noted above, their economic weight, participation, and importance in the world economy (except for the exceptional role of American money distributed by the Europeans), was far less than that of many other regions in the world, in particular of East and South Asia, but probably also of Southeast and West Asia. Second, the available historical, economic, and social literature has already devoted an immense amount of ink and attention to Europe and the Americas, and of the relation of Africa to both, which is all out of proportion to their relatively small importance in the world economy before 1800. Moreover, far too much of the literature (including Frank 1978a, b) has been written from an excessively Eurocentric perspective, which the present book is intended to help correct and replace. Therefore it seems only right and proper to focus on those other regions and their relations that have been neglected out of all proportion to their real weight and importance. That

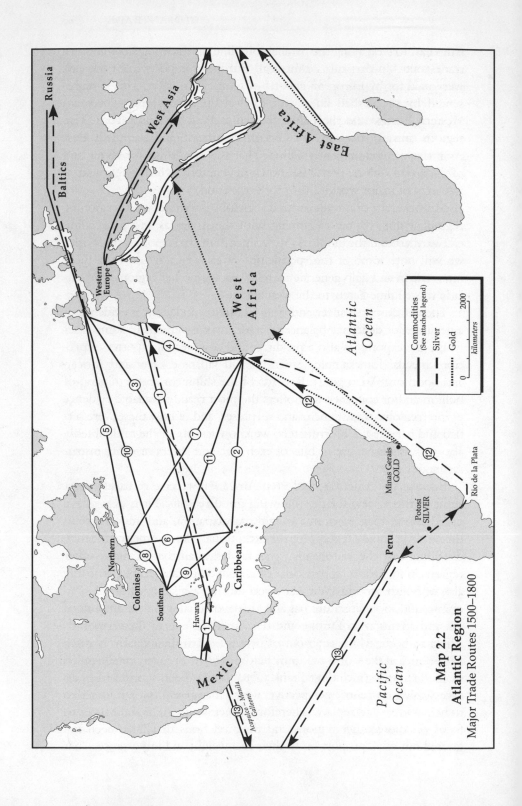

Russia

Baltics

West Asia

East Africa

Western Europe

West Africa

Atlantic Ocean

Commodities (See attached legend)
— Silver
····· Gold

0   2000
kilometers

④

③

①

⑤

⑩

⑦

⑪

②

⑫

Minas Gerais
GOLD

Potosí
SILVER

Rio de la Plata

Northern

Colonies

Southern

⑧

⑥

⑨

Havana

①

Peru

Mexic

Acapulco – Manila
Galleons

⑬

⑬

Pacific Ocean

**Map 2.2
Atlantic Region**
Major Trade Routes 1500–1800

MAP 2.2 ATLANTIC REGION
[brackets indicate re-export/onward-shipment]

Principal exports and imports

ROUTES

	Westward	Eastward
1. MEXICO - HAVANA - EUROPE	manufactures	SILVER
2. WEST AFRICA - CARIBBEAN	slaves	rum
3. CARIBBEAN - WESTERN EUROPE	manufactures	sugar, molasses [SILVER]
4. WEST AFRICA - EUROPE	(north) guns [textiles]	(south) [cowries]
5. NORTHERN COLONIES - BRITAIN	manufactures	raw materials [money]
6. NORTHERN COLONIES - CARIBBEAN	(north) molassses [SILVER]	(south) manufactures, naval stores transport / services

ROUTES

	Westward	Eastward
7. NORTHERN COLONIES - WEST AFRICA	transport / services rum	- - -
8. NORTHERN COLONIES - SOUTHERN COLONIES	(north) food, tobacco	(south) manufactures, services
9. SOUTHERN COLONIES - CARIBBEAN	molasses	slaves
10. SOUTHERN COLONIES - EUROPE	manufactures	rum, tobacco
11. SOUTHERN COLONIES - WEST AFRICA	- - [bought/paid via North. Col.]	slaves
12. SOUTH AMERICA - WEST AFRICA	slaves	GOLD, SILVER
13. MEXICO & PERU - MANILA Galleon to CHINA		SILVER

is not to say, of course, that this modest effort here can hope thereby to right the wrongs that have been done. The third reason for giving short shrift to Europe, the Americas, and Africa is that the purpose here is not so much to right such wrongs by examining different "regions"; their identification is in any case arbitrary, as was noted above. The more important purpose is to demonstrate the nature, kind, and changes in the *relations* among these regions.

Thus, the real object and fourth reason for the choices made below is to add to a basis for the inquiry into the structure and dynamic world economy and system *as a whole*. As cannot be repeated often enough, it is the whole (which is more than the sum of its parts) that more than anything else determines the "internal" nature of its parts and their "external" relations among each other. So we begin our historical around-the-world-in-eighty-pages by going predominantly eastward around the globe, starting in the Americas but always keeping this holistic perspective in mind.

THE AMERICAS

We have already examined the reasons for the "discovery" and incorporation of the Americas into the world economy and the impact on its native peoples, beginning with their population decline from about 100 million to 5 million people. For the rest of the world, the early impacts were mostly the Americas' contribution of new plants, the export of plantation crops, and of course the production and export first of gold and then of large amounts of silver. Gold exports started from the "discovery" in 1492 and large-scale silver exports by the mid-sixteenth century. To what extent this American production and export of silver declined, only slackened off, or indeed even increased during the seventeenth century has been the subject of much debate. Either way, production and trade appears to have continued to increase during the "seventeenth century crisis," either despite (or perhaps because of?) less stimulus from European-supplied American money or making still better use of its supply. During the eighteenth century, the production and export of bullion increased again (or continued its rise still farther), and so did the production and trade of other goods around the world.

Over these same centuries and especially during the eighteenth century, the well-known "triangular" trade across the Atlantic developed into a significant adjunct of the Afro-Eurasian trade and the world economic division of labor (see map 2.2). Actually, there were several related transatlantic triangles in operation. The most important one coordinated European, and especially British, manufacturing exports, including many re-exports of textiles and other goods from India and China to the Americas and Africa; African exports of slaves to the Caribbean and the South and North American slave plantations; and primarily Caribbean exports of sugar and secondarily North American exports of tobacco, furs, and other commodities back to Europe. In the seventeenth and even more the eighteenth centuries, North America, the Caribbean, and Africa also became ever more important export markets (which were still not available in Asia) for European manufactures, including especially guns to Africa for use in rounding up the supply of slaves. There was also a large European re-export of Asian goods, especially of Indian textiles to Africa, the Caribbean, but also to the Spanish colonies in Latin America.

However, there were also other related triangles, which involved particularly the North American colonies as importers of sugar and molasses from the Caribbean in exchange for exports of grain, timber, and naval stores to the latter and the export to Europe of rum produced with the imported molasses. The most important secondary trade in these triangular trades, however, was trade itself, including shipping, financial services, and the slave trade. The earnings from this trade served especially the American colonists to cover their perennial balance of trade deficits with Europe and to accumulate capital themselves. The literature on this transatlantic trade is vast (for my own analysis, see Frank 1978a) and much more abundant than on the quantitatively much greater and more important trans- and circum- Afro-Eurasian trade. Yet far too neglected in this literature is how much the attraction of North America continued to be its own role as a waystation to the East. The continually sought-after Northwest Passage to China defined much of the history of Canada, which in turn was valued as a conduit and counterpoint to the United States and its also still intermediary position. As recently as 1873, a Canadian Tory paper welcomed a contract for a railroad to the Pacific for "bringing the trade of India, China and Japan to Montreal by the shortest route and the cheapest rate possible" (Naylor 1987: 476).

AFRICA

African population was at about 85 million in 1500 but was still only about 100 million two and a half centuries later in 1750, of which about 80 and 95 million respectively were south of the Sahara (see tables 4.1 and 4.2 in chapter 4 below). Of course, the slave wars and trade intervened to subtract population and especially men (thus changing the ratio in favor of women, but also subtracting fertile women) from the slaving areas. Moreover, slaving was not limited to the Atlantic slave trade from West and Southwest Africa, but included intra-African slaving as well as in and from East Africa to Arab lands. However, the earlier suggestions of 100 million slaves exported by the slave trade have long since been revised downward to about 10 million and then up again to about 12 million; and the direct demographic impact appears not to have been very substantial (Patrick Manning: personal communication). Whether it had a more indirect one is hard to tell, although population and socioeconomic growth seems to have slowed relative to earlier centuries. It is certainly remarkable that African population remained stable while population throughout most of Eurasia expanded rapidly. That raises the question whether Africa, far from being further incorporated, was rather relatively more isolated from the worldwide forces stimulating the growth of production and population elsewhere (which of course also decimated the population in the Americas).

In the fifteenth century, intra-African trade far outweighed the better known African-European-transatlantic trade (Curtin 1983: 232). Moreover, trans-Saharan trade grew in the succeeding centuries (Austen 1990: 312). West African long-distance trade—especially of gold—had been oriented northward across the Sahara (especially but not only on the heralded Timbuktu-Fez route) to the Mediterranean (see map 2.3). This trade was supplemented, but never replaced, by maritime trade around Senegal and then also by the slave trade across the Atlantic, both from northwest and southwest Africa.

That is, Africa's participation in transatlantic trade neither initiated its far-flung trade relations and division of labor, nor did it replace trans-Saharan trade. On the contrary, in Africa (and as we will note below in West, South, Southeast, and East Asia as well), the new maritime trade instead complemented and even stimulated the old and still ongoing overland trade. As Karen Moseley (1992: 536) aptly observes, "the form and content of the new trade, . . . at least until the eighteenth century, was very much an extension of preexisting patterns." "When the region was integrated into both desert and oceanic commercial systems, Sudanic trade and industry reached its peak" (Moseley 1992: 538, quoting Austen 1987: 82). So trans-Saharan trade continued to thrive in general, and in particular its transport of slaves from West

Africa grew from 430,000 in the fifteenth century to 550,000 in the sixteenth, and to over 700,000 in each of the seventeenth and eighteenth centuries (Moseley 1992: 543, 534, also citing Austen 1987). There always also was some west-east trade, including the legendary amounts of gold carried by "pilgrims" via or from the Maghreb overland via Libya or through the Mediterranean to Egypt and Arabia.

In West Africa, cowrie shells became a major medium of exchange. They were produced in the Maldive Islands, were in use as money in South Asia, and Europeans brought them to Africa to buy slaves for export. The import of cowrie shells increased massively—and later again decreased—concomitantly with the slave trade. The demand for cowries was African, so that they were imported into Africa, where cowrie shell money co-existed with and even displaced gold dust and gold and silver coins and sometimes became regionally dominant. Like metal and all money elsewhere, cowries served to expand economic activity and commercialization into the interior, especially among the poorer people. However, cowries could not again be exported, since Europeans and others refused to accept them in payment. This one-way cowrie trade therefore helped to marginalize Africans from world trade as a whole (Seider 1995; for further discussion of cowries, see chapter 3 on money). However, textiles were an important, and often more important, medium of exchange within Africa; but the imported cloth of higher quality was monetized less than African cloth was (Curtin 1983: 232).

East African trade, which had been described in Roman times in the *Periplus of the Erytrean Sea,* was predominantly oriented northward to the Fertile Crescent and eastward across the Indian Ocean. In the period under discussion in this book, exports were primarily "natural" products, especially ivory and gold, but also slaves; and the imports were Indian textiles and grains, Arabic earthenware, Chinese porcelain, and cowrie shells from the Maldives for use as money. East African ports served as conduits for trade between southern Africa, especially Zimbabwe and Mozambique, and northern Africa and/or Indian Ocean ports. The shipping and trade was largely in Arab and also Indian hands, although even Americans from New England were active on the southeast African and Madagascar coasts, if only as privateers:

The Americans switched between looting, preying on Arab or French ships and exchanging Indian textiles, ropes, sailcloth, arms or munitions against coral, beads, or other products in use in other slave-markets. For, besides to Madagascar, the Americans traded at Mozambique, Bela Goa Bay, the Swahili coast and—if we are to believe Defoe—even at Mogadishu. The hold would contain, in addition to the inevitable arms and rum, a good array of other goods since it was unknown how much and where products had been traded by the French, Dutch and metropolitan English competitors. (Barendse 1997: chap. 1)

EUROPE

The major importers and re-exporters of both silver and gold bullion were western and southern Europe, to cover their own perpetual and massive structural balance of trade deficits with all other regions, except with the Americas and Africa. Of course, the Europeans were able to receive African and especially American bullion without giving much in return, and much of that they provided as intermediaries in their re-export of Asian goods. Western Europe had a balance of trade deficit with—and therefore re-exported much silver and some gold to—the Baltics and eastern Europe, to West Asia, to India directly and via West Asia, to Southeast Asia directly and via India, and to China via all of the above as well as from Japan.

An indication of the European structural balance of trade deficit is that gold and silver were never less than two-thirds of total exports (Cipolla 1976: 216). For instance in 1615, only 6 percent of the value of all cargo exported by the Dutch East India Company was in goods, and 94 percent was in bullion (Das Gupta and Pearson 1987: 186). Indeed, over the sixty years from 1660 to 1720, precious metals made up on the average 87 percent of VOC imports into Asia (Prakash 1994: VI-20). For similar reasons, the British state, representing also manufacturing and others interested in "export promotion," obliged the British East India Company by its charter to include British export products of at least one-tenth of the value of its total exports. Yet, the company had constant difficulty to find markets even for this modest export, and most of that went only as far as West Asia. Later, a small amount of broadcloth woolen textiles were placed in India for use not in clothing but as household and military goods, such as rugs and saddles. Most European exports were of metal and metal products. Unable to fill even its 10 percent export quota, the company had to resort to over- and under-invoicing to reduce "total" exports, and it was under constant pressure to find financing for its Asian imports in Asia itself. Therefore, it engaged in the intra-Asian "country trade," which was much more developed and profitable than the Asia-Europe trade.

In summary, Europe remained a marginal player in the world economy with a perpetual deficit despite its relatively easy and cheap access to American money, without which Europe would have been almost entirely excluded from any participation in the world economy. Europe's newfound sources of income and wealth generated some increase in its own production, which also supported some growth of population. That began to recover from the disastrous fourteenth-century decline in the fifteenth century, and for the next two and a half centuries Europe's population grew at an average of about 0.3 percent a year, to double from 60 or more million in 1500 to 130 or 140 million in 1750. By Eurasian standards however, European population growth was relatively slow; for in Asia in general and in China and India in particular, population grew significantly faster and to much higher totals (see tables 4.1 and 4.2).

WEST ASIA

West Asia (or more properly, the many different regions and cities scattered throughout the Ottoman and Safavid Persian empires and contiguous regions) contained an interlocking series of productive and commercial centers of its own. Ottoman population grew in the sixteenth century but leveled off after that, and by Eurasian standards West Asian population as a whole seems to have remained rather stable at about 30 million (see table 4.1).

Since time immemorial, the location of West Asia made it into a sort of commercial and migratory turntable between the Baltics/Russia/Central Asia to the north and Arabia/Egypt/East Africa to the south, and especially between the transatlantic/West African/ Maghreb/European/Mediterranean economic centers to the west and all of South, Southeast, and East Asia to the east. Productive centers were widely scattered, and trade among them, as well as between them and the rest of the world, was both maritime and overland. There was also a combination of overland, maritime, and riverine trade, which were transshipped at many cities in West Asia. For centuries the Persian Gulf route to and from Asia had favored Baghdad as a meeting place and transshipment center of caravan, riverine, and maritime trade from and to all directions. Alternatively and in perpetual competition with the same,

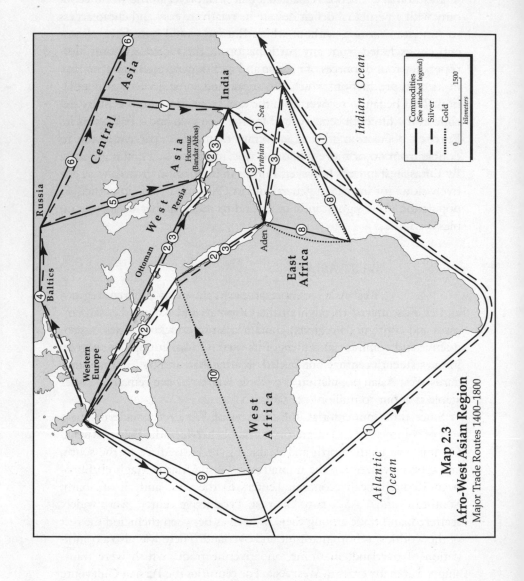

Map 2.3
Afro-West Asian Region
Major Trade Routes 1400–1800

Principal exports & imports

ROUTES
Westward   Eastward

1. EUROPE - ASIA, MARITIME AROUND AFRICA
silk, cotton textiles,   SILVER
pepper, spices,

2. EUROPE - WEST ASIA via MEDITERRANEAN
silk, cotton textiles   SILVER, GOLD
[pepper, spices, ceramics] metal products, wool textiles,
coffee
Some products from route 3 below were also shipped further westward via route 2

3. WEST ASIA - INDIA via PERSIAN GULF & RED SEA & ARABIAN SEA
silk, silk text., cot. textiles,   minerals, metal/prods.,
spices, pepper, rice,   copper, lumber, horses,
dyes/indigo, ivory,   carpets, luxury goods,
shawls, blankets, paper,   pearls, fruits, dates,
gumlace, saltpeter,   dye woods, aromatics, incense,
iron & steel products,   salt, fish, coffee, wine,
housewares, wood & glass,   arms, coral, rosewater,
rice, pulses, wheat, oil,   SILVER
ships [sold to Britain]

4. EUROPE - BALTICS - RUSSIA
grains, timber, furs,   wool textiles,
iron, flax, hemp   SILVER

ROUTES
Westward   Eastward

5. RUSSIA - WEST ASIA
(north)   (south)
cot. textiles, carpets,   furs, hides/leather,
satin [dyes/indigo]   SILVER

6. RUSSIA - CENTRAL ASIA - CHINA
silk, tea, paper,   clothing, drugs,
precious stones/jade,   horses, camels, sheep,
cotton, furs, swords,   medicines/ginseng,
arms, sugar, tobacco,   paper money, jade,
grains & food   SILVER

7. CENTRAL ASIA - INDIA
(north)   (south)
cot. textiles, silk text.,   horses, camels, sheep
wheat, rice, pulses,   SILVER
cotton, indigo, tobacco

8. EAST AFRICA - ARABIA & INDIA
rice, cot. text. [ceramics]   slaves, ivory, GOLD

9. WEST AFRICA - EUROPE
(north) GOLD   (south)
guns [cowries, cot. textiles]

10. WEST AFRICA - WEST ASIA
GOLD

the Red Sea route favored Cairo, the Suez region and of course Mocha and Aden near the Indian Ocean. Trade was in the hands mostly of Arabs and Persians and—as also elsewhere in Asia—of merchants from the Armenian diaspora, based especially in Persia.

The Ottomans. The European view that the Ottoman Empire was a world onto itself and "virtually a fortress" (Braudel 1992: 467) is more ideological than factual. Moreover, the "traditional" Euro-centric put-down of the Ottomans as stuck-in-the-mud Muslim military bureaucrats only reflects historical reality insofar as it is an expression of the very real commercial competition that the Ottomans posed for European commercial interests and ambitions. Although the same Braudel also called the Ottoman Empire "a crossroads of trade," it had a far more important place and role in the world economy than Europeans like Braudel recognized.

The Ottomans did indeed occupy a geographical and economic crossroads between Europe and Asia, and they sought to make the most of it. The east-west spice and silk trade continued overland and by ship through Ottoman territory. Constantinople had developed as and lived off its role as a major north-south and east-west crossroads for a millennium since its Byzantine founding. That also made it attractive for conquest by the Ottomans, who renamed it Istanbul. With a population of 600,000 to 750,000, it was by far the largest city in Europe and West Asia and nearly the largest in the world. As a whole, the Ottoman Empire was more urbanized than Europe (Inalcik and Quataert 1994: 493, 646). Other major commercial centers, which vied with each other over trade routes, were Bursa, Izmir, Aleppo, and Cairo. The fortunes of Cairo had always depended on the Red Sea route as an alternative to the Persian Gulf one. In the late eighteenth century, the competition between Caribbean and Arabian coffee undermined Cairo's prosperity.

Of course, the Ottomans like everybody else had no desire to choke off the goose that laid (or at least attracted) any golden eggs through transit trade. Particularly important was the transit trade of money even though "world economic and monetary developments often had consequences for the Ottoman monetary system . . . [which] was often vulnerable to and adversely affected by the large movements of gold and silver" which passed through from west to east (Pamuk 1994: 4). Moreover, the Ottomans were linked not only with Europe to the west but also directly with Russia to the north and Persia to the east:

Imperative economic interdependency compelled both [Ottoman and Persian] sides to maintain close trade relations even during wartime. . . . The impact of the expansion in the use of silk cloth and the silk industry in Europe cannot be underestimated. It formed the structural basis for the development of the Ottoman and Iranian economies. Both empires drew an important part of their public revenues and silver stocks from the silk trade with Europe. The silk industries in the Ottoman Empire . . . depended on imported raw silk from Iran. . . . Bursa became a world market between East and West not only for raw silk but also for other Asian goods as a result of the revolutionary changes in the network of world trade routes in the fourteenth century [and remained so through at least the sixteenth century]. (Inalcik and Quataert 1994: 188, 219)

However, the Ottoman court and others also had their own resources—and transcontinental trade connections—to import large quantities of distant Chinese goods, of which over ten thousand pieces of porcelain in only one collection today is testimony.

The wealth of the Ottoman Empire also derived from substantial local and regional production and commercialization, interregional and international specialization, division of labor, and trade. The Ottoman economy involved substantial intersectoral, interregional, and indeed international labor migration among the private, public, and various semipublic enterprises, sectors, and regions. Evidence for these comes from, among others, studies by Huri Islamoglu-Inan (1987) and Suraiya Faroqhi (1984, 1986, 1987) of silk, cotton and their derived textiles, leather and its products, agriculture in general, as well as mining and metal industries. For instance, Faroqhi summarizes:

First of all, the weaving of simple cotton cloth was in many areas a rural activity. Secondly, it was carried out in close connection with the market. Raw materials in quite a few cases must have been provided commercially, and linkages to distant buyers assured. In passing, a further document . . . reveals that here lay an opportunity for profitable investment. (Faroqhi 1987: 270)

Furthermore, the Ottomans expanded both westward and eastward. This expansion was motivated and based not only politically and militarily but also, indeed primarily, economically. Like everybody else, be they Venetians, French, Portuguese, Persians, Arabs, or whatever, the Ottomans were always trying to divert and control the major trade routes, from which they and especially the state lived. Therein, the main Ottoman rivals were these same European powers to the west and their Persian neighbors to the east. The Ottoman Muslims fought, indeed sought to displace, the Christian Europeans in the Balkans and the Mediterranean, where economic plums were to be picked, obviously including control of the trade routes through the Mediterranean. However, the Balkans also were a major source of timber and dye wood, silver, and other metals, and the conquest of Egypt assured the Ottomans a supply of gold from Sudanese and other African sources.

A realistic approach to this problematique from a wider world economic perspective is offered by Palmira Brummett (1994). She studies Ottoman naval and other military policy as an adjunct to and battering ram for its primarily commercial regional interests and world economic ambitions:

> The Ottomans were conscious participants in the Levantine trading networks among which their empire emerged. Their state can be compared to European states on the bases of ambitions, commercial behaviours, and claims to universal sovereignty. The Ottoman state behaved as merchant, for profit, and to create, enhance, and further its political objectives. These objectives included the acquisition and exploitation of commercial entrepôts and production sites. . . . Pashas and vezirs, far from disdaining trade, were attuned to commercial opportunities and to the acquisition and sheltering of wealth to which those opportunities could lead. . . . There is evidence of the direct participation of members of the Ottoman dynasty and of [the administrative-military class] *askeri* in trade . . . particularly of long established grain export. . . . Also important were the Ottoman investments in the copper, lumber, silk, and spice trades. It is clear that the Ottomans were attracted by the prospect of capturing the oriental trade, rather than simply by the possibilities of territorial conquest, and that state agents urged the sultans to conquest for commercial wealth. Ottoman naval development was directed to the acquisition and protection of that wealth. (Brummett 1994: 176, 179)

Eastward, the first obstacle to Ottoman ambitions for a greater share of the South Asian trade were the Mamluk traders from Egypt and Syria. However, many Mamluks were quickly put out of business—with Portuguese help. Arab traders also continued to do Indian Ocean business under Ottoman sovereignty, and there were few Turks in the trade. The next major obstacle, especially for Turkish-manned trade to the

East, was the Safavid empire in Persia. That obstacle was never overcome, despite the Ottoman-Safavid wars and notwithstanding the tactical alliance of convenience between the Ottomans and the Portuguese
against the Persians. Nonetheless, the Portuguese had their own ambitions in the Indian Ocean. They competed with both the Ottomans and
Persians for the same trade. The Portuguese intervention did substantially eliminate the Venetian monopoly position in the silk trade and
aided the Ottomans in establishing their own substantial monopoly
position, at least in the Levant trade (Attman 1981: 106–7, Brummett
1994: 25).

Incidentally, these shifting tactical diplomatic, political, and military
alliances and competitive maneuvering or outright war in pursuit first
and foremost of commercial advantage belie the myth of alleged common fronts and interests between the Christian West on the one hand
and the Muslim East on the other. Muslims (Mamluks, Ottomans, Persians, Indians) fought with each other, and they forged shifting alliances
with different European Christian states (for example, Portuguese,
French, Venetian, Hapsburg), which also vied with each other all in
pursuit of the same end: profit. The Muslim Persian Shah Abbas I sent
repeated embassies to Christian Europe to elicit alliances against their
common Ottoman Muslim enemies, and later made commercial con-
cessions to the English in compensation for their help in throwing the
Portuguese out of Hormuz. Before that, however, the Portuguese had
supplied the Muslim Safavids with arms from Muslim India to use
against the Muslim Ottomans.

So only when it was convenient, "the use of religious rhetoric . . .
was a strategy employed by all the contenders for power in the Euro-
Asian sphere. It served to legitimize sovereign claims, rally military and
popular support, and disarticulate the competing claims of other states"
(Brummett 1994: 180). A case in point was the alliance among the Muslim Ottomans, Gujaratis in India, and Sumatrans at Aceh, to which the
Ottomans sent a large naval mission as part of their common commercial rivalry against the Portuguese. Also incidentally, this "business" of
ever-shifting alliances and wars of all against all also has another interesting implication: there is no foundation in fact for the alleged differences between European states and those in other parts of the world in
their international behavior. That demolishes still another Eurocentric
fable about European "exceptionality."

So in conclusion and contrary to the conventional wisdom, we must
agree with Faroqhi when he summarizes that

Trade between the Ottoman Empire and the Indian subcontinent, as well as Ottoman-Iranian commerce and interregional
trade within the Empire itself . . . [largely] used the Asian land
routes, and their control by the Ottoman state was a factor staving
off European economic penetration. . . . The Ottoman Empire
and Moghul India have both been placed in the category of "gunpowder empires." But they share an even more significant feature:
they were both cash-taxing empires, and as such they could not
exist without internal and external trade. (Faroqhi 1991: 38, 41)

Safavid Persia. Persia was less vulnerable, perhaps both
because its location gave it an even stronger trading position and because it had more of its own sources of silver, which it coined—also for
circulation among the Ottomans.

Routes criss-crossed the Iranian plateau linking east with west,
the steppes of Central Asia and the plains of India with the ports
of the Mediterranean and north and south, down the rivers of
Russia to the shores of the Persian Gulf carrying trade from the
East Indies, India and China to Europe. Along the roads were
strung the main towns, their sites determined as much by geographical and economic factors as political. It is notable that the
main trading routes, while fluctuating in importance, remained
almost constantly in use throughout (Jackson and Lockhart 1986:
412).

Moreover, Persian overland and maritime trade was more complementary than competitive, as we observed also in the Sahara and will again
in India. Indeed, the caravan trade between India and Persia flourished
through the eighteenth century and carried as much merchandise as the
sea route. Merchants also diversified risks by sending some shipments
through Kandahar and other inland hubs and others via Hormuz/
Bandar Abbas (Barendse 1997, I).

At Hormuz, long before the Portuguese arrived there, a mid-
fifteenth-century observer reported the arrival of "merchants from the
seven climates" (Jackson and Lockhart 1986: 422). They arrived from
Egypt, Syria, Anatolia, Turkestan, Russia, China, Java, Bengal, Siam,
Tenasserim, Socotra, Bijapur, the Maldives, Malabar, Abyssinia, Zanzi-
bar, Vijayanagara, Gulbarga, Gujarat, Cambay, Arabia, Aden, Jidda,
Yemen, and of course from all over Persia itself. They came to exchange
their wares or buy and sell them for cash and to a lesser extent on credit.
Merchants were in good standing. Persian trade with India and the East

was particularly high at the end of the fifteenth century. Persia became the major West Asian producer and exporter of silk, at costs that were lower even than either those of China or later of Bengal (Attman 1981: 40). Major importers were Russia, Caucasia, Armenia, Mesopotamia, the Ottomans, as well as the Europeans via the Ottomans. This trade generated important earnings of silver and other income for the Persian producers from Russia, Europe, and the Ottomans, but also made profits for the Ottoman middlemen. Shah Abbas I (1588–1629) and his successors did all they could to promote and protect trade, including battling against the Ottomans, importing and the protecting Armenian artisans and merchants from embattled Ottoman territories, and recovering Hormuz from the Portuguese. The Ottoman-Safavid war of 1615–1618 and indeed other on-and-off conflicts between Persia and the Ottomans between 1578 and 1639 were over control of the silk trade and its alternative routes. The Persians sought to bypass the Ottoman intermediaries, and the latter to cement their position. Persian trade then turned increasingly eastward across the Indian Ocean, and after the fall of the Safavid monarchy in 1723, Persian silk was largely replaced by that from Syria.

First the Portuguese and after them the Dutch traded in and around Persia. Persian silk and some wool were the main items in European demand. They were paid for with Asian spices, cotton textiles, porcelain, assorted other goods, and European metal products—and gold. Chronic and recurrent commercial conflicts between Europeans and the Shah as well as with private traders in Persia generated frequent diplomatic and occasional military conflicts. However, the Europeans mostly lacked both the commercial bargaining power and political military power to get their way.

> To say, for example, that the Dutch East India Company (VOC) made Persia subservient to its worldwide trading connection is to state a belief that would not have been shared by either Dutchmen or Persians. It is therefore sometimes necessary to look at historical reality—at how things probably really were. . . . [This] shows that Europeans did not order Persians about, but rather the other way around. . . . The Europeans might take action in the face of such a situation, and in fact they did, but they were unable to create a structural improvement of their situation throughout the entire 140 years that the VOC was present in Persia. (Floor 1988: 1)

To summarize the trade of West Asia as a whole, it had a balance of trade surplus with Europe, but a balance of trade deficit with South,

Southeast, and East Asia (and probably with Central Asia, across which silver moved predominantly eastward, but gold westward). West Asia covered its balance of trade deficits to the East with the re-export of bullion derived from its balance of trade surplus with Europe, the Maghreb and via it with West Africa, and gold from East Africa, as well as some of its own production of both gold and silver, especially in Anatolia and Persia. An observer wrote in 1621:

> The Persians, Moores, and Indians, who trade with the Turkes at Aleppo, Mocha, and Alexandria, for Raw Silkes, Drugs, Spices, Indico, and Calicoes; have alwaies made, and still doe make, their returnes in readie money; for other wares, there are but few which they desire from foreign partes . . . [which] they do yearly vent in all, not for above 40. or 50. thousand pounds sterling [or only 5 percent of the cost of the above mentioned imports that had to be paid for in specie]. (cited in Masters 1988: 147)

Nonetheless, Chaudhuri writes that

> whether or not the Islamic world [of West Asia] suffered a perpetual deficit on its balance of trade is debatable. There is little doubt that its trade to India, the Indonesian archipelago, and China was balanced by the export of precious metals, gold and silver. [However] the Middle East appears to have enjoyed a financial surplus with the Christian West, Central Asia, and the city-states of eastern Africa. The favorable balances materialised in the form of treasure, and what was not retained at home as a store of wealth flowed out again in eastward directions. (Chaudhuri 1978: 184–45)

INDIA AND THE INDIAN OCEAN

We may visualize a sort of necklace of port-city emporia strung around Asia (see map 2.4):

> The most important of these port-cities were, going clockwise, Aden and later Mocha, Hormuz, several in the Gulf of Cambay (at different times Diu, Cambay, and Surat), Goa, Calicut, Colombo, Madras, Masulipatam, Malacca and Aceh. All no doubt rose and fell in importance during our period, but certain common characteristics can be mentioned. In all of them the population was exceedingly diverse, including usually representatives of all the major seafaring communities of the Indian Ocean, and sometimes from outside: Chinese in Malacca, Europeans in most

of them. . . . all of these port cities also acted as transhipment centres. Some with unproductive interiors, such as Hormuz and Malacca, had this as their almost exclusive role, but even exporting
ports funnelled on goods from elsewhere. Politically all these port
cities had a large, or at least a necessary, degree of autonomy.
Some were completely independent. (Das Gupta and Pearson
1987: 13)

The geographical and economic center of this Indian Ocean world was
the Indian subcontinent itself. Much of it was highly developed and
already dominant in the world textile industry before the Mughal conquest. However, that conquest further united, urbanized, and commercialized India, notwithstanding the imperial Mughal's alleged financial
dependence on agriculture and its tax yields. In fact by the seventeenth
century, the principal Mughal capitals of Agra, Delhi, and Lahore each
had populations of some half million and some of the commercial port
cities listed above had 200,000 inhabitants each. Urbanization in cities
over 5,000 reached 15 percent of the population. This was significantly
higher than later Indian urbanization in the nineteenth century and
dwarfs the 30,000 inhabitants of European-controlled enclave cities in
Asia such as Portuguese Malacca and Dutch Batavia (Reid 1990: 82).
Total population in the Indian subcontinent also expanded, more than
doubling in two and a half centuries from between 54 and 79 million in
1500 to between 130 and 200 million in 1750 (see tables 4.1 and 4.2).
Other estimates are some 100 million in 1500, 140 to 150 million in
1600, and 185 to 200 million in 1800 (Richards 1996).

Turning to India, Chaudhuri explains that

> taken as a whole, the caravan and seaborne trade of India was
> oriented more toward exports than imports, and the favorable
> balance was settled in precious metals. . . . India's trade to the
> Middle East was dominated by the import of treasure, just as ex-
> ports to South East Asia were balanced by imports of spices, aro-
> matics, and Chinese goods. . . . There was even considerable re-
> export of silver from the subcontinent in the direction of Java,
> Sumatra, Malaya, and China. . . . Large quantities of cotton tex-
> tiles were exported to Manila and were then sent to Spanish
> America by way of the galleon trade to Acapulco. The returns
> were made largely in silver. (Chaudhuri 1978: 185)

So, India had a massive balance of trade surplus with Europe and some
with West Asia, based mostly on its more efficient low-cost cotton textile production and also of course on pepper for export. These went

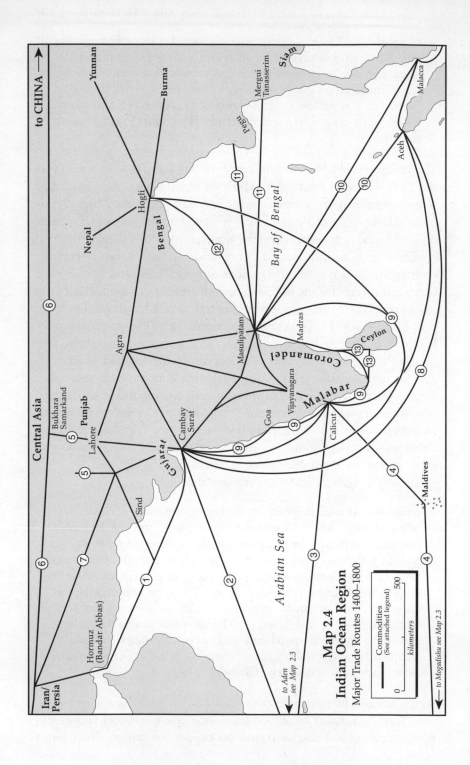

Map 2.4
Indian Ocean Region
Major Trade Routes 1400–1800

Commodities
(See attached legend)

0   500
kilometers

to Aden
see Map 2.3

to Mogadishu see Map 2.3

to CHINA →

Yunnan

Burma

Siam

Mergui
Tanasserim

Malacca

Pegu

Aceh

Nepal

Bengal

Hogli

Bay of Bengal

Central Asia

Bukhara
Samarkand

Punjab

Lahore

Agra

Masulipatam

Madras

Ceylon

Coromandel

Vijayanagara

Malabar

Goa

Calicut

Gujarat

Cambay
Surat

Sind

Iran/
Persia

Hormuz
(Bandar Abbas)

Arabian Sea

Maldives

MAP 2-4 INDIAN OCEAN REGION
[also see legends to Maps 2-3 and 2-5]

ROUTES Westward	Eastward
1. INDIA-WEST ASIA cotton textiles, dies, indigo, silk, silk textiles, iron & steel products, housewares, wood & glass prods., rice, pulses, wheat, oil [spices, pepper, ceramics] aromatics, incense, shawls, blankets, paper, gumlace, saltpeter	dye woods, salt, pearls, minerals, metal/prods., copper, lumber, horses, carpets, luxury goods, fruits, dates, arms, coral, rosewater, dye woods SILVER
2. GUJARAT-GULF same as 1	wine, opium, pearls, aromatics, incense, SILVER, GOLD
3. MALABAR-GULF pepper, rice [spices]	GOLD
4. MALABAR-EAST AFRICA rice, cowries	ivory, slaves, fish, GOLD
5. GUJARAT/PUNJAB-CENTRAL ASIA [northward] cotton & silk textiles, pulses, rice, wheat, indigo, tobacco	[southward] horses, camels, sheep, cotton
6. WEST-CENTRAL-EAST ASIA silk, tea	horses

ROUTES Westward	Eastward
7. GUJARAT-SIND-PUNJAB-WEST ASIA cotton textiles, wheat, indigo	SILVER
8. GUJARAT- SOUTHEAST ASIA spices, [sugar, silk, ceramics] GOLD	cotton textiles coral, copper, glass [re-exports from Aden/Gulf] SILVER
9. INDIAN INTER-REGIONAL [not fully represented] exchanges among most major Indian products along maritime and overland trade routes among Punjab, Sind, Gujarat, Malabar, Vijayanagara, Coromandel, Bengal	
10. COROMANDEL - SOUTHEAST ASIA tin, sugar, metals, elephants, [ceramics, silk] GOLD	cotton textiles, slaves, rice, diamonds, SILVER
11. COROMANDEL - BURMA/SIAM tin, elephants, woods, SILVER	cotton textiles
12. COROMANDEL- BENGAL silk, cotton textiles, rice, sugar	
13. CEYLON - INDIA elephants, cinnamon, jewels, pearls	rice

westward to Africa, West Asia, Europe, and from there on across the Atlantic to the Caribbean and the Americas. However, India also exported food staples, like rice, pulses, and vegetable oil both westward (as had been the case as early as the third millennium B.C.—see Frank 1993) to the trading ports of the Persian Gulf and Red Sea (which also depended on Egypt for grain supplies), and eastward to Malacca and elsewhere in Southeast Asia. In return, India received massive amounts of silver and some gold from the West, directly around the Cape or via West Asia, as well as from West Asia itself. Mocha (which has given its name to coffee) was called "the treasure chest of the Mughal" for the silver from there. Since India produced little silver of its own, it used the imported silver mostly for coinage or re-export, and the gold for coinage (of pagoda coins), jewelry, and hoarding.

India also exported cotton textiles to and imported spices from Southeast Asia. The same route was used to exchange cotton textiles for silk and porcelain and other ceramics with China. However, India seems to have had a balance of trade deficit with Southeast Asia, or at least India re-exported silver to there, and especially to China. However, the vast bulk of this trade was in Muslim Indian hands and on Indian-built shipping, although some was also in Arab and Southeast Asian—also Muslim—hands. A very small, albeit in the eighteenth century growing, share was in one or another European country's ships, which however employed Asian captains, crews, and merchants as well (Raychaudhuri and Habib 1982: 395–433, Chaudhuri 1978).

Inland trade moved by water and overland. Ubiquitous short-haul (or, small-boat) shipping went all along and around the coasts of India. Inland waterways were available in many parts of India, especially in the south. Even in the north, shipping was built in many provinces, including Kashmir, Thatta, Lahore, Allahabad, Bihar, Orissa, and Bengal. Caravans numbering from ten to forty thousand pack and/or draught animals at a time moved overland. Combinations of all of the above crisscrossed the subcontinent and were transshipped to and from long-distance maritime trade. "We see the relation between activities on land and sea as asymmetric. Most of the time sea activities had less influence on those on land than vice versa" (Das Gupta and Pearson 1987: 5). Almost all the port cities were in organic symbiosis with the caravan routes into and from their respective hinterland interiors and sometimes also with distant transcontinental regions, especially in Central Asia. Indeed, Chaudhuri (1990a: 140) suggests that the continental overland trade and the Indian Ocean maritime trade should be viewed as mirror images of each other.

In southern India, the inland capital of Vijayanagara was for a long time the focal point of trade to and from Goa in the west, Calicut in the south, and Masulipatam and Pulicat on the Coromandel coast to the east. These and many other port cities, and of course especially those with no or relatively unproductive hinterlands, were highly dependent on staple food imports. These came via other port cities from father up or down the coast, but often also from ports with access to rice and other grain producing areas thousands of miles distant. Moreover, the first and last named port cities and Vijayanagara also had overland connections to the north, both to inland centers such as Hyderabad and Burhanpur and to the west Indian port of Surat (or at other times Cambay), which in turn were entrepôts for the Punjab and Central Asia (for more details see Subrahmanyam 1990). However,

> the trade of Central Asia had no such direct connections with the sea, and yet the whole region itself exercised a vital influence on the lives of the people closer to the monsoon belts of the Indian Ocean. In terms of direct relationships, the Central Asia caravan trade was complementary to the trans-continental maritime commerce of Eurasia. (Chaudhuri 1985: 172)

Moreover, there was the India-China trade across Nepal and Tibet, which had been going on for more than a millennium. Bengal and Assam exported textiles, indigo, spices, sugar, hides, and other goods to Tibet for sale to merchants there, who took them on for sale in China. Payment was in Chinese products, tea, and often gold (Chakrabarti 1990). (I have discussed some of these Central Asian routes and their "Silk Road" history in Frank 1992; Central Asia is covered in a separate section below in this chapter.)

Different Indian regions also traded and had balance of trade surplus and deficits with each other. The major coastal regions (Gujarat, Malabar, Coromandel, and Bengal) all traded with each other—and with Ceylon—and also served each other as entrepôts in transoceanic and continental caravan trade. They also competed with each other as "exporters" to the interior of India, where their market areas overlapped. However in general, the interior had an export surplus with the coastal ports and in exchange received imported goods and coin, which had been minted from imported bullion (or melted-down foreign coins) in or near the ports. Silver tended to move north into regions governed by the Mughals, and gold went south, especially to Malabar and Vijayanagara. Below we look more closely at some major Indian regions.

North India. North India was active in interregional and inter-"national" trade with Central and West Asia, as we have already noted. B. R. Grover summarizes:

> Trade in the industrial products of many a region of north India was well established. Most villages . . . produced a variety of piece goods. . . . The industrial products of commercial regions in many a province of north India were exported to other places. (Grover 1994: 235)

Many are itemized in the legends to the maps.

Gujarat and Malabar. The west coast of India on the Indian Ocean/Arabian Sea was the site of the major port-city entrepôts of Diu, Cambay (and then Surat) in Gujarat, as well as the Malabar coast, including the Portuguese entrepôt at Goa. They were the major ports of call for monsoon-driven coast-hugging ships from the Red Sea and Persian Gulf, as well as for ships on some circum-African maritime routes from Europe and for regional shipping to the Indus estuary and northward to the Sind. Cambay/Surat were also the turnaround points for the overland caravan trade with Persia, Russia, Central Asia, the Punjab, and the southeasterly inland regions of India; and they supplied rice and/or wheat to most of them. Moreover, the Gujarat and Malabar ports maintained trade relations with Coromandel and Bengal on the east side of the Indian subcontinent, and with Southeast Asia, China, and Japan. Their manufacturing industries specialized in the production and export of textiles, especially westward and northward. Over and above their imports of horses, metals, consumer and other goods (see legends to maps 2.3 and 2.4) from these directions, their balance of trade surplus with these regions was covered by the inflow of silver. Some of that was, however, re-exported to cover deficitary maritime import trade from the East. From there, Gujarat was both an importer for itself and its hinterland and very importantly for transshipment westward to West Asia, the Mediterranean, and Europe—and from there to Africa and the Americas. Nonetheless, most trade was in Indian hands, although some was also in Arabian and Persian hands. Even as late as the eighteenth century only about 12 percent of Surat trade was European (Das Gupta and Pearson 1987: 136).

Coromandel. The Coromandel coast, which faces the Bay of Bengal on the east of India, had many important centers of production and export, although perhaps only about one-tenth of its production was for export. A major export was cotton textiles eastward to Southeast Asia and China, from which it imported spices, porcelain, and gold. Another role was its entrepôt function, both in trade with and among other regions of India and worldwide, most of which was also in Indian hands. However, the Dutch and later other Europeans also used the Coromandel locations and resources for their own Indian and worldwide operations. Coromandel "domestic" Indian trade was especially with Bengal to the northeast, from which it imported food grains and silk, and with Gujarat to the northwest, as well as of course to the interior. However, its geographical location and productive diversity in textiles, pepper, indigo (for dyes), rice, iron/steel, diamonds, and other commodities too numerous to mention here (see legends to maps 2.4 and 2.5 for a partial list) as well as slaves made Coromandel the major way station for international and indeed intercontinental trade both eastward and westward. It also imported Persian and Arabian luxury consumer goods and horses from the west for transshipment eastward.

From the east, Coromandel imported spices, woods, elephants, lead, zinc, tin, and especially copper and gold, some for transshipment further west. Eastward the trade was with continental and island Southeast Asia and especially to Aceh and Malacca, China and Japan as well as to Manila and on to Acapulco (and of course with neighboring Ceylon both as a trading partner and as another way station). Westward, Coromandel was the major area not only of transshipment but also of reprovisioning and exchange of commodities and precious metals for trade with the Maldives. From there—and also directly—trade was with Africa, with port cities along the Persian Gulf and the Red Sea and from there to the Mediterranean and/or around South Africa to Europe—and then on across the Atlantic to the Americas. Coromandel also traded with Goa and Cambay/Surat, both for Indian interregional trade and as way stations on the world trade routes. Of course, Coromandel ports also served as entrepôts for the inland trade, but in competition with ports elsewhere on the Indian coast (Arasaratnam 1986).

Bengal. The most productive region of all came to be Bengal. It exported cotton and silk textiles and rice to most of the other regions of India. Some goods went southward to and along the Coromandel coast, and goods went or continued over to Cambay/Surat on the west coast, as well as overseas westward to West Asia and Europe and eastward to Southeast Asia and China. Hence, Bengal absorbed silver and gold from all directions, including overland from Tibet/Yunnan/Burma and across the Bay of Bengal from Burma. Bengal supplied 20 percent of Indian and 15 percent of all the English East India Company's (referred to hereafter by its acronym, EIC) imports in 1670, about 35 percent of both in 1700, but almost 80 percent of Indian and 66 percent of all imports by 1738–1740. By 1758–1760 just after the Battle of Plassey, the Indian share of EIC trade was 80 percent. Then the share of the total declined to 52 percent, as the Chinese share rose from nothing a century earlier to 12 percent in 1740 and 34 percent by 1760. However, by then part of the Bengali exports were opium, with which the EIC replaced some of the silver as its medium of payment to China (Attman 1981: 51).

An interesting observation in the light of the recurrent Bengal famines since 1770 is Chaudhuri's (1978: 207) observation that up through the early eighteenth century Bengal could always be depended on as a supplier of food when crops failed in other regions. Another interesting observation is Perlin's (1983: 53) on "the lack of any serious regional monographs on [Bengali or other Indian] textile industries, in the seventeenth or eighteenth centuries, of a kind [that have been] long legion in the European historiography" (Ramaswamy 1980 and recently S. Chaudhuri 1995 seem to be exceptions).

SOUTHEAST ASIA

Southeast Asia has been far too neglected by historians, who tend to devote no or only the briefest attention to it before 1500 and after that focus mainly on European activities there. Therefore, it may be well to take a longer look back into the history of Southeast Asia and its relations with other parts of the world. Domesticated rice dates from 3000 B.C., Bronze Age archaeological finds from 1500 B.C., and Iron Age ones from 500 B.C. (Tarling 1992: 185). Southeast Asian world trade ties also date back several millennia. On the basis of his research on the manufacture of beads (which survive in the archaeological record better than most things) Peter Francis (1989, 1991: 40) shows that Arikamedu in eastern India was an 'Indo-Roman trading-station' but looked east far more than it looked west." Documentation from the Chinese Eastern Han dynasty also attests to significant trade with Southeast Asia in the second century A.D., and there is also evidence of the same from the second century B.C.:

By the early Christian era these trade routes reached out to bring together the previously rather separate Southeast Asian exchange systems, linking them into a vast network stretching from Western Europe, via the Mediterranean basin, the Persian Gulf and the Red Sea, to India, Southeast Asia and China . . . [in] what has been called the World System. (Glover 1991)

Southeast Asia was one of the world's richest and commercially most important regions. Significantly however, the most developed productive and trading area in Southeast Asia was located on the eastern side of the peninsula at what the Chinese called Fu-nan on the South China Sea, and not on the Indian Ocean side of the Isthmus of Kra. However, from the perspectives of the Chinese, Indian, Arab, and European "civilizations," not to mention the later Portuguese, Dutch, and other European interests, Southeast Asia was only a way station populated by peoples of little account and little more. Even Abu-Lughod (1989: 282 ff.) does not give Southeast Asia its due, treating it as little more than a region of "peripheral" entrepôts between China and India.

Yet the archaeological and historical evidence speaks for a vast Southeast Asian region of highly civilized and productive peoples in their own right long before as well as long after the birth of Christ. Highly developed societies, economies, and polities came and went both on the mainland and in island Southeast Asia. The most notable of these were Viet and Champa in Vietnam, Angkor in Khmer Cambodia, Pegu in Burma, Ayutthaya in Siam, Srivijaya on Sumatra and, after its decline, Majapahit. They had extensive economic and cultural relations among each other and with India and China. Sumatran Srivijaya and for some time its capital Palembang was dominant over a vast insular and peninsular area from the seventh to the thirteenth centuries. Java was reputed to be the richest place on earth in the thirteenth century, and the Mongols invaded Southeast Asia and sought but failed to exploit its riches. After the decline of Srivijaya, the Javanese Majapahit empire controlled almost the entire area of central Indonesia in the fourteenth and fifteenth centuries. They competed for and attempted to monopolize the economy and trade of the South China Sea.

The *Cambridge History of Southeast Asia* summarizes:

The Southeast Asian region was eulogized as a land of immense wealth; developments there were of crucial importance to the entirety of world history in the pre-1600 period. Writers, travellers, sailors, merchants, and officials from every continent of the

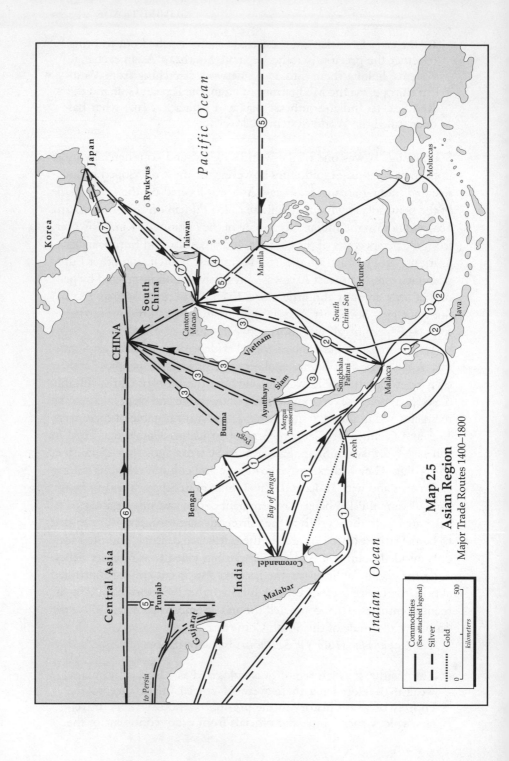

Map 2.5
Asian Region
Major Trade Routes 1400–1800

Commodities
(See attached legend)

Silver

Gold

0   500
kilometers

Pacific Ocean

Indian Ocean

Central Asia

CHINA

Korea

Japan

Ryukyus

Taiwan

South China

Canton
Macao

Vietnam

Siam

Ayutthaya

Tanasserim

Mergui

Pegu

Burma

Bengal

Bay of Bengal

Coromandel

India

Malabar

Gujarat

Punjab

to Persia

Songkhala
Pattani

South China Sea

Manila

Brunei

Java

Moluccas

Malacca

Aceh

MAP 2-5 ASIAN REGION
[brackets indicate re-export/onward-shipment]

ROUTES

North - Westward South - Eastward

1. INDIA-SOUTHEAST ASIA

pepper, spices, rice, sugar, elephants, tin, copper, other metals, cinnamon, teak, rubies, GOLD

cot. textiles, silk textiles, slaves, diamonds, rice, iron & steel/prods., diamonds, shipping/services [SILVER]

2. ARCHIPELAGAN SOUTHEAST ASIA - CHINA

pepper, spices, tin, rice, sugar, fish, salt, aromatic woods, resins, lacquer, tortoise shell, pearls, precious stones, amber, jade, birdsnests, jaggery, jasper, cutch, tin [SILVER]

silk/textiles, ceramics, tea, cloth, satin, velvet, paper, fruit, drugs, arms & powder, copper & iron products, gold/silver thread, zinc, cupro-nickel

see also route 3 for partial commodity overlap/duplication

3. CONTINENTAL SOUTHEAST ASIA - CHINA
(north)

rice, sugar, cotton, rubies, amber, jade, deer & tiger skins, timber, ships, woods, jaggery, paper, cutch, betelnut, birdsnests, shark fins, tobacco,

ceramics, lacquerware, silk/textile, clothing, arms & powder, copper cash, quicksilver, copper & iron products, lead, zinc, cupro-nickel, salt, fruit, rhubarb, tea,

ROUTES

North - Westward South - Eastward

3. CONTINENTAL SOUTHEAST ASIA - CHINA, cont.
(south)

pepper, sappan wood, tin, lead, saltpeter, SILVER

satin, velvet, brocades, thread, paper, dyes, carpets, shoes, stockings, housewares, labor, shipping/services

4. SOUTHEAST ASIA - JAPAN [VIA TAIWAN & RYUKUS]
(north)

spices, pepper, tin, sugar, medicines [cot. textiles]

(south)
copper, sulphur, camphor, swords, shipping, SILVER

5. CHINA - MANILA GALLEON - ACAPULCO/ MEXICO PERU

SILVER

silk/textiles, ceramics, quicksilver

6. CENTRAL ASIA - CHINA

silk/textiles, tea, arms, clothing, ceramics, medicines, paper money

horses, camels, sheep, jade, medicines [SILVER]

7. JAPAN - CHINA

SILVER
copper, sulphor, camphor, swords, iron

silk/textiles, cot. textiles, sugar, skins, woods, dyes, tea, lead, manufactures eastern hemisphere knew of Southeast Asia's wealth, and by the second millennium of the Christian era, most were aware of its power and prestige. . . . Until the nineteenth-century "industrial age," all world trade was more or less governed by the ebb and flow of spices in and out of Southeast Asia . . . By contrast, the early history of Southeast Asia and its international significance is not appreciated in the contemporary age. (Tarling 1992: 183)

Southeast Asia's geographical location also made it a natural crossroads and meeting point for world trade, not to mention migration and cultural exchange. That is because it lies between China and Japan to the north, South Asia to the west, and the Pacific to the east. At the beginning of the fifteenth century, the narrowest part of the Malay Peninsula at the Isthmus of Kra was used for portage between the Bay of Bengal and the South China Sea (and today it is being considered for a pipeline and/or canal). It was replaced by a sea route through the straits of Malacca and Singapore between the southern end of the Malay Peninsula and the island of Sumatra. That was in turn complemented by still another sea route to the China Sea around the south of Sumatra and through the Sunda Strait separating it from Java (see map 2.5). For centuries, most shipping used the entrepôts in Southeast Asia as turn-around points at which cargo was transferred to and exchanged for that coming from the other direction.

The coastal trading ports, riverine settlements, and their agrarian hinterlands were always intertwined; and port and inland polities waxed and waned in response to the ups and downs of these relations as well as the shift of trade routes.

"When we look with care at the factors critical to the early modern era in Southeast Asia, however, most of them begin before the arrival of European fleets" (Reid 1993:10). The "long sixteenth century" (1450–1640) expansion, renowned in Europe and the Americas, probably started even earlier in Southeast Asia (in 1400) in response to increasing demand from East Asia, especially China, South and West Asia and then also from Europe for spice and pepper. Several hundred thousand workers were incorporated into the boom in production and trade, which—with a three-decade lull after 1500—lasted until at least 1630. Imports of American silver and Indian textiles peaked between 1600 and 1640, when Southeast Asia was still a trading partner equal to others (Reid 1993: 11, 17). The peak of the Southeast Asian trading boom from 1580 to 1630 coincided with and was also generated by the simultaneous economic expansions in and demand by Japan, China, India, and Europe. Several spices were almost exclusive to some islands and Southeast Asian pepper displaced Indian pepper because its costs of production were a third less than Indian costs. However, cotton was an even more widespread cash—and export—crop. Cash cropping in the countryside and urbanization to commercialize the same also implied large-scale maritime imports of staple foodstuffs (Reid 1993: 7–16; also see Tarling 1992: 463–68). After 1662, Tongkin also entered the world market as a major exporter of ceramics.

By 1600, Southeast Asia had a population of 23 million (Tarling 1992: 463), or about one-fifth to one-fourth of all of China, and they traded with each other as well as with others worldwide. At least a half dozen trade-dependent cities—Thang-long in Vietnam, Ayutthaya in Siam, Aceh on Sumatra, Bantam and Mataram on Java, Makassar on Celebes—each counted around 100,000 inhabitants plus a large number of seasonal and annual visitors (Reid 1990: 83). Another half dozen cities had at least 50,000 inhabitants. Malacca also had 100,000 inhabitants, but that number declined to between 25,000 and 33,000 after the Portuguese took over. So during this period, Southeast Asia was highly urbanized, both relative to many other parts of the world, including Europe, and to later centuries (Tarling 1992: 473–75).

Archipelago and Islands. The division of labor and pattern of trade in Indonesia and adjacent regions combined three interrelated axes of interisland and peninsular short-haul trade, regional trade with India and China/Japan/Ryukyu Islands, and world trade with West Asia, Europe, and the Americas. All three axes depended not only on the exchange of products from afar, but also on the productive capacities and specializations within Indonesia and Southeast Asia. Following B. Schrieke (1955), Ashin Das Gupta summarizes for the fifteenth century:

> Essentially it was a pattern of east-west exchange of goods within the Indonesian archipelago with Javanese rice being carried everywhere. The central fact of Indonesian trade was that two major products—pepper and spices—were located at the two extremities of the archipelago. Pepper was produced in Sumatra, Malaya, west Java and Borneo. Spices—cloves, nutmeg and mace—were available only in the eastern island groups of the Moluccas and Bandas. Java produced rice, salt, salt-fish and a variety of foodstuffs as well as some cotton, thread and textiles. . . . Rice and

other Javanese product were carried by Javanese traders and junk-owners to Sumatra to have them exchanged for pepper and other foreign goods. Pepper was then taken to Java and further on to Bali in order to collect in exchange Balinese cotton fabrics which were in great demand in the spice islands. In the final stage the Javanese sailed out to the Moluccas and Bandas carrying rice, and other Javanese products, Balinese cloth, along with Indian textiles and Chinese porcelain, silk and small coins. . . . A marked feature of Indonesian trade was the intertwining of inter-island and inter-national trade. (Das Gupta 1987: 243)

Southeast Asia's international trade is summarized by Anthony Reid:

The pattern of exchange in this age of commerce was for South-east Asia to import cloth from India, silver from the Americas and Japan and copper-cash, silk, ceramics and other manufactures from China, in exchange for its exports of pepper, spices, aromatic woods, resins, lacquer, tortoise shell, pearls, deerskin, and the sugar exported by Vietnam and Cambodia. (Reid 1993: 23)

By the late seventeenth century, Java also exported important amounts of sugar to Japan, Surat, Persia (where it forced out Bengali sugar), and as far as Europe (Attman 1981: 41).

Moreover, several Southeast Asian ports—as also the Ryukyu Islands then or Hong Kong today—became important entrepôts in trade among China, Japan, other parts of Eurasia, and the Americas, espe-cially when direct trade was restricted but never eliminated by China and Japan. Even the minor entrepôt of the Vietnamese port of Hoi-an illustrates the connections among overlapping markets:

Vietnam found itself a junction for the world flow of precious metals. . . . Ships from Japan brought large amounts of silver and copper cash which went mainly for silk, sugar, aloeswood, deer-skins, rayskins, and ceramics. Japanese traders controlled the local silk and sugar markets by prepayment with imported cash. The Chinese merchants gathered during this four month "fair" and traded their silk, copper cash, and tutenag for the Japanese silver and the goods of Southeast Asia. The Vietnamese welcomed [all these] . . . and drew revenue from the exchanges which took place on their soil. The Portuguese mingled with the Chinese traders . . . [and] brought American and Persian silver via Goa as well as American silver from Manila and Japanese silver. The Dutch, also carrying American silver, made contact with the Chinese in Hoi-an. . . . (Whitmore 1983: 380, 388)

The Japanese also established a merchant colony at the regional entre-pôt of Ayutthaya (near modern Bangkok) in Siam until many of them were massacred and the others expelled in 1632. Indeed a few years earlier, a Portuguese visitor had reported, perhaps with some exaggeration, that of the 400,000 households in Ayutthaya, 100,00 were foreigners from all over (Lourido 1996a: 24). The city was an entrepôt for extensive trade not only with Japan and of course Macao/Canton, but also with archipelago Southeast Asian ports and Pattani on the east coast of the Malay Peninsula. Moreover, Ayutthaya maintained overland connections with Mergui/Tenasserim on the western side of the peninsula and from there northward to Pegu in Burma and westward across the bay to Bengal, Coromandel, and other parts of India (see map 2.5). The oft-cited Portuguese Tome Pires observed "over one hundred junks leaving for China, Ainam, Lequois, Cambodia and Champa . . . Sunda, Palembang and other islands, Cochinchina and Burma and Jangoma [Chiangmai]. From the Tenasserim side Siam also traded with Pase, Pedir, Kedah, Pegu, Bengal; and Gujarati came to its ports every year" (quoted in Lourido 1996a: 25–26). Rui D'Avila Lourido (1996a: 29) himself summarizes: "Siam was, in economic terms, a 'half-periphery' of the Chinese trade, but at the same time, was a centre of its own economic region, with all the countries of the Gulf of Siam's recognizing its own economic region."

However, the major entrepôt was Malacca, control of which offered a stranglehold on the throat of Venice, as Pires observed. Malacca was founded in 1403 as Ming Chinese sea power expanded and Zheng He (Cheng Ho) began his celebrated seven voyages (from 1405 to 1433) with three-hundred-ship fleets carrying 27,000 men to India, Arabia, and even to East Africa. Most Chinese shipping, however, used Malacca as its turnaround point, though that was also temporarily halted in 1433, as the Chinese state turned inward to counter renewed Mongol threats. Nonetheless, Malacca continued to prosper and attracted more and more Gujaratis, of whom one thousand came to live there and several thousand more came and went each year in trade with Cambay. They were joined by Turks, Armenians, Arabs, Persians, and Africans, who also used Malacca as a trading center with Southeast and East Asia. It became the world's biggest spice emporium and sent most of them on to China. However, Malacca also served as a point of distribution of Indian textiles throughout Southeast Asia—and via Manila on to the Americas. Its food supply came from Java and India.

The Portuguese capture of Malacca in 1511 had far-reaching consequences. Although they themselves never numbered more than 600 residents and averaged only 200, the Portuguese sought but failed to monopolize the Malaccan trade and through it other trade as well. However, the Portuguese did succeed in driving many Muslims out of Malacca to Johore in Malaya, Brunei in Borneo, Bantam in Java, and especially to Aceh on Sumatra. All of these centers competed for the Malaccan trade and with each other. One result was to open an alternative trade route to Java and the China Sea around the other side of Sumatra. That favored Bantam in Java, which catered to the China trade, and especially the development of Aceh on the westernmost tip of Sumatra. It soon imposed itself in the sixteenth century and attracted the Gujarati, Coromandel, and Bengali trade. Malacca was correspondingly weakened, and in 1641 the Dutch took it over from the Portuguese, with the help of Malacca's rival, Johore.

However, soon after the Dutch sought to establish themselves more firmly in the spice-producing Moluccas and in Java, where they had established their headquarters at Batavia in 1619. Like the Portuguese before them, the Dutch tried to monopolize spice production and trade. In the vain effort to do so and to practice price maintenance, they repeatedly destroyed spice trees in the islands, spice stocks in Batavia, and even in Amsterdam. So, the most far-reaching and deep-going large-scale European presence in Asia was undoubtedly in Southeast Asia, or more properly in Malaya and Indonesia. Yet even there, indigenous production and trade continued; and none of the Europeans were successful in their repeated attempts to control, let alone monopolize, it.

For the fifteenth and sixteenth centuries, J. C. van Leur (1955: 126) estimates Southeast Asian trade to have been carried on some 480 large and medium-sized ships, weighing between 200 to 400 tons. Of these, 330 to 340 medium-sized ships plus many more small ones handled the Indonesian interisland trade, and 115 ships the China and India trade. Elsewhere, he estimates the shipping tonnages for the year 1622: Indonesian, 50,000 tons; Chinese and Siamese, 18,000; Achinese, 3,000; Coromandel, 10,000; and Dutch, 14,000 (or less than 15 percent of the 95,000-ton sum) (Van Leur 1955: 235). Another undated estimate yields 98,000 tons, of which 50,000 tons are Indonesian and 48,000 others, which he attributes by percentages to the following: China, 18 percent; Siam, 8 percent; Far India, 8 percent; northwest India, 20 percent; Coromandel, 20 percent; Aceh, 0.6 percent; Pegu (in Burma), 10 percent; and Portugal, 6 percent; plus another 10 percent for trade with Japan (Van Leur 1955: 212).

Even in the eighteenth century, the bulk of the spice exports still went to China, and most of them remained in Asian hands. In Southeast Asia, notably, these "hands"—and heads—normally included women, who regularly traveled on trading ships and engaged in large-scale commercial as well as other market transactions at home and abroad. Significantly however, much of the China trade was in the hands not of Southeast Asians (and certainly not of Europeans) but of Chinese. Manila and Batavia have been called "Chinese colonial towns" (Wills 1993: 99, 100). Many Chinese also came to settle as artisans, craftsmen, and merchants and so constitute the now-renowned overseas Chinese diaspora in Southeast Asia (Tarling 1992: 482, 493–97).

Chinese junks from the provinces of Guandong, Zhejiang, Fujian, Tchekian, and Kiannan traded with Japan, the Philippines, the Solo Islands, Sulawesi, Celebes, the Moluccas, Kalamatanon-Borneo, Java, Sumatra, Singapore, Rhio, the east coast of the Malayan Peninsula, Siam, Cochin China, Cambodia, and Tongkin. The eastern coastal route connected Fujian, opposite Taiwan, with the Philippines and Indonesia. The western route connected especially Guandong along the coast with mainland Southeast Asia. Of 222 junks counted at one time (not dated but presumably not long after 1800), 20 each went to Japan, Cochin China, and Tongkin; and about 10 each to the Philippines, Borneo, Sumatra, Singapore, and Cambodia. In addition numerous smaller junks left from Hainan Island (Hamashita 1994a: 99).

Mainland. This survey of trade between Southeast Asia and other regions has privileged the island or archipelago regions over the continental ones and especially their overland trade. The reason is not that the former were much more active or important than the latter, but that the evidence is more abundant. Maritime trade was of greater interest to Europeans, who kept contemporary records; and recent historical, especially underwater, archaeology has also concentrated in these regions. Nonetheless, Burma, Siam, and Vietnam also maintained far-reaching maritime, riverine, and overland caravan trade relations with each other and archipelago Southeast Asia, and perhaps more importantly with India and China (see map 2.5). But this trade has left fewer records, or at least they have not been subjected sufficiently to studies by nineteenth- and twentieth-century chroniclers and scholars. Since most of these records are physically and/or linguistically beyond my reach, I confine myself here to reporting on the still on-going survey and analysis of the literature by Sun Laichen (1994a, b) and Lourido (1996a, b).

Sun (1994a) records three periods of particularly active trade between Burma and China, after the Yuan conquest in the late thirteenth
century, another in the late fourteenth and early fifteenth century
(which corresponds to our observations about the expansion elsewhere
of production and trade since about 1400), and one that began at the
end of the eighteenth century. Although trade with China also took the
form of some "tribute" missions (examined in the section on China
below), Sun emphasizes that contemporaries as well as later scholars
were quite aware of their commercial motives. Any temporary interrup-
tion of this trade for political or climatic reasons made "people run out
of daily necessities" in Burma. It imported much silk, salt, iron and
copper utensils, arms, and powder, as well as cloth, satin, velvets, brocades, thread, carpets, paper, fruits, tea, and copper-cash from China.
In turn, Burma exported amber, rubies, and other precious stones, jade,
ivory, fish, birds' nests, shark fins, jaggery, jasper, catechu, betel nuts,
tobacco, and, certainly by the eighteenth century but probably also earlier, raw cotton to China.

Sun's sources record substantial caravans of beasts of burden, 30
boats on the Irrawaddy River, and 100 to 150 ships plying other Burma-
China trade. Thus in value terms, Burma's abundant maritime trade
was two to three times that of its nonetheless significant overland caravan trade, some of which was also, presumably, in contraband imports
of prohibited metals and arms exports from China. This trade was in
turn tied into numerous Burmese trading fairs, which for instance in
Mong Mit were held daily on a small scale and every five days on a large
scale. Additionally, Burmese mines attracted Chinese entrepreneurs,
merchants, and labor in the several tens of thousands, who produced
metals both for the domestic market and for export to China. That
permitted Burma to cover its otherwise unfavorable balance of trade
and payments, which like its internal trade was progressively monetized
through copper coin, cowries, but also silver and its coinage.

Similar trade, migratory, and other relations flourished between
Vietnam and China. Vietnam imported silk, sugar, tea, cloth, shoes,
stockings, paper, dyes, lamp oil, betel nuts, candy, and medicines
as well as the usual copper-cash. Vietnam in turn exported wood,
bamboo, sulfur, medicines, dies, salt, rice, and lead. Mining was even
more extensive in Vietnam than in Burma, and yielded copper, lead,
and probably zinc and silver, some of which was also exported to China.
Miners and related craftsmen in Vietnam reportedly numbered upward
of several hundred thousand, many of which were Chinese who were

expulsed by growing unemployment and poverty at home and attracted by opportunities in Vietnam and elsewhere in Southeast Asia (Sun 1994a).

Siamese trade deserves special consideration. Not only was most of it concentrated on the Chinese market, but it was in Chinese junks or in Chinese-manned Siamese shipping, which was treated as "domestic" trade by the Chinese authorities themselves (Cushman 1993). The pattern of trade was the usual. Siam exported commodities, especially rice, cotton, sugar, tin, timber and woods, pepper, cardamom, and some high-value luxury goods like ivory, rhinoceros horn, sappan wood, benzoin, and deer and tiger skins, but also lead and silver. The principal value added was probably the production and export of Siamese ships. Jennifer Cushman (1993: 78) explains that "Siam's exports should not be seen as marginal luxuries, but as staple products intended either for popular consumption or for the manufacture of consumer goods by the Chinese." Chinese exports were primarily manufactures such as ceramics, textiles, fans, paper and books, brass and copper wares, and preserved fruits for popular consumption in Siam.

Siamese ports and especially Ayutthaya (on the river north of Bangkok) also served as important north-south and east-west emporia for interregional transshipment. However, as elsewhere in Southeast Asia, another important Chinese "export" to Siam, especially from Fujian, was people: laborers, artisans, entrepreneurs, and merchants (Viraphol 1977, Cushman 1993).

To summarize its position in international trade, Southeast Asia exported spices and tin of its own production to Europe, West Asia, and India. It also re-exported imports from India to China, which was its major customer, some eight times more than Europe. Additionally, Southeast Asia exported forest products, cotton, and gold from its own production to India, China, and Japan. Southeast Asia received silver from India, some of which it also re-exported to China via Malacca. So, Southeast Asia had a balance of trade surplus with India (and of course with West Asia and Europe) but a balance of trade deficit with China.

The "domestic" economic consequences for Southeast Asia are summarized by Reid:

> The entire period 1400–1630 was one of rapid monetization and commercialization of the economy, with the most rapid expansion in the period 1570–1630. A large proportion of the population, by any contemporary standard, was drawn into production

and marketing for the world economy and came to rely on long-distance imports for such everyday items of consumption as cloth, ceramics, utensils, and coinage. Trade occupied a relatively high share (again by contemporary standards) of Southeast Asian national income and made possible a degree of urbanization probably higher than was achieved again before the twentieth century. Within these cities were communities that devoted themselves wholly to trade and commerce, and such institutions as bottomry, profit-sharing, and lending for interest were well established. In a number of crucial areas, however, China, India, and Japan were economically more advanced than Southeast Asians, even though their techniques [including embryonic banks] were known to many urban Southeast Asians. (Reid 1993:129)

Nonetheless, Southeast Asia also had a financial system with a "sophisticated and reliable money market" where money could be borrowed at interest rates of about 2 percent a month, similar to those in Europe (Reid 1990: 89; Tarling 1992: 479). (The "real revolution" in Europe had been, as Cipolla [1976: 211–12] suggested, the sharp decline in the interest price of money, thanks to the big increase in the latter's American supply.)

The productive contributions of Spanish Manila in the Philippines and of Vietnam and Taiwan as well as of Portuguese Macao on the South China coast were far more modest than others in Southeast Asia. However, they contributed important entrepôt functions, especially in the China and Japan trade. Chinese vessels trading to Manila alone numbered between thirty and fifty a year. Over 60 percent of Mexican transpacific imports from Manila had Chinese origins and included Chinese quicksilver, which was always in short supply but essential for mining and refining silver in the Americas (some of which then returned to China). To promote this trade at the beginning of the sixteenth century, Manila had upward of 27,000 (some say 30,000) Chinese residents. They were however victims of several pogroms, including one in which as many as 23,000 (some say 25,000) were massacred in 1603 and again in 1640 (Yan 1991, Quiason 1991). The roles of these entrepôts in the transfer of money is reviewed in chapter 3.

JAPAN

Recent research offers

evidence that important economic developments were occurring in Japan as early as the thirteenth century. Several scholars have shown that Japan was deeply enmeshed in a network of foreign trade with other parts of Asia at this early period. . . . Trade with China and Korea became an important part of the Japanese economy. . . . During the fifteenth and sixteenth centuries foreign trade grew rapidly in intensity and trade ventures were extended to other parts of the Far East, even as far as the Straits of Malacca. (Sanderson 1995: 153)

Korea, Japan, and the Ryukyu Islands, which are south of Japan by 500 miles and opposite the Chinese coast, were in the first circle of China's tributary center-periphery system. However, the Japanese were also a serious would-be competitor of China and sought to press any competitive advantages they could muster, particularly when the Chinese experienced "times of trouble," such as with the Mongols and/or internally. Stephen Sanderson also notes that "it seems that Japan was involving itself in a vigorous Far Eastern trade at basically the same time that late Sung and early Ming China was withdrawing from world trade and declining economically. These events are undoubtedly connected. A large economic vacuum was created, and Japan was quick to fill it. Japan picked up impetus where China left off." (Sanderson 1995: 154)

After 1560, Japan became a major producer and exporter of silver and then copper to China and Southeast Asia, but also of some gold and considerable sulfur, as well as such goods as camphor, iron, swords, lacquer, furniture, sake, tea, and high quality rice as far as India and West Asia. In return, Japan received Chinese silks and Indian cotton textiles, as well as a whole gamut of other producer and consumer goods like lead, tin, woods, dyes, sugar, skins, and quicksilver (used for smelting its own silver) from Korea, China, and Southeast Asia. As Satoshi Ikeda (1996) suggests, the Japanese and European positions with regard to Asia and especially to China were analogous: the former imported manufactures from the latter and exported silver to pay for them (albeit Japan produced its silver at home, while Europe plundered it from its American colonies). The bulk of Japanese cargo was carried on Chinese ships; and only some of it was carried first by the Portuguese and then by the Dutch who came to fetch Japanese silver, copper, and other exports. Ryukyu-based traders and ships also served as intermediaries, both with China and with Southeast Asia. Japan also established a domestic and export ceramics business in competition with China. Taking advantage of the transition from the Ming to Qing dynasties and the temporary political holdouts in southern China, Japan after 1645 reduced its ceramics imports from China by 80 percent and from 1658 became a significant exporter itself, both to Asian and to Persian Gulf and European markets.

In the seventeenth and eighteenth centuries, Reid (1993) notes that Japan's economic advances matched those of the advanced European countries.

> For Japan the period 1570–1630 was a unique moment when the country was unified, cities prospered as the nuclei of flourishing internal trade, and exceptional quantities of silver were extracted from the mines to form the basis of a vigourous trade with Southeast Asia. Japanese vessels were still forbidden to trade directly with China, so the exchange of Japanese silver for Chinese silk and other goods had to take place in Southeast Asian ports, notably Manila and Hoi An (known to Westerners as Fiafo, central Vietnam). Throughout the period 1604–35 about ten Japanese vessels a year were licensed to trade with the south, the largest number going to Vietnam (124 ships during the thirty-one years), the Philippines (56), and Siam (56). In 1635 this activity was stopped abruptly . . . [but] Japanese trade remained high throughout the rest of the century, but only through the tightly controlled Dutch and Chinese trade at Nagasaki. (Tarling 1992: 467–68)

Nonetheless, Japanese exports have been estimated to have reached 10 percent of its GNP (Howe 1996: 40). Between 1604 and 1635 the Japanese recorded 355 ships sailing officially to Southeast Asia, where the Japanese controlled the trade of Siam (Klein 1989: 76). Over about the same period, Japanese imports of Chinese silk quadrupled to 400,000 kilos; and even after the mid-century economic and political crisis in China, 200 ships arrived in Nagasaki every year in the 1650s (Howe 1996: 37, 24).

Japanese population doubled from 16 million in 1500 to between 26 and 32 million in 1750 (see tables 4.1 and 4.2). However, Christopher Howe (1996) has population growing at 0.8 percent a year and more than doubling to 31 million between 1600 and 1720 alone. The earlier demographic study by Susan Hanley and Kozo Yamamura (1977) put the population at 26 million in 1721. After that, all sources show population leveling off in Japan.

The course of Japanese economic development in the second half of the seventeenth and during the eighteenth centuries has been the subject of some dispute. Recent research has revised the earlier opinion that "seclusion" resulted in "stagnation." Although population stabilized in Japan (while it continued to grow in many other parts of Asia), Japanese agricultural and other production also continued to grow. Therefore, per capita income increased during the eighteenth century, according to the more recent calculations of Hanley and Yamamura (1977) and Howe (1996).

Howe (1996) still subscribes to the thesis that Japanese foreign trade declined especially after 1688 and remained low throughout the eighteenth century. However, Ikeda (1996) reports on important new Japanese scholarship, which shows that the policy of seclusion did not result in less foreign trade at all. Chinese silk imports continued, indeed even increased until 1660, and did not end until 1770. Moreover, silk imports via Korea and the Ryukyus sometimes exceeded those via Nagasaki, and unauthorized trade with South China remained beyond official control. Trade also continued to flourish between Japan and Southeast Asia, including Burma. Contrary to earlier suppositions, even Japanese silver exports now seem to have continued until the middle of the eighteenth century. Of course, foreign ships, especially from China, continued to call on Japan.

In conclusion, Japan's population grew rapidly and then stabilized, and its economy commercialized and urbanized extensively, as these and other sources testify (for example, *The Cambridge History of Japan* edited by John Hall 1991). We will review Japan's population growth and some of its institutions in chapter 4. Here I only wish also to make note of Japan's spectacular urbanization. In the century and a half after 1550, the number of cities with over 100,000 population increased from one to five. By the eighteenth century the urban population of Japan was higher than in contemporary China or Europe. Osaka/Kyoto and Edo (now Tokyo), each had populations of at least one million, and the latter reached 1.3 million inhabitants (Howe 1996: 55). By the late eighteenth century, 15 to 20 percent of the population was urbanized (Howe 1996: 55, also 63); and 6 percent of the population—or even 10 to 13 percent according to Sanderson (1995: 151, citing Spencer)— lived in cities over 100,000 in Japan, when it was still 2 percent in Europe (Hall 1991: 519). Indeed, with only 3 percent of the world's population, Japan accounted for 8 percent of the inhabitants of cities over 100,000 in the world. So on the evidence, the view of Tokugawa and even earlier Japan as "stagnant" and "closed," not to mention "feudal," must be rejected. Indeed, we must revise even the notion that the arrival of Commodore Perry "opened" Japan in 1853 and that the Meiji Restoration in 1868 spelled an abrupt break from its Tokugawa past. Like Rome, modern Japan was not built in a day or even in a century.

CHINA

Ming and Qing China experienced massive increases of production, consumption, and population, which were only briefly interrupted at the time of the Ming/Qing transition in the mid-seventeenth century. The latter is examined in chapter 5 below. Here we examine some aspects of Chinese production and trade, and especially what place they had and the role they played in the world economy as a whole. China had undoubtedly been the economically most advanced region of the world under the Song dynasty in the eleventh and twelfth centuries. To what extent that may have been changed by the Mongol invasion and during the Yuan dynasty is beyond our temporal scope here. The question we must address, however, is the place and role in the world of the Chinese economy during Ming and Qing times from 1400 to 1800. The evidence presented below challenges the widespread supposition that China was an economic world only onto its own, especially after the Ming reversed naval expansion in the fifteenth century and the Qing imposed limitations on maritime trade in the seventeenth century.

It is true that Chinese maritime expansion, especially under Zheng He after 1403, was halted in 1434. The reasons have been the subject of much speculation, but both the earlier expansion and then the later recoil were certainly related to Chinese relations with the Mongols and others in the continental northeast and the Ming transfer of the capital to Beijing near the frontier in order better to control renewed Mongol threats. The opening of the Grand Canal in 1411 to provision especially distant Beijing and the border outposts with rice from the centers of production and population in the Yangzi Valley also diminished the previous reliance on the coastal sea route, and therewith the merchant marine and navy. The political economic conflicts of interest between the southern maritime and northern continental orientations and interests were increasingly resolved in favor of the latter. The concomitantly increasing challenge of Japanese, but also Chinese, pirates and smuggling at sea reinforced the hand of those who sought their fortunes inland and led to the imposition of further limitations on maritime commerce, until—catering to southern interests especially in Fujian—these were abandoned again in 1567. At the same time in 1571, China retreated from confrontation with the Inner Asian Mongols, reduced the size of its army by over two-thirds, and (again) switched to a policy of negotiated appeasement toward the nomads on its northwest frontier.

Yet the southeastern maritime trade had never stopped. Indeed, illegal trade, which soon became mixed up with "Japanese" (but really more Chinese) piracy, prospered so much that its volume exceeded the official "tribute" trade by far (Hall 1991: 238). The trade to and from the southeast China coast experienced periodically renewed minibooms; and it revived and prospered between at least 1570 and about 1630, by which time Ming state finances also took a nose-dive (examined in chapter 5).

Population, Production, and Trade. Estimates for Ming China's population vary. The 1393 census was 60 million, but the real number was probably higher (Brook 1998). For 1500, William Atwell (1982) suggests 100 million. Others give that estimate only for a century later, in 1600. However, for that date John King Fairbank (1992: 168) says 150 million, and Timothy Brook (1998) regards 175 million possible. Ho Ping-ti's (1959) careful *Studies on the Population of China* suggests that the real population mostly exceeded the officially recorded number, and in the 1740s it did so by at least 20 percent (Ho Ping-ti 1959: 46). All sources agree that the population doubled or more during Ming rule, when the Chinese economy expanded rapidly. After the mid-seventeenth century crisis (discussed in chapter 5) growth of population, urbanization, and production resumed. The composite population estimates in table 4.1 are 125 million in 1500 (the lower estimate in table 4.2 is 100 million), 270 million (or 207 million) in 1750, and 345 million (or 315 million) in 1800. Thus in these three centuries population in China may have tripled, which is far more than its rise in Europe. There were large cities (although less so than half a millennium earlier in Song times) with Nanjing at a million and Beijing at over 600,000 population in the late Ming dynasty during the early seventeenth century. By 1800 Canton (now Guangzhou) and its neighboring sister city Foshan had a million and a half residents by themselves (Marks 1997a), which about equals the urban population of all of Western Europe put together.

This growth of production and population in China was fueled by imports of Spanish American and Japanese silver, and it was supported first through the introduction of early maturing rice that permitted two harvests per year and then by the expansion of arable land and food crops through the introduction of American-derived maize and potatoes, which could grow where rice could not. In the early to mid decades of the seventeenth century, the economy and polity were however temporarily troubled, perhaps in part because of this population increase but also for climatic reasons (see chapter 5). Population and production slowed down and temporarily even declined, but they recovered again toward the end of the seventeenth century and accelerated throughout the eighteenth century to about 300 million by 1800, or nearly triple (Eberhard 1977: 274).

A convenient summary of Chinese agricultural, commercial, and industrial expansion is offered by Bin Wong:

> The broad features of increased cash cropping, handicrafts and trade are well known in the Chinese and Japanese literature. . . . Most famous are the expanding cotton and silk industries of the Lower Yangzi region near Shanghai, the two principal handicraft industries that join rice and other cash crops to create China's richest regional economy. To feed the population of this area, rice grown in the upstream provinces of Anhui, Jianzxi, Hubei and especially Hunan and Sichuan moves down the Yangzi River. Other cash corps and handicrafts, like cotton, indigo, tobacco, pottery and paper, emerge in parts of these provinces as market expansion connects increasing numbers of locales.
>
> Market expansion was most salient along the Yangzi River, but hardly limited to this vast area. In south and southeast China, cash crops and handicrafts expanded in several areas. The Pearl River delta in Guangdong produced sugar cane, fruits, silk, cotton, ironware, and oils from sesame and tung plants. Along the southeast coast, sixteenth-century foreign trade ties stimulated cash crop production in tea and sugar. (Wong 1997)

Lingnan, that is South China, and particularly Guangdong and Guangxi provinces, as well as Fujian, prospered. Economic growth in these provinces was stimulated by foreign trade, especially their export of silk and porcelain in return for silver. A provincial governor may have exaggerated when he said that a thousand ships come and go from Guangdong every year, but an English captain referred to five thousand junks and small boats outside Guangzhou in 1703 (Marks 1996: 62). Robert Marks analyzes the impact of this external trade on domestic trade, the commercialization of agriculture, and the environment during the sixteenth through the eighteenth and into the nineteenth centuries. In the last four decades of the sixteenth century, the number of food markets increased by 75 percent, or much faster than population, in Guangdong (Marks 1996: 61). Marks summarizes:

Commercialization of the economy was a powerful force remaking the landscape. Not only did peasant farmers in the Pearl River delta dig up rice paddies to make way for fish ponds and mulberry tree embankments [which were productively, commercially and to some extent ecologically mutually supportive and necessary to feed the silkworms], but their consequent need for food transformed much of the agricultural land in the rest of Lingnan into monocropping, export-oriented rice regions. . . . The peasant farmers of the Pearl River delta grew nonfood crops, pushing rice production into the river valleys. There, peasant farmers subsisted on sweet potatoes and maize grown on more marginal lands in the hills, shipping rice grown in paddies downstream to the Pearl River delta. . . . [However] the system as a whole was not sustainable without greater and greater inputs from outside. (Marks 1996: 76)

Nonetheless, rice came to be in short supply anyway. Commercialized agriculture, including sugar cane and for a while cotton, occupied up to half the arable land in Guangdong, which produced only half the rice it needed in the early eighteenth century. Therefore, increasing amounts of rice had to be imported from elsewhere, including from Southeast Asia. In response, the central government in Beijing offered more and more tax exemption incentives to promote the reclamation of ever more marginal land and to clear hilly land. This led to increased deforestation, soil erosion, and other environmental damage.

China in the World Economy. Two related factors, already mentioned in the discussion of the trade patterns above, were perhaps of the greatest significance for the world economy. One was China's world economic preeminence in production and export. China was unrivaled in porcelain ceramics and had few rivals in silk, which was China's largest export product, mainly to other Asian buyers and secondarily for the Manila-Americas trade (Flynn and Giraldez 1996). The other important factor, also emphasized by Dennis Flynn and Arturo Giraldez (1994, 1995a, b) was China's position and function as the final "sink" for the world's production of silver. Of course, the two were related in that China's perennial export surplus (until the mid-nineteenth century) was settled primarily through foreigners' payment in silver.

However, the Chinese magnet for silver also had another source: the Ming abandoned the previous Yuan and even earlier Song dynasties' partial reliance on paper money. In times of crisis, its printing had been abused with inflationary consequences. The Ming discontinued the printing and later also the use of paper money and relied on copper-cash and silver bullion. Moreover, increasing shares and ultimately all payments of revenue were transformed into a "single-whip" tax in silver. This Chinese public demand for silver and the large size and productivity of the Chinese economy and its consequent export surplus generated a huge demand for, and increase in the price of, silver worldwide.

Therefore, Flynn and Giraldez (1994: 72) barely exaggerate when they write that "there would have been neither the same type of 'price revolution' in Europe and China nor a Spanish Empire [which lived from its sales of silver] in the absence of the transformation of Chinese society to a silver base in the early modern period." Indeed, except that production of goods in general responded sufficiently in China itself to keep inflation under control there, as I will argue in chapter 3.

First the Portuguese and then the Dutch arrived at the ports of East Asia, seeking to profit from the Chinese (and Japanese) economic expansion by inserting themselves as middlemen in the trade between China and its neighbors. Of course, they and others also introduced a number of important American crops to China, some of which like maize and tobacco would significantly increase Chinese agricultural production and consumption.

We may now inquire into where and how China's vast and productive economy fit into the world economy. We have already noted China's exports of silk, porcelain, and quicksilver and, after 1600, tea. However, China was also the source of zinc and cupronickel, both of which were used as alloys for coinage elsewhere. The contemporary observer Botero remarked that "the quantity of silk that is carried out of China is almost not credible. A thousand quintals of silk are yearly carried thence for the Portuguese Indies, for the Philippines they lade out fifteen ships. There are carried out to Japan an inestimable sum . . . " (cited in Adshead 1988: 217).

Ming China had a virtual monopoly in porcelain and other ceramics (still called china to the present day) on the world market. Yet over 80 percent of Chinese ceramics exports went to Asia, including over 20 percent to Japan, and 16 percent in volume but up to 50 percent in value of high-quality goods to Europe. However, the Ming-Qing transition occasioned a more than two-thirds decline in ceramics exports after 1645. Exceptionally during the 1645–1662 period, the Fujian-based Zheng family that still remained loyal to the Ming had almost complete control over this now much reduced export trade. The reduced ceramics export lasted until 1682, after which it recovered both absolutely and to a lesser extent relatively. In the meantime, Japan and after 1662 the Vietnamese Tongkin also entered the market as major exporters (Ho Chuimei 1994: 36–47). Briefly, Tongkin also afforded supplies of silk to the Dutch to carry to Japan in exchange for silver (Klein 1989: 80). China also shipped silk to Batavia for re-export to Japan, along with silk that had arrived from Bengal. In return, China imported cotton textiles from India (some of them for re-export), spices, sandalwood, and other timber for ships or the ships themselves from Southeast Asia, and silver from everywhere. At the same time, China also produced vast quantities of cotton textiles for itself as well as some for export also to Europe. Jesuit visitors to Shanghai in the late seventeenth century estimated that it alone had 200,000 weavers of cotton and 600,000 spinners to supply them with yarn (Ho Chuimei 1959: 201).

Takeshi Hamashita (1988, 1994b) has recently proposed an interesting interpretation of a separate Chinese-based Asian world-economy in his articles on "The Tribute Trade System and Modern Asia" and "Japan and China in the 19th and 20th Centuries." Hamashita (1988: 7–8) argues for recognizing "Asian history [as] the history of a unified system characterized by internal tribute/tribute-trade relations, with China at the center . . . [which was] an organic entity with center-periphery relations of southeast, northeast, central and northwest Asia . . . connected with the adjacent India trade area." Hamashita centers his analysis on the ancient Chinese "tribute" system that survived into the nineteenth century:

> The ideal of Sinocentrism was not solely a preoccupation of China but was substantially shared throughout the tribute zone. . . . Satellite tribute zones surrounding the Chinese-dominated one had a historical existence of their own which continued. . . . Thus all these countries maintained satellite tribute relations with each other that constituted links in a continuous chain. The other fundamental feature of the system that must be kept sight of is its basis in commercial transactions. The tribute system in fact paralleled, or was in symbiosis with, the network of commercial trade relations. For example, trade between Siam, Japan and southern China had long been maintained on the basis of profits from the tribute missions, even when much of the non-tribute trade was scarcely remunerative. . . . The story of the commercial penetration of Chinese merchants into South-East Asia and the emigration of "overseas Chinese" is historically intertwined with the building of this trade network. Commercial expansion and the

tribute-trade network developed together. Trade relations in East and South-East Asia expanded as tribute relations expanded. It should be noted that this tribute trade functioned as an intermediate trade between European countries and the countries of East Asia. . . . Tribute relationships in fact constituted a network of tribute trade of a multilateral type, absorbing commodities from outside the network. . . . To sum up, the entire tribute and interregional trade zone had its own structural rules which exercised systematic control through silver circulation and with the Chinese tribute system at the centre. This system, encompassing East and South-East Asia was articulated with neighbouring trade zones such as India, the Islamic regions and Europe. (Hamashita 1994a: 94, 92, 97)

We may note especially that Hamashita (1988: 13) recognizes that "in fact, it is quite legitimate to view tribute exchange as a commercial transaction . . . [which] in reality embraced both inclusive and competitive relations extending in a web over a large area." Indeed, Central Asian merchants were known often to bring phony credentials as "political emissaries" who paid "tribute" as a fig leaf for humdrum commercial trade. European travelers like the Jesuit Matteo Ricci had already remarked on it centuries earlier, and Ming documents freely admitted the same (Fletcher 1968). Similarly, the Japanese also used tributary forms of fealty to enjoy profitable, and where possible monopoly, trade with China. Other authors as well insist that, "tributary" or not, "Chinese traders to Siam were invariably moved solely by commercial motives" (Viraphol 1977: 8, also see pp. 140 ff.). Cushman (1993) observes the same.

Hamashita also argues that "the foundation of the whole complex tribute trade formation was determined by the price structure of China and . . . the tribute trade zone formed an integrated 'silver' zone in which silver was used as the medium of trade settlement" of China's perennial trade surplus (Hamashita 1988: 17).

Hamashita's rendition of the Chinese tribute trade system follows that of the Ming and Qing institutional codes. They distinguished and ranked—and, in response to changing circumstances, modified—geographical groupings of "tributaries" and specified their respective allowable ports of entry. These ranged from Korea and Japan in the north through various parts of Southeast Asia in the south and India in the east, and also included Portugal and Holland. However ideologically intent on regarding the celestial Middle Kingdom as the center of the earth, the Chinese were also realistic and pragmatic enough to recognize that commercial trade and its quid pro quos were a form of what they liked to term "tribute," which others had to pay to them.

Therein however, the Chinese courts were then (and Hamashita is now), essentially realistic: others preponderantly did have to pay China for readily available exports that it considered of less value than the massive amounts of scarce silver shipped into China every year. That these payments were ideologically called "tribute" did not change their essential function, which indeed did express the commercial "tribute" in silver that others, including of course the Europeans, were obliged to pay to the Chinese in order to trade with them. Their ranking of these tributaries in concentric circles with China in the center may seem excessively ideological to us, but it rather accurately expressed an under-lying reality: the entire system of multilateral trade balances and imbal-ances, including the subsidiary roles of India and Southeast Asia relative to China's industrial superiority, acted as the magnet that resulted in China being the ultimate "sink" of the world's silver! These bullion settlements of commercial transactions (call them "tribute" if you will) and the center-periphery relations with and among Korea, Japan, Southeast Asia, India, West Asia, and Europe and its economic colonies played a central role in the world economy right through the eighteenth century. Hamashita calls them a "continuous chain of satellite tribute relations" among these regions. China's central position probably did permit its internal price structure to exert significant influence—which bears more attention than it has received—though it seems more doubtful that it alone was able to "determine" all other prices in Asia, let alone in the world economy, as Hamashita claims.

On the other hand, Hamashita (1988: 18) is right when he insists that in order to do any business at all, Westerners had little choice other than to participate in the already established "tribute trade network . . . as the basis of all relations in the region . . . [and establish] a working base within it." However, that is saying little more about de facto trade with China than what was the rule everywhere in Asia: the only choice the Europeans had was to attach their trading wagon to the much larger Asian productive and commercial train, which was steaming ahead on an already well-established track (or rather caravan and maritime network). Moreover, the Chinese "tribute trade network" in East and Southeast Asia was—and for two millennia already had been—an integral part of this wider Afro-Eurasian world economic network. What the Europeans did, was to plug the Americas into it as well. However as already men-tioned, there is also evidence that the Chinese themselves had already done so to some extent—and precisely also to obtain scarce means of payment!—centuries before Columbus set sail. See for instance Hans Breuer's *Columbus Was Chinese* (1972).

The economic and financial results of the "China trade" were that China had a balance of trade surplus with everybody else, based on its unrivaled manufacturing production and export of silks, porcelain, and other ceramics. Therefore, China, which like India had a perpetual silver shortage, was *the* major net importer of silver and met much of its currency needs out of imports of American silver, which arrived via Europe, West Asia, India, Southeast Asia, and with the Manila Galleons directly from Acapulco. China also received massive amounts of silver and copper from Japan and some through the overland caravan trade across Central Asia (see chapter 3). Gold was both imported to and exported from China, depending on changing gold/silver/copper price ratios. In general over the centuries, silver moved eastward (except westward from Japan and Acapulco via Manila), and gold moved westward (except eastward from Africa) over both overland and maritime routes. Some eastward-moving gold even reached Europe.

So, the Sinocentric international order also absorbed commodities from outside China's East and Southeast Asian "tributary" network. That means that this network itself was part of the *world* economy/system, and not a separate world onto its own, as Hamashita would have it. However, Hamashita is essentially right and so were the Chinese themselves in their perspective of a "Sinocentric international order . . . [which] in fact constituted a network of tribute trade of a multilateral type, absorbing commodities [especially silver] from outside the network" (Hamashita 1988: 14). The dispute is only about how far-reaching the economy was, of which China was central.

Ikeda (1996) also makes much of Hamashita's "model" of a Sinocentric East Asia to counter received Eurocentrism and to offer a perspective that accommodates the resurgence of China today. However, Ikeda also limits himself to describing a second, Sinocentric "world-economy" in East and Southeast Asia and barely to the "European world-economy." Ikeda speculates on the past, present, and probably glorious future of this Asian "world-economy," but he is still unwilling or unable to see that both and other regional "world-economies" as well were all part and parcel of a single global world economy. That global economy may have had several "centers," but if any of them (pre)-dominated over the others in the system as a whole, it was the Chinese (and not the European!) center. "China, not Europe, was the center of the world" writes Brook (1998) in the introduction to his study of Ming economy and society.

Some other observers have also noted the possibility that the China may have been central to the entire world economy: Frederic Wakeman (1986: 4,17) writes that "according to Chaunu, the Chinese domestic [seventeenth-century] crisis may actually have helped precipitate the global crisis: 'It is the ups and downs of trade with the Chinese continent which commands the ups and downs of the galleon trade itself.' ... The Chinese polity and the society it governed were thus able to recover from the seventeenth-century crisis sooner than any major power in the world." Dennis Flynn's focus on silver also leads him to recognize the centrality of China at least in the world silver market. Thus, Flynn and Giraldez(1995c) plead for "reserving a central place for China" and by extension its East Asian tributary system, which included perhaps two-fifths of the world's population, in the world silver trade. Elsewhere Flynn and Giraldez (1995b: 16, 3) go on to say that "we view silver as a crucial driving force underlying the emergence of global trade" and therefore "we argue that the emergence of a new monetary and fiscal regime within Ming China was the driving force behind global trade in the early-modern period . . . in the context of a Sino-centered world economy." That was certainly very much the case. However, neither China's—nor anybody else's—hunger and thirst for silver would then (and still does not now) translate into effective demand for silver or money, unless there was (and is) an equivalent effective supply forthcoming, for which there is a demand by those who can pay in silver or other money. So equally or even more significant is that China did effectively produce this supply of goods (including also some gold) thanks to the high productivity/low cost competitiveness of its manufactures on the world market.

Thus, we can and should make an even stronger case than Hamashita does: the entire world economic order was—literally—Sinocentric. Christopher Columbus and after him many Europeans up until Adam Smith knew that. It was only the nineteenth-century Europeans who literally rewrote this history from their new Eurocentric perspective. As Braudel observed, Europe invented historians and then put them to good use in their own interests but not those of historical accuracy or objectivity.

CENTRAL ASIA

The history of mostly Islamic Central Asia during the period 1400 to 1800 is largely dismissed by the *Cambridge History of Islam:*

> Central Asia was thus isolated from the early sixteenth century
> . . . and therefore led an existence at the margin of world history.
> . . . The discovery of the sea-route to East Asia rendered the Silk
> Road increasingly superfluous. . . . From the threshold of modern
> times Central Asian history becomes provincial history. This justi-
> fies us in giving no more than a rapid sketch of the following
> centuries. (Holt, Lambton, and Lewis 1970: 471, 483)

This dismissal is unacceptable, both in principle and on factual grounds.
To begin with, the peoples of Islamic Central and Inner Asia certainly
were not "at the margin of world history," if only because the Timurid
dynasty descended from Tamerlane, who had made his capital in Samarkand. Also, the major Muslim states and regimes of the Ottomans in
Turkey, the Safavids in Persia, and the Mughals in India were formed
by people who had arrived from Central Asia. Indeed, the Mughals
considered themselves to be—and continually imported many high
level administrators and other members of the intelligentsia—from
Central Asia (Foltz, 1996, 1997). Moreover, Inner Asian Mongols gave
rise to the "Chinese" Yuan dynasty, much of whose administrative
structure was inherited by the Ming, who were then displaced by the
Manchus, also from Inner Asia.

Regarding the economy and caravan trade of Central Asia, Rossabi
(1990: 352) refers to their "decline" but also observes their continuation
into the early seventeenth century and adds that there is a "paucity of
precise information about this commerce." Actually, evidence is not all
that scarce; Russians and Central Asians have marshaled quite a lot of
it during Soviet times, as surveyed by Eli Weinerman (1993). Alas however, the evidence is difficult to interpret since it was used and misused
for largely ideologically motivated debates in accord with Soviet political interests. To legitimize Soviet power in Central Asia, it was convenient to contrast it favorably with czarist contributions to the "decline
of Central Asia." When Central Asian nationalism challenged Moscow's
rule and the latter wanted to defuse it, the Soviets argued that even
Russian czarist rule had not been so bad after all. Then the evidence
was marshaled to show that the seventeenth-century "decline" in Central Asia was overcome and reversed in the eighteenth century. Related
debates pitted Russians and Central Asians against each other about
whether the former or the latter themselves deserved the credit for the
"recovery" and/or whether the earlier "decline" was only a Russian
myth in the first place.

Additionally, the debates about decline and/or progress in Central
Asia were also a function of the perennial dispute about "modes of

production" and "capitalism." Did "capitalism" germinate and flourish indigenously in Central Asia? Was it strangled or promoted there by Russian colonialism? How does Soviet power and/or ideology serve anticolonialism and the "noncapitalist" and then "socialist" path in the "Third" World—and in Central Asia? Here is yet another illustration of how literally misleading these "mode of production" categories are: as is argued in chapters 1 and 7, they distract our attention from what really went on. The political/ideological motivation and underpinning of this still ongoing debate renders the "evidence" marshaled by all sides rather suspect for our more "innocent" use, although readers of Russian may be able to separate some grain out from all that chaff. I am obliged to turn to other sources.

Rossabi, like Niels Steensgaard (1972), observes that transcontinental caravan trade was *not* replaced by circum-Asian maritime trade. One reason is that the maritime route around Africa did not lower transportation costs, and another was that these costs accounted for a small proportion of the final selling price anyway (Menard 1991: 249). Therefore, the Portuguese round-the-Cape trade was brief and was soon again replaced by the trans-Central and West Asian route. Steensgaard (1972: 168) estimates that European consumption of Asian goods coming by caravan was double that brought around the Cape by ship.

Both authors do observe declining trans-Central Asian trade in the seventeenth century. Rossabi attributes this decline to two main factors: severe drought (the "Little Ice Age") and political upheaval, including especially that which ended the Ming dynasty in 1644 and replaced it by the Manchus, the fall of the Timurid empire in western Central Asia, and problems with Mughal rule in northern India. Chinese tribute trade missions to the Tarim Basin oases did decline at the end of the sixteenth century, and even more so before 1640 during the last decades of Ming rule, when Turfan also sought to assert control over the northern Tarim Basin trade routes. Mongol-Ming relations also deteriorated again (Rossabi 1975, 1990). However, one student attributes at least some of the decline also to more distant problems among the Safavids along the other end of the line in Persia (Adshead 1988: 196–67).

It is easy to accept Rossabi's empirically based observation that "the common assumption that seaborne commerce superseded caravan trade needs qualification" (Rossabi 1990: 367). More doubtful is his claim in the next sentence that the seventeenth-century decline must be due to "the political disruptions that afflicted most of the Asian regions through which caravans travelled. . . . In sum, the decline of central

Asian caravan trade cannot be attributed solely to economic considerations." Perhaps, but why could the cause-effect relation not have been the other way around, that is, drought and economic decline generated political conflict? That has generally been even more true elsewhere and at other times, and could more plausibly explain why "commerce via northwest China declined considerably" (Rossabi 1975: 264). In East and South Asia however, climatic problems were especially severe only in the decade of the 1630s. Both the early and late seventeenth century were periods of marked economic expansion in both China and India. That renders the thesis of such "decline" doubtful also in Central Asia. This is all the more the case inasmuch as trans-Central Asian trade revived again along with the eighteenth-century trade expansion and "commercial revolution" elsewhere. Steensgaard (1972) observed that trade then shifted to a more northerly route between Russia and China.

Similarly, Fletcher (1985) also rejects the argument (or rather the assumption) that transcontinental trade was replaced by maritime trade, but he does notice "nomadic economic decline" beginning in 1660 in Outer Mongolia. Like Steensgaard also, he remarks on the establishment of more northerly trade routes by Russian traders also serving a growing population in Siberia. Since 1670, the Russians increasingly displaced "Bukhariot" traders (who were not only from Bukhara), who previously had a corner on the more southerly long-distance routes across Central Asia. Fletcher stresses three additional factors: One is the seventeenth-century demographic decline, which was common to much of Eurasia (and plays the key role in Jack Goldstone's 1991a demographic/structural analysis of crisis after 1640, examined below). Another factor were the advances in military (that is, gun) technology, which made warfare much more expensive and put nomad bands at a—since then permanent—competitive disadvantage with larger/richer states/empires, as proposed by Hess (1973).

A third factor cited by Fletcher is that intraregional trade expanded in various parts of Eurasia. This regionalism may have diminished the market for trans-Central Asian trade. However, that did not deprive particular parts or regions of Central Asia of economic functions as suppliers and markets for regions contiguous to them, which were growing economically and commercially. Thus, we have already observed above that both the spice and the silk trades actually made increasing use of caravan trade routes through parts of Central Asia. These were contiguous and complementary to the Persian Gulf and Red Sea trade routes between Asia and Europe. Similarly, the Mughal expansion southward through the Indian subcontinent generated a large demand for horses, for military and other purposes. Various regions in Central Asia were their "natural" suppliers, both in the west along with Persia and farther east in Tibet and Yunnan. Travelers like Marco Polo and Ibn Batuta had already remarked on these Central Asian regions' very profitable sale of horses southward into India, as analyzed by John Richards (1983) for the thirteenth and fourteenth centuries. The horse trade continued, however, in later times as well. Reportedly, 100,000 horses a year were exported from Central Asia in the early seventeenth century, of which 12,000 alone were for the Mughal's stables (Burton 1993: 28).

Similarly, regional trade persisted—in its age-old fluctuating fashion—between the Mongols and China, although the Mongols' last serious military threat seems to have been repelled by the Ming. To do so however, the Ming had to turn their attention northward—and even move their capital to Beijing—and sacrifice many commercial maritime opportunities in the South after they halted further trade missions, such as Zheng He's in 1433. This regionalization and the new methods and costs of warfare, which may be the explanation for the events, are analyzed by Isenbike Togan (1990):

> the aim of this paper is to bring a further qualification to the decline of the Silk Routes by demonstrating that trade and traders did not cease to function [in the seventeenth century], and that, instead, state formations that were playing the role of intermediaries along the Silk Routes were eliminated. Their elimination was due to the expansion of the sedentary empires of the early modern age. It was the moment [1698] when two of these empires, the Chinese and the Russian, came to direct contact with each other . . . that the intermediaries lost their function. As a result, the merchants, in this case the [Bukharan] Muslim merchants of the Silk Routes, became merchants of the empires who were involved much more with internal trade within these empires than with transcontinental trade, as was the case earlier. (Togan 1990: 2)

However as Adshead (1993: 179) suggests, these developments also meant that the seventeenth-century decline of trans-Central Asian caravan east-west trade was complemented if not replaced by regional north-south trades, so that "Central Asia did not decline" (Adshead 1993: 200). Rossabi (1975: 139–65) catalogs Chinese imports from Central Asia as horses, camels, sheep, furs, swords, jade, ginseng and other medicines, as well as gold and silver. He lists Chinese exports of textiles, clothing, drugs, tea, paper, porcelain, and after the late fifteenth century some silver instead of the previously listed export of paper money, which could be used for purchases only in China itself.

Trade between Russia and Central Asia also continued to prosper and indeed in the eighteenth century to grow. First, the caravans from Central Asia also had to carry some gold and silver in settlement for their purchase of Russian exports. However in the later eighteenth century, the exchange became more balanced as Central Asians exported more cotton and textiles to the Russians. Then the balance of trade turned to favor Central Asia, and Russia itself had to export precious metals to the Central Asians and then also to China (Attman 1981: 112–24). Accordingly, one czar after another issued edicts prohibiting the export of precious metals and coin. Beginning in the mid-seventeenth century and all the more so in the eighteenth century, the Russian state sought to reserve trade to its subjects and to exclude Bukharan and other Central Asian competition (Burton 1993).

In his (1993) survey of Bukharan trade from 1559 to 1718, Burton also includes trade by non-Bukharans. His maps and text provide trade routes and substantial trade—and therefore division of labor—of commodities for sumptuary as well as daily use (far too many to list here). Particularly noteworthy, however, are slaves from all over (including Germany and eastern Europe, but especially "non-Christian" ones from the west and "non-Muslim" Hindu ones from the south); horses and other livestock as well as hides, skins, and furs; fibers and textiles of all sorts; indigo and other dyes; metals and metal wares and especially small arms; porcelain and other ceramics; food of all sorts including grains, sugar, fruits, and especially rhubarb; medicines; tea and tobacco; precious stones; and of course precious metals and coins. The trade routes connected Central Asian emporia such as Khiva, Bukhara, Balkh, Samarkand, Kabul, and many others. Northward they went via Astrakhan and Orenburg to Moscow and onward from there to eastern and western Europe. Westward, they went to Persia, the Levant, and Anatolia and/or via the Black Sea route to Istanbul and the Mediterranean. Southward, they went into India. Eastward, they went along the old Silk Road to China and northeastward to Siberia and on to China. Burton (1993: 84) concludes, "throughout the period reviewed [Central Asians] continued to ply their trade, regardless of dangers and difficulties. They carried an enormous variety of goods, and were always able to adjust to changing circumstances. They continued to trade with Muscovy and Siberia even after the Tsars [imposed impediments]."

After the rapid Russian advance through Siberia in the first half of the seventeenth century, Sino-Russian competition for Central Asian and Siberian trade and territory and political power waxed and waned. The Russians seemed more intent on (long-distance) trade, and the Chinese were apparently more concerned with political control, which offered regional/local tribute and trade. By mutual agreement therefore, Russian trade was safeguarded but its political power in the region was ceded to China in the 1689 Treaty of Nerchinsk, until the latter again lost control in 1858–60 (and only regained any of it in the mid-twentieth century). Indeed, the Western Mongols gained control of the oases along the northern branch of the Silk Road through the Tarim Basin (which the Chinese had controlled only off and on since Han times). Another competitive struggle for this vital area ensued until the Qing regime finally annexed the by now largely Muslim Xinjiang Uygur to China. (These Muslims' interest in regaining independence has only been heightened by the recent separation of the Muslim Soviet Central Asian republics.)

RUSSIA AND THE BALTICS

Russia and the Baltics occupied positions in the structure of international trade and payments analogous to those of the Ottomans and Persia in West Asia. That is, Russia and the Baltics consistently exported more furs especially, but also timber, hemp, grain, and other commodities toward Western Europe than they imported textiles and other manufactures. The favorable trade balance was settled in precious metals, derived largely from the Americas. The same pattern characterized the Russian-Baltic and Baltic-Northwest European trade itself (which included important Swedish exports of copper, iron, and later timber).

The Baltic Sea was one of the three major east-west trade routes. The others from Russia were the more northerly maritime route through the Arctic Sea and the overland route through East-central Europe. However, north-south trade routes also ran through Russia, especially along the major rivers, into the Ottoman and Persian empires. Astrakhan, at the Volga delta to the Caspian Sea, became an important international trading center. To promote this trade and to exclude the Muslims more, Russians planned—but never built—a Volga-Don canal. Southward, Russia exported mostly furs, leather, and some metal products, and imported primarily silk, satin, cotton, indigo, and other dyes. The balance of trade was heavily against Russia, which in settlement had to re-export some of the silver and some gold it received through its Baltic and European trade surplus.

To promote domestic commerce and to compete better in international commerce, the czar favored merchants and permitted their municipal self-government. He also sent consuls to Europe and Asia and, of course, sought to establish an important position for Russia in the Baltic trade. The construction of St. Petersburg (named after St. Peter, not the czar) and of the road to it across the swamps from Moscow against fierce political opposition from the latter city were only some of the related measures designed to substitute Russian-controlled trade through the Baltics for foreign-controlled trade via Archangel (which therefore declined by 90 percent). However, Peter also sought, but failed, to build a combination fluvial-canal system to link the Baltic, Black, White, and Caspian seas. Moreover, "all this emphasis on Baltic commerce tends to obscure the development of Moscovite trade with the east. . . . [in which] Turkey, Persia, the central Asian khanates, and China played important roles as well," not to mention Peter's interest to benefit from the flourishing India trade (Oliva 1969: 129). There were permanent settlements of over 300 Indian merchants in Astrakhan, and smaller ones in Moscow, Narva, and elsewhere; and Indian textiles were sent to Siberia and from there to what is today the Chinese city of Kashgar (Barendse 1997: chap. 1).

By the end of Peter the Great's reign, there were at least 200 large industrial enterprises in the Moscow region, of which 69 were in metallurgy, 46 were related to textiles and leather, and 17 for gunpowder. The production of pig iron was greater than in England and grew to exceed that of all Europe by 1785 (Oliva 1969: 124). Peter's economic policies also generated an overall balance of trade surplus of 0.8 million rubles between exports of 2.4 million and imports of 1.6 million rubles in 1725 (Oliva 1969: 130).

Moreover, with Russian expansion into and through Siberia beginning rapidly in the first half of the seventeenth century, the export of furs from Siberia increasingly complemented those from European Russia. Therefore, money flowed farther eastward as well and helped open up Siberia. At the eastern end of Siberia and Eurasia, the Russians became important customers for silk and then tea from China. The czarist governments sought trading privileges in the eastern Russian-Central Asian-Chinese regional trade both for the Russian state and private merchants.

We noted above that in the late seventeenth and early eighteenth centuries, transcontinental trade was diverted from the more southerly routes across Central Asia to more northerly ones through Russia. In

part, this change followed or accompanied the Russian settlement of
Siberia. In part, as a consequence of the same, there was increasing
cross-border and Sino-Russian trade. In part also, Russian rulers since
Ivan the Terrible in the mid-sixteenth century had been trying to shift
or entice the Silk Road to pass through Russian territory (Anisimov
1993: 255). Bukharan traders, both itinerant and resident in Siberia, initially received encouraging privileges and protection. However, they
were subject to more and more constraints and eventually prohibitions
as Russian merchants increasingly petitioned their state to constrain and
then eliminate this foreign competition. These petitions became particularly insistent in the mid-seventeenth century, during the monetary
and trade crisis (discussed in chapter 5; also see Burton 1993: 54). They
also cropped up again at the end of the seventeenth century, during the
reign of Peter the Great.

The market was reserved for Russians, and Bukharans were increasingly eliminated after Peter the Great signed the Sino-Russian Treaty of
Nerchinsk in 1689, agreeing to Chinese political privileges in return for
Russian ones for trade in Siberia and with China. Precious metals
flowed in both directions at the same time, though later mostly bullion
went westward and coins eastward (Attman 1981: 114–24). However,
Peter the Great prohibited the export of precious metals and any goods
other than Russian ones (Burton 1993: 76–81).

Peter the Great was determined to protect and expand Russian trade
in the east and to the south. He wrote to his ambassador to Persia (cited
in Anisimov 1993: 255): " . . . is it possible to make some obstacle to the
Smyrna and Aleppo trade, where and how?" Moreover, he had other
related ideas: war against Persia in 1722 (taking advantage of its temporary weakness due to troubles at the Safavid palace) and then with Turkey in 1723, with whom he sought to partition Persian territories and
trade routes, all for commercial reasons. When he captured Baku on
the Caspian Sea, he was "toasted joyfully" for having "entered upon the
path of Alexander the Great"—to India! (Anisimov 1993: 259).

The magnet was the riches and trade of India, and it became an obsession with Peter the Great to find a water route thither. He sought
one or another via the Caspian Sea, the Oxus and other rivers, and
inquired about diverting rivers and constructing connecting canals. He
even engaged in ocean-borne adventures via Madagascar. And via Madagascar also, he dispatched an ambassador on an ill-fated mission to
India with the instructions to approach the Mughal and "by all means
. . . incline him to allow commerce to be conducted with Russia" (cited

in Anisimov 1993: 262). As his ambassador to Persia, Artemy Volynsky, later recalled "according to His Majesty's designs, his concern was not for Persia alone. For, if matters had succeeded for us in Persia and his exalted life had continued, of course he would have attempted to reach India, and he nurtured intentions even to the Chinese state, which I was honored from his Imperial Majesty. . . . to hear myself" (Anisimov 1993: 263). Moreover, the czar also sent the Danish navigator Vitus Jonassen Bering (for whom both the strait and the sea have been named) to seek a passage between the Russian far east and the Americas. Yet all these commercial and imperial policies to benefit from the riches of Asia had to await some satisfactory settlement of the czar's Baltic and European ambitions, in whose pursuit among other things he had built St. Petersburg. And still today Russia remains torn and may yet be torn apart by conflicting interests between East and West.

SUMMARY OF A SINOCENTRIC WORLD ECONOMY

This chapter has demonstrated beyond reasonable doubt that there indeed was a globe-encircling worldwide trading system and division of labor. It bound agricultural hinterlands and peripheries to their respective provincial and regional metropolitan centers and maritime port and/or inland emporia cities. These in turn developed and maintained dense and far-reaching interprovincial, interregional, and world systemic international economic relations. These are most visible through traders and trade, and in their resultant imbalances of trade. However, the former also reflect widespread interregional and intersectoral complementarities and competition in the global division of labor. All of these in turn also reflect the relative—and indeed absolute—weight and dominance of the Asian economies, and of China in particular. This global Sinocentric multilateral trade expanded through the infusion of American money by the Europeans. Indeed, that is what permitted Europeans to increase their participation in the global economy, which until and even through the eighteenth century remained dominated by Asian production, competitiveness, and trade.

The international division of labor and relative sectoral productivity and regional competitiveness in the world economy are reflected in the global pattern of trade balances and money flows.

In the structure of the world economy, four major regions maintained built-in deficits of commodity trade: the Americas, Japan, Africa, and Europe. The first two balanced their deficit by producing silver money for export. Africa exported gold money and slaves. In economic terms, these three regions produced "commodities" for which there was a demand elsewhere in the world economy. The fourth deficitary region, Europe, was hardly able to produce anything of its own for export with which to balance its perpetual trade deficit. Europe managed to do so primarily by "managing" the exports of the three other deficitary regions, from Africa to the Americas, from the Americas to Asia, and from Asia to Africa and the Americas. The Europeans also participated to some extent in trade within Asia, especially between Japan and elsewhere. This intra-Asian "country trade" was marginal for Asia but nonetheless vital for Europe, which earned more from it than from its own trade with Asia.

Southeast Asia and West Asia also produced some silver and gold money, which contributed to balancing their trade. Unlike Europe however, they were also able to produce some other commodities for which there was an export demand. Both Southeast and West Asia also realized "export" earnings from their respective locations at the southeastern and southwestern trade turntables of the Asian core economies. To some extent, so did Central Asia.

The two major regions that were most "central" to the world economy were India and China. That centrality rested primarily on their outstanding absolute and relative productivity in manufactures. In India, these were primarily its cotton textiles that dominated the world market, and to a lesser extent its silk textiles, especially in Bengal, India's most productive region. Of course, this competitiveness from manufacturing also rested on productivity of the land and in transport and commerce. They supplied the inputs necessary to supply raw materials to industry, food to workers, and transport and trade for both, as well as for export and import.

The other, and even more "central" economy was China. Its even greater centrality was based on its greater absolute and relative productivity in industry, agriculture, (water) transport, and trade. China's even greater, indeed the world economy's greatest, productivity, competitiveness, and centrality were reflected in its most favorable balance of trade. That was based primarily on its world economic export leadership in silks and ceramics and its exports also of gold, copper-cash, and later of tea. These exports in turn made China the "ultimate sink" of the world's silver, which flowed there to balance China's almost perpetual export surplus. Of course, China was only able to satisfy its insatiable "demand" for silver because it also had an inexhaustible supply of exports, which were in perpetual demand elsewhere in the world economy.

Returning to our fourteenth-century point of departure and particularly to Abu-Lughod's (1989) "thirteenth-century world system," we can observe some "regional" patterns, which persist in the world economy through the eighteenth century. These regional patterns may be summarized in several not mutually exclusive ways. None of them, however, correspond to the received image of a "capitalist world-economy" that began in Europe and only then expanded to "incorporate" one region after another elsewhere in the world until the West dominated them all.

Two possible regionalizations of the world economy are illustrated by the headings and much of the text of this chapter. Following the introductory warning that all regions must be rather arbitrarily defined, chapter sections are designated "The Americas," "Africa," "Europe," and so on. Alas, most accounts of "world" economic history have hardly extended beyond these three. This chapter undertakes to show that they were only relatively minor players in the world economy, which extended over many regions in Asia as well. Of course, for other purposes, each of these regions could be subdivided by points of the compass, or by core/peripheral, continental/insular, highland/lowland, cold/warm, wet/dry, or other geographical and ecological, terms, as well as by economical, political, or cultural designations.

Or they could be grouped into Atlantic, Indian Ocean, China Sea, Inner Asian, and other larger regions, as well as North/South Atlantic, North/South China Sea, and so on. Of course, it is the Atlantic region that has received the lion's share of attention in most previous accounts, although I contend that the others merit far more recognition and study, both relatively and absolutely. De facto, the present chapter focuses on these larger regions, devoting half or more of its attention in each section to the economic relations of a region with its neighboring regions to the east and west. For instance, the account of "India" identifies the division of labor and trade among Gujarat, Coromandel, Bengal, Ceylon, and so on and stresses their respective close-knit economic relations and division of labor with Africa and Central, West, Southeast, and East Asia.

In this way, we can also observe the continuance over the centuries of the essentials of Abu-Lughod's (1989) "thirteenth-century world system." Recall that in her account of the world economy, Abu-Lughod identifies three major regions—and within each of these some minor ones—in eight mutually overlapping regional ellipses that covered

Afro-Eurasia. These include regions centered—going from west to east—on Europe, the Mediterranean, the Red Sea, the Persian Gulf, the Arabian Sea, the Bay of Bengal, the South China Sea, as well as Inner Asia. We have seen how all of these regions continued to play more or less major, but not equal, roles in the world economic division of labor and system of "international" trade, despite the addition of an Atlantic ellipse in the sixteenth century.

However, we have also seen that among these regions some were certainly more equal than others and that their relative positions also underwent some cyclical or other temporal changes. Although the Atlantic Ocean displaced the Baltic and Mediterranean seas as the preponderant locus of European trade in the eighteenth century, it still did not begin to match the importance of the Indian Ocean and the China Sea regions in the world economy and its trade. A number of works by mostly Asian historians, cited above and also in the chapters that follow, are helping to put the Indian Ocean economy on the map, as its important place and role in history well merits. This chapter's section on China in particular argues that there was a Sinocentric subsystem in East Asia, whose economic weight in the world has been grossly underestimated, even when it has been recognized at all, which itself has been all too rare. The work of Hamashita (1988, 1994) and the proposed research by him and by Arrighi and Selden (1996) are designed to help remedy this serious deficiency. The present account can also contribute to the elucidation of the structure and transformation of this East Asian "regional" economy. For instance, this account stresses the long-standing bilateral relations of China with Central Asia and the trilateral ones with Korea and Japan, and the significant roles of the coastal regions of China, of emporia and other ports on the South China Sea and in Southeast Asia and the Ryukyus, and of the trading diasporas especially of overseas Chinese, who not incidentally continue to play vital roles today.

Of course, the emphasis here has been on the global economy and within it of China's and Asia's preponderant place and role in the world economy. Thus another "regionalization" of the world economy may emerge, which can be visualized in the form of concentric circles. Among these, China (and within that the Yangzi Valley and/or South China) would form the innermost circle. The East Asian tribute/trade system studied by Hamashita (1988, 1994) would form the next circle, which beyond China included at the very least parts of Central Asia, Korea, Japan, and Southeast Asia. However, we have seen that the boundaries of this circle as well were porous and uncertain, and Hamashita himself recognizes its extension to South Asia. In turn of course South Asia had millennial-old close relations with West Asia and East Africa, as well as with Central Asia, which in turn became increasingly enmeshed with Russia and then with China. These regions could be said to form a next outer band, which we can then perhaps identify as an Asian, or Afro-Asian, regional circle. To what extent this (Afro-)Asian economy had an identifiable economic structure and dynamic of its own has not really been investigated yet(and is not examined in the present account).

The focus of this book is the world economy as a whole, into whose global outer circle we must place the Asian economic circle as well. Within this global circle, we can then successively view the smaller concentric Asian, East (and South?) Asian, and Chinese economic circles. Europe and, across the Atlantic, the Americas would then occupy their rightful places in the outer band of the concentric circles, since Asia also had economic relations with Europe and, through its mediation, with the Americas. These economic relations included the trade from Asia directly across the Pacific, examined further in chapter 3 on money, which also deals with the Manila Galleon trade between Acapulco in Mexico (or El Callao near Lima) and Manila in the Philippines. Apart from focusing on China, East Asia, and Asia respectively as major world economic regions, such a concentric-circle mapping of the global economy also puts Europe and even the Atlantic economy in their marginal place.

Chapter 3 goes on to examine the flow into Asia and especially China of the new American money supplied by the Europeans and how that affected the world economy as a whole. The unequal structure and uneven dynamic of this single world economy and the intersectoral/interregional/international competition within it also generated the incentives for and a process of global economic "development" through increased global production. These developments are examined in chapter 4, where more evidence for the primacy of Asia in the world economy is examined. Chapter 4 also shows how the technological and institutional changes—in Asia as much as elsewhere—made this world development possible. This world (economic) history must also be analyzed and can only be adequately comprehended as a single global process studied everywhere at the same time simultaneously. Chapter 5 therefore begins to analyze several such simultaneous developments, which show that the Asian economic expansion continued into the mid-eighteenth century. Chapter 6 then explores the reasons for the subsequent decline of Asia and the related rise of Europe.

CHAPTER 3

Money Went Around
the World and Made
the World Go Round

Since the first discovery of America, the market for the produce of its silver mines has been growing gradually more and more extensive . . . [and] the greater part of Europe has been much improved. . . . The East Indies is another market for the silver mines of America, and a market which . . . has been continually taking off a greater and greater quantity of silver. . . . Particularly in China and Indostan, the value of the precious metals . . . was much higher than in Europe; and it continues to be so. . . . Upon all these accounts, the precious metals are a commodity which it has always been, and still continues to be, extremely advantageous to carry to India. There is scarce any commodity which brings a better price there . . . because in China, and the greater part of the other markets in India, . . . ten, or at most twelve ounces of silver will purchase an ounce of gold; in Europe it requires from fourteen to fifteen ounces. . . . The silver of the new continent seems in this manner to be one of the principal commodities by which the commerce between the two extremities of the old one is carried on, and by means of it, in great measure, that those distant parts of the world are connected with one another.

Adam Smith ([1776] 1937: 202, 204, 205, 206, 207)

World Money: Its Production and Exchange

An Afro-Eurasian-wide market for gold and silver has existed since time immemorial. The great fourteenth-century historian Ibn Khaldun observed that "if money is scarce in the Maghrib and Ifriquiyah, it is not scarce in the countries of the Slavs and the European Christians. If it is scarce in Egypt and Syria, it is not scarce in India and China. . . . Such things . . . have often been transferred from one region to another" (Ibn Khaldun 1969: 303). Caribbean gold was added by the

Spaniards from the voyages of Columbus and his followers. A major new infusion of America silver began with the discovery of the silver mines at Potosí in Peru (now Bolivia) in 1545 and at Zacatecas in Mexico in 1548. This new silver made a far-reaching impact on the world economy, beginning in 1600 if not earlier in various parts of Asia. For instance in 1621, a Portuguese merchant observed in a treatise on silver that it "wanders throughout all the world in its peregrinations before flocking to China, where it remains, as if at its natural center" (cited by von Glahn 1996a: 433). How silver went around the world has also been summarized more recently:

> The usual pattern of trade with the Far East was to transship some of the silver imported either from Europe or from Mexico . . . on the China-bound ships and exchange it for gold or commodities in China which were then imported back to India and the proceeds used to purchase return cargo for Europe. (Chaudhuri 1978: 182)

> In fact, American silver was so ubiquitous that merchants from Boston to Havana, Seville to Antwerp, Murmansk to Alexandria, Constantinople to Coromandel, Macao to Canton, Nagasaki to Manila all used the Spanish peso or piece of eight (*real*) as a standard medium of exchange; the same merchants even knew the relative fineness of the silver coins minted at Potosí, Lima, Mexico, and other sites in the Indies thousands of miles away. (TePaske 1983: 425)

So, "no one disputes the existence of a world market for silver. The issue is how to model it" (Flynn 1991: 337). "The price of silver in Peru . . . must have some influence on its price, not only at all the silver mines of Europe, but at those of China," observed Adam Smith ([1776]1937: 168). He regarded the matter important enough to devote sixty-four pages of his book to "A Digression on the Variations in the Value of Silver during the Course of the Four Last Centuries" and to discuss its effects in numerous places elsewhere in his book.

The existence and operation of a global world market is reviewed in chapter 2. Money and especially silver money was the blood that flowed through its circulatory system and oiled the wheels of production and exchange. Every kind of money acted as a store of value and as a medium of exchange both among other types of money and for other commodities. The multiplicity of coin types, in various denominations and purity, were exchanged or arbitraged against each other and against all other goods. Thus, this arbitrage of money and its exchange for commodities all around the globe also made the world market operationally practical for practically all goods!

MICRO- AND MACRO-ATTRACTIONS IN THE GLOBAL CASINO

Perhaps it is necessary to address the question first of *why* this money moved around the world, where and when it did, and indeed why it was produced in the first place. A later section examines the worldwide consequences of the flow of money around the globe. In chapter 2, the main "answer" to the question of where and why the money moved was that it was used to "settle the accounts" of the trade deficit at each link of the chain by those who wanted to import from the next link but did not have enough to export in return. Therefore, they had to settle the difference in money. However, that still leaves at least three related questions unanswered: (1) Why did some want to import commodities without having enough export commodities to pay for them? (2) Why did others want to export commodities they produced and be paid for many of them with money, rather than in other commodities? That is, why did they have a demand for money? (3) Why was this money produced in the first place? After all, to produce, transport, safeguard, mint, and exchange this money required considerable expenditure of labor, materials, and also of money itself.

It is easiest to offer an answer to the last question, and that answer will be a guide as well to answering the other two. Money was produced because it (in the form of silver, gold, copper, coins, shells, and the like) was—and remains—a commodity like any other, the production, sale, and purchase of which can generate a profit just as any other commodity can—only easier and better! Of course to be profitable, the costs of production, transport, and so on have to be lower than the anticipated sale price. And so generally this was the case, except if and when the supply of silver, for instance, increased so much or so rapidly as to drive its sale price down below the costs of production. That did happen sometimes to Spanish (American) and other producers. Then they had to find technological or other ways to reduce costs of production and/or to reduce the amount of production and supply until the price again rose enough to cover their costs. The same was true for gold, copper, cowries, textiles, food, and all other commodities.

Once the money was produced, it could be sold at a profit wherever its price was higher—in terms of some other commodity, be that some other kind of money or whatever. Since the price of the money was largely determined by supply and demand, both locally and worldwide, the money traveled from here to there if and when the supply was high here relative to its supply and demand there. That made the price of silver lower here where the supply was higher relative to demand and the price higher there where the demand was higher relative to the supply, and attracted the silver from here to there. Therefore, it was in the profit-making interest of any private company, or public (or state) producer to send the money from a low-price market here to a high-price market there, even and especially if the low- price market was at home and the high-price one was somewhere else — like half way around the world.

That was one, indeed often the *main,* business of the major trading companies and state governments, as of course it was of bankers, money lenders, and often of merchants, consumers, indeed anybody and every-body. The supply price of silver was relatively low where it was abun-dant at the mine head, especially in the Americas, and it was relatively higher farther and farther around the world to Asia. So that is why and where the silver money went on its predominantly eastward journey around the world, although it also went westward across the Pacific and from Japan across the China Sea. And that was the primary, indeed almost the only, world economic business of the Europeans, who were not able to sell anything else — especially of their own noncompetitive production — in the thriving markets of Asia. Asians would buy nothing else from Europe other than the silver it got out of its colonies in the Americas.

That this monetary arbitrage had a long history and became world-wide not long after the incorporation of the Americas into the world economy can be illustrated as follows. From the eleventh to the six-teenth centuries, during the Song dynasty, later under Mongol rule, and during much of the Ming dynasty, the predominant direction of monetary metal exports was of silver and copper from China to Japan and of gold from Japan to China. Reflecting changes in supply and demand from the sixteenth century onward, this flow was essentially reversed, as Japan became a major exporter of silver and then of copper, and an importer of gold (Yamamura and Kamiki 1983). In China, the gold/silver ratio increased (that is, gold increased and silver decreased in relative values) from 1:8 around 1600 to 1:10 at both mid and end century, and then doubled to 1:20 toward the end of the eighteenth century (Yang 1952: 48). However, the gold/silver ratio usually re-mained lower and sometimes far lower, and the price of silver far higher, in China than elsewhere in the world. As Han-Sheng Chuan explained in his 1969 article on the inflow of American silver into China,

> from 1592 to the early seventeenth century gold was exchanged for silver in Canton at the rate of 1:5.5 to 1:7, while in Spain the exchange rate was 1:12.5 to 1:14, thus indicating that the value of silver was twice as high in China as in Spain. (cited in Flynn and Giraldez 1994: 75)

Similar ratios were observed in 1609 by the Spaniard Pedro de Baeza, who also noted that arbitrage between them offered a profit of 75 or 80 percent (von Glahn 1996a: 435).

In the 1590s also, the gold/silver ratio was 1:10 in Japan and 1:9 in Mughal India (Flynn and Giraldez 1994: 76). As long as the relative price of gold was lower and that of silver was almost two times higher in China, silver was attracted to China and exchanged for gold, which was exported. European trading company spokesmen, quoted below, testified to China as one of their sources of gold. As is well known, from the early sixteenth century onward, first Portuguese and then Dutch middlemen were very active in this Sino-Japanese trade, and drew large profits—and precious metals themselves—from it. A Portuguese memo in about 1600 indicates a profit of 45 percent between Portuguese Macao on the China coast and Japan (von Glahn 1996a: 435).

The Europeans then used these profits to support their trade between various parts of Southeast, South, and West Asia and Europe and the Americas. Their merchants and trading companies, especially the Dutch East India Company (usually known by its Dutch initials, VOC) and then also the English East India Company (EIC), engaged in gold/silver/copper arbitrage as major and essential parts of their worldwide business dealings. Of course, they also arbitraged with or exchanged these metals to buy and sell all the other commodities in which they, like the Asians also, traded in Asia and around the world.

Copper coin was the most predominant and widespread currency of daily use in most of Asia, though it was gradually and partially displaced by silver. So there was at least a trimetallic world market, which however was predominantly on a de facto silver standard. Or rather, the more rapidly increasing world supply of silver, and its concomitant decline in price relative to gold and copper (as well as other monetary commodities), induced and permitted the silver standard increasingly to impose itself in the world market economy.

The rapid increase in the world supply of silver produced especially by the Americas and Japan lowered its price relative to that of gold.

However, gold/silver ratios varied regionally, reflecting differences in supply and demand, as did those of silver and copper, which was in greater use for minor coinage. Trimetallic gold/silver/copper and indeed multimetallic and commodity arbitrage extended all around the world and everywhere locally. This arbitrage also included especially cowrie shells, textiles, and other media of exchange, as well as baser metals such as lead, tin, and iron.

Cowrie shells were in much demand as currency and for the slave trade in Africa; and cowries and badam (an inedible almond) were also in widespread use at the most popular level in many parts of India, where they competed with copper coin. The high cost of mining copper and of minting copper coins, relative to that of silver or even gold ones, allowed cowries, which did not have to be minted, to displace coins at the lowest end of the market when copper shortages or coining costs rendered the latter too expensive in India and parts of China. When on the other hand, the slave (and later the palm oil) trade grew and absorbed more shells in Africa, relatively fewer went to India, where some were again replaced in circulation by copper coin in low-value transactions.

Indeed following the "lowly" cowrie around is illustrative of several themes in this book. Cowries were already in use in West Africa when Ibn Batuta reported their gold exchange values in the fourteenth century. By the seventeenth century, their gold exchange value had fallen, presumably because of the intervening increase in their supply relative to that of gold. First the Portuguese and then also the Dutch and English brought them to West Africa in large numbers, which rose and declined with the slave trade. The cowries took two main routes from their centers of production in the Maldives, where they were purchased by Indians and Europeans. One was to Bengal and the other was to Ceylon, at both of which they were then transferred to and used as ballast in European ships bound primarily for England and Holland. From there they were reshipped to the coasts of West and Southwest Africa in payment for slaves. The contemporary John Bardot observed in 1732 that

> according to the occasion of several trading nations of Europe . . . to carry on their traffic at the coast of Guinea and of Angola; to purchase slaves or other goods of Africa . . . proportionately to the occasion the European Guinea adventurers have for those cuaris [cowries], and the quantity or scarcity there happens to be of them, either in England or in Holland, their price by the hun-

dredweight is higher or lower. (quoted in Hagendorn and Johnson 1986: 47)

So the price of cowries reflected supply and demand changes both in
Europe and in Africa as well those emanating in the producing islands,
the Maldives, and in the "consuming" regions of South and East Asia.

Another eighteenth-century observer complained that "formerly
Twelve thousand Weight of these Cowries would purchase a cargo of
five or six Hundred Negroes; but these lucrative times are no more . . .
[so that now] there is no such thing as having a Cargo under twelve or
fourteen Tuns of Cowries" (quoted in Hagendorn and Johnson 1986:
111). Similarly, a merchant in West Africa complained that prices for a
slave had increased from 100 to 136 pounds of cowries, or from 12 to 16
guns, or from 5 to 7 rolls of Brazilian tobacco, or from 25 to 36 pieces
of Silesian linen, or from one anker of French brandy to one and a half,
or from 15 to 150 pounds of gunpowder (Hagendorn and Johnson
1986). Not only was there cowrie inflation, but relative prices of commodities also changed, and apparently those of brandy and gunpowder
rose most of all!

During the apogee of the eighteenth-century slave trade, there were
26 million pounds, or 10 billion individual shells, of registered cowrie
imports, in decade totals averaging from 2 to 3 million pounds but rang-
ing from about 1 to 5 million pounds (Hagendorn and Johnson 1986:
58–62). So, as Perlin (1993: 143) remarks, even the lowly cowrie shell
connected economic, political, and social processes and events in the
Indian and Atlantic oceans and the lands and peoples adjoining them
on all sides. For all of them were part and parcel of a single global
marketplace, in which supply and demand regulated relative prices.
These differential and fluctuating world prices were arbitraged and
"balanced" even in terms of cowries and between them and metallic
currencies (including most importantly, copper) or other currencies
and among these and all other commodities as well.

Money, as Perlin also insists, no more than any other commodity, is
paid out only to balance a trade deficit. No, money is also a commodity
like any other in its own right; and it is the demand for money that
makes possible both the market supply of goods and the use of the
money to purchase them. So, this universal practice of arbitrage in itself
already reflects—or helped create—a world market in every sense of the
term. To observe as Flynn and Giraldez (1991: 341) do that "the 'world
market' was really a series of interconnected regional markets dispersed

and overlapping around the globe" does not alter anything fundamental, precisely because these "markets" *were overlapping and interconnected*.

But why and how did this money make the world go round? Why did anybody—indeed everybody!—want this money so much as to drive up its price, and in Asia and especially in China to keep the money that arrived from elsewhere? Because people and companies and governments there were able to use money to buy other commodities, including precious metals such as gold and silver. Both at the individual and firm micro-level and at the local, regional, "national," and world economic macro-level, money literally oiled the machinery and greased the palms of those who produced or ran that machinery in manufacturing, agriculture, trade, state expenses, or whatever. No less and no more than anywhere else, either then or today. That is, the money supported and generated effective demand, and the demand elicited supply. Of course, additional demand could only elicit additional supply where and when it could. That is, there had to be productive capacity and/or the possibility to expand it through investment and improved productivity.

The argument here is that *that* expansion was possible and did happen, especially in many parts of Asia. Otherwise, the Asians would not have demanded and bought the additional foreign and domestic money either by supplying commodities or other money for it. If supplies of commodities had not been able to expand, any increased demand for them would just have driven up the price of existing commodities through what is called inflation—and/or there would not have been demand to import this additional new money in the first place! That is, the new silver and copper money, not to mention the additional credit it supported, increasingly monetized and stimulated production in the world, regional, "national," and many local "economies," that is in these parts of the single global economy.

The macro-supply part of this argument has been made by all those who have emphasized that the production and/or export of money was necessary to cover deficits in the balance of trade. The macro-demand part of this argument has been emphasized particularly by Perlin (1993, 1994) and others like myself, who observe that this money really did oil the wheels of production and trade and was not just "dug up in the Americas to be buried again in Asia." The related and complementary micro supply-and-demand argument is that individual producers and companies or even public producers and traders had to have their own profit interests to induce them to do their part in oiling or monetizing macro supply and demand around the world. This argument has been stressed particularly by Flynn (1986), Flynn and Giraldez (1995c), but also by Perlin, who contends that "a demand-centric framework incorporates the question of supply; that is, it establishes a broader, more inclusive, and also far more complex, range of empirical phenomena that need to be taken into account in an adequate explanation" (Perlin 1994: 95).

The combination of these arguments here supports my thesis that there was only *one world economy/system* and that it had its *own structure and dynamic*. Money played an important part during the period of global development from 1400 to 1800. Money went around the world and made the world go round in this global casino in which it supplied and vastly increased the lifeblood that fueled and oiled the wheels of agriculture, industry, and commerce.

DEALING AND PLAYING IN THE GLOBAL CASINO

Among the main exporters of precious metals were the Spanish American colonies and Japan. Europe, the Ottomans, Persia, and India also were exporters, but they largely though not entirely reexported precious metals that they had themselves imported.

Africa and Southeast Asia produced and exported gold. China produced copper coin predominantly for domestic use but also for export to Southeast Asia and elsewhere. China also produced and exported gold, which Japan and others imported. Japan became probably the world's major copper exporter from the mid-seventeenth century onward. Daily and small transactions in East, Southeast, and South Asia were mostly in copper coin. Asians no less than Europeans devoted enormous amounts of economic, social, political, military, and other "energy" and attention to this money business, which often was more profitable than any other. The world's major and some minor producing and exporting regions of monetary silver, gold, copper, and tin, which were exchanged and arbitraged against each other, are summarized in table 3.1.

So for silver, the major producers and exporters were Spanish America and Japan; and of gold, the major producers were Africa, Spanish America, and Southeast Asia. Effectively, the world economy was on a silver standard, although gold and copper, and to a much lesser extent tin and cowrie shells, were also mutually interchangeable. The

Table 3.1 *Monetary Metal Producing and Exporting Regions*

	Major Producers	Minor Producers
Silver	Mexico Peru Japan	Northeast Europe Persia Central Asia Burma/Siam/Vietnam
Gold	West and Southeast Africa Spanish America (in 16th c.) Brazil (in 18th c., from 1690) Southeast Asia	Japan Persia China
Copper*	Japan Sweden	
Tin*	Malaya	

* Copper and tin were sometimes alloyed; both were used for low-value coinage.

Ottomans, Ming China, and India used large quantities of silver to support their currency systems, ultimately sustained by the huge and cheap production of American, but also Japanese, mines.

As had been the case for millennia, gold predominantly moved through Central Asia and to and around South Asia from east to west, in the direction opposite to that of silver, which moved from west to east. On the Indian subcontinent, gold moved to the south and silver to the north. Both were exchanged not only for each other but of course also for other commodities, as well as for local and especially imported foreign coins and other forms of currency. This profitable arbitrage was big business not only for Venetians and later Spaniards, Dutch, and other Europeans, but equally so for Ottomans, Persians, Indians all around the subcontinent, Southeast Asians, Japanese, and Chinese. Bullion and coins were produced and transported often halfway around the world and over other long distances. Sometimes these metals went as a single shipment, but more usually they were transmitted through chain-linked stages. The precious and also some baser metals were bought and sold in the form of bullion and coin like any other commodity to generate profit. That in turn was converted into and invested in other commodities, also including other currencies and of course wage, slave, and other "forms" of labor.

TePaske (1983) describes the chain-linked movement of silver:

The bullion flowed out of Spain to England, France, and the Low Countries for purchase of manufactured goods unavailable in Castile. From English, French, Flemish or Dutch ports Spanish pesos were transshipped through the Baltic or Murmansk into Scandinavia or Russia and traded for furs. In Russia . . . [silver] went southeastward along the Volga into the Caspian Sea to Persia, where it was sent overland or by sea to Asia. Spanish-American bullion also flowed out of Spain through the Mediterranean and eastward by land and water routes to the Levant. India procured its American silver by means of traffic from Suez through the Red Sea and into the Indian Ocean, overland from the eastern end of the Mediterranean through Turkey and Persia to the Black Sea, and finally into the Indian Ocean, or directly from Europe on ships rounding the Cape of Good Hope following the route discovered by Vasco da Gama. The latter way was also used by Portuguese, Dutch, and English ships to carry Spanish American treasure directly to Asian ports to exchange for Asian goods. Lastly—and long ignored—American silver found its way to the Orient by way of the Pacific route from Acapulco to Manila. (TePaske 1983: 433)

In India, Spanish American silver began to arrive via West Asia and around the Cape of Good Hope by the beginning of the seventeenth century. The Mughal empire was financed and maintained with silver, and its coinage and currency was henceforth heavily dependent on the influx of silver from abroad. Most of it ultimately came from the Americas and arrived via Europe and the Levant over the Persian Gulf or Red Sea routes, but some also originated in Ottoman lands and Safavid Persia. Most of the silver arrived, not by sea around the Cape of Good Hope, but by caravan and via either the Red Sea or the Persian Gulf from Egypt, the Levant, Turkey, and Russia (Brenning 1983: 479, 481, 493). At Surat, for a time India's most important port, the big trading companies (which were by no means the only suppliers) brought about half of the silver arriving from the west. Of that, less than 30 percent arrived via the Cape of Good Hope and most came via the Red Sea, the Persian Gulf, and overland, including from Russia. In 1643–1644, more than half the silver arrived via the Red Sea and the Persian Gulf (Steensgaard 1990a: 353). Another 20 percent came from Japan, via Taiwan, where the Dutch VOC had exchanged it for gold. Silver also flowed into the Punjab from Central Asia and probably into Bengal from Tibet/Sichuan/Yunnan and Burma. The British EIC also brought gold from the east to India and paid for it with silver. Gold also flowed into India, especially to the south of the subcontinent, both from West Asia and from Japan and China in East Asia and especially from Southeast Asia. However, India was only the penultimate "sink" for the world's silver, since India itself had to re-export some silver further eastward to remit it especially to China.

Chapter 2 offers evidence of the onward shipment of silver from India to Southeast Asia and China. However, John Richards (1987: 3) claims that Mughal silver coin sent eastward soon returned augmented by gold from Southeast Asia. Thus, unlike the Ottoman Turkish and the Safavid Persian empires, according to Richards, the Mughal empire was able to export enough goods to pay for its imports, so that it had no need for any net specie export, which instead flowed in to augment its own supply.

Increased inter- and intra-Asian trade and specie shipments by Indians and other Asian themselves, however, reduced the Europeans' share from half in 1640 to only one-fifth by 1700. Yet in 1715 during an already existing "silver famine," a Spanish treasure fleet succumbed to a Caribbean hurricane, and "the economic shock waves reverberated all the way to India" (Day 1987: 159). Arguments and evidence regarding an important "silver famine" around 1640 are examined in chapter 5.

THE NUMBERS GAME

The world's stock and flows of money and their increase have been the subject of many estimates and their revisions from Alexander von Humboldt and Earl Hamilton to the present—and presumably will continue to be re-estimated in the future. It would be impossible to review or evaluate let alone to add to them here. Fortunately that is not necessary in order to inquire how some of this money oiled the wheels of commerce among the world's major regions—and affected their relations to each other.

Braudel and Spooner (1967) have estimated the existing stocks in Europe in 1500 to have been about 3,600 tons of gold and 37,000 tons of silver. Raychaudhuri and Habib (1982: 368) have revised these estimates downward, to 3,600 tons of gold and 35,000 tons of silver in the entire Old World in 1500. Ward Barrett's (1990) summary of world bullion flows from 1450 to 1800 reviews a number of previous estimates (by Alexander von Humboldt, Earl Hamilton, Adolf Soetbeer, Michel Morineau, B. H. Slichter van Bath, and others, including Nef, Attman, TePaske, Kobata, Yamamura and Kamiki cited in the references) and concludes that from 1493 to 1800, 85 percent of the world's silver and 70 percent of its gold came from the Americas.

Silver. Disregarding variations over time and summarizing Barrett's estimates, in the sixteenth century American silver production was about 17,000 tons or an annual but of course rapidly growing average of 170 tons a year. In the seventeenth century annual average production rose to 420 tons a year or 42,000 tons for the century, of which about 31,000 tons arrived in Europe, with roughly one-quarter on public and three-quarters on private account (TePaske 1983). Europe in turn shipped 40 percent of this silver, or over 12,000 tons, to Asia, of which 4,000 to 5,000 tons each were transported directly by the Dutch VOC and the British EIC. Additionally, another 6,000 tons went to and via the Baltics, and 5,000 tons to and via the Levant, both of which kept some but also remitted some further eastward to Asia. In the eighteenth century, American average annual production was 740 tons for a total of 74,000 tons. Of these, 52,000 tons arrived in Europe and over 20,000 tons, or still 40 percent, were shipped onward to Asia.

Thus according to Barrett, in the seventeenth and eighteenth centuries, about 70 percent of the American production of silver arrived in Europe, and 40 percent of that was shipped on to Asia. TePaske (1983) estimates a higher—sometimes much higher and growing—retention of silver by the Americans themselves. From a world monetary point of view, this would only mean that the effective costs of production and its administration and defense in the Americas, as well as the provision of markets there, was that much higher. However, Flynn and others suggest that most of the silver that did not arrive in Europe was not retained in the Americas, but was shipped to Asia across the Pacific instead.

So by Barrett's estimates, of the 133,000 tons of silver produced in the Americas beginning in 1545 and until 1800, about 100,000 tons or 75 percent arrived in Europe. Of these in turn, 32,000 tons or 32 percent of European receipts (or 24 percent of American production) arrived in Asia. But since this onward shipment to Asia really started only around 1600, after that it represented about 40 percent of European receipts. By this estimate then, over the whole period Europe kept 68,000 tons; and the Americas retained less than 33,000 tons since some silver was also lost at sea. However, as we will note below, some of this American "retained" silver was also shipped across the Pacific directly to Asia.

American production thus increased world silver stocks by 17,000 tons or by half the total in the sixteenth century, by 42,000 tons or by another 80 percent to 1700, and by another 74,000 tons or again by almost 80 percent to 1800. That means that the world stock of silver increased from about 35,000 tons in 1500 to 168,000 tons in 1800, or by nearly five times. Yet this amount still does not include the 15 percent of the total world silver, which according to Barrett was produced elsewhere. Most of that, and perhaps more, was produced by Japan, as we will note below.

Artur Attman (1986a: 78) also compiles estimates from many sources and arrives at somewhat different totals for the last two centuries. Attman's figures are in rix-dollars, whose equivalents, according to his appendix, are 1 rix-dollar = 25 grams of silver, or 1 million rix dollars = 25 tons (25 million grams) of silver. Attman estimates American production at an average of 13 million rix-dollars (equivalent to 325 tons per year or 32,000 tons) in the seventeenth century and 30 million rix-dollars (750 tons per year or 75,000 tons) in the eighteenth century. Of these, Attman estimates shipments of about 75 percent to Europe, and remissions of these in turn of over 60 percent (compared to only 40 percent estimated by Barrett) of European receipts. If we take the average of the two estimates, at least a half and an ever rising share of American production was sent to the East. Of this half of American production, in turn over half of the also growing share was shipped directly to South and East Asia, while over 20 percent was remitted to the Baltics and another 20 percent to the Levant/West Asia—which in their turn however also had to remit a portion of their imports farther eastward (Attman 1981: 77). Thus, by Attman's estimates, the amount and share of American silver that ended up in Asia was even higher, that is, 48,000 tons rather than the approximately 32,000 tons we get by adding up the figures from Barrett (1990).

However, at least another 15 tons of silver annually, or 3,000 tons more, were shipped on the Manila Galleons from Acapulco in Mexico and earlier also from Peru directly to Manila. Almost all of this silver was then transshipped to China. However, the transpacific shipments of silver may have been much greater. Transpacific shipments averaged around 20 tons annually from 1610 to 1640 and then fell to less than 10 tons per year in the next two decades (Reid 1993: 27). Atwell (1982: 74) also mentions annual Acapulco-Manila shipments of 143 tons, and 345 in 1597. However, Pierre Chaunu estimated that as much as 25 percent of American silver was shipped directly across the Pacific (cited in Adshead 1988: 21). Han-Sheng Chuan in turn estimates shipment of as much as 50 tons of silver a year (or as much as through the Baltics) in the seventeenth century, all of which, of course, ended up in China (cited in Flynn and Giraldez 1995a: 204, 1995b:16, Flynn 1996).

A large but unknown share of the transpacific silver trade was contraband and so not registered. To maintain its monopoly rake-off in Spain itself, the Spanish crown tried to restrict the direct transpacific Manila Galleon trade, so an unknown share of it went as unregistered contraband. For this reason also, Flynn and Giraldez (1995b,c) believe the amount of transpacific silver is still underestimated. That would also mean that much of the Spanish American silver that according to Te-Paske did not make its way across the Atlantic did not really stay in the Americas but was shipped across the Pacific instead. Therefore, Flynn suggests the transpacific shipments of silver may well have sometimes equaled the amount of silver flowing to China via Europe. Flynn mostly uses Chuan's estimates of 2 million pesos, or 50 tons, of silver a year, which is already three times more than the 15 tons mentioned above. Atwell (1982: 74), citing a Chinese source, estimates 57 to 86 tons a year. However, Flynn also asks if it is "possible that over 5 million pesos [125 tons] per year traversed the Pacific? Supporting evidence does exist for such lofty figures", and he goes on to suggest that the transpacific trade may not have declined in the seventeenth century as the trans-Atlantic one did (Flynn and Giraldez 1994: 81–82).

The big Asian supplier was Japan. It produced and supplied 50 tons a year between 1560 and 1600, and between 150 to 190 tons a year from 1600 to 1640, peaking at 200 tons in 1603 (Atwell 1982: 71 and Reid 1993: 27). Reid tabulates estimates from several sources to arrive at 130 tons a year from 1620 to 1640, declining to 70 tons a year in the 1640s, 50 tons in the 1650s, and 40 tons a year in the 1660s. Von Glahn (1996a: 439, table 3.1) constructs estimates of nearly 4,000 tons, and cites Yamamura and Kamiki's estimates of about 8,000 tons for the nearly one hundred years from 1550 to 1645. Japan had imported Korean engineers and technology to respond to the rising demand for and price of silver. Japan then became a major world producer and exporter of silver during the eighty years from 1560 to 1640. After that, Japanese silver production has been supposed to have declined, and copper production and exports to China increased instead. However, recent Japanese research reported by Ikeda (1996) and data cited by von Glahn (1996a) suggest that Japanese exports of silver continued until at least the mid-eighteenth century.

Noteworthy also is that Japanese silver exports to China were more than three to ten, and on average six to seven, times greater than that which arrived across the Pacific from the Americas. In any case the perhaps 8,000- or 9,000-ton total of Japanese silver exports between 1560 and 1640 must be compared with the about 19,000 tons received by Europe from the Americas (estimate from Barrett) plus the over 1,000 tons shipped across the Pacific during the same period. That is, Japan alone contributed 8,000 or 9,000 tons out of this 28,000-ton total, or almost 30 percent. Flynn and Giraldez (1995a: 202) suggest that it was 30 to 40 percent at its peak.

A couple of students of the era (Flynn 1991) have proposed the counterfactual speculation of how different the world—including Europe—would have been without this major Japanese contribution to world liquidity, especially to China. Or alternatively, without the American contribution and its competition with Japan, would the latter have been able to parlay a concomitantly much stronger position on the world silver market into an economic and/or also political conquest of China and Southeast Asia? The Europeans—for lack of any means of payment—would have been virtually excluded from world trade. Either one—and a fortiori both—of these eventualities would have made all subsequent world history very different from what it has been. Be that as it may, we must agree with Yamamura and Kamiki's (1983: 356) plea that "serious reexamination of the role played by Japan in the monetary system of the world during this period is long overdue." Therefore from this world monetary perspective, all allegations about Japan's or China's isolation from the world economy are again belied by the evidence.

Yet the amount and share of the world's silver that ended up in China must have been even higher than all of the above estimates, since China received an unknown part of the remaining world supplies of silver as well. Reid (1993: 27) constructs estimates of about 6,000 tons in the 1601–1640 period, or 150 tons a year, in East Asia, of which 4,500 tons came from Japan; almost all the total ended up in China. For the period 1641–1670 this total supply declined to an average of 80 tons a year, or 2,400 tons total, of which 53 tons a year, or about 1,600 tons, came from Japan.

Thus between 1600 and 1800 and using Barrett's estimates, continental Asia absorbed at least 32,000 tons of silver from the Americas via Europe, 3,000 tons via Manila, and perhaps 10,000 tons from Japan, or a total of at least 45,000 tons. Using Attman's estimates of proportionately higher European remissions to Asia, the latter would have received 52,000 tons directly from Europe plus a share of the trans-Atlantic shipments of silver then remitted to and via the Baltics and the Levant, plus the transpacific shipments. That adds up to 68,000 tons, or half the silver production accounted for in the world between 1500 and 1800. However, Asia (outside of Japan) also produced silver for its own use, particularly in Asia Minor, Persia, and Central Asia, some of which was also remitted to China. Moreover, some silver was also produced in Yunnan and other parts of China for its own use.

So China received and used a very significant share of the world's supply of silver. Much came from Japan, some across the Pacific via Manila, and some arrived in China from the Americas via Europe, the Levant, and West, South, and Southeast Asia as well as from and through Central Asia. By Reid's (1993: 27) admittedly incomplete estimates, the European traders supplied about 14 percent of the Chinese silver imports between 1610 and 1630, then 10 percent until 1660, and 40 percent in the decade of the 1660s. Chaunu's early estimate was that one-third of the original American silver ended up in China and another third in India and the Ottoman Empire (cited in Adshead 1993). Frederic Wakeman (1986: 3) suggests that even as much as half of all American silver may have ended up in China.

The production and flow of silver around the world is graphically consolidated in map 3.1, primarily by averaging the estimates of Barrett and Attman. It shows American production of 17,000 tons in the sixteenth century, almost all of which were shipped to and remained in Europe. For the seventeenth and eighteenth centuries, the map shows American production of 37,000 and 75,000 tons respectively, of which 27,000 and 54,000 tons were shipped to Europe, for a two-century total of 81,000 tons. Of these European receipts of silver, about half (or 39,000 tons) were in turn remitted onward to Asia, 13,000 in the seventeenth century and 26,000 in the eighteenth. This silver ultimately went predominantly to China. Moreover, between 3,000 and 10,000 tons, and maybe up to 25,000 tons, were also shipped directly from the Americas to Asia via the Pacific; and almost all of this silver also ended up in China. Additionally, Japan produced at least 9,000 tons of silver, which were absorbed by China as well. Therefore over the two and a half centuries up to 1800, China ultimately received nearly 48,000 tons of silver from Europe and Japan, plus perhaps another 10,000 tons or even more via Manila, as well as other silver produced in continental Southeast and Central Asia and in China itself. That would add up to

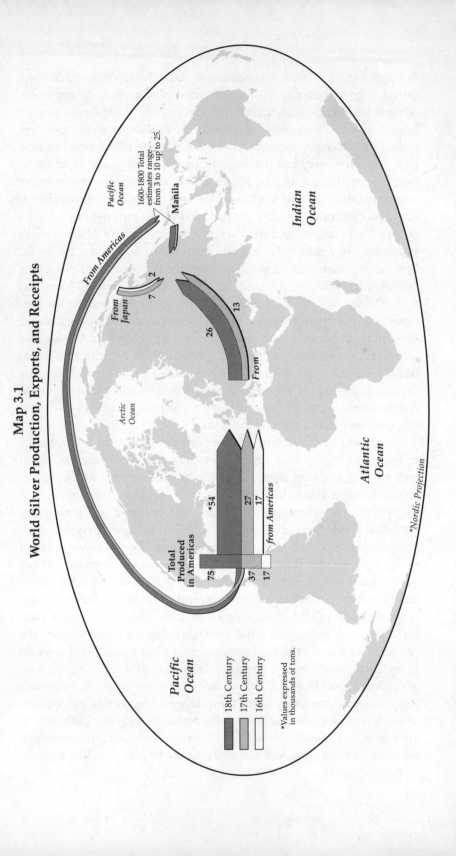

Map 3.1
World Silver Production, Exports, and Receipts

Pacific Ocean

Indian Ocean

1600–1800 Total estimates range from 3 to 10 up to 25.

Manila

From Americas

From Japan

2

7

13

26

From

Arctic Ocean

Atlantic Ocean

Nordic Projection

Total Produced in Americas

*54

27

17

from Americas

75

37

17

Pacific Ocean

18th Century

17th Century

16th Century

*Values expressed in thousands of tons.

some 60,000 tons of silver for China or perhaps half the world's tallied production of about 120,000 tons after 1600 or 137,000 tons since 1545.

New estimates have been independently constructed by von Glahn (1996a). He uses data on silver shipments where available; and where not, he estimates them by converting 80 percent of the values of Chinese exports to imports of silver, calculated in metric tons. His total from all sources, including Japan, America via Manila, and the Indian Ocean (but not including overland across Asia) are about 2,200 tons for 1550 to 1600 and 5,000 tons for 1600 to 1645, or a total of 7,200 tons for the nearly one hundred years from 1550 to 1645. The estimates for the second period and therefore also for the whole period are 20 to 30 percent lower than those of Yamamura and Kamiki, probably in part because von Glahn uses data for commodity exports and converts them into imports of silver at a constant ratio of 80 percent. The legitimacy of this estimation procedure is questionable, however, insofar as over time the supply of silver increased, thus driving down its value in terms of other commodities. In that case the use of a constant conversion ratio of commodities to silver would result in an underestimate of the quantity of silver that was paid to China for these commodities and could help account for von Glahn's estimates being lower than all others. For more discussion in my review of his book, see Frank (1998b).

Combining some of the above estimates for the production and remission of silver from the mid-sixteenth to the mid-seventeenth centuries suggests production of some 30,000 tons in the Americas and about 8,000 tons in Japan, for a total of 38,000 tons. If we again subtract the uncertain amount that remained in the Americas and/or was lost in transit, the 7,000 to 10,000 tons that ended up in China certainly represent a very appreciable share. That is, even this very conservative estimate by van Glahn leaves China with between one-fourth and one-third of total world silver production. That is still more than any of the shares left for the use individually of Europe and West, South, and Southeast Asia, not to mention Africa and Central Asia. (We have even less evidence for the last two, although some additional silver also reached China through the latter region).

Gold. Gold was supplied to the world market in the sixteenth century from the Caribbean, Mexico, and various Andean regions, from both previously existing and newly opened mines. Minas Gerais in Brazil had a major gold boom from 1690 to the mid-eighteenth century. However, there was also non-American production

of gold, about 30 percent of the world's total, as Barrett noted. As had
been the case for centuries before 1500, the bulk of this gold came from
Africa, mostly from West Africa, which exported perhaps some 50 tons
in the sixteenth century and nearly 100 tons, or a ton a year, in the
seventeenth century. This gold export declined to 60 tons in the eighteenth century, before it ceased near the end of the century (Barrett
1983: 247, Curtin 1983: 240, 250).

Other supplies of gold came from Nubia, which exported gold via
Egypt to Constantinople/Istanbul and from Ethiopia to Egypt, the Red
Sea, and India. Zimbabwe, which for a millennium had been an important source of gold for the world, reached its peak production of
one ton during the fifteenth century. The Ottomans also produced and/
or received gold (but absolutely if not relatively more silver) from the
Balkans, Rumelia, Crimea, Caucasia, and the Urals. Gold was also produced in and exported from various parts of Southeast Asia, such as
mainland Yunnan, Burma, Malaya, Thailand, Champa (Vietnam), and
in some islands, especially in Sumatra. Some of this Southeast Asian
gold went northward to East Asia, and some westward to South Asia.
China also produced gold and, during much of the period from 1400
to 1800, exported it in exchange for silver.

Credit. Both the availability and scarcity of metallic currency stimulated an "unprecedented expansion of credit: loans, securi-
ties, bonds, credit transfers, bank-money, paper money and negotiable
obligations—all were employed on an increasing scale to avoid the use
of precious metals" (Parker 1974: 531). However, it is likely—as elsewhere and at other times as well—that the amount of credit also increased and decreased in tandem with the availability and scarcity of
metallic currency and bullion to back it up. Politicians especially may
have wanted to replace scarce real money by credit and paper. However, that same scarcity made or allowed money lenders to increase the
rate of interest price that they charged for their money and credit—and
thereby to limit the effective amount of credit. Indeed then as now, it
usually took real (metallic) money to make or get paper money and
credit.

But the bullion was mainly needed as a collateral on the loans of
the Companies: the trade of all Companies and of the *Estado [da
India]* floated on the credit of Indian bankers. If the *Compagnie
des Indes* did not receive bullion its shaky credit would collapse

and one would be unable to buy and sell anything. . . . To obtain loans and honour their bills of exchange merchants therefore had to remit bullion from abroad. Bullion not only served as collateral for the traffic in bills within India but between India and the Middle East as well. It was usual for merchants operating from Kerala and Gujarat to draft bills on Mocha and Aden; for merchants from Surat to draft bills on Kung—the major centre for banking within the Gulf. Yet this traffic in paper depended upon a steady flow of coin from the Middle East.

A lack of bullion, in turn, hampered the collection of land revenue in Gujarat; rural credit-rates would mount and so would the discount on bills of exchange drafted from Surat on Burhanpur or Ahmedabad to transfer the land revenues. For the land revenues and the incomes of nobles from their *mansabs* were largely remitted through bills too. (Barendse 1997: chap. 6)

If it is difficult to make or get reliable estimates of metallic money, it is all the more likely that we will never know how much the wheels of commerce, investment, and production were also oiled by credit—or indeed themselves produced credit, in its myriad of forms. Yet, credit must have been very significant, even if direct evidence about it is scarce and for the period from 1400 to 1800 a bit tardy, at least in the secondary literature. For instance between 1740 and 1745, bills of exchange accounted for about 20 percent (and commodities and precious metals 80 percent) of the British and Dutch East India companies' export payments for what they imported (Steensgaard 1990c: 14). Many bills, including British, were settled on the Amsterdam money market. These companies themselves also borrowed heavily on the money markets in Asia, which financed their exports. In Asia itself, bridging credits advanced to growers of indigo or merchants of coffee were normally made for periods up to twelve months, and for the supply of textiles for three or four months (Chaudhuri 1990b: 8). Chapter 4 discusses the role of credit in its examination of market and financial institutions.

How Did the Winners Use Their Money?

In a word, did they hoard the money (as the fable goes), or did they spend it, and if so on what?

THE HOARDING THESIS

For readers brought up in the Western tradition reaching from David Hume and Adam Smith to Immanuel Wallerstein today, it may be well to reexamine the thesis that "the money was dug up in the West only to be buried again in the East." Under the title *Spenders and Hoarders,* Charles Kindleberger writes: "This brings us to the central issue, whether the traditional view that hoarding in India and China was a reflection of lack of financial sophistication or that their use of precious metals was much the same as that in Europe" (Kindleberger 1989: 35).

To deal with this issue, Kindleberger examines a wide variety of sources, some of which indicate that there also was some hoarding in Europe and many that indicate that there also was much "spending" in Asia. Nonetheless, all analysis to the contrary notwithstanding, Kindleberger is unwilling to abandon the traditional thesis:

> Given this fascination with gold, it is hard to accept the experts' opinion—those of Chaudhuri, Perlin, Richards—that India did not have a strong propensity for hoarding gold, but needed silver imports to use as money. . . . It is difficult to accept the argument of the experts that the East is no different from the West. (Kindleberger 1989: 63, 64)

I find it difficult to accept Kindleberger's skepticism, which seems based in part on his claim that gold was never used as money in India, which at least for the south of India is not true. Moreover, albeit referring to copper coin, money had a "startling velocity and range of circulation . . . [and] travelled from the outer frontier provinces of the empire to its heartland within one year of minting. This is a startling feature of the Mughal system," which also contradicts "anyone accustomed to thinking of ordinary coin as circulating within circumscribed localities and regions" (Richards 1987: 6–7).

Kindleberger continues:

> What needs to be explained is why the silver stops when it comes to China. . . . It is hard in the light of this admittedly spotty and anecdotal evidence [of nonmonetary use mostly of gold in China] to share the conclusion of the experts that the Chinese appetite for silver was dominated by monetization and that the notion that the Chinese hoarded more that other countries is questionable. Monetization was important, especially in taxation. . . . (Kindleberger 1989: 71)

Despite this contemporary monetary expert's best efforts (including numerous references to anecdotes in newspapers from the 1930s to the 1980s) to keep the hoary old hoarding thesis alive, Kindleberger is unable to offer either a convincing theory or any persuasive evidence against the "argument of the experts that the East is no different from the West."

Perhaps even more alarming is the recent echo of the hoary hoarding thesis by Wallerstein (1980: 108–9): not only does he write (citing a 1962 source for the single quotes that follow) that "coin or bullion brought into Asia (and Russia) was largely used 'for hoarding or jewellery' and the 'balance of trade' (if one refuses to think of silver as a commodity) was *persistently* unfavourable and largely bilateral for a long period of time." But to make matters still worse, he continues in the very next sentence: "These two facts are precisely evidence that the East Indies remained *external* to the European world-economy. . . . [That is] the distinction between trade within the capitalist world-economy and trade between any particular world-system and its external arena [his emphasis]." I say "alarming" in two senses of the word. First, this Wallerstein citation in and of itself should be sufficient to alarm us about the limitations of his *European* world-economy/system perspective and theory, which renders him and others unable to take account of the real world, as I already argued with voluminous chapter and verse citations from both him and Fernand Braudel in Frank (1994, 1995). Om Prakash (1995: 8–9) also remarks that there is no good theoretical or empirical basis for Wallerstein's contention that the influx of the same silver served and was necessary for the expansion of investment and capitalism in Europe but that in Asia it could have had no more than a decorative function for the aristocracy.

However, it is also alarming that Wallerstein's European blinders seem to oblige him both to be blind to and to misinterpret the very evidence which otherwise itself would pull the rug out from under his own theory. For, contrary to Wallerstein, the world-wide flow of money to Asia and Russia is evidence precisely that they *were* parts of the same world economy as Europe and the Americas.

INFLATION OR PRODUCTION IN THE QUANTITY THEORY OF MONEY

The injection of new American (overwhelmingly silver) bullion and also Japanese silver and copper provided new liquidity and credit formation. That in turn facilitated an important, perhaps dramatic, increase in worldwide production, which rose to meet the new monetary demand. This "pull" factor therefore encouraged further industrial success and development in China, India, Southeast Asia, and West Asia (including Persia). As Chaudhuri observed,

> the economies of the two great empires of Asia benefited from the expansion of economic relations with the West. The huge influx of bullion . . . was only one indication of the growth in income and employment. The export of textiles turned the coastal provinces of India into major industrial regions, and the bullion imported by the Companies passed directly into circulation as payment for the exported goods. (Chaudhuri 1978: 462)

A favorite economist's tool is the Fisher equation $MV = PT$. That means that the (increase in) the quantity of Money multiplied by the Velocity of its circulation in use equals the (increase of) the Prices of goods and services, multiplied by the (increase of) the Transactions of their production and sale. The quantity theory of money has it that if the quantity of money increases while its velocity and the number of transactions stay the same, then the prices of the goods and services transacted must rise proportionately to the increase in money. Hamilton and others observed that in the sixteenth century new American money arrived in Europe, and prices rose. That was called the great "price revolution." Ceaseless debates have ensued about whether the amount of new money that arrived was really what Hamilton had calculated it to be, whether the velocity of its circulation changed as well, to what extent production and transactions also increased, in what sequence these events occurred, and therefore what really explains the rise of prices in Europe—and how much they really rose, and just when. Jack Goldstone (1991a, b) reviews many of the arguments and makes a persuasive case that the price inflation in Europe (outside of Spain) was generated by increases in population and demand rather than by new supplies of money from the Americas.

The debate spilled over also to refer to Asia, first because some of the American money left Europe again, and second because it arrived in Asia and thereby also increased the supply of money there. So the question becomes whether the new American money and/or population increases also generated inflation in Asia.

The effects of the new money on prices in India have been the subject of dispute. Aziza Hasan (1994) argues that silver imports did lead to price inflation. Her estimates show silver in circulation tripling between 1592, when inflows became significant, and 1639. Since production could not have kept this pace, prices must have risen, she reasons. After also examining price changes for a few commodities, though "we have little information about the prices of commodities of mass consumption" (Hasan 1994: 175), Hasan concludes that there was a significant price inflation. As we will see, Irfan Habib and others share this thesis at least in part.

However, Brenning (1983) challenges the thesis that India, like Europe earlier, was visited by a "price revolution" in the seventeenth century. Rather, Brenning contends, although there were brief periods of price rises in the 1620s and again the mid-1650s and 1660s, on the whole prices remained fairly stable at other times and only rose moderately over the whole seventeenth century. Indeed after their mid-century increase, prices stabilized after 1670 just when silver imports again accelerated. Brenning (1983: 493) appeals to "powerful local developments affecting regional monetary history," but he does not spell them out. However, even Habib (1987: 138–89) equivocates on whether there indeed was inflation and, if so, how so:

> The problem of the impact of the seventeenth-century silver "inflation" on the structure of Mughal Indian economy cannot be elucidated properly until one is able to establish in what coined metal, and at what time, payments were being made. There is the further question of whether the quantities of silver flowing into the country caused a rise in the price-level (or a depreciation in the value of silver) approximately proportionate to the additions they were making to the existing stock. (Habib 1987: 139)

Habib himself is otherwise inclined. Prices in terms of silver did not rise proportionately with its increased supply, and prices and wages in terms of the more commonly used copper did not rise at all. As silver became increasingly available, it declined in value relative to copper and in the seventeenth century increasingly replaced it as the medium of exchange. Moreover, the demand for copper was increased by its use to make bronze cannons. Moreover, Habib stresses that the influx of silver also reduced its price relative to that of gold. The value of the rupee certainly declined in terms of silver and gold, and it first rose and then also declined in terms of copper. "The agreement between the earlier trends in agricultural and silver prices is remarkable" (Habib 1963a: 89).

This evidence and analysis weakens even further the thesis that India suffered from inflation, since prices of goods were more a reflection of the reduced price of silver as a commodity itself (measured against gold and copper currency) rather than of a generalized inflationary price rise of all commodities. Indeed, Prakash (1995: 13) observes that "a considerable body of work done over the last two decades . . . has consistently negated the possibility of a general price rise." Rene Barendse's (1997) study relating to the Dutch VOC also shows no overall inflationary increase in Indian prices or wages. The most systematic inquiry into the prices of precious metals is Sanjay Subrahmanyam's (1994) review of previous writers and of the evidence in general as well as that specifically for Bengal, Surat, Masulipatam, and Agra. He also concludes that

> overall then, the Indian evidence suggests that price inflation was at best sporadic, and limited to specific regions and specific commodities. . . . The case for a Price Revolution remains unproven. . . . The empirical materials do not support such a hypothesis. . . . [Indeed] rates of interest . . . showed a downward trend. (Subrahmanyam 1994: 209, 53–54)

Moreover, Subrahmanyam also reviews the analogous discussion for the Ottoman Empire and comes to the same conclusion, amended by Goldstone's (1991a) thesis that population growth pushed prices up. Elsewhere, Goldstone (1991b) argues similarly that inflation was maintained at low levels and that it was practically nonexistent in China, except during the mid-seventeenth century. The reason is that increases in output and velocity of circulation absorbed the growth in the supply of money. He also suspects substantial hoarding, or at least sterilization of silver, in Europe through use as conspicuous consumption in the form of silverware and plates. Of course, as usual, he attributes inflation to population growth. (We return to these issues in chapter 5.)

In China also, production and population increased, but the new money did not drive up prices significantly faster than the growth of population. Even for highly monetized South China, Marks (1997a, 1996) and Marks and Chunsheng (1995) found that, apart from some brief temporary periods of rapid inflation in the price of rice, over the centuries the rise in rice prices closely matched that of the growth of population; and the prices of other commodities tended to decrease. Moreover, they cite the findings of other scholars to the effect that "virtually all households responded to high [purchase] prices by reducing fertility and to low prices by increasing fertility." Therefore, "if all Chinese peasants controlled their fertility in response to economic condi-

tions, then the rise in population . . . may well have been a direct response to significant advances in economic growth." Although their
reference is to the eighteenth and nineteenth centuries, the same can
hold equally for earlier centuries as well.

To conclude this review of whether there was inflation or not in Asia
in general, we must agree with Subrahmanyam:

> In the absence of widespread and rapid inflation of commodity
> prices in terms of major coinage metals in south and west Asia (at
> least at rates corresponding to the inflation of western Europe), it
> is evident that the rate of increase of money supply must largely
> be decomposed in terms of the rate of change of output, and that
> of the inverse of the income-velocity of money. (Subrahmanyam
> 1994: 218)

"The weight of the evidence" suggests there was no inflation in southern India (Subrahmanyam 1990a: 349) nor in Bengal, as Richard Eaton
(1993: 204–6) stresses. Nor was there sustained inflation in China, to
which we will return below.

That is, in terms of the $MV = PT$ Fisher equation, the evidence
suggests strongly that throughout most of Asia the increased arrival of
money from the Americas and Japan did not substantially raise prices,
as it did in Europe. In Asia instead, the infusion of additional new
money generated increased production and transactions, as well as rais-
ing the velocity of money circulation through more extensive commercialization of the economy. What might be argued is that in proportion
to the size of its population and economy, Europe not only received
but even retained more new money that circulated around its economy
than was the case in the much larger and more populous Asia. That
might account for some of the higher rate of inflation in the European
than in the Asian economies. Yet, not even this reasoning would be
sufficient to undercut the present argument that the new money served
to increase production and also population more in Asia, as we argue
in chapters 4 and 6.

Moreover, prices should have risen more in Asia if Goldstone
(1991a,b) is right that the growth of population more than that of the
money supply drives prices up. But population rose significantly faster
and more in Asia and especially in China than in Europe, as we note in
chapter 2 and document in chapter 4. Yet the real price revolution was
essentially limited to Europe. This observation lends further support to
our inferential argument that the massive arrival of new American and

Japanese money stimulated production and population more in Asia than in Europe. However, there is also direct evidence that this money stimulated the expansion of production, settlement, and population in Asia, and how it did so.

MONEY EXPANDED THE FRONTIERS OF SETTLEMENT AND PRODUCTION

The evidence and reasoning about prices discussed above lends support to the thesis that the inflow of money stimulated expansion both of consumer demand for and the productive supply of goods in Asia. Let us examine some of the direct evidence as well.

In India. In India, the expansion of production was most strikingly evident in Bengal and Bihar after their conquest by and incorporation into the Mughal empire (Richards 1987: 5). Indeed, among prices in India, those in Bengal were relatively low and remained stable between 1657 and 1714, despite the large inflow of silver money from abroad (Prakash 1994: V-165). Prakash attempts various possible explanations in terms of the quantity theory of money. If the large increase in the supply of money did not evoke a corresponding increase in prices, it must have been because the velocity of circulation or turnover of the money supply increased with the progressive monetization of the economy and/or the amount of production increased. Prakash concludes that although increased money turnover may have absorbed or sterilized some of the increase in its supply, output must also have increased either through a better utilization of installed capacity to produce and/or through improved allocation of resources. However, Prakash does not seem to consider the possibility, indeed the probability, that production also rose as more resources were mobilized and productive capacity and production itself were increased. Yet he estimates that the number of workers in the Bengali textile industry grew to one million, of which no more than 10 percent were engaged in production for export by the British and Dutch East India companies (Prakash 1994: vii-175, 197). So the bulk of the productive expansion must have been for a combination of the Asian-managed internal and export markets. To give credit where credit is due, more recently Prakash (1995: 13) does refer to growing population and "a substantial net increase in output, income and employment. A rising output would occasion a growing need for money." However, he sees these as the counterpart of an increase in exports, and even in this passage he still regards the "need for money" as derivative from the increase in output.

Moreover, after the Mughal decline and its regional replacement by Maharashtra rule, "the use of money, not barter, had spread to all levels of society in Maharashtra, and secondly, . . . all rural folk were tied into larger regional and world economies by a wcb of moncy, credit and market transactions" (Richards 1987: 11). Richards is commenting on the findings of Perlin (1987, 1993), who himself summarizes that "briefly the documents [very detailed and prolonged research in private and governmental accounts of an extremely local level of economic life] reveal a society in which monetisation had developed to a relatively remarkable extent [accessible to relatively large numbers of people], and in marked contrast to what we know of conditions in early colonial times" (Perlin 1993: 178–89). Elsewhere Perlin (1983: 75) is more specific:

> Villagers . . . not only engaged in local market transactions in money, but were also paid daily and monthly money wages for agricultural labour, craft production, soldiery, and household service. I would argue that the import of copper and cowries indicates precisely the existence of vigorous, highly monetized, local market centres of this kind. . . . It is also important to demonstrate that such monetary "communications" also integrated areas primarily concerned with agricultural production with the rest of the subcontinent, and thereby with events and relationships on an international scale. . . . But it is also important to underline the fact that documentation exists with which to test it, although [it is] as yet astonishingly neglected. (Perlin 1983: 75, 74)

However, Perlin (1983: 78) also observes that "in contrast, early colonial rule led to a substantial reduction in the level of monetary life." B. R. Grover (1994: 252) also observes that with the onset of British colonialism, there is a "definite deterioration in the commercial life in India, in comparison to conditions in the seventeenth century."

The question is how this money fertilized—indeed opened up—the fields of agriculture, oiled the wheels of manufacturing, and of course greased the palms of trade into the farther reaches and among "subsistence" peasants. In Keynesian terms, the new means of payment generated new effective demand and thereby called forth additional production also in the domestic markets in Asia.

Eaton (1993) examines the spread of Islam in tandem with deforestation to clear the way to grow cotton for—and rice to feed the workers in—the textile industry in Bengal. The frontier was colonized to supply the growing Bengali production and export of textiles in the sixteenth and again at the end of the seventeenth and beginning of the eighteenth centuries. However, all of these, including the initial clearing of the jungle (as in the Amazon today) were financed by "countless intermediaries who were, in effect, capitalist speculators, or classical revenue farmers" (Eaton 1993: 221). They funneled the expanding supply of money, which was derived from the influx of silver from the outside, into the interior and even to the frontier of Bengal.

However, Bengal was only the newest frontier that was opened up and made productive with—if not by!—the new money; it was by no means the only one.

> Extensive tracts of country became populated and settled by peasant populations during this long period, not only in the upland regions of the Deccan, but even in the Ganges basin itself; in Gujarat, where the countryside became more intensely settled, new villages were established, and the interstices between old ones filled in. As Hambly remarks in *The Cambridge Economic History of India*, it was also a period of accelerated urban growth at all levels, from small market town to major concentrations such as Agra. . . . The Punjab became an important centre of textile production, its products finding their way to the Middle East, Persia and central Asia. . . . Hambly has recently remarked that urban growth in the seventeenth and eighteenth centuries was closely linked to the development of textile production. (Perlin 1983: 67, 71)

The development of textile production and the growth, distribution and processing of cotton and dyes for textile production, and of course the production and distribution of food for the producers and traders, were all stimulated or even rendered possible by the massive infusion of new money. This influx of silver and the growing demand it generated was not inflationary precisely because they stimulated a concomitant increase in supply. The "long sixteenth century" cyclical expansion began in about 1400 and continued well into the eighteenth century. There was no "seventeenth-century crisis," as we observe in chapter 5.

In China. Probably even more spectacular were the economically expansive effects of the infusion of silver into the Chinese economy from the mid-sixteenth century onward. The Ming economy was increasingly monetized on a silver standard and expanded rapidly

at least through the 1620s. This expansion was only temporarily interrupted during the climatological/demographic/economic/political crisis
and change from the Ming to Qing dynasties in the middle of the century (examined in chapter 5). However, the economy recovered again
and resumed its expansion from the late seventeenth century onward
through the eighteenth century.

The stimulatory and expansive effects of silver and trade were most
dramatically notable in South China. Suffice it here to offer only a tip-
of-the-iceberg indication of commercialization and economically rational choice in South China: in Marks's (1997a) study, a contemporary
governor general is quoted as asserting that "all trade is conducted in
silver, and it circulates throughout the province." Merchants advanced
capital (presumably also derived directly or indirectly from exports and
the import of silver) to peasant producers in return for later receipt of
their crop (Marks 1997a). Marks offers numerous summary accounts,
among which the following two are particularly revealing:

> The silver flowed back to China [in return for its exports]. . . . By
> 1600, this trade resulted in an annual inflow of perhaps two hun-
> dred thousand kilograms of silver into the coastal economies of
> south and southeast China, from Ningpo south to Guangzhou.
> The increased demand for silk induced significant changes in land
> use patterns . . . [and] by 1700 about half of the forest cover had
> been removed [to cultivate mulberry trees as food for silk worms,
> cotton, sugar, and rice in the low lands and maize and sweet pota-
> toes on higher ground]. (Marks 1996: 60, 59)

> The Nanyang [South China Sea] demand was mostly for Chinese
> manufactured goods produced either in or around areas like Gu-
> angzhou [Canton], or gathered in that great emporium from
> other parts of the empire. The impact of increased export trade
> upon Lingnan's [South China] agricultural economy was indirect,
> mediated by the need to import raw cotton: rather than growing
> cotton, peasant farmers grew sugar cane which, after being refined
> and processes, was exchanged for cotton from central and north-
> ern China. After being spun and woven, much of the cotton was
> then exported to Nanyang. The increased demand for cotton tex-
> tiles thus drove the substitution of sugar cane for rice [in the same
> irrigated fields, while producing cotton would have required
> clearing another kind of land and although that] . . . did not result
> in [or require] the clearance of more land to grow sugar cane for
> sale in the market, it did decrease the amount of rice produced in
> and around the Pearl River delta, and thus increased the market

demand for rice. A similar conversion of rice paddies to a non-food, commercial crop occurred when the demand for silk increased. (Marks 1997a)

That is, it was economically rational—and market-institutionally quite feasible—that "peasant farmers who responded to the commercial impulse did so by converting existing rice paddies to sugar cane or sericulture, rather than clearing or creating new fields on which to grow commercial crops [like cotton]" (Marks 1997a). The institutional aspects of this process are examined further in chapter 4.

Thus, in South China the process was analogous to that in Bengal. The agricultural and settlement frontiers expanded along with their commercialization, stimulated by demand from the outside which also generated local demand—and supply—and which were financed by the inflow of new money from abroad.

Elsewhere in Asia. An analogous process also occurred in both mainland and island Southeast Asia, as documented and analyzed by Reid (1993). Moreover, as Victor Lieberman, a student especially of mainland Southeast Asia, writes of the sixteenth and seventeenth centuries,

Larger domestic aggregate demand and the extension of settlement to frontier zones with unique agricultural and mineral products encouraged internal exchange, as reflected in the proliferation of local markets, growing interprovincial complementarity, and monetization . . . [including the] diffusion of "capital" cultures into the countryside, and the simultaneous infiltration of some provincial forms of capital usage. Maritime trade, firearms, and imported bullion reenforced and modified these processes in complex ways. . . .

[the] eighteenth century saw either a resumption or acceleration of population growth, land reclamation, and commercial exchange in key sectors of the mainland. These movements drew strength both from external demand, most obviously in Thailand and southern Vietnam and . . . from a constellation of internal forces similar to those which operated before 1680.

(Lieberman 1996: 800–801, 802)

In Japan also, silver and copper production expanded rapidly during this period and supported exceptional growth in agricultural and manu-facturing production, construction, urbanization, commerce, and commercialization (except for the 1630s and 1640s, two decades of climatic problems and monetary and economic difficulties examined in chapter 5). A sixteenth-century writer observed that by then there was no one "even among peasants and rustics . . . who have not handled gold and silver aplenty" (cited in Atwell 1990: 667). The observer may have exaggerated, but the tendency is confirmed by other contemporary observers, whose accounts all indicate that, when these contemporary observers wrote, monetization, commercialization, and economic growth had significantly grown to greater levels in Japan—even during their own lifetimes. Moreover, Ikeda (1996) also cites Japanese research to the effect that European trade, which means more than anything the money the Europeans brought, increased production and migration *within* Asia and for *intra*-Asian trade.

Regarding the Ottoman Empire and the world economy, a number of authors in the volume edited by Huri Islamoglu-Inan (1987) refer to inflation; but only one, Murat Cizakca, investigates it. And his findings seem to disconfirm the others' allegations about inflation and instead help confirm my general thesis that it was not so much prices as production that rose in Asia. Cizakca shows that this "supply-side" expansion of production and population was also visible during the sixteenth and seventeenth centuries in the Ottoman lands. He makes a detailed study of prices in the silk industry in Bursa between 1550 and 1650. He does indeed find sharply increasing prices in the first half of this period. But they are limited to raw silk, and they stabilize again in the seventeenth century, although European silver continued to arrive. Yet, silk-cloth prices remained remarkably stable over even more than this entire period (Cizakca 1987: 249–51). Cizakca's own "interpretation of [the] observations . . . [and] conclusion" are that the initial rise of the price of silk itself was due primarily increased European demand, which the new supply of silver permitted the latter to buy also from Turkey. This European demand may have fallen off again during Europe's "seventeenth-century crisis." On the other hand, Cizakca explains "the relatively small increase in silk-cloth prices" in that "the increase in prices was retarded by a considerable increase in the supply of cloth . . . [in particular] the domestic supply of cloth may have increased as a result of internal developments, such as the expansion of traditional urban or rural industries" (Cizakca 1987: 254).

In summary, the evidence suggests that the growing supply of new money especially from the Americas and Japan stimulated production and supported population growth in many parts of Asia. I suggest that we can and should similarly interpret the economic expansions of the Ottoman Empire (especially in Anatolia and the Levant), of the Safavid empire in Persia, and of course also of Russian expansion and settlement in Siberia. Also noteworthy is Steensgaard's (1990c: 18 ff.) observation that major states in Eurasia responded to extraordinary fiscal strains with almost simultaneous fiscal reforms in the late sixteenth century: Japan, China, India, the Ottomans, France, Spain. The only common factor he can see to account for this "coincidence" is the sudden increase in the money supply, although (related?) increases in population and in production may have been other factors. Moreover, we observe in chapters 5 and 6 below that this economic expansion continued right through the seventeenth and much of the eighteenth centuries.

Another observation is most significant for challenging received Eurocentric perspectives and interpretations of developments in this period. The evidence suggests that the new money which the Europeans brought over from the Americas probably stimulated production and supported population growth *more* in many parts of Asia than it did in Europe itself. This conclusion is supported by at least two observations. One is that the new money drove prices up more in Europe than in Asia, where increased production was better able to keep pace with the growing purchasing power generated by the additional money. The reservation to this observation is only that per capita more new money arrived in Europe and less in Asia. However, the comparative examination of the development of population, production, trade, and technology in chapter 4 can help to allay this reservation.

Moreover, a second observation here can help neutralize this reservation and in turn strengthen the proposition about Asia's continued superiority over Europe: as we see in chapter 6, population grew *more* in Asia, where it rose by about 6 percentage points of the world total, than in Europe where it remained stable (about 20 percent of the world total). Yet in 1750, Asia's still less than 66 percent of world population produced 80 percent of world GNP (see chapters 4 and 6). That suggests Asians must have been *more* productive than Europeans, Africans, and Americans. This is consistent with the thesis in the present chapter that the new money was able to stimulate production more in Asia than in Europe, precisely because the Asian economies were *more* flexible and productive than the European ones. More evidence in support of this proposition is supplied in the next chapter.

CHAPTER 4

The Global Economy

Comparisons and Relations

---

*Although it is difficult to "measure" the economic output of early modern Asia . . .
every scrap of information that comes to light confirms a far greater scale of
enterprise and profit in the East than in the West. Thus Japan, in the second half of
the sixteenth century, was the world's leading exporter of silver and copper, her 55,000
miners surpassing the output of Peru for the former and for Sweden of the latter.
Though Western sources tend to stress the role of eight or so Dutch ships which docked
in Japan each year, in fact the eighty or so junks from China were far more
important. It was the same in south-east Asia: the Europeans . . . [and] their ships
were outnumbered ten-to-one by Chinese vessels; and the Europeans' cargoes
consisted in the main, not of Western wares but of Chinese porcelain and silk.*

*The output of both commodities was stunning. In Nanking alone, the ceramic
factories produced a million pieces of fine glazed pottery every year, much of it
specifically designed for export—those for Europe bore dynastic motifs, while those for
Islamic countries displayed tasteful abstract patterns. . . . In India, the city of
Kasimbazar in Bengal produced, just by itself, over 2 million pounds of raw silk
annually during the 1680s, while cotton weavers of Gujarat in the west turned out
almost 3 million pieces a year for export alone. By way of comparison, the annual
export of silk from Messina . . . Europe's foremost silk producer[,] was a mere 250,000
pounds . . . while the largest textile enterprise in Europe, the Leiden "new drapery,"
produced less than 100,000 pieces of cloth per year. Asia, not Europe, was the centre of
world industry throughout early modern times. It was likewise the home of the
greatest states. The most powerful monarchs of their day were not Louis XIV or Peter
the Great, but the Manchu emperor K'ang-hsi (1662–1722) and the "Great Moghul"
Aurangzeb (1658–1707).*

The Times Illustrated History of the World (1995: 206)

Quantities: Population, Production, Productivity, Income, and Trade

The so-called European hegemony in the modern world system was very late in developing and was quite incomplete and never unipolar. In reality, during the period 1400–1800, sometimes regarded as one of "European expansion" and "primitive accumulation" leading to full capitalism, the world economy was still very predominantly under Asian influences. The Chinese Ming/Qing, Turkish Ottoman, Indian Mughal, and Persian Safavid empires were economically and politically very powerful and only waned vis-à-vis the Europeans toward the end of this period and thereafter. Therefore, if anything, the modern world system was under Asian hegemony, not European. Likewise, much of the real dynamism of the world economy lay in Asia throughout this period, not in Europe. Asians were preponderant in the world economy and system not only in population and production, but also in productivity, competitiveness, trade, in a word, capital formation until 1750 or 1800. Moreover, contrary to latter-day European mythology, Asians had the technology and developed the economic and financial institutions to match. Thus, the "locus" of accumulation and power in the modern world system did not really change much during those centuries. China, Japan, and India in particular ranked first overall, with Southeast Asia and West Asia not far behind. The deficitary Europe was clearly of less significance than Asia in the world economy in all respects. Moreover, its economy was based on imports and not on exports, which were the sine qua non of industrial ascendance, then as now. It is also difficult to detect even any significant change in the relative position among the Asian powers, Europe included. Europe did not emerge as a Newly Industrializing Economy (NIE) challenging Asia until the late eighteenth and early nineteenth centuries. Only then and not before did the world economic center of gravity began to shift to Europe.

The preponderance of Asian economic agents in Asia and of Asia itself in the world economy has been masked not only by the attention devoted to "the rise of the West" in the world, but also by the undue focus on European economic and political penetration of Asia. This chapter will document and emphasize how very out of focus this perspective of European expansion is in real world terms. However, the argument is not and cannot remain confined to mere comparisons between Europe and Asia or its principal economies in China and India.

The analytically necessary emphasis must be shifted to the worldwide economic *relations,* in productivity, technology, and their enabling and supporting economic and financial institutions, which developed on a global scale—not just on a regional, let alone European, scale. Contrary to the Eurocentric perspective, the Europeans did not in any sense "create" the world economic system itself nor develop world "capitalism."

POPULATION, PRODUCTION, AND INCOME

Data on world and regional population growth before the nineteenth century, or even the twentieth, are admittedly speculative. Examination of a sizable variety of sources and the relatively small variations in their estimates nonetheless affords a clear and very revealing picture of world and comparative regional population growth rates. Still used are the estimates for the seventeenth and eighteenth centuries by A. M. Carr-Saunders (1936) and his revisions of Walter Willcox (1931), who in turn also revised his own earlier estimates (see Willcox 1940). Carr-Saunders's work has been slightly modified in various publications of the Population Division of the United Nations (1953, 1954, and later). Colin Clark (1977) constructs estimates using the above plus nine other sources; his tabulation is summarized below in table 4.2. M. K. Bennett (1954) relies on many of the same sources as well as others to make his own estimates. His data are the most comprehensive and detailed and are the source for table 4.1. These estimates were compared and found to be very similar to a variety of others that are not specifically used here and whose sources are not cited, if only because they group their regions differently (for instance including all of Asiatic Russia in "Europe"). However, the estimates are checked for the key year 1750 by comparing them with John Durand's (1967, 1974) evaluations of many population series, as well as against those by Wolfgang Kollman (1965) reproduced in Rainer Mackensen and Heinze Wewer (1973).

All of these world and regional population growth estimates reveal essentially the same significant story, so that we will not err much by using the figures from Bennett (1954). World (as well as European) population declined in the fourteenth century and resumed its upward growth from 1400 onward. World population grew by about 20 percent in the fifteenth century and by about 10 percent in the sixteenth century (all figures cited here are rounded percentages of the totals listed in table 4.1). However, subtracting the precipitous post-Columbian population decline in the Americas (which these tables

Table 4.1 *World and Regional Population Growth (in millions, rounded)*

Region	Year										
	1000	1200	1300	1400	1500	1600	1650	1700	1750	1800	1850
Europe	42	62	73	45	69	89	100	115	140	188	266
All Asia	168	203	216	224	254	292	319	402	508	612	743
Asiatic Russia	3	7	8	9	11	13	14	15	16	17	19
Southwest Asia	32	34	33	27	29	30	30	31	32	33	34
India	48	51	50	46	54	68	80	100	130	157	190
China (major)	70	89	99	112	125	140	150	205	270	345	430
Japan	4	8	11	14	16	20	23	27	32	28	33
Southeast Asia,	11	14	15	16	19	21	22	24	28	32	37
Africa	50	61	67	74	82	90	90	90	90	90	95
The Americas	13	23	28	30	41	15	9	10	11	29	59
World Total	275	348	384	373	446	486	518	617	749	919	1,163

SOURCE: M. K. Bennett (1954: table 1)

underestimate in comparison to the more than 90 percent decline cited in chapter 2), in the rest of the world population still grew by 16 percent in the sixteenth century. Then world population growth accelerated to 27 percent in the seventeenth century, or 29 percent outside of the Americas. The mid-seventeenth century seems to have been a period of inflection and even further acceleration, so that in the century from 1650 to 1750 world population growth increased to 45 percent. These significant increases in world population growth were supported by concomitant increases in production, which were fueled by increases in the world supply and distribution of money, as argued in chapter 3.

The regional distribution and variation in this population growth is significant as well. In the fifteenth and sixteenth centuries, population growth was relatively fast in Europe at 53 and 28 percent respectively, so that Europe's share of world population rose from 12 percent in 1400 to 18 percent in 1600. After that however, the European share of world population remained almost stable at 19 percent until 1750, when it finally began to increase to 20 percent in 1800 and 23 percent by 1850. Yet at the same time from 1600 onward, population rose more and faster in Asia. Having been about 60 percent of world population in the fifteenth and sixteenth centuries, Asia's share of world population rose from 60 percent in 1600 to 65 percent in 1700, 66 percent in 1750, and 67 percent in 1800, according to Bennett's estimates. That is because population grew at about 0.6 percent a year in the previously already more densely populated Asia, while in Europe it grew at only 0.4 percent per year. According to the later figure of Livi-Bacci (1992: 68), the rate of population growth in Europe was only 0.3 percent. That is, in relative terms Europe population grew at only half or two-thirds of what it did in the much larger Asia, where absolute growth was of course much greater still. This faster growth of population in Asia is also confirmed by Clark (1977), whose estimates of the Asian shares of world population are about 54 percent in 1500, 60 percent in 1600, and 1650, and 66 percent for 1700, 1750, and 1800. Mackensen and Wewer (1973) and Durand (1967, 1974) also confirm the 66 percent estimate for the share of all of Asia for 1750.

Moreover, population growth was even faster in Asia's most important regions and economies: 45 percent from 1600 to 1700 and even 90 percent over the century and a half from 1600 to 1750 in China and Japan, and 47 and 89 percent in India during the same periods—compared with 38 and 74 percent respectively in all of Asia, and only 29 and 57 percent in Europe. Clark's estimates (see table 4.2) suggest

Table 4.2 *World Population (in millions, rounded)*

Year	1200	1500	1600	1650	1700	1750	1800
World	348	427	498	516	641	731	890
Europe	51	68	83	90	106	130	173
Asia	248	231	303	311	420	484	590
China	123	100	150	100	150	207	315
Japan	12	16	18	22	26	26	26
India	75	79	100	150	200	200	190
Africa	61	85	95	100	100	100	100
Americas	23	41	15	13	13	15	25
Oceania	1	2	2	2	2	2	2

SOURCE: Colin Clark (1977: table 3.1)

Clark's table 3.1 also includes estimates for A.D. 14, 350, 600, 800, 1000, and 1340 as well as additional detail since 1500.

an even greater gap in population growth rates: 100 percent in India from 1600 to 1750, and after its mid-century crisis (see chapter 5), also in China from 1650 to 1750, compared with only 56 and 44 percent during the same periods in Europe. Only in the rest of Asia, that is in Central Asia (partly represented by Asiatic Russia in table 4.1), and West and Southeast Asia, was population growth slower, at 9 and 19 percent. For Southeast Asia, Bennett estimates 28 million in 1750 and 32 million in 1800, while Clark suggests 32 million and 40 million for the same dates but is apparently including Ceylon. Durand (1974) regards even this last estimate as too low. Thus for the 1600–1750 period, Southeast Asian population growth would have been 33 percent according to Bennett (table 4.1) and 100 percent according to Clark (table 4.2), that is the same as in China and India, which seems more reasonable from the evidence of their close economic relations reviewed in chapter 2. According to Durand's (1974) suggestion, population growth in Southeast Asia was higher still, and thus would also have been much higher than in Europe during this same 1600–1750/1800 period.

Thus, population grew more slowly only in West and perhaps in Central Asia, and in Africa; and it was of course negative in the Americas. Total African population remained stable at 90 million (other estimates, including table 4.2, suggest stability at 100 million) over the three centuries from 1500 to 1800 and therefore was a declining share of world totals. As a result of the Columbian "encounter" and "exchange" of course, in the Americas population declined absolutely by at least 75 percent (but by 90 percent according to the more careful estimates cited in chapter 2). Therefore it declined relative to the growing world total between 1500 and 1650, and then grew only slowly till 1750.

In summary, and all variations and doubts about population estimates notwithstanding, during the period from 1400 until 1750 or even 1800 population grew much faster in Asia, and especially in China and India, than in Europe. Alas, we lack estimates of total and regional production for this same period, but it stands to reason that this much faster population growth in Asia can have been possible only if its production also grew faster to support its population growth. The theoretical possibility that production or income per capita nonetheless remained stable in Asia and/or declined relative to those in Europe seems implausible in view of our review in chapter 2, and is empirically disconfirmed by the estimates below of world total and comparative regional production in GNP terms and per capita incomes.

Hard data on global production and income are of course also hard to come by for this period, both because they are difficult to find or construct and because few people have been interested to do so. However, a number of scholars have taken the trouble to construct estimates for part of the eighteenth century because they have wanted to use them as a base line to measure more recent Western and world economic growth, in which there is more interest. So much the better for us, since these estimates also offer some indication of world and regional production and income for at least the end of our period.

Braudel (1992) cites world and regional GNP estimates by Paul Bairoch for 1750. Total world GNP was US $155 billion (measured in 1960 US dollars), of which $120 billion or 77 percent was in "Asia" and $35 billion in all the "West," meaning Europe and the Americas, but also including Russia and Japan because of how Bairoch grouped his estimates (to highlight subsequent growth in the "West"). If we reallocate Japan and Siberian Russia to Asia, its share of world GNP was then surely over 80 percent. Out of $148 billion GNP in 1750, Bairoch himself allocates $112 billion or 76 percent to what is in the "Third" World today, including Latin America, and $35 billion or 24 percent to the countries that are today "developed," including Japan. For 1800, after the beginning of the industrial revolution in England, Bairoch's corresponding estimates are a total of $183 billion, of which $137 billion or 75 percent were in the part of the world that is today underdeveloped. Only $47 billion, or only 33 percent of world GNP, was in what are today's industrialized countries (Bairoch and Levy-Leboyer 1981: 5). More than another half-century later in 1860, total GNP had risen to $280 billion, and the respective amounts were $165 billion or almost 60 percent for today's "Third" World and $115 billion or still only just over 40 percent for the now developed countries (recalculated from Braudel 1992: 534).

Thus, in 1750 and in 1800 Asian production was much greater, and it was more productive and competitive than anything the Europeans and the Americas were able to muster, even with the help of the gold and silver they brought from the Americas and Africa. If Asia produced some 80 percent of world output at the end of our period in the eighteenth century, we can only speculate on what the proportions may have been at the beginning or in the middle of that four-hundred-year period. Were they the same, because over four hundred years production in Afro-Asia and Europe together with the Americas grew at the same rate? Or was the Western proportion lower and the Afro-Asian one even higher, because Europe grew faster and its American colonies threw their output into the balance? The comparative population growth rates cited above must incline us against either of these hypotheses. Rather the reverse, the Asian share of the world total was lower in the fifteenth century and then grew because the Asian economies grew even faster in the following centuries than the Europeans did. The evidence on relative population growth rates above, as well as scattered evidence in chapters 2 and 3, and our argument about higher inflation in Europe than in Asia, all support this last hypothesis: production also grew faster in Asia than in Europe! Moreover, if inflation and prices were higher in Europe than in Asia, perhaps they may also have introduced an upward bias into Bairoch's calculations of GNP in the West, relative to the East. In that case, the gap in real production and consumption between Asia and Europe and America may have been greater still than the 80:20 ratio cited above.

Particularly significant is the comparison of Asia's 66 percent share of population, confirmed by all above cited estimates for 1750, with its 80 percent share of production in the world at the same time. So, two-thirds of the world's people in Asia produced four-fifths of total world output, while the one-fifth of world population in Europe produced only part of the remaining one-fifth share of world production to which Africans and Americans also contributed. Therefore on average Asians *must* have been significantly more productive than Europeans in 1750! A fortiori, the most productive Asians in China and India, where population had also grown much faster, must have been that much more productive than the Europeans. In Japan between 1600 and 1800, population increased by only about 45 percent, but agricultural output doubled, so productivity must have increased substantially (Jones 1988: 155). By 1800, wages of cotton spinners, per capita income, life expectancy, and stature or height of people was similar in Japan and England, but by the early nineteenth century, average quality of life may have been higher in Japan than in Britain (Jones 1988: 160, 158).

Indeed, Bairoch's estimate of per capita GNP for China in 1800 is (1960) US $228, which compares rather well with his estimates for various years in the eighteenth century for England and France, which range from $150 to $200. By 1850, China's GNP had declined to $170 per capita, and of course India's GNP also declined in the nineteenth century and probably had already declined in the last half of the eighteenth century (Braudel 1992: 534).

Indeed, all per capita income estimates also disconfirm the Eurocentric prejudices of those who might wish to argue that the greater production observed for Asia only reflects its higher population compared to that of little Europe. Bairoch (1993) reviews estimates of worldwide differentials in per capita income. As late as 1700 to 1750 he finds a maximum worldwide differential of 1 to 2.5. However he also cites a later estimate of 1 to 1.24 by Simon Kuznets, estimates of 1 to 2.2 and 2.6 by David Landes, and 1 to 1.6 or 1.3 or even 1.1 by Angus Maddison. Bairoch also reviews seven other estimates including contemporary eighteenth-century views, and himself arrives at an estimate of 1 to 1.1, or virtual parity of incomes or standards of living around the world.

Perhaps the most important standard of living "index"—the years of expectancy of life itself—was similar among the various regions of Eurasia (Pomeranz 1997: chap. 1, pp. 8–12). It was certainly not low in China if septuagenarians were common—and in 1726 nearly one percent of the population was over seventy years of age, including some more than one hundred years old (Ho Ping ti 1959: 214).

According to estimates by Maddison (1991: 10), in 1400 per capita production or income were almost the same in China and Western Europe. For 1750 however, Bairoch found European standards of living *lower* than those in the rest of the world and especially in China, as he testifies again in Bairoch 1997 (quoted in chap. 1). Indeed, for 1800 he estimates income in the "developed" world at $198 per capita, in all the "underdeveloped" world at $188, but in China at $210 (Bairoch and Levy-Leboyer 1981: 14). Ho Ping-ti's (1959: 269, 213) population studies have already suggested that in the eighteenth century the standard of living in China was rising and peasant income was no lower than in France and certainly higher than in Prussia or indeed in Japan. Gilbert Rozman (1981: 139) also makes "international comparisons" and concludes that the Chinese met household needs at least as well as any other people in premodern times. Interestingly, even the per capita consumption of sugar seems to have been higher in China, which had to use its own resources to produce it, than in Europe, which was able to import it cheaply from its slave plantation colonies (Pomeranz 1997: chap. 2, pp. 11–15). For India, Immanuel Wallerstein (1989: 157–8) cites evidence from Ifran Habib, Percival Spear, and Ashok V. Desai, all to the effect that in the seventeenth century per capita agricultural output and standards of consumption were certainly not lower and probably higher than contemporary ones in Europe and certainly higher than Indian ones in the early and mid-twentieth century. Ken Pomeranz (1997) however suggests that European standards of consumption were higher than Asian ones.

That is, all available estimates of world and regional population, production, and income, as well as the discussion above on world trade, confirm that Asia and various of its regional economies were far more productive and competitive and had far and away more weight and influence in the global economy than any or all of the "West" put together until at least 1800. If this was not due only to Asia's greater population, as its ratios of population to production and its per capita income figures show indirectly and inferentially, how was this possible? Part of the answer lies in ample direct evidence on Asia's greater productivity and competitiveness in the world economy, to which we turn below. Moreover, Asia's preeminence was also rendered possible by technology and economic institutions, which we examine in the final two sections of this chapter.

PRODUCTIVITY AND COMPETITIVENESS

We have some direct evidence on Asia's absolute and relative productiveness and competitiveness, especially in industrial production and world trade. K. N. Chaudhuri (1978) rightly observes that the demand for industrial products, even in a pre-machine age, measures the extent of specialisation and the division of labour reached by a society. There is no question that from this point of view the Indian subcontinent and China possessed the most advanced and varied economies in Asia in the period from 1500 to 1750. (Chaudhuri 1978: 204–5)

Not only in Asia, however, but in the world!

It is clear that Asia's absorption of silver, and to a lesser extent gold for a limited period in the seventeenth century, was primarily the result of a relative difference in international production cost and prices. It was not until the large-scale application of machinery in the nineteenth century radically altered the structure of production costs that Europe was able to bridge the effect of the price differentials. (Chaudhuri 1978: 456)

Yet it has also been argued that Indian competitiveness in textiles was not so much due to more advanced or sophisticated mechanical productive equipment. Kanakalatha Mukund (1992) agues that the Indians' advantage lay in the highly developed skills of their (handicrafts) workers. That in turn was due in part to the also high degree of specialization in and subdivision among the various productive processes. Moreover, Indian competitiveness was also based on an organizational structure that permitted rapid flexible adaptation to shifting market demands for types and styles of textiles that were produced and exported. Additionally, India was preeminent in the growth and quality of its long-staple cotton and in the chemical technology and industry to dye it. Finally, costs of production were low because wages were low, because wage-good foodstuffs for the producers were cheap; and in turn that is because Indian agriculture produced them efficiently at low cost.

Chaudhuri summarizes some of the industrial production in Asia:

The three great crafts of Asian civilisations were of course textiles, cotton and silk, metal goods including jewellery, [and] ceramics and glassware. There were in addition a whole range of subsidiary craft manufactures which shared all the attributes of industrial technology and organization: paper, gunpowder, fireworks, bricks, musical instruments, furniture, cosmetics, perfumery; all these items were indispensable parts of daily life in most parts of Asia. . . . The surviving historical material, whether relating to the process of manufacturing or the system of distribution, shows quite clearly that most Asian craft industries involved intermediate stages, and the separation of functions was social as well as technical. In the textile industry before a single peace of chinz or muslim reached the hands of the public, it needed the services of farmers growing raw cotton, harvesters, those who ginned the cotton fibre, carders, spinners, weavers, bleachers, printers, painters, glazers, and repairers. . . . A list of historical objects fashioned from metal itself would be a long one. Agricultural tools and implements, metal fastenings, doors and locks in buildings, cooking utensils, heavy and fine armaments, religious artifacts, coins, and jewellery. . . . An active and varied trade developed in all parts of Asia in coarse cloth, earthenware pottery, iron implements, and brass utensils. Ordinary people as well as the well-off bought these simple goods of everyday use. . . . (Chaudhuri 1990a: 302, 319, 323, 305)

As a joke has it, a puzzled customs officer wondered about the guy who kept crossing the border with wheelbarrows that appeared empty. It took quite a while until the customs officer got wise to what the guy was doing: he was smuggling wheelbarrows! Well, it was no joke but serious business that the preponderant majority of shipping, albeit with goods of whatever origin and engaged in legal as well as contraband trade among Asian ports, was on Asian ships built with Asian materials and labor of West, South, East, and Southeast Asian origin and financed by Asian capital. Thus, shipping, naval and port construction, and their maintenance and finance were in and of themselves already a major, continuing, and growing "invisible" industry all around Asia, which dwarfed all European interlopers probably until the nineteenth-century advent of the steamship.

An analogous "invisible industry" was coinage—minting and re-minting—for local, regional, and national use, and also very much so for export. The production, assaying, and exchange of gold, silver, copper, tin, iron, and other metal coins, specie in bar and other bullion form, and of cowrie shell, badam, and other currencies (including textiles) was big business for state and private interests, to which Frank Perlin (1993) and others have devoted extensive studies. In principle, coins could be accepted at face or weight value, although not entirely so in case they may have been debased; bullion had to be assayed for weight and purity, which implied a business cost but also provided still another state or private business opportunity.

In world economic terms China, not India, was the front-runner, exporting huge quantities of valuable commodities and importing vast quantities of silver. India, however, does not seem to have been far behind China in this regard, being the seat of very significant industrial centers, particularly in cotton textiles, and importing huge quantities of bullion, particularly gold (for which India was a "sink"). We have already countered in chapter 3 the Eurocentric myth that the Asians just hoarded the money they received. On the contrary, Asians *earned* this money first because they were *more* industrious and more productive to begin with; the additional money then generated still more Asian demand and production.

West Asia too seems to have continued to prosper both from its own industrial base, in cotton and silk textiles for instance, and from transshipments of commodities between Europe and the rest of Asia. Both Southeast Asia and Central Asia appear to have prospered, largely on the transshipments of bullion and goods between regions, but in the case of Southeast Asia, also in terms of its locally produced silk, exported especially to Japan.

Europeans were able to sell very few manufactures to the East, and instead profited primarily from inserting themselves into the "country trade" within the Asian economy itself. Europe's source of profits was overwhelmingly derived from the carrying trade and from parleying multiple transactions in bullion, money, and commodities in multiple markets, and most importantly, *across the entire world economy*. Previously, no one power or its merchants had been able to operate in *all* markets simultaneously or systematically to integrate its activities between all of them in such a coherent logic of profit maximization. The main key for the European ability to do so was their control over huge supplies of bullion. Their naval capabilities were a much smaller and long indecisive factor; and their imperial or private company forms of commercial organization were not so different from those of their competitors, as we will note below. Europeans did arbitrage the differentials in exchange rates between gold and silver across all the countries of Asia, and placed themselves in a middleman role in some trade circuits, particularly between China and Japan in the sixteenth and early seventeenth centuries. Nonetheless in world economic terms, for at least three centuries from 1500 to 1800 the most important, and indeed almost only, commodity that Europe was able to produce and export was money—and for that it relied on its colonies in the Americas.

One thing is very clear: Europe was not a major industrial center in terms of exports to the rest of the world economy. Chapters 2 and 3 demonstrate that in fact Europe's inability to export commodities other than money generated a chronic balance of payments deficit and a constant drain of bullion from Europe to Asia. Only Europe's colonial sphere in the Americas explains its viability in the world economy, without which it could not have made good its huge deficits in the commodities trade with Asia. Even so it never had enough money to do so as the poor Europeans wished, for as a Dutch trader reported home in 1632, "we have not failed to find goods . . . but we have failed to produce the money to pay for them" (Braudel 1979: 221). This problem was not overcome until the end of the eighteenth century and especially the nineteenth century, when the flow of money was finally reversed, go to from East to West.

WORLD TRADE 1400–1800

In view of the above documentation about Asian population, production, productivity, competitiveness, domestic and regional trade, and their continued growth, it should come as no surprise that international trade was also predominantly Asian. Yet the mythology has grown up that world trade was created by and dominated by Europeans, even in Asia. We confront below the several reasons for this myth.

The Portuguese, and after them Europeans generally, have "bewitched" historians into devoting attention to themselves all out of proportion to their importance in Asian trade. Giving credit where credit is due, this enthrallment with the Portuguese, the Dutch, and the British is due in part to the fact that it is they who left the most records of Asian trade. Of course, these records also reflect their own participation and interests, more than those of their Asian partners and competitors.

The Eurocentric position about European participation in Asian trade has however become subject to increasing revision. W. H. Moreland's (1936: 201) now classic *A Short History of India* argued that "the immediate effects produced by the Portuguese in India were not great." The next major salvo came from a former Dutch official in Indonesia, J. C. van Leur (1955), who challenged the then still dominant Eurocentric view in a series of comments:

the general course of Asian international trade remained essentially unchanged. . . . The Portuguese colonial regime, then, did not introduce a single new economic element into the commerce of southern Asia. . . . In quantity Portuguese trade was exceeded many times by the trade carried on by Chinese, Japanese, Siamese, Javanese, Indians . . . and Arabs. . . . Trade continued inviolate everywhere. . . . The great intra-Asian trade route retained its full significance. . . . Any talk of a European Asia in the eighteenth century [a fortiori earlier!] is out of the question. (Van Leur 1955: 193, 118, 165, 164, 165, 274)

Indeed, asserts van Leur (1955: 75),"the Portuguese Empire in the Far East was actually more idea than fact," and even that had to give way to reality, as M. A. P. Meilink-Roelofsz (1962) repeatedly observes, despite her defense of the Europeanist position. She in turn challenges the van Leur thesis in her carefully researched text on the European influence on Asian trade, which she explicitly claims was greater and earlier than van Leur allows. Yet her own evidence, and her repeated disallowance of the real impact of the Portuguese, seem to lend even more support to "van Leur's thesis that it was only about 1800 that Europe began to outstrip the East" (Meilink-Roelofsz 1962:10). Her own research concentrates especially on insular Southeast Asia, which experienced the greatest European impact in Asia; and yet even there she shows that indigenous and Chinese trade successfully resisted the Dutch.

Now, more and more scholarship—for example, Chaudhuri (1978), Ashin Das Gupta and M. N. Pearson (1987), Sinnappah Arasaratnam (1986), and Tapan Raychaudhuri and Irfan Habib (1982)—has confirmed van Leur's message that Asian trade was a flourishing and ongoing enterprise into which the Europeans only entered as an added and relatively minor player.

Asian pepper production more than doubled in the sixteenth century alone, and much of that was consumed in China (Pearson 1989: 40). Of the relatively small share, certainly less than a third, that was exported to Europe, sixteen times more spices were transported overland by Asians through West Asia than went around the Cape on Portuguese ships in 1503, and even by 1585 almost four times as much went by the Red Sea route as the Cape route (Das Gupta 1979: 257). Even though shipping was their forte, the Portuguese never carried more than 15 percent of the Moluccan cloves to Europe, and the vast bulk of Southeast Asian pepper and other spices was exported to China. Moreover, some ships flying Portuguese flags were really owned and run by Asians, who used that "flag of convenience" to benefit from the lower customs duties accorded Portugal in some ports (Barendse 1997: chap. 1). Yet with all their military and political strong-arm attempts to "monopolize" trade and to charge tribute tolls to others, Portugal's nonetheless very small share of inter-Asian trade provided 80 percent of their profits, and only 20 percent came from their trade around the Cape of Good Hope, which they had pioneered (Das Gupta and Pearson 1987: 71, 78, 84, 90; Subrahmanyam 1990a: 361). This is illustrated by the itemized documentation in a Portuguese book published in 1580, which records in Portuguese cruzados just how profitable particular routes and voyages were. For the relatively short Macao-Siam, Macao-Patane, and Macao-Timor trips, the profits were 1,000 cruzados each; for Macao-Sunda, 6,000 to 7,000 cruzados; and for Goa-Malacca-Macao-Japan, 35,000 cruzados. By comparison, for the entire Lisbon-Goa voyage via the Cape of Good Hope the owner received 10,000 to 12,000 cruzados and the ship's captain 4,000 cruzados (cited in Lourido 1996a: 18–19).

Though so important for the Portuguese, their share of the exports of silver from Japan was never more than 10 percent of the Japanese total between 1600 and 1620 and only briefly rose to a maximum of 37 percent in the 1630s (Das Gupta and Pearson 1987: 76). In India also, even at the height of their sixteenth-century "penetration" of Asia, the Portuguese handled only some 5 percent of Gujarati trade. Despite their base at Goa, Portuguese procurement was less than 10 percent of southwestern Indian pepper production. The maintenance of Portugal's *"Estado da India"* cost its taxpayers and the state more than its direct earnings from India, although its private merchants did benefit from it, as other European "servants" did from their companies (Barendse 1997: chap. 1).

The small Portuguese trade in East and Southeast Asia was replaced by the Dutch. Yet despite all their efforts to monopolize trade at least in parts of Southeast Asia, the Dutch never succeeded in doing so, as we observe in chapter 2. Indeed, even the inroads that the Dutch made primarily at the expense of the Portuguese were again replaced by the Chinese and other East Asians, whose domination of their seas—not to mention their lands—was never seriously challenged. From the late seventeenth century onward, "European penetration was actually reversed" (Das Gupta and Pearson 1987: 67). Europeans were outcompeted by the Chinese, whose shipping between 1680 and 1720 increased threefold to Nagasaki and reached its maximum at Batavia, when the 1740 massacre of Chinese took place (Das Gupta and Pearson 1987: 87). For instance, in the four years after shipping was legally reopened again in 1684, Nagasaki received an average of nearly 100 Chinese ships a year, or two a week; over the longer period to 1757, the average was still over 40 a year. In 1700, Chinese ships brought over 20 thousand tons of goods to South China, while European ones carried away 500 tons in the same year. In 1737 it was 6 thousand tons, and not until the 1770s did Europeans transport 20 thousand tons (Marks 1997a).

Trade from the sixteenth to the nineteenth centuries in the East China Sea, bordering Korea, Japan, and the Ryukyus, and the South China Sea around Southeast Asia is illuminated in an essay by Klein (1989). He finds that Europeans never achieved any control, much less domination, or even a partial monopoly. In the East China Sea, trade was exclusively in Asian hands; Europeans hardly entered at all. In the South China Sea, first the Portuguese and then the Dutch Europeans achieved at best a foothold by taking advantage of regional disturbances until the mid-seventeenth century. However, even that was reduced to no more than a toehold (later including the British), with the economic and political recovery of East Asia in the second half of the seventeenth and through the eighteenth centuries. Klein concludes that

> The European penetration into the maritime space of the China seas during the sixteenth and seventeenth centuries had only been possible due to the peculiar development of the domestic and regional power relations in the area itself. Its influence on the region's economy had been marginal. Its commercial effects on the world economy had been only temporary, restricting themselves to the rather weak and limited European trading network in Asia. After the region regained a new balance of power in about 1680, its internal maritime trade experienced a new era of growth within a well established framework of traditional institutions. This trade and its institutions were gradually eroded during the later part of the eighteenth century . . . [but included] European commerce . . . [that] also fell prey to disintegration. The establishment of European hegemony in the nineteenth century found no base in what had happened in pre-industrial times . . . [but was based on] entirely new conditions and circumstances. (Klein 1989: 86–87)

Even at the other, western end of Asia, where commercial access was easier for the Europeans,

> the Arabian seas were part of an ancient, larger network of exchange between China, South-East Asia, India, the Middle East, . . . [where] Europeans were tied to pre-existing arrangements, relating to foreign traders . . . [who] were collaborating with Asians reluctantly, for the degree of mutual trust should not be exaggerated. (Barendse 1997: chap. 1)

Turning to the significance of Asian trade in world trade as a whole, one of the European historians after van Leur most sympathetic to Asia is Niels Steensgaard (1972). He also agrees that Portugal changed little in the Indian Ocean and that much more important—indeed *the* event of the sixteenth century—was the conquest of Bengal by Akbar in 1576. (Steensgaard 1987: 137).

So it is surprising to read that Steensgaard (1990d) regards Asian trade through the Indian Ocean to have been "marginal" and of little importance. "The point may seem like restating the obvious," he adds, dismissing Asian trade by noting Moreland's (1936) and Bal Krishna's estimates of 52,000 to 57,000 tons and 74,500 tons, respectively, of long-distance trade annually at the opening of the seventeenth century. He compares that with half a million or closer to a million tons of shipping capacity in Europe. However, the weight of traded cargoes versus shipping capacity are hardly commensurate measures. Steensgaard himself notes that these Indian Ocean trade figures exclude coastal shipping, which was both greater per se and an integral part of long-distance trade that also relied on relay trade. Yet European ships primarily plied the Baltic and Mediterranean coasts for distances no longer, and mostly less so, than those along the Indian Ocean or the Southeast Asian seas for that matter. So this comparison hardly seems adequate to evaluate the relative weights of India (let alone Asia) and Europe in world trade.

Moreover, as noted in chapter 2, Asian overland and maritime trade were more complementary than competitive, as Barendse also observes:

> The relation between land and seaborne trade is a complex one: the choice between them partly depended upon the circuits covered, partly on "protection rent." Trade along the caravan roads was not substituted by trade overseas. In some cases seaborne trade might even stimulate caravan trade. In others, commerce partly shifted to the sea routes, particularly where overland trade became dangerous, like in India in the late seventeenth century. . . . Trade on the coast depended on that of the hinterland. Many fairs were mere satellites on the coast of metropolises in the interior: thus Barcelore of Vijayanagara, Dabhul of Bijapur and—as its name indicates—Lahawribandar of Lahore. The centres of both manufacture and government were located in the hinterland; the bulk of the agricultural production was redistributed there. (Barendse 1997: chap. 1)

We observed in chapter 2 that overland trade also flourished and grew. In India and to and from Central Asia, caravans of oxen, each carrying from 100 and 150 kilograms and numbering 10 to 20 thousand animals, were not uncommon and caravans as large as 40 thousand animals were not unknown (Brenning 1990: 69, Burton 1993: 26). Caravans could also include a thousand or more carts, each drawn by ten to twelve oxen. Caravanserai, rest stops located at a day's distance from each other, accommodated up to 10 thousand travelers and their animals (Burton 1993: 25). In the seventeenth century, just one of the merchant communities, the Banjaras, transported an average of 821 million ton miles over an average of 720 miles a year. By comparison, two centuries later in 1882, all Indian railways carried 2,500 ton miles (Habib 1990: 377).

By all indications, Asia's trade with Europe, though growing over these centuries, still remained a very small share of Asians' trade with each other (even including their long-distance trade). Sir Joshua Childe, the director of the British East India Company, observed in 1688 that from some Indian ports alone Asian trade was ten times greater than that of all Europeans put together (cited in Palat and Wallerstein 1990: 26).

In view of this review of trade in Asia and especially the analysis of trade in the China seas by Klein (1989), it is noteworthy that Carl-Ludwig Holtfrerich (1989: 4) claims, in his introduction to his edited volume of papers in which Klein's work appears, that "Europe dominated throughout the whole period." Holtfrerich goes on to claim (1989: 5, table 1.2) a European share of all world trade at 69 and 72 percent in 1720 and 1750 respectively, leaving only 11 and 7 percent for India in those two years (an additional 12 percent is claimed for Latin America and 8 percent for "Other" during each of the tabulated time periods).

This unabashedly Eurocentric claim is disconfirmed by the evidence discussed in the present book, as well as by Klein's (1989) analysis on Chinese and not European trade in the China seas. Moreover, in the period 1752–1754 according to figures from Steensgaard (1990d: 150), the relatively small exports to Europe from Asia (which were a very small share of Asia's trade) remained higher than Europe's imports from the Americas. (European exports to the Americas were higher, but of course the Europeans were still unable to compete successfully with their exports elsewhere, that is in Asia). Indeed, even in 1626 an anonymous Iberian observer wrote a "Dissertation" whose title claims to "Demonstrate . . . the Greater Importance of the East Indies than the West Indies by Virtue of Trade, and therefore we Find the Causes of Why the Oriental Trade is lost and Spain is Reduced to the

Abject Poverty that we [now] Witness" (translated from Lourido 1996b: 19).

Terry Boswell and Joya Misra (1995) offer another graphic illustration of how these Eurocentric blinkers not only hide most of the world economy and trade from (Western) view but also distort the perception even of the European "world-economy." First they write that, in Wallerstein's and their view "despite trade connections, Africa and Asia remained external [to the world-system]. Neither logistics not long waves should apply to them." Then they disagree with Wallerstein: "We think it reasonable to consider East Asian trade a leading sector in the world-system, even if Asia itself is external" (Boswell and Misra 1995: 466, 471). So they include "East Asian trade" in their calculations of "global" trade, only to find that "thousands of ships were engaged in the Baltic trade, compared to only hundreds in the Atlantic and Asian." Since the latter journeys were longer, they allot each of them greater weight in their estimations of total "global trade"(Boswell and Misra 1995: 471–2). Alas, their myopia allows them to see and include in their "global" trade only the hundreds of ships in the East-West trade, and not to see nor count any of the thousands in the intra-Asian trade, which Holtfrerich (1989) at least included even if he vastly underestimated them. However, Boswell and Misra also fall into another trap of their own making. First they argue that the observation that "East Asian trade showed a different [cyclical] pattern from the Atlantic and global trades supports considering the latter external" (Boswell and Misra 1995: 472). They do not even consider the possibility that the divergence of "East Asian trade" from East-West trade may be compensatory, as in a see-saw. That would make their observation evidence of the opposite: Asia and its trade would be not "external" but rather internal to the system! Then they argue that their own further investigation of cyclical ups and downs accidentally shows exactly that: "This finding suggests the Asian trade is more central to the capitalist world economy than expected" (Boswell and Misra 1995: 478)! Of course, what they "expected" is a function of their own Eurocentric blinkers, but it turns out that these distort even their own analysis of the "European world-system," as well as of course blinding them to the existence of a much larger world economy and trade in Asia.

In conclusion, the Asian economy and intra-Asian trade continued on vastly greater scales than European trade and its incursions in Asia until the nineteenth century. Or in the words of Das Gupta and Pearson in their *India and the Indian Ocean 1500–1800,*

a crucial theme is that while the Europeans obviously were present in the ocean area, their role was not central. Rather they participated, with varying success, in an on-going structure. . . . [In]
the sixteenth century, the continuity is more important in the history of the Indian Ocean than the discontinuities which resulted
from the Portuguese impact. (Pearson and Das Gupta and Pearson
1987: 1, 31)

Even the European(ist) Braudel had long insisted that the world economic center of gravity did not even begin to shift westward until *after*
the end of the sixteenth century, and it did not arrive there until the
end of the eighteenth century and during the nineteenth. Indeed, "the
change comes only late in the eighteenth century, and in a way it is
an endogamous game. Europeans finally burst out, and changed this
structure, but they exploded from within an Asian context" (Das Gupta
and Pearson 1987: 20).

Thus, despite their access to American money to buy themselves into
the world economy in Asia, for the three centuries after 1500 the Europeans still remained a small player who had to adapt to—and not
make !—the world economic rules of the game in Asia. Moreover,
Asians continued to compete successfully in the world economy. How
could they do so if, as the received Eurocentric "wisdom" has it, Asians
lacked science, technology, and the institutional base to do so? The answer is that Asians did not "lack" any of these and instead often excelled
in these areas. So let us turn now to examine the development of science, technology, and institutions in the real world and how they too
differ from what Eurocentric mythology alleges.

Qualities: Science and Technology

EUROCENTRISM REGARDING SCIENCE AND
TECHNOLOGY IN ASIA

The received Eurocentric mythology is that European
technology was superior to that of Asia throughout our period from
1400 to 1800, or at least since 1500. Moreover, the conventional Eurocentric bias regarding science and technology extends to institutional forms, which are examined in the following section. Here I
focus on the following questions: (1) Were science and technology on
balance more advanced in Europe or in Asia, and until when? (2) After

importing the compass, gunpowder, printing, and so on from China, was technology then developed indigenously in Europe but no longer in China and elsewhere in Asia? (3) Was the direction of technological diffusion after 1500 from Europe to Asia? (4) Was technological development only a local and regional process in Europe or China or wherever, or was it really a global process driven by world economic forces as they impacted locally? To preview the answers that will emerge below, all of them contradict or at least cast serious doubt on the received Eurocentric "wisdom" about science and technology.

Technology turns out not to be independently parallel. Instead, technology is rapidly diffused or adapted to common and/or different circumstances. In particular, the choice, application, and "progress" of technology turns out be the result of rational response to opportunity costs that are themselves determined by world economic and local demand and supply conditions. That is, technological progress here *and* there, even more than institutional forms, is a function of world economic "development" much more than it is of regional, national, local, let alone cultural specificities.

Nonetheless an oft-cited student of the subject, J. D. Bernal (1969) attributes the rise of Western science and technology to the indigenous rise of capitalism in the West (which he accounts for in the same terms as Marx and Weber). Robert Merton's now classic 1938 discourse on "Science, Technology, and Society" is entirely Weberian and even linked to the latter's thesis about the Protestant ethic and the "Spirit of Capitalism." That in itself should make his derivative thesis on science and technology suspect, as already argued in chapter 1; for another critical discussion, see Stephen Sanderson (1995: 324 ff.). Coming full circle, Rostow's (1975) "central thesis" on the origins of modern economy is quite explicit: it all began in modern Europe—with the scientific revolution.

The study of the history and role of this scientific and technological revolution seems to be much more ideologically driven than the technology and science that allegedly support it. For instance, Carlo Cipolla (1976: 207) favorably cites one of the Western "experts" on the history of technology, Lynn White, Jr., who asserts that "the Europe which rose to global dominance about 1500 had an industrial capacity and skill vastly greater than that of any of the cultures of Asia . . . which it challenged." We have already seen above that Europe did *not* rise to "dominance" at all in 1500 if only because exactly the opposite of White's Eurocentric claim was true.

The second volume of the *History of Technology* edited by Charles Singer et al. (1957: vol. 2, 756) recognizes and even stresses that from A.D. 500 to 1500 "technologically, the west had little to bring to the east. The technological movement was in the other direction." Reproduced there is a table from Joseph Needham (1954) that traces the time lags between several dozen inventions and discoveries in China and their first adoption in Europe. In most cases, the lag was ten to fifteen centuries (and twenty-five centuries for the iron plow moldboard); in other cases the lag was three to six centuries; and the shortest time lag was one century, for both projectile artillery and movable metal type. "It was largely by imitation and, in the end, sometimes by improvement of [these] techniques and models . . . that the products of the west ultimately rose to excellence" (Singer et al. 1957: vol. 2, 756).

However, these accounts are themselves also excessively European-focused. There was indeed much technological diffusion; but during the millennium up to 1500 it was primarily back and forth among East, Southeast, South, and West Asia, and especially between China and Persia. Before any of this technology reached Europe at all, most of it had to pass via the Muslim lands, including especially Muslim Spain. The Christian capture of Toledo and its Islamic scholars and important library in 1085 and later of Córdoba significantly advanced technological learning farther "westward" in Europe. The Byzantines and later the Mongols also transmitted knowledge from east to west.

Singer's third volume, covering the period 1500–1750, is explicitly devoted to the West. Without any further comparisons, the assertion is made that "it is certain, however" that the balance had already shifted by 1500, so that "granted the immense European naval and military superiority, European control of the Far East was an almost inevitable consequence." Moreover, it is claimed that there was a "generally higher level of technical proficiency in Europe in the seventeenth century compared with the rest of the globe"; this is attributed to a European and especially British more "liberal social system," being "united in religion" and other such differences in "civilization." Also mentioned is that all this is "in no way inconsistent with an inferiority" in silks and ceramics, but cotton textiles and other industries are not mentioned (Singer et al. 1957: vol. 3, 709–710, 711, 716, 711)

However, this reference to alleged sociocultural superiority is no more than the same Eurocentric prejudice that we already challenged in chapter 1 and will have to reject after the examination below of institutions also. In principle, it could indeed have been the case that

Europe lagged behind in the important ceramics, silk, and cotton industries and yet had advanced more in other technologies. However, the
History of Technology does not offer the slightest comparative evidence
for what is taken for "granted," and we will observe below that the
evidence from elsewhere does *not* support the suppositions in this multivolume history. Indeed only a quarter of a century later, David Arnold
(1983: 40) was already able to observe that "there is now much greater
awareness than formerly of the relative narrowness of the technological
gap between Europe and China, India and the Muslim world in the
fifteenth and sixteenth centuries."

The Eurocentric treatment of the history of science is similar, although there is serious doubt that science, as distinct from inventors
working on their own, had any significant impact on technology in the
West before the middle of the nineteenth century. The received and
excessively Eurocentric treatment of science is illustrated by several well
known multivolume histories. A. C. Crombie's (1959) review of medieval and early modern science from the thirteenth to seventeenth centuries does not even mention any science outside of Western Europe. The
first volume of Bernal's (1969) *Science in History,* devoted to its emergence up through the Middle Ages, gives some credit to China and less
to West Asia. However, Bernal's second volume, which begins with
1440, makes no further reference to science outside Europe. Only in
volume 1 does he mention that, thanks to Needham (1954–), "we are
beginning to see the enormous importance for the whole world of Chinese technical developments" (Bernal 1969: vol. 1, 311). Alas, when Bernal was writing Needham had only just begun his major work. So in
the very next paragraph, Bernal repeats the same old litany, and even
cites Needham in support, that "this early technical advance in China,
and to a lesser extent in India and the Islamic countries, after a promising start came to a dead stop before the fifteenth century, and . . . resulted in . . . a high but static technical level" (Bernal 1969: vol. 1, 312).
Accordingly, Asia disappears from Bernal's second volume. We observe
below that the real world evidence is otherwise.

The more recent comprehensive review by H. Floris Cohen, *The
Scientific Revolution. A Historical Inquiry* (1994), seems more promising
at first sight; but on closer inspection it too is ultimately almost equally
disappointing. Cohen does importantly distinguish between science
and its use in technology, and he reviews the large body of literature
on "the Great Question" of why "The Scientific Revolution" took place
in Europe and not elsewhere. Much of his review, of course, reflects the
same inquiries cited above as well as others, from Weber and Merton to

Bernal and Needham. However, Cohen takes Needham seriously enough to devote sixty-four pages to the discussion of his work and another thirty-nine pages to Islamic and other "nonemergences" of early modern science "outside Western Europe," in a section that takes up one-fifth of his text.

Yet the thread that runs through Cohen's entire review of "the Great Question" is that something about the embedment of science in society was unique in and to Europe. That is, of course, the Weberian thesis and its resurrection by Merton as applied to science. Alas, it was also originally Needham's Marxist and Weberian point of departure. As Needham found more and more evidence about science and technology in China, he struggled to liberate himself from his Eurocentric original sin, which he had inherited directly from Marx, as Cohen also observes. But Needham never quite succeeded, perhaps because his concentration on China prevented him from sufficiently revising his still ethnocentric view of Europe itself. Nor does Cohen succeed.

For, the more we look at science and technology as economic and social activities not only in Europe but worldwide, as Cohen rightly does, the less historical support is there for the Eurocentric argument about the alleged role of the (European!) scientific revolution in the seventeenth or any other century before very modern times. Another interesting and useful example is "Why the Scientific Revolution Did Not Take Place in China—Or Didn't It?" by Nathan Sivin (1982). Sivin examines and effectively rebuts several of the same Eurocentric assumptions about this issue, but he neglects to raise the also crucial question of what impact the scientific revolution had on the development of technology, if any.

Neither does Cohen, whose review of this "revolution" and its role is even more marred by both his point of departure and his final conclusion. To begin with, Cohen seems to accept the proposition that science emerged only in Western Europe and not elsewhere. Therefore, he as much as dismisses Needham's claim that by the end of the Ming dynasty in 1644 there was no perceptible difference between science in China and in Europe. Yet Cohen's own discussion of works by Needham and others about areas outside Europe shows that science existed and continued to develop elsewhere as well. That of course stands to reason if the alleged "East-West" social and institutional differences were far more mythical than real, and it is also confirmed by other evidence cited below. But if there still was science elsewhere as well, then what is the purpose of Cohen's focus on it primarily in Europe?

Maybe even more significant, however, is that Cohen never troubles to inquire if and how science impacted on technology, even though he insists on the distinction between the two. Yet the evidence is that in Europe itself science did not really contribute to the development of technology and industry at all until two centuries after the famed scientific revolution of the seventeenth century.

To inquire into the alleged contribution of Western science to technology in general and to its industrial "revolution" in particular, it is apt to paraphrase the opening sentence of Steven Shapin's (1996) recent study of the subject: "There was no seventeenth century scientific revolution, and [this section of] this book is about it." Authoritative observers from Francis Bacon to Thomas Kuhn conclude that, whether "revolutionary" or not, these scientific advances appear to have had no immediate impact on technology whatsoever and certainly none on the industrial "revolution," which did not even begin until a century later.

Bacon had observed "the overmuch credit that hath been given unto authors in sciences [for alleged contributions to] arts mechanical [and their] first deviser" (cited in Adams 1996: 56). Three centuries later the author of *The Structure of Scientific Revolution* (1970) commented that "I think nothing but mythology prevents our realizing quite how little the development of the intellect need have had to do with that of technology during all but the most recent stage of human history" (Kuhn 1969; cited in Adams 1996: 56–57). All serious inquiries into the matter show that this "stage" did not begin until the second half of the nineteenth century and really not until after 1870, that is two centuries after the scientific "revolution" and one after the industrial "revolution." Shapin himself devotes a chapter to the question of "What was the [scientific] knowledge for?" His subtitles refer to natural philosophy, state power, religion's handmaid, nature and God, wisdom and will, but not to technology other than also to conclude that "It now appears unlikely that the 'high theory' of the Scientific Revolution had any substantial direct effect on economically useful technology in either the seventeenth century or the eighteenth" (Shapin 1996: 140).

Also, Robert Adams's (1996) *Paths of Fire: An . . . Inquiry into Western Technology* reviews any and all relations between technology and science, including the "seventeenth century scientific revolution." He cites numerous observers regarding particular technologies as well as technology and the industrial revolution in general. On the basis of these observers and his own work, Adams concludes on at least a dozen occasions (1996: 56, 60, 62, 65, 67, 72, 98, 101, 103, 131, 137, 256) that scientists and their science made no significant visible contribution to new technology before the late nineteenth century. Adams writes that "few if any salient technologies of the Industrial Revolution can be thought of as science based in any direct sense. They can better be described as craft based in important ways"; and he concludes that "scientific *theories* were relatively unimportant in connection with technological innovation until well into the nineteenth century" (Adams 1996: 131, 101). Adams's most generous conclusion is that "it must be emphasized that scientific discovery was not the only initiating or enabling agency behind waves of technological innovation, nor was it apparently a necessary one" (Adams 1996: 256). Through the eighteenth century in Britain only 36 percent of 680 scientists, 18 percent of 240 engineers, and only 8 percent of "notable applied scientists and engineers" were at any time connected with Oxford or Cambridge; moreover, over 70 percent of the latter had no university education at all (Adams 1996: 72). Instead, Adams and others trace technological advances primarily to craftsmanship, entrepreneurship, and even to religion. Indeed, Adams credits technology with far more contribution to the advancement of science than the reverse.

Finally, even Nathan Rosenberg and L. E. Birdzell, who attribute the West's growing "rich" only to European developments, recognize that

> evidently the links between economic growth and leadership in science are not short and simple. Western scientific and economic advance are separated not only in time [by 150 or 200 years between Galileo and the beginnings of the industrial revolution], but also by the fact that until about 1875, or even later, the technology used in the economies of the West was mostly traceable to individuals who were not scientists, and who often had little scientific training. The occupational separation between science and industry was substantially complete except for chemists. (Rosenberg and Birdzell 1986: 242)

On the other hand, Newton believed in alchemy; and in one example of the use of scientific measure in Europe, the Venetian Giovan Maria Bonardo found in his 1589 study, *The Size and Distance of All Spheres Reduced to Our Miles,* that "hell is 3,758 and 1/4 miles from us and has a width of 2,505 and 1/2 miles [while] Heaven is 1,799,995,500 miles away from us" (cited in Cipolla 1976: 226).

So the overwhelming evidence is that the alleged contribution of seventeenth-, eighteenth-, or even early nineteenth-century science to technology or to the industrial revolution is no more than "mythology" as Kuhn aptly termed it. And so what is the relevance of this entire "Great Question" about the seventeenth-century "scientific revolution" to our other "Grand Question" about "the Decline of the East" and "the (temporary) Rise of the West"? Not much, at least not within our present time frame before 1800. Therefore, it is just as well and most welcome that Cohen (1994: 500) himself ends by asking "Is the (fifty-year old concept of the) 'Scientific Revolution' going the way of all historical concepts?" "Perhaps" he answers, for "the concept has by now fulfilled its once useful services; the time has come to discard it. After all, historical concepts are nothing but metaphors, which one should beware to reify." Amen!

Except alas, not so fast: this Eurocentric mythology still seems to be alive and well also among Asians, whose resulting distortions of developments in science and technology are even more alarming. For instance, Aniruddha Roy and S. K. Bagchi (1986: v) call Irfan Habib a pioneer in medieval technology studies in India. Yet Ahsan Qaisar (1982) records his deep gratitude to Habib for suggesting his own research in *The Indian Response to European Technology and Culture (A.D. 1498–1707)*. Indeed, Habib himself also contributes a chapter on the same theme to the book edited by Roy and Bagchi. Elsewhere, Habib (1969:1) himself writes that "it would be foolish, even if detailed evidence has not been studied, to deny that India during the seventeenth century had been definitely surpassed by Western Europe [in technology]." Habib does bring some of the evidence, to be examined below. As we observed in chapter 3, Prakash (1994) disputes much of Habib's reasoning and himself disputes many alleged differences between Asia and Europe and avows that Asia played a widely underestimated key role in the early modern world economy. Yet even Prakash (1995: 6) writes that "Europe had an undoubted overall superiority over Asia in the field of scientific and technical knowledge."

Roy McLeod and Deepak Kumar (1995) also inquire into Western technology and its transfer to India from 1700 to 1947; despite the 1700 date in their subtitle, they explicitly disclaim any attention to the precolonial era; and yet, as we note below, some of their contributors (Inkster, Sanpal) do deal with that period. Even so, the editors permit themselves to introduce their book with unsubstantiated claims that are challenged by the evidence—cited below—from at least one of their own contributors. Yet the editors write that "technological change" in pre-British India "certainly was no match to what was happening in

Europe. The whole technical process was skill- and craft-oriented [but not so in Europe, we may ask]; the output was excellent (for example, in steel and textile), but limited to local markets [if so, how then did India dominate world markets, we may ask]. European travellers . . . were wonder-struck by some Indian products, but invariably critical of Indian customs" (McLeod and Kumar 1995: 11–12). Yet, even their first contributor, Ian Inkster examines and rejects arguments of India's alleged inferiority on cultural grounds. The editors claim that these and other "prefixes" (better prejudices!) "point to the weakness of the Indian economy as compared to proto-industrial Europe, Tokugawa Japan, or even Ming China" (McLeod and Kumar 1995: 12). Alas, they see reality in reverse; for, on all the evidence in the present book, the order of economic "weakness" and strength was the reverse, with China strongest, Europe weakest, and Japan and India in between.

What is noteworthy is that all of these texts by Asian scholars inquire only into technological diffusion from Europe to India and its selective adoption there—not the other way around. Yet as we will note below, diffusion went in *both* directions; and adoption and adaptation in *both* places as well as elsewhere responded to *common* world economic development mediated by local circumstances.

For China, Joseph Needham's (1954–) monumental multivolume *Science and Civilization in China* is well known, although perhaps insufficiently examined because of its large bulk and detail. A four-volume extract has been prepared by Colin Ronan (1986), and Needham (1964) himself has written a summary, "Science and China's Influence on the World." He explicitly challenges the dismissal by others: "In technological influence before and during the Renaissance China occupies a quite dominating position. . . . The world owes far more to the resilient craftsmen of ancient and medieval China than to Alexandrian mechanics, articulate theoreticians though they were" (Needham 1964: 238). Needham lists not only the well-known Chinese inventions of gunpowder, paper and printing, and the compass. He also examines co-fusion and oxygenation iron and steel technology, mechanical clocks, and engineering devices such as drive-belts and chain-drive methods of converting rotary to rectilinear motion, segmental arch and iron-chain suspension bridges, deep-drilling equipment; and paddle wheel boats, foresails and aft sails, watertight compartments and sternpost rudders in navigation, and many others.

Moreover, Needham insists that scientific investigation was well accepted and supported and that technological innovation and its application continued through the early modern period, also in fields like astronomy and cosmology, and in medical fields like anatomy, immunology, and pharmacology. Needham explicitly denies the European notion that the Chinese only invented things but did not wish to or know how to apply them in practice. Although he examines some apparently parallel developments in East and West, he also speculates on the possible channels and extent of their mutual influence and interchange.

There are also similar studies and findings for India, albeit on a lesser scale than Needham's monumental work. For instance, G. Kuppuram and K. Kumudamani (1990) have published a history of science and technology in India in twelve volumes, and A. Rahman (1984) has edited another collection on the same topic. Both works testify to the continued development of science and technology in India not only before 1500 but also since then. Dharampal (1971) collected eighteenth-century accounts by Europeans, who testify to their interest in and profit from Indian science and technology. Indian mathematics and astronomy were sufficiently advanced for Europeans to import astronomical tables and related works from India in the seventeenth and eighteenth centuries. In medicine, the theory and practice of inoculation against smallpox came from India. The export of Indian science and technology relating to shipbuilding, textiles, and metallurgy are noted below.

Similarly, S. H. Nasr (1976) and Ahmand al-Hassan and Donald Hill (1986) have written and edited histories testifying to the development and diffusion of Islamic science and technology from the earliest to recent times. George Saliba (1996) provides multiple examples of important Arab scientific influences on the Renaissance, not only before and during this period but into the seventeenth century. Only one example from Saliba is that Copernicus knew and had documents about Arab theories, which made crucial inputs to his own "revolution."

So it is not enough to just go on "granting the immense European naval and military superiority," as does Singer, or claiming that it "would be foolish, even if detailed evidence has not been studied, to deny" European technological superiority in other fields, as does Habib. Better to examine the evidence of Asian capacities with a bit more care, as Goody (1996) and Blaut (1997) begin to do, especially in these two fields. Another area of superiority mentioned in Singer's history of technology are coal and iron, while Habib and others also refer to printing and textiles. Upon any inspection, not only will we find that technology was far "advanced" in many parts of Asia, but it continued to develop in the centuries after 1400. That was the case especially in the globally more competitive military and naval technologies. Moreover, the alleged "Ottoman decline" is contradicted by a comparative examination of technologies in precisely these two areas (Grant 1996), as chapters 5 and 6 show in other respects as well. However, advanced technologies were also the case in more "local" arenas such as hydraulic engineering and other public works, iron working and other metallurgy (including armaments and especially steel-making), paper and printing, and of course in other export industries such as ceramics and textiles.

Guns. I say "other" export industries because arms and shipbuilding *were* important export industries. Not for nothing have the Ottomans, Mughals, and the Chinese Ming/Qing been termed "gunpowder empires" (McNeill 1989). They developed the latest and best in armaments and other military technology, which every ruling elite in the world sought to buy or copy it if it could use and afford it (Pacey 1990; see also chapter 5). Nonetheless, both Cipolla (1967) in his *Guns and Sails* and McNeill (1989) in his *The Age of Gunpowder Empires 1450–1800* repeatedly claim that European guns, especially when mounted on ships, were and remained far superior to any others in the world.

On the other hand, both Cipolla and McNeill themselves bring some contrary evidence. Both discuss the rapid development of Ottoman military technology and power. The Ottomans (but also the Thais) excelled in arms production, as Europeans and Indians recognized and also copied, adapting and reproducing Ottoman small and large arms technology to their own circumstances and needs. "Until about 1600, therefore, the Ottoman army remained technically and in every other way in the very forefront of military proficiency," avers McNeill (1989: 33). Cipolla (1967) acknowledges the same high degree of Ottoman military technology in his Chapter 2, and Jonathan Grant's (1996) comparative examinations confirm it. Although all three authors signal Ottoman military weaknesses (and defeat against Russia) in the seventeenth century, the first two also stress that European development of military technology could not begin to shift the balance of land-based power anywhere in Asia before the second half of the eighteenth century.

On the seas and at the coasts, their naval artillery did give Europeans some military technical advantages, but never enough to impose even a small part of the economic monopoly they sought, as Cipolla and

McNeill also recognize. The Ottoman Sultan said that even the 1571 European naval victory at Lepanto only singed his beard (quoted in Cipolla 1967: 101). The Portuguese sixteenth-century incursions in the Arabian Sea, the Indian Ocean, and the China Sea, using their bases at Hormuz, Goa, and Macao respectively, were only limited and temporary. The seventeenth-century Dutch offensive did much to displace the Portuguese but failed to impose the monopoly they sought in Asian waters, even in "Dutch" Southeast Asia, as we observed above.

Nor did their guns afford the Europeans any significant military impact in or on China and Japan, although there was some reverse diffusion of artillery technology. The Eurocentric fable that Chinese invented gunpowder but did not know how to use it is completely belied by Needham's (1981) evidence. He details widespread Chinese military use of powder for propulsion and also in incendiary devices and flamethrowers since at least A.D. 1000. Moreover, the Chinese also developed and used rockets with fifty and more projectiles, including two-stage rockets whose second propulsion was ignited after the first stage was in the air. Originally, the rocket launchers were stationary, but then they were made mobile as well. Europeans did not put gunpowder to military use until the late thirteenth century, and then only after they had themselves been victimized by the same in the eastern Mediterranean. Similarly, the Chinese and the Japanese also rapidly adopted and adapted advanced foreign gun technology, as Geoffrey Parker (1991) describes:

> Firearms, fortresses, standing armies, and warships had long been part of the military tradition of China, Korea, and Japan. Indeed, both bronze and iron artillery were fully developed in China before the spread westward to Europe around 1300. However . . . by 1500 the iron and bronze guns of Western manufacture—whether made by Turkish or Christian founders—proved to be both more powerful and more mobile than those of the East. . . . they attracted both attention and imitation [when] they may have arrived in China as early as the 1520s, perhaps with one of the numerous Ottoman diplomatic missions to the Ming Court. . . . For most Chinese, Western-style firearms were first encountered in the hands of pirates operating from Japan against Fukien in the late 1540s. . . . European weaponry was adopted on China's northern frontier before 1635. (Parker 1991: 185, 186)

European "superiority," if any, was limited to naval gunnery and then only temporarily. It may be true, as Governor-General Coen observed in 1614 that "trade cannot be maintained without war, nor war without trade" (cited in Tracy 1991: 180). However, Coen was Dutch, and he was trying to establish control in some small Indonesian islands, where doing so seemed a relatively practical proposition. Yet even there, the Dutch—like the Portuguese before them—never managed to impose economic monopoly control over the spice trade. If and when Europeans had any superiority in land-based military technology, it was not and could not be effectively used anywhere in Asia—without its being immediately copied and adapted. One of the reasons sometimes adduced for the relatively limited European incursions in Asia has been that (in distinction to the Americas and later in Africa) they were militarily incapable of penetrating inland beyond a few coastal ports. That may be true. However, although Tracy (1991) and his contributors like Parker (1991) try to revive this "explanation," it unjustifiably leaves the much greater strength of most Asian economies out of account. Moreover, as is still true today when nuclear arms do not remain a monopoly for long, any and all armaments technology was rapidly diffused to anyone in a position to pay for it.

Ships. Shipbuilding was certainly among the "high-technology" industries of sixteenth-century Europe (Pacey 1990: 72). Yet, no one questions the fact that in earlier centuries Chinese ships were bigger, better, far more numerous, and traveled father. One case in point is Zheng He's commercial fleets to Africa in the early 1400s. These fleets used much bigger and many times more ships than did either Columbus or Vasco da Gama (who, almost a century later, had to hire an Arab navigator). Another case is the comparison between the Mongol/Chinese fleet that attacked Japan in 1274 and the Spanish "Invincible" armada sent against Britain in 1588. Both were defeated by weather rather than by the defenders, but the Chinese one had over 2,000 ships and the Spanish one 132.

Did European ships outstrip the Chinese, especially after the institution of the official Ming policy to turn away from the sea? The conventional European answer in the affirmative is far from certain. Needham (1964) examines navigation in his fourth volume, which Ronan (1986) summarizes. They quote a European observer who argued in 1669 that "there are more Vessels in China than in all the rest of the known World. This will seem incredible to many Europeans"; but the observer goes on to explain why he is certain of his numbers (Ronan 1986: 89). Also cited in Needham's massive survey and Ronan's summary are various seventeenth- and eighteenth-century European navigators and sailors who register their astonishment at the quality of Chinese ships. In addition there are cataloged a whole series of Chinese nautical, navigational, propulsion, steering, and equipment technologies that matched or were better than, *and* that were being copied and adapted by, other contemporaries. These innovations included the shape of the hull, its compartmentalization into watertight sections, and pumping mechanisms both for bailing water out and for dousing shipboard fires caused in battle. Needham sums up with the following:

> the conclusion that this indicates a clear technical superiority of Chinese seamanship seems almost unavoidable. . . . All that our analysis indicates is that European seamanship probably owes far more than has been generally supposed to the contributions of the sea-going peoples of East and Southeast Asia. One would be ill-advised to undervalue [them]. (Ronan 1986: 210, 272)

Indeed, the Spaniards bought ships in the Philippines and also had their own maintained and repaired there, using technology and workmanship that antedated their arrival (Pacey 1990: 65–68, 123–28). The British East India Company and its servants did the same, although to a lesser extent (Barendse 1997: chap. 1).

The evidence is inescapable that the same is true with regard to South Asian shipbuilders. Unlike Chinese and European shipbuilders, Indian ones did not used iron nails to secure the planks in their ocean-going ships. If only because of the shortage and expense of iron, Indians adopted this technology only sparingly, although they did adopt foreign technology where advisable (Sangwan 1995: 139). They used fiber ties and caulking instead. For that and other reasons, Indian-built ships were much more durable, as Europeans of the day certified, praising the quality of Indian-built ships—see for example the quotes in Qaisar (1982: 22) and Sangwan (1995: 140). Moreover, Europeans bought many Indian-built ships for their own use, both because they were more durable and because they were cheaper than European ones, approximately 1,000 pound sterling less for a 500-ton ship in 1619 (Qaisar 1982: 22).

The British East India Company also maintained its own shipyards in Bombay (to which it recruited shipwrights from Surat), building large ships there and elsewhere in India after 1736. The Portuguese and then the Dutch had already done the same before the British; indeed, Amsterdam protected its own shipbuilding industry by prohibiting

Dutch purchase of large ships in India. Shipbuilding costs in India were 30 to 50 percent lower than in Portugal, Holland, and Britain. Moreover, Indian-built ships were better suited for the waters of the Indian Ocean, where their useful life was double and triple that of European-built ships (Barendse 1997: chap. 1). In the last two decades of the eighteenth century, the British EIC *and* the Royal Navy commissioned at least 70 ships to be built there and in the first two decades of the nineteenth century about 300. A contemporary observed:

> We do find many reasons inducing us to build the shipping in this country, where tymber, iron worke, carpenters are very cheape. The building [is] farre more substantial than in England, and more proper for these parts, in regard they will require noe sheeting and chalking more than the decks. (quoted in Barendse 1997: chap. 1)

Satpal Sangwan (1995:140) concludes that "India-built ships of this period were of equal quality, if not superior, to ships built anywhere in the world." Edmond Gosse concurs: "there would be no exaggeration in averring that they build incomparably the best ships in the world" (quoted in Barendse 1997: chap. 1). However, they were less likely to be equipped with guns, though even that increased as competition demanded. To discourage pirates, some Indian ships were built to look like more heavily armored European ships (Barendse 1997: chap. 1). In short, as Pacey observes:

> Asia was thus characterized by superior manufacturing technologies. . . . Some Indian [shipbuilding] techniques were distinctly better than those of their European counterparts by the early eighteenth century. . . . It is striking how eagerly Indians and Europeans learned from each other. . . . The dependence of Europeans on Indian and Filipino shipbuilders is thus part of a pattern in which westerners exploited Asian knowledge and skill. (Pacey 1990: 67–69)

Despite his skepticism about Indian technology in general, even Habib (1969:15–16) concedes that India experienced "what is practically an unchronicled revolution" in shipbuilding, which was in some respects superior to that of Europe. Nonetheless, he insists that it did not eliminate the lag he claims it had.

There can be no doubt that Asians also used and adapted European shipbuilding techniques and navigational skills and even personnel.

That only shows that in the competitive navigation industry as in various others technological progress and development was worldwide and world-driven economically. Moreover, "as long as there was an 'alternative' or 'appropriate' indigenous technology which could serve the needs of Indians to a reasonable degree, the European counterpart was understandably passed over" (Qaisar 1982: 139).

Printing. Printing is of particular interest not only as an important industry per se, but also as a service industry for the transmission of knowledge, including of course of science and technology, as well as a reflection of some degree of cultural "rationality" and social "openness." It is therefore significant that wood-block printing was invented and used in China up to half a millennium earlier than elsewhere. Color printing began in China in 1340, and five-color printing was in use there in the 1580s and widespread (certainly far more than in the West) in both China and Japan in the seventeenth and eighteenth centuries. Movable metal type came from Korea and was soon introduced elsewhere, though not into the Islamic world for a long time. In China, as Brook (1998) suggests, printing may not have changed much in the strictest technical sense. However, economically and socially speaking, printing, publishing, and literacy expanded enormously and surely had much more widespread effects than in Europe—including even the counterfeiting of paper money until the Ming withdrew it from circulation.

Textiles. A main locus of the industrial revolution of course was the textile industry. We have already observed the Chinese, Persian, and Bengali world economic preeminence in silk and Indian predominance in cotton. They were the highest-quality and lowest-cost producers in the manufacturing industries, competing even more successfully worldwide than in armaments and shipbuilding. As was noted above, textile production also had widespread linkages to the agricultural, machinery, transportation, vegetable dye and mineral-derived chemical industries, not to mention finance. To be a high-quality/low-cost producer and seller of textiles, competitive production in and coordination among all these ancillary industries was necessary. India excelled in all of them.

Moreover, it could not do so by standing still but only by maintaining its competitiveness through continued technological progress and cost reduction. It maintained a competitive lead for at least the four centuries between 1400 and 1800. India also imported new technologies, particularly for dyeing, as well as skilled workmen from Ottoman and Persian sources. A Mughal book listed seventy-seven different processes for producing forty-five shades of color. India also exchanged new technology in the porcelain industry with China and Persia. The British in turn copied their fundamental dyeing techniques from India (Chapman 1972: 12).

Curiously, Habib (1969) denigrates Indian technology and denies its progress even in textiles, although he concedes that there was no built-in resistance to technological change. Yet Vijaya Ramaswamy (1980) examined some evidence regarding particular textile techniques mentioned by Habib and reported that they had been introduced in India long before Habib supposed. Ramaswamy concludes:

> it would be quite erroneous to speak of technological development, at least in the [Indian] textile industry, as having been in spurts and as the result of external agents . . . or [imported] from Europe in the sixteenth-seventeenth centuries. Skill specialization and low labour costs were far from being the only merits of the Indian industry and, as has been demonstrated at some length, there was a gradual development in indigenous textile technology although it was interspersed with certain imported techniques. (Ramaswamy 1980: 241)

There can or should be no doubt that in the world's most competitive industry, textiles, the choices offered to consumers as well as the selection of the techniques of production anywhere in the world were adopted and were changed in reference to those everywhere else in the world. The incentives for the industrial revolution in Britain, particularly in the textile industry, are further examined in chapter 6 below.

Suffice it in this regard here to quote Pacey (who in turn is citing Braudel):

> Labour was plentiful in the Indian textile areas and wages were low. There was little incentive, therefore, for Indian merchants to mechanize production. As Braudel puts it, the incentive "worked the other way round." New machines were invented in Britain to try to equal Indian cloth both in cheapness and quality, and there were transfers of dyeing techniques. . . . Processes which had been in used for centuries in India, Iran and Turkey were extended quite rapidly [in Britain] with many new applications. (Pacey 1990: 121, 120)

We will return to Braudel's own argument in our chapter 6 discussion of the world economic competition that underlay the industrial revolution in Britain. As we will see, like any Newly Industrializing Economy in East Asia today, Britain began its own industrialization through import substitution for the domestic market by protectionism and other stimulation of the domestic cotton textile industry. Then, Britain proceeded to export promotion to the world market. By 1800, four out of seven pieces of cotton cloth produced in Britain were exported (Stearns 1993: 24); these in turn accounted for one-fourth of all British exports — and for one-half by 1850 (Braudel 1992: 572).

Metallurgy, Coal, and Power. European superiority is widely alleged especially in metallurgy and the associated mining of coal and its use for fuel and mechanical power (including the use of mechanical power in mining coal). To begin with, this development was primarily part and parcel of the industrial revolution only since the nineteenth century. Up through most of the eighteenth century, no one used much coal. As long as charcoal was still widely available and cheap, there was little incentive to replace it by more costly coal, and all the less so in those regions, especially in South Asia, where coal was not readily available. In Britain, the price of charcoal rose significantly during the first half of the eighteenth century while the price of coal dropped until by mid century it became cheaper to smelt iron with coal than charcoal (Braudel 1992: 569).

The Chinese also had coal, and if they mined it less, it was presumably for cost calculations and surely not for lack of appropriate technology. For the Chinese had long since developed and excelled in all sorts of analogous hydraulic engineering and other technology used in the construction and maintenance of their extensive canal system and other public works. Unfortunately for the Chinese and unlike Britain however, ample deposits of coal in China were located very far from the centers of its potential industrial use, as Pomeranz (1997) emphasizes. Moreover, their wood-fueled iron metallurgy had long been centuries ahead of everybody else.

Steel-making was also highly developed in Japan, India, and Persia in the sixteenth and seventeenth centuries. Indeed, there are several accounts of British import of samples of Indian *wootz* steel, which specialized British laboratories found equal to that of Sweden and superior to any made in Britain in 1790. Moreover, among the ten thousand Indian furnaces at the end of the eighteenth century, many still produced comparable iron and steel both faster (in two and a half hours instead of four) and cheaper than the British did in Sheffield (Dharampal 1971, Kuppuram and Kumudamani 1990).

Mechanical devices, also containing metal parts, were developed and put to use where abundant human labor was not cheaper. Watermills were in use in China, India, and Persia; and they supplied power for a variety of irrigation, agricultural, industrial, and other uses. Many regions in Asia excelled in irrigation and other improvements as well as in the clearing and development of agricultural land. Particularly significant for productivity in agriculture was the early development in India and widespread use of the drill plow.

We will argue below that productivity, and by implication appropriate technology, in agriculture was certainly as "advanced" in China and India as anywhere in Europe. Asians were certainly able to feed more people (per hectare of available arable land); and we will see evidence below that southern Chinese agriculture was more efficient than any in Europe.

Transport. Russel Menard (1991: 274) looks for a possible "European transport revolution" between the fourteenth and eighteenth centuries and concludes that there was none. Freight charges hardly fell, and it was cheaper goods, including those from Asia, rather than lower transport costs that made goods more accessible. At the same time, transportation, both by water and overland and also with reliance on mechanical devices, was well developed in many parts of Asia. Pomeranz (1997) can find no European advantages over Asia in overland transport in general and specifically finds that ton miles estimated by Habib for India exceed those estimated by Werner Sombart (1967) for Germany by more than five times in total number and are possibly only a little less per capita.

In 1776, Adam Smith (1937: 637–8,) compared Chinese and Indian canal and fluvial low-cost transport with that in Europe and declared the former superior. Asian use of substantial human labor in transport was economical given its availability. However, infrastructural investment in ports, canals, roads, caravanserai, and their maintenance and protection was also large and to all intents and purposes efficient and competitive within China, India, Central Asia, Persia, and in the Ottoman Empire. "International" transport across and around Asia was all the more so developed and competitive; and as we observe again and again below, Europeans took advantage of and benefited from this "development" through their own participation.

In short, it is far from established, as is so often supposed, that

European "technological superiority" can be dated from 1500 onward. Comparisons of European and Asian technologies certainly cast more than doubt on this Eurocentric thesis.

WORLD TECHNOLOGICAL DEVELOPMENT

However, this thesis about European superiority is even more doubtful on two other and more important grounds. One is that, as we have noted, there could be no such superiority in Europe or any one other place, if only because of the very substantial diffusion of technology back and forth. This happened through the purchase or theft of items containing technology; their copy and adaptation; the transfer of productive processes and organization, through both voluntary and forced (by slavery) displacement and engagement of skilled craftsmen, engineers, and nautical personnel; through publication; and through industrial espionage.

Moreover, to permit increased output and export Asians also needed and fomented technological development. Thus, the fifteenth and early sixteenth centuries witnessed not only growing production and export in China, but also significant increases in productivity and technological progress to support that export production. This occurred especially in the ceramics, silk, and cotton industries, the printing and publishing industry (where copper/lead alloys for casting movable characters were developed), sugar manufacturing, and both irrigated and dry agriculture (including the processing of agricultural products and the introduction of new crops from the Americas). There can be no doubt that India also developed improved technology and increased productivity in the sixteenth and seventeenth centuries, especially in the textile and arms industries, where competition required and stimulated the same.

The other and still more important reason that casts even more than doubt on the thesis of European technological superiority is derivative from the above observations: there was no *European* technology! In the worldwide division of labor in a competitive world economy, national, regional, or sectoral technological superiority could not be maintained as long as at least some other real or potential competitors had sufficient interest and capacity to acquire such technology as well. That is, technological development was a *world economic process,* which took place in and because of the structure of the world economy/system itself. It is true that this world economy/system was and still is structurally unequal and temporally uneven. However, it is not true that technological or any other "development" was essentially determined either locally, regionally, nationally, or culturally; nor that any one place or people had any essential "monopoly" or even "superiority" within this world economy/system. Still less was or is it the case, as we observe below, that any such alleged "superiority" was based on "exceptional" institutions, culture, civilization, or race!

Mechanisms: Economic and Financial Institutions

If trade and consumption, based on production, productivity, and technology were both absolutely and relatively so advanced in many parts of Asia, it stands to reason that the necessary institutional "infrastructure" must also have been in place there to permit and facilitate economic development. This observation casts serious prima facie doubt on the Eurocentric "wisdom," received from Marx, Weber, and their many disciples, that the "Asiatic mode of production" was stagnant and literally useless, while European institutions were progressive. Nonetheless, let us compare some of these economic and financial institutions and inquire into their pedigree and provenance.

First however, it may be well to address the role of institutions in general and of political or state institutions in particular. History, the social sciences, and economics, not to mention the public in general, all have a long tradition of focusing on institutions to which they sometimes explicitly albeit often only implicitly attribute the determination of all sorts of human behavior and historical events. There even is a self-styled "institutional economics" associated with Thorstein Veblen and others, and the economics Nobel laureate Douglass North has made a career of institutional analysis of economic history in general and of "the Rise of the West" in particular. Moreover, one and all devote their preferential attention to legal, political, and—in short—state institutions.

The alleged importance of these institutions for the "explanation" of history, including economic history, the rise of the West, and capitalism, has been a central tenet of classical and Marxist political economy, Weberian sociology, and most historiography and "political" history such as that defended by Himmelfarb (1987) in the West. As though that were not enough, many have inveighed to "bring the state back in"

(Skocpol 1985). The European state and its legal and other institutions have often been allotted much or even all of the credit for the rise of capitalism, the West, the industrial revolution, modernization, and all that. Those who subscribe to these "explanations" will find the economic analysis and its treatment of institutions and the state insufficient or inadequate in this book.

No matter that chapters 2, 3, and the preceding sections of chapter 4 have already made numerous references to states and their intervention in the economy. Thus, the state in China, Japan, India, Persia, and the Ottoman Empire was shown to have made massive investments in and organized the maintenance of canals and other transport infrastructure; expanded, settled, and reclaimed arable land; run para-state economic enterprises; made trade and other economic policy; not to mention lent military support to and promoted "national" economic interests. So the alleged incapacity of the "despotic oriental" state to promote economic development in Asia is quite inconsistent with the historical evidence.

Another version of Eurocentric "theory" refers to the international state *system*. It is alleged that the "warring states" in Europe (but not in China!) and their "international system" after the Peace of Westphalia in 1648 institutionalized some kind of cooperative competition that developed the economies—or at least armaments technology—in Europe, but not in Asia. The evidence, alas, disconfirms this international state system proposition as well. Granted that the Ming/Qing and Mughal states were bigger than the small European ones; but that does not make them less active or relevant, and they were also involved in wars. In Southeast Asia, as in Europe, city and "national" states also competed with each other. And as was observed in chapter 2, in West Asia and between the Ottoman and Safavid empires and among them and the European ones as well economic, political, and military competition was the rule. Whether the present account devotes sufficient attention to these political and institutional factors or not is debatable.

However, the problem lies not so much in any insufficient attention to institutions as it does in the sufficiency or not of the economic analysis of these institutions. For a major thesis of this book is precisely that institutions are *not* so much determinant of, as they are derivative from, the economic process and its exigencies, which are only institutionally instrumentalized rather than determined. That is, the institutions are the derivative and adaptive instruments and not the cause or—contra Polanyi—the social embedment of the economic process. And the proof of the pudding lies not in the institutional recipe but in the analytic eating. The reader will have to judge to what extent this book's world, regional, and sectoral economic analysis can account for and is more or less explanatory of events and the historical process than are the institutions within which they occur. According to this account, the institutions have to and do adapt to economic exigencies if the latter do not give rise to these institutions in the first place.

In this regard there is much comfort (at least for the author if not for the reader) to find belatedly another author, Graeme Snooks, who now argues that institutions

> do not play a fundamental *causal* role. The point of the book is that the dynamics of human society is driven by fundamental economic forces—the "primary dynamic mechanism"—and that institutions respond to these forces—through the "secondary mechanism"—rather than driving them. (Snooks 1996: 399; italics in the original)

Regarding the collapse of human societies—and by extension "the Decline of the East," to which we return in chapter 6—Snooks writes that such collapse is

> an outcome of changes in fundamental economic forces operating through the dynamic strategies, not the outcome of institutional problems arising from social complexity. It is true that institutional problems reenforce fundamental problems, but they are largely a reflection. . . . (Snooks 1996: 399)

Moreover, Snooks also writes about the industrial revolution and "the Rise of the West" and specifically of its institutional analysis by Douglass North, which is

> diametrically opposite my own in terms both of methodology and interpretation. . . . He focuses upon the role of institutions in leading the growth process, whereas I focus upon the role of fundamental economic forces which determine both the progress of society and its institutional and ideological change. (Snooks 1996: 131)

In the industrial revolution,

> the reason for the [technological] paradigm shift is the continuing drive of economic agents in a highly competitive environment together with fundamental change taking place in factor endowments—the relative factor prices—of natural, human, and physical resources. (Snooks 1996: 403)

That will also be the economic basis for my analysis of "the Rise of the West" and its industrial revolution in chapter 6. Here we will examine and compare some earlier economic and financial institutions and suggest how they were themselves shaped by the highly competitive economic environment in the global economy. We will see how they adapted to that environment and thereby facilitated—but neither determined nor prevented—economic growth in many parts of Asia as well, or indeed even more, than in Europe before 1800.

COMPARING AND RELATING ASIAN AND EUROPEAN INSTITUTIONS

The final section of this chapter neither attempts nor pretends to be a history or even a survey of financial and commercial institutions. I wish to address the question, or rather the common presumption, that such institutional development was more "advanced" in Europe than elsewhere, that Europe "exported" its institutions, and that others ultimately had to and did adopt them as well. That is the message of almost the entire European/Western historiography and social theory, or rather assumption, regarding this matter. They reach at least from Marx and Weber and Western economic historians to social scientists and publicists still following this line today. Much of what has been written has been based on pure ignorance of and/or prejudice about conditions outside Europe, or on hearsay, despite Weber's many studies of religion, society, and institutions in Europe and Asia. Such earlier authorities have been the basis, largely, for the "authority" of later and contemporary observers. Hardly any of them have taken the trouble to look for themselves, or even to ask themselves whether the received "theory" is or could be plausible in the face of other generally known evidence—which it cannot.

Alas, the direct evidence about these institutions outside Europe is fragmentary, and there are relatively few historians and social theorists who have even troubled to look at what there is. Nonetheless a number of Asian historians offer evidence on institutional organization, mostly as background or asides to their studies of economic events. I have cited them extensively elsewhere in this book, and we may usefully call upon their testimony regarding the institutions that made them possible. A few other (mostly Western) historians of a more general perspective have sought to construct some inductive summaries based on these studies as well as their own experience. However they in turn also bring their Western Eurocentric perspective with them and seek to overcome it only to varying degrees. I refer principally to van Leur (1955), Steensgaard (1972, 1990c), Braudel (1979, 1992), Mark Elvin (1973) on China, and lately especially Perlin (1990, 1993, 1994), who does reject Eurocentrism entirely.

The argument below will appeal to their authority. An exhaustive or even fragmentary survey of the institutional landscape is now beyond my scope and capacity. However, the received Eurocentric institutional accounts and theories also rely excessively on the "authority" of testimony, alas often false testimony. My selection too will be frankly partisan: for, I will argue, if the productive and commercial structure and process really was as the evidence reviewed elsewhere in this book shows, then we must ask what kind of institutional organization could or must have existed, to make that possible.

Pursuing this task therefore involves posing the following questions and seeking answers to them, among others: What economic, productive, commercial, trade, and financial activity was there? This entire book is an attempt to outline and summarize that activity. What kind of financial/commercial and other economic and political or social institutions here and there made that possible? We will cite some of the evidence, appealing mostly to authority. What is the history of these institutions, and especially, were they "endogenous" or at least already long preexisting in this or that region? In answer, we will and can adduce circumstantial evidence at best. How do these institutions compare between here and there? In answer, we will appeal both to authority and to if-then arguments of plausibility.

GLOBAL INSTITUTIONAL RELATIONS

Beyond this "comparative" issue, there lies another still more important relational one. Were these institutional developments largely independent of each other and reflections of different or similar cultural or other regional histories and circumstances? Or were these institutions common responses to common problems and challenges? Or was there an interdependent institutional development as part of a common interdependent economic structure and process? And if so, did this interdependence diffuse from here to there, and in particular from Europe to elsewhere? Or, was the interdependent institutional development around the world part and parcel of an interdependent world economic structure and process? That is the crucial question,

which goes a step beyond the observation by Pomeranz (1997) that European and Western economic institutions themselves evolved in response to the needs of trade. But so did Asian ones, as Prakash (1995:
12) aptly observes: "I need hardly stress that there was an important
organic link between the rise in the supply of money and the growth of
banking forms in the Mughal Indian economy." But the supply of, not
to mention the demand for, money in India as elsewhere in the world
was of course itself a function of the operation of the global economy.

It may be difficult to offer enough convincing evidence to make a
persuasive case of the derivative and adaptive transformation of institutions and their relations on a worldwide basis, but then maybe "posing
the right question is already more than half of getting the right answer."
Or in the words of Perlin, "we need to consider . . . to ask questions
about the possible existence, at the same particular moment in 'world'
history, of similar, even identical forces operating on these different
types of local political economy, thus of larger structural forces" (Perlin
1990: 50). Perlin continues:

> We need to move beyond comparison in an attempt to draw
> broader structural conclusions. Thus it may be argued that the
> context of societal growth and developing proto-capitalist rela-
> tionships [in India] formed an essential precondition for the in-
> creasing European involvement in the subcontinent . . . together
> with similar developments occurring elsewhere in Asia . . . and
> formed part of the preconditions for the development of a system
> of international exchanges and dependencies in which Europe es-
> tablished an increasing hegemony. . . . In short, commercial man-
> ufactures in Europe and in Asia formed dependent parts of wider
> international developments. The rise of merchant capital in differ-
> ent parts of the world, of market-oriented manufactures in Eu-
> rope, Asia and North America, the incorporation of the ex-
> panding systems of peasant production into international
> commodity circuits, all these need to be considered in terms of a
> framework of relevance comprising the growth of international
> commerce and the division of labour. (Perlin 1990: 89–90)

That is, of course, the purpose of this entire book—and indeed also of
Frank and Gills (1993), which covers a much longer time period. We
pursue this goal below with regard to some financial and commercial
institutions in the early modern period.

To explain my intent, it may be well to begin by appealing to some
authorities: under the heading "The World outside Europe," Braudel

(1979: 114) writes "To ask whether Europe was, or was not, at the same stage of exchange . . . is to ask a crucial question." His answer, as we will see, is that Europe *was* at the same stage, or rather that "other densely-populated regions of the world—that is other privileged areas" were also at the same stage or level. That is, implies Braudel, Marx, Weber, and their followers got it wrong.

One thing is certain: the major structural or even institutional changes in the world economy were not due to any diffusion of institutions from Europe. For instance,

> the coming of the Western traders broadened the market for Asian ceramics but did not alter its basic pattern. . . . Perhaps the business would not have been so well recorded, but otherwise the market development in the South Seas would have been pretty much the same. As noted previously, the demand for common wares in the South Seas had been persistent ever since the fourteenth century. (Ho Chuimei 1994: 48)

Moreover, commercial organization was not all that different either:

> It was the Zhengs [in southern China] who first hit on the idea of marketing Japanese [ceramic] wares abroad in 1658: the [Dutch] VOC reacted fast enough to do the same thing the next year. . . . The Zheng networks of commercial and political intelligence must have been at least as effective as those of either of its main enemies, the Manchus and the Dutch. . . . Arguably, the Zheng organization had some of the same traits as the VOC. (Ho Chuimei 1994: 44)

Thus, we must agree with Chaudhuri when he insists that

> division of labour, industrial production, and long-distance trade were part of the social community from pre-historic times. It will be difficult to find a society in any age or place which did not have some of the features of an exchange economy based on the concept of relative values, money use, and the market. Communities practising subsistence agriculture and industrial production almost certainly co-existed with those that were subject to the influence of the market mechanism and the control of capital. . . . The capitalism of trade, in spite of the absence of fixed capital, was a fact of daily life for the Asian artisan and farmer alike. . . . Capitalism as a commercial activity was universal in the Indian Ocean. . . . Of course, the long-distance trade of the Indian Ocean was a capitalistic activity, however that may be defined. . . .

Weavers, spinners, silkworm-rearers, metal-smiths, and the own-
ers of spice plantations, all received their rewards through the
price mechanism. The link between long-distance trade, commercial capitalism, and production for the export market remained
strong. . . . (Chaudhuri 1978: 207, 220, 214, 222)

And that economic link was worldwide.

For further evidence, we may quote from Chaudhuri's review of the
institutional forms and organization of manufacturing production in
various parts of Asia:

An expanding and flexible labour force able to switch occupations
between agriculture and industry was to be found both in China
and India. . . . Asian history is full of examples revealing the constant movements and migrations of craftsmen from one locality
to another in search of better opportunities. . . . Migration and
movements provided common remedy against natural disasters,
political oppression, and shrinking economic opportunities. . . .
There are numerous references in our sources which show that in
all parts of India and China at a time of commercial depressions,
the unemployed industrial worker turned to agricultural work
such as helping with the harvest in order to earn a wage. . . .
Whether it was in the Middle East, India, or China a clear vertical
link appeared between marketing and industrial production. . . .
Dominance of artisans by merchants was a reality wherever the
force of competition on the buying side weakened. The historical
sources also demonstrate that Asian merchants, whether they
were operating in India, the Middle East, or China, intervened
directly in industrial production as a result of particular commercial needs. . . . The real explanation for the development of certain
areas as export producers [is that] industrial location even in the
age of non-mechanized production is strongly influenced by relative costs of labour, wage goods, and capital which are distributed
unevenly over space. . . . There were entire regions in the Middle
East, India, and China which produced textiles intended for export both within and outside the national frontiers. . . . Many
parts of Asia had developed industries with all the attributes of an
export-oriented demand, and it was not until the latter half of the
eighteenth century that Europe was able to challenge. . . .
(Chaudhuri 1990a: 313, 306, 299, 318, 303, 309, 310–311, 301)

Janet Abu-Lughod (1989: 12 ff.) also noted the "striking similarities
[which] far outweighed differences" in levels and institutions of economic development throughout Eurasia in the thirteenth century. Inso-

far as there were differences, Europe lagged behind. She cites Cipolla to the effect that ever since the decline of Rome, Europeans had been an "underdeveloped area . . . a land of barbarians" and remained so still in the thirteenth and fourteenth centuries (Abu-Lughod 1989: 99: also see Cipolla 1976: 206). Strangely however and without giving any evidence beyond the time frame of her book, Abu-Lughod claims that Europe had pulled considerably ahead by the sixteenth century. The evidence supports her judgment about the earlier centuries, but belies it about the later one.

Even the European Braudel recognized that

> Everywhere from Egypt to Japan, we shall find genuine capitalists, wholesalers, rentiers of trade, and their thousands of auxiliaries, commission agents, brokers, money-changers and bankers. As for the techniques, possibilities or guarantees of exchange, any of these groups of merchants would stand comparisons with its western equivalents. (Braudel 1992: 486)

In his second volume of *Civilization and Capitalism,* Braudel (1979: 219) avers that "the European presence changed nothing in this respect. The Portuguese, Dutch, English and French traders all borrowed from Muslims, from Banyans [in India] or from the moneylenders of Kyoto [in Japan]." Indeed, the Europeans borrowed not only the money to use in Asia, but they borrowed it through and from the existing local financial institutions, whose operations they ipso facto also adopted. Braudel refers to Werner Sombart as "the most outspoken defender" of the thesis of the exceptionalism of European rationalism, but then goes on to ask whether

> Finally, when one is considering the range of rational instruments of capitalism, should one not also make room for other instruments besides double-entry bookkeeping: bills of exchange, banking, stock exchanges, markets, endorsements, discounting, etc.? But of course all these things were to be found outside the western world and its sacrosanct rationality. . . . More significant than the innovating spirit of entrepreneurship were the increased volume of trade. . . . Like Europe, the rest of the world had for centuries had the experience of the necessities of production, the laws of trade and the movements of currency. (Braudel 1979. 575, 581)

Indeed, it was *world* production, trade, and currency movements that offered the attraction and possibility for Europe to expand its own production and trade to begin with—and for three centuries after the

Europeans discovered the American money with which to participate in this world economy. So the necessary economic, productive, trade, commercial, and financial institutions had to exist previously and then also had to persist and to develop in order for Europeans to get in on the game. Indeed as Pomeranz (1997) repeatedly observes, the same can be said about property rights and legal institutions, which also were established and developed in various parts of Asia.

In India. However, rather than trying to detail these in-stitutional forms, it would seem legitimate here to appeal to a small sampling of authorities, beginning with South and Southeast Asia:

> [India's] banking system was efficient and well organized throughout the country, and the hundis and bills of exchange is-sued by the great business and financial house were honoured ev-erywhere in India, as well as in Iran, and Kabul [Afghanistan] and Herat and Tashkent and other places in central Asia. . . . There was an elaborate network of agents, jobbers, brokers, and middle-men . . . a very rapid and ingenious system of communicating new and market prices had been evolved. (Nehru 1960: 192)

If modern India's first prime minister may have been influenced by some partiality to his country in his *Discovery of India,* then the same could be equally expected of the Portuguese Tome Pires, who advised that

> "those of our people who want to be clerks and factors ought to go . . . and learn" from the Gujarati Indians in Cambay because there "the business of trade is a science in itself." (Pires [1517?] 1942/44: 42)

Two more recent authors make similar observations:

> there is evidence of a highly developed class (the *shroff* or *sarafs*) [a term that was itself derived from Arabic—see Habib 1976: 392] dealing with currency, commercial credit, loans, insurance of goods, etc. . . . [which] were undoubtedly closely connected with the rural petty bourgeoisie . . . [which was] an important link in the transmission of a definite share of the agrarian surplus to the commercial classes. . . . It is not clear if the Portuguese introduced any organizational changes in India's commerce and industrial production even in limited areas or sectors. . . . To all appearance, they made use of the existing machineries of [production and commerce]. (Ganguli 1964: 57, 68)

From the late sixteenth century on, the portfolio capitalist—an entrepreneur who farmed revenue, engaged in local agricultural trade, commanded military resources (war animals, arms and human labor), as well as on more than one odd occasion has a flutter in the Great Game of Indian Ocean commerce—was a characteristic feature of the Indian political economy. (Bayly 1990: 259)

To provide at least one illustration and some local color, it may be useful to cite an interested contemporary participant-observer. Gerard Aungier, the president of the English factory at Surat, reported to his EIC London home office in 1677 that

> we take due notice of what you advise touching the low price of pepper in Europe and your orders to bring it down here also; wherein we have not been wanting to use our best endeavours; but without success. For there is so great a consumption of pepper in these countries and so many dealers therein, who transport it to foreign parts, as well that of Deccan as a [sic] Malabar, that it is impossible to lower the price to the rates you limit. (quoted in Chaudhuri 1994: 275)

B. R. Grover's (1994: 219–55) comprehensive review of rural society in north India during the seventeenth and eighteenth centuries stresses that commerce pervaded India into its farthest reaches, well distant from the coast, the ports, and the Europeans. In one example about insurance rates, Habib (1969: 71) indicates the efficiency and security of such commerce and the transport that underlay it in west and east India: insurance rates in the mid-seventeenth century for distances of 315, 550, and 675 miles (as the crow flies, that is rather less than on the ground) were 0.5, 2.5, and 1 percent of the value of insured goods, respectively.

Habib's discussions (1969, 1980, 1990) of the economy of Mughal India and of merchant communities in precolonial India leave no doubt about the "development" of commerce and finance. The market was open and competitive. There were large-scale traders as well as small-scale "peddlers." Credit was widespread. Ahmadabad merchants made payments and settled debts almost entirely in paper, and almost any order or promise of payment could be turned into discounted commercial paper (Habib 1969: 73). Another indication of the "development" of the financial market is that rates of interest varied from a half to one percent a month, which was not significantly different from English and Dutch rates (Habib 1990: 393).

Another author summarizes:

[European] Company officers documented a complex, changing, and highly differentiated landscape of agrarian commodity production in south India. . . . Scholars support a line of argument . . . [that] spatially differentiated but widespread trade expansion, capital accumulation, labour specialisation, and productive diversification generated commercial resources for state revenue during three centuries before British rule . . . [and] produced the commercial economy that states tapped for revenue. (Ludden 1990: 236, 216–17)

Local producers and distributors of both agricultural and manufacturing products were tied into a complex system of advance payments on credit and/or materials. "In fact" writes Perlin (1983: 73), "credit and finance operated in terms of a complex ordering involving lenders at different organizational and social levels . . . [which] encompassed a relatively large proportion of the agricultural product," not to mention the manufacturing output.

These mechanisms and institutions allowed high rates of appropriation by providing means for large numbers of producers to survive climatic and price fluctuations, to which high taxation and rents, and low real prices for marketable commodities, made them especially vulnerable . . . [and] provided continuity in space and time, enabling commercial transactions to multiply. (Perlin 1983: 98)

Manufacturers received raw materials and or credit to acquire them, employed artisans, and paid them wages. Other artisans worked for state monopolies, also on a wage basis, and still others worked independently (Ganguli 1964: 47 ff.). All of them were part and parcel of an organized "system" of finance, credit, distribution, trade, and production for the local, regional, and export market—which had of course long been and continued to be part and parcel of the *world* market. When the Europeans entered, as for instance the Dutch VOC did near Agra, it was into a "triangular network, covering large distances, and a framework for company transfers between several other places, [that] is merely the tip of an organisational complex of remittance facilities and advance crediting that includes much of the Indian sub-continent and extends well beyond" (Perlin 1990: 268).

Burton Stein's (1989) review of some of this same evidence from India's precolonial economy once again confirms its widespread commercialization as well as both extensive and dense productive and commercial relations between the countryside and towns and among ubiquitous small and larger urban commercial centers. Elsewhere, Stein and Sanjay Subrahmanyam, (1996) note in the introduction to their collection, *Institutions and Economic Change in South Asia,* that the unifying thread among the collected papers is that economic actors and institutional structures were continually undergoing economic change in relation to each other and in response to changing economic circumstances and imperatives. Stein (1989) also signals that India's well-developed financial system provided much of the capital used not only by Indian producers and traders themselves, but also by both the EIC and private European traders for their own operations within India and beyond.

One of the extensions of Indian trade for centuries—indeed millennia (Frank 1993a)—had been westward to Central Asia, Persia, Mesopotamia, Anatolia, the Levant, Arabia, Egypt, and East Africa. Of course, analogous—and related—productive, commercial, and financial institutions had been operative there as well. Arab and Muslim trade had flowered during the European Dark Ages, and continued to do so in early modern times, even though the Arab traders themselves were subject to increasing competition from both the west and the east. For instance, Ibn Khaldun, already quoted regarding merchants and commerce from non-Arabic lands, also wrote about Muslim and other trade in the fourteenth century:

> when goods are few and rare, their prices go up. On the other hand, when . . . they will be found in large quantities, the prices will go down. . . . Commerce means the attempt to make a profit by increasing capital, through buying goods at a lower price and selling them at a higher price, whether these goods consist of slaves, grain, animals, weapons, or clothing. The accrued amount is called profit. . . . It has thus become clear that gains and profits, in their entirety or for the most part, are realized from human labour. . . . Furthermore, God created two minerals, gold and silver, as a measure of value for all capital accumulations. These the inhabitants of the world, by preference, consider treasure and property. Even if, under certain circumstances, other things are acquired, it is only for the purpose of ultimately obtaining (gold and silver). All other things are subject to market fluctuations. . . . Profit may come from merchandise and its use in barter; merchants can make such profit either by travelling around with

(merchandise) or by hoarding it and observing the market fluctuations that effect it. This is called commerce. . . . Commerce is a
natural way of making profits. However, most of the practices
and methods are tricky and designed to obtain the (profit) margin
between purchase price and sale prices. This surplus makes it possible to earn profit. Therefore, the law permits cunning in commerce, since (commerce) contains an element of gambling. (Ibn
Khaldun 1969: 298–300)

Abu-Lughod (1989: 201–9) devotes a section to Islam and business in
which she examines many financial instruments and economic institutions. Muslim "commercial techniques" have been surveyed by Abraham Udovitch (1970) among others, and the compatibility of Islam
with capitalism and commerce has been the theme of Maxime Rodinson (1970, 1972), though the very fact that Muslims, not to mention
Mohammed himself, had been merchants for ages should be enough
evidence. Bruce Masters (1988) is at pains to distinguish Ottoman from
European economic policies in his study of Aleppo. Nonetheless, his
account of the caravan trade, merchants, commercial institutions,
money, credit, and investment all testify to the thoroughgoing commercialization and monetization of the Ottoman economy. His examination of court records involving loans "provide us with a painfully
clear vision of the cycle of debt that linked the rural areas to various
wealthy and influential individuals in the city" (Masters 1988: 156–67).
Moreover, Masters also stresses the active and independent participation of women in the Ottoman economy.

Elsewhere also, Indian Muslim and other trade and traders had well-
established and still growing positions in and through Southeast Asia,
where Malay and other peoples had also developed their own commercial and financial institutional structures, into which they admitted Arabs, Persians, Indians, and later Europeans coming from the west and
Chinese coming from the north.

In China. That the Chinese (as well as the Japanese and
others) were linked in this international division of labor and trade is
beyond doubt, and that they held a position of productive superiority
is one of the theses of this book. We have reviewed some of China's
foreign and long-distance trade above. In this regard of course, "long-
distance overseas trade for the Chinese was no different than for other
trading peoples," as Wang Gungwu (1990: 402 ff.) observes. Despite
official Ming restrictions, overseas trade from South China continued,

and "overseas Chinese" communities as well as foreigners participated in it. Particularly important ones, especially Hokkiens, resided in Nagasaki, Manila, and Batavia, all to manage the China trade.

However, the Chinese must also have had the requisite complementary productive, commercial, and financial institutions at home. Curiously, the institutional base seems to be better established for the earlier Song and Yuan times (Yang 1952, Ma 1971, Elvin 1973) than for the later Ming and Qing times. Nonetheless, Perlin (1990: 280) writes that "all of my reading of Chinese circulation forms suggests a spatial organization of physical moneys and moneys of account very similar in its principles to those of pre-colonial India, the near and middle East, early-modern Europe, or Spanish America." In an earlier work, Perlin (1983: 66) writes that "Late pre-colonial south Asia, like China in the same period, was subject to a fundamental process of change affecting most of its major social, economic and government features." That was, of course, the same development of the same global economy in which they all participated, and Europe too! So it need not appear strange that in her review of Chinese "business practices and institutions," Abu-Lughod (1989: 309 ff.) cites Kato as observing that the Chinese "Hang" merchants' associations resembled European guilds.

We have already observed in chapter 2 that the Chinese economy since Song times in the eleventh and twelfth centuries had been industrialized, commercialized, monetized, and urbanized far in excess of any other in the world. Looking back over these centuries up until the eighteenth century, Elvin (1973) summarizes:

The Chinese economy had become commercialized. One sign of this development was the increased complexity of the structure of business. . . . [Other signs were] the growth of money-shops and remittance banks, the guilds of merchants engaged in inter-regional trade . . . [and] the growing density of the local market network. . . . Nor was entrepreneurship absent. Here is an account of how the price of fuel was reduced. . . . We may thus conclude that the last three centuries of pre-modern Chinese history saw the creation of much larger units of private economic organization than ever before, and that the change here was qualitative as well as quantitative. In particular, rural industries were coordinated through a market network of rapidly increasing density, and urban industry, supplied with materials and customers through this network, developed new structures to handle large numbers of employees. (Elwin 1973: 172, 299, 300)

For instance, Elvin describes the iron works in the Hubei/Shaanxi/Sichuan region, where six or seven furnaces gave employment to a thousand men and also quotes a contemporary account about Jingdezhen (Ching-te-chen), the great porcelain-making center in Jiangxi (Kiangsi) province:

> Tens of thousands of pestles shake the ground with their noise. The heavens are alight with the glare from the fires, so that one cannot sleep at night. The place has been called in jest "The Town of Year-Round Thunder and Lightening." (Elvin 1973: 285)

Elvin concludes that

> Economic enterprise would thus seem to have been alive in late traditional China. There certainly was keen awareness of comparative costs, and this could demonstrably have its effects upon the kind of technology used [as for instance using evaporation techniques instead of boiling to make salt, since firewood had became increasingly scarce and expensive]. . . . It is therefore reasonable to assume that perfectly rational short-run considerations lay behind many or most choices of technique. (Elvin 1973: 300)

Shortages of good hardwood trees, which were felled to build ships, raised the price of wood so much in South China that shipbuilding moved to Siam and Malaya, where such wood was much more plentiful and cheaper (Marks 1997a).

Referring to South China, Marks (1996: 77) also notes that "by the middle of the eighteenth century so much of Lingnan's agroecosystem had become commercialized that a larger portion of food entered the market, and markets operated more efficiently, than in England, France, or the United States at the same time." Ng Chin-Keong (1983) also testifies to far-reaching commercialization not only in eighteenth-century Amoy (Xiamen) that is the specific subject of his study, but also of its province, Fujian. Moreover, he reviews Fujian's complex relations of trade and migration with Taiwan across the straits, with Canton and Macao down the coast and with the Yangzi Valley rice-growing regions as far upstream as Chongqing [Chungking] and beyond in Sichuan, as well as with Manchuria. Beyond analyzing government intervention in the market to stabilize prices through the seasonal and other sale of food stocks, he summarizes that "rice shipments within the coastal network had gone beyond the sole purpose of relief and had become highly commercialized" (Ng 1983: 130). The commercial development and institutions of the Yangzi Valley region were already noted following Wong (1997) in chapter 2.

Pomeranz (1997: chap. 1, pp. 30–31) notes that Chinese farmers placed a larger percentage of their production on the market, which was also more competitive, than did farmers in Western Europe. At the same time, Chinese farmers were also freer to engage in handicrafts production for the market. Pomeranz also shows that rights over property and sale of land were greater in China than in Western Europe.

Moreover, there was increased regional specialization in agriculture (Gernet 1982: 427–8), also in cash crops, especially mulberry leaves as food for silkworms. This and much other agricultural production was increasingly commercialized, not the least to serve the industrial and export economy. For instance, the prices of mulberry leaves needed to feed silkworms could fluctuate from morning to noon to evening. Land was bought and sold, particularly to merchants who wanted to gentrify, so much that landlords came to be called "silverlords" (Brook 1998).

A 1609 quotation from a Chinese contemporary, Zhang Tao, may be enough to give some of the flavor:

> Those who went out as merchants became numerous and the ownership of land was no longer esteemed. Men matched wits using their assets, and fortunes rose and fell unpredictably. . . . Those who enriched themselves through trade became the majority, and those who enriched themselves through agriculture were few. The rich became richer and the poor, poorer. Those who rose took over, and those who fell were forced to flee. It was capital that brought power; land was not a permanent prospect. . . . One man in a hundred is rich, while nine out of ten are impoverished. The poor cannot stand up to the rich, who though few in number, are able to control the majority. The lord of silver rules heaven and the god of copper cash reigns over the earth. (cited in Brook 1998)

Nonetheless, the institutional structure of agriculture and the market for its products in China was remarkably responsive to changing ecological and economic circumstances and social needs, and apparently more so than during this same time in England. Grain prices varied inversely to harvest supplies in both countries. However, they were less volatile in South China than they were in England, not because the market worked less, but because it worked better! In South China, cropping was increased by planting two corps a year, harvest yields were relatively stabilized by increased irrigation, and supplies were regulated through local storage and interregional trade. Marks's (1997a) comparisons suggest that "peasant farmers, state bureaucrats, and grain merchants of South China managed better than their English counterparts to even out adverse effects of climate upon their respective agricultural economies." Marks attributes this to "improved technology as represented by irrigation works, the state granary system, and an efficient market mechanism [which] served to lessen the impact of climatic changes upon harvest yields and rice prices in South China"—more and better than in eighteenth-century England.

After many careful comparisons between market institutions in China and various parts of Western Europe, Pomeranz also concludes:

> when we turned to factor markets for land and labor we found, surprisingly, that China seemed to conform to modern European ideas of efficient economic institutions at least as well as pre-1800 Western Europe. . . . Thus, it seems likely that the use of labor in China, like that of land, conformed to the principles of "market economy" at least as well as in Europe, and quite likely somewhat better. . . . Moreover, China's much-maligned patterns of family labor use seem, upon closer examination, to have been as responsive to shifting opportunities and price signals as those of Northwestern Europe. Far from being unique, then, the most developed parts of Western Europe seem to have shared crucial economic features—commercialization, commodification of goods, land, and labor, market-driven growth, and adjustment by households of fertility and labor allocation to economic trends—with other densely populated core areas in Eurasia. . . . (Pomeranz 1997: chap. 1, pp. 51–52).

Indeed, the state provided tax, market, and other incentives not only to clear and settle new land, but also to encourage the migration of tens of millions of peoples to labor-scarce areas.

Moreover, Pomeranz also compares long-distance grain shipments in China and Europe, all of which had then to be distributed by commercial institutions through some kind of market network. In North China in the eighteenth century, long-distance grain trade yearly fed 6 to 10 million adult males. That was ten to fifteen times the normal, and some three times the peak, amounts of grain trade through the Baltic. Indeed, imports into a single southern Chinese province fed more people than the entire Baltic trade (Pomeranz 1997: chap. 1, pp. 5).

Elvin (1973) notes how these developments also generated and supported urbanization (and vice versa), which also was absolutely and relatively greater in China than elsewhere, except for a time in Japan. Two cities of around 5 million population each have been reported for Song times (Frank and Gills 1993: 177, citing Gernet 1985). In the early modern period, Elwin finds a rate of urbanization of 6 to 7.5 percent with an urban population of 6 million inhabitants, which "undoubtedly understates big city population." China still was the most urbanized country in the world, though it then ceded that pride of place to neighboring Japan. By 1900, however, the Chinese urban population had declined to about 4 percent of total population, that is, significantly less than it has been in the thirteenth century (Elvin 1993: 175, 178).

In summary, it should be clear that contrary to Eurocentric myth, "all entrepreneurs in intercontinental trade [which included much regional and local trade as well] acted rationally and made the best possible use of their resources, not only the East India companies and the Liverpool slave trader, but also the Indonesian or Malabar pepper farmer, the Indian merchant or the African slave exporter" (Steensgaard 1990c: 16). Therefore, there is no basis in historical fact for the latter-day Eurocentric put-downs (nor the Polanyi-type elevation) of Asians and Africans. They are certainly not held back by any "Asiatic mode of production" (Marx) or by a "hydraulic/bureaucratic society" (Wittfogel) or by the lack of "rationality" or even irrationality (Weber, Sombart). Equally irrelevant are the categories of "redistributive" (Polanyi) and other "traditional" societies (as per Lerner, Rostow, and all Western Modernizationists).

The same Eurocentric myopia still pervades those who study the "modern world-system." For instance, an issue of Wallerstein's *Review* carries an otherwise innovative article on cycles by Tony Porter (1995). Following Angus Cameron, Porter identifies and analyzes long "logistic" cycles spanning almost the entire period from A.D. 1000 to the present day and relates "global" finance and hegemony in the context of cycles including "world production." Unfortunately, his data on the latter are taken from Joshua Goldstein (1988), whose "world" is limited to Europe. No matter, for so are Porter's financial institutions and "hegemonies." The fact that there also were important financial institutions and innovations as well as economic cycles, but no hegemonies, in the world economy outside Europe does not seem to concern Porter. Yet the Dutch and other European financial institutions he analyzes were intimately related to and dependent on those in Asia, as we have noted above and in chapter 2. Porter's nearly total blindness toward Asia in his "model of innovation in global finance" also distorts and vitiates the analysis of history "as it really was" in Europe and its alleged separate "world-economy" itself. Alas, much the same must be said of Giovanni Arrighi's (1994) otherwise magisterial and prize-winning but also still too Eurocentric book on (exclusively) European financial innovations, *The Long Twentieth Century* (see discussion below in chapter 6).

The implications of all this for the thesis of the alleged European origin of capitalism, we may leave for consideration in the concluding chapter 7—after we have had the opportunity to examine still more evidence that casts doubt on this proposition, which is as dubious as it is widespread.

In summary, this chapter has examined population, production, income, productivity, trade, technology, and economic and financial institutions around the globe, compared them among major regions, and argued that all of them were related and generated as part of the market structure and developmental dynamic of a single global economy. We have noted that, comparatively speaking, development in many parts of Asia was not only far ahead of Europe at the beginning of our period in 1400, but continued to be so still at the end of this period in 1750–1800. Moreover historically speaking, our survey shows that contrary to the received "wisdom" in and from Europe, its "takeoff" after 1800 was not based on any exceptional European scientific, technological, and institutional "preparation." Still less were developments in Europe based on any alleged "head start" gained during its "Renaissance," let alone on any spurious "inheritance" of superior rationality and science from Greece and Judaism. All this received "wisdom" is no more than Eurocentric ideology based on mythology, and not on real history or social science. On the contrary, even minimally adequate scholarship must derive "the Rise of the West" from the prior and contemporaneous development of "The rest" in and of the world. That is what will be demonstrated in the chapters that follow.

To conclude our "comparative" analysis and before proceeding with our global one however, it will be useful to present the comparative conclusions by another student of the timing of Asia's "decline" and Europe's "rise." Rhoades Murphey tried to evaluate the relative "effectiveness" of the East and the West through estimates of a combination of military strength, economic prosperity or expansion, technological growth, and political cohesion:

In many respects the West did attain a rising level of effectiveness, beginning perhaps in the late seventeenth or early eighteenth centuries, and this tended to coincide in time with a falling level of effectiveness on the part of most Asian traditional [sic!] orders. Both the Western rise and the Eastern decline were absolute, and their temporal coincidence shaped the pattern of confrontation. (Murphey 1977: 5)

Murphey drew an ascending curve for the "West" and a descending one for "Asia," and they crossed in 1815. For India, he would put the crossover earlier, around 1750 or even before, and later for China. That is, Murphey's impressionistic but quite independent estimation of Asian and European global "effectiveness" also supports the contention in the present book of Asian preponderance in the world until at least 1800.

These findings so far only form the basis for the analysis that follows: In chapter 5 we analyze how different parts of the world economy responded simultaneously to the same, often cyclical, global economic forces. That analysis in turn sets the stage for our inquiry in chapter 6 of when and why the Asian economies almost simultaneously declined and how and why the West "rose" not only in *relation* to Asia, but how these were the global, regional, and sectoral consequences of the structure and dynamic of the whole world economy itself. Let us then turn to the world economic structural and cyclical forces, which reversed this East-West relationship only in and apparently also only for the nineteenth and twentieth centuries.

CHAPTER 5

Horizontally Integrative Macrohistory

The fact remains, however, that the field of history, as it is cultivated at most European and American universities, produces a microhistorical, even parochial outlook. . . . Historians are alert to vertical continuities (the persistence of tradition, etc.) but blind to horizontal ones. . . . However beautiful the mosaic of specific studies that make up the "discipline" of history may be, without a marcohistory, *a tentative general schema of the continuities, or at least, parallelisms in history, the full significance of the historical peculiarities of a given society cannot be seen. . . . Integrative history is the search for and description and explanation of such interrelated historical phenomena. Its methodology is conceptually simple, if not easy to put into practice: first one searches for historical parallelisms (roughly contemporaneous similar developments in the world's various societies), and then one determines whether they are causally interrelated. . . . To find interconnections and horizontal continuities of early modern history, one must look underneath the surface of political and institutional history, and examine developments in economics, societies, and cultures of the early modern period. If we do this, it may appear that in the seventeenth century for example, Japan, Tibet, Iran, Asia Minor, and the Iberian peninsula, all seemingly cut off from one another, were responding to some of the same, interrelated, or at least similar demographic, economic and even social forces.*

Joseph Fletcher (1985: 39, 38)

The structure of the global economy and world system is outlined in the preceding chapters, but the proposition that it has its own temporal dynamic has been only implicit. Therefore, this chapter uses some analytical apparatus to inquire into this temporal dynamic and to distinguish among various kinds of temporal and possibly cyclical movements. For, if there indeed was a single globe-encompassing world economic system with its own structure of interlinkages among its regions and sectors, then it stands to reason that what happened in one of them should or at least may have had repercussions also in one or more others. We observed in chapter 3 how the circulation of money around the global economy affected its participants even at its farthest reaches. Moreover, we saw in chapter 4 how this global economic structure and process helped shape and modify even "local" institutions and generate new technological adaptations to changing circumstances. Indeed, not only can one part of the system affect another, but the interlinked structure and dynamic of the whole system may affect any and even all of its parts.

Therefore to account for and understand any local or regional process, it may also be necessary to inquire into how those processes are affected by and respond to contemporary events elsewhere and/or to simultaneous processes in the world economic system as a whole. For this reason I pleaded long ago that

> however useful it may be to relate the same thing through different times, the essential (because it is both the most necessary and the least accomplished) contribution of the historian to historical understanding is successively to relate different things and places at the same time in the historical process. The very *attempt* to examine and relate the simultaneity of different events in the whole historical process or in the transformation of the whole system—even if for want of empirical information or theoretical adequacy it may be full of holes in its factual coverage of space and time—is a significant step in the right direction (particularly at a time in which this generation must "rewrite history" to meet its need for historical perspective and understanding of the single historical process in the one world today). (Frank 1978a: 21)

Since that time and shortly before his untimely death, Joseph Fletcher made the even stronger plea reproduced above in the epigraph to this chapter. So we must try to start doing what he counseled but was not able to do. Moreover, Joseph Schumpeter (1939) wrote that economic or business cycles are not like tonsils that can be extirpated, but rather are like the heartbeat of the organism itself. There is also substantial evidence in Braudel and Wallerstein that the world economy has a cyclical heartbeat of its own. Even scattered evidence suggests that this cyclical heartbeat has been so common to widely distant—and supposedly autonomous—areas of the world as to constitute still another important indication that they were truly part and parcel of a single world economy.

George Modelski has suggested that we must first define the system in which we seek to locate the cycles. Yet, operationally it may well be the other way around: identifying simultaneity of cycles across far-flung areas can also offer prima facie evidence of the extension and bounding of the system, as I have argued even for Bronze Age world system cycles (Frank 1993a). Much more evidence to this effect should, and surely could, be brought to light and analyzed for the modern world system. Unfortunately, only a very few historians have troubled to find and present evidence on whether and how cycles coincided across the sup-posed boundaries of world-economies. However, Modelski and Thompson (1996) have now adopted the same procedure to identify world systemic linkages and dimensions. That can reveal so much about whether several world-economies really did form a single world econ-omy—which hardly any historians think existed! Let us nonetheless make at least some stabs in the dark at inquiring into such a horizontally integrative macrohistory, to use Fletcher's terminology, and see what light it can shed on our concerns.

Simultaneity Is No Coincidence

To make an excursion to a time partly before our period, let us briefly examine Immanuel Wallerstein's (1992: 587) account of European-wide cyclical decline from 1250 to 1450, in a pattern "clearly laid out and widely accepted among those writing about the late Middle Ages and early modern times in Europe." In his own review of the same period Fernand Braudel, noting the decline of the Champagne fairs at the end of the thirteenth century, says

> these dates also coincide with the series of crises of varying dura-tion and seriousness affecting the whole of Europe at the time, from Florence to London, heralding what was to become, in con-junction with the Black Death, the great recession of the four-teenth century. (Braudel 1992: 114)

But was this decline limited to Europe? No! Janet Abu-Lughod (1989) and Barry Gills and myself (1992; also in Frank and Gills 1993) discuss its repercussions throughout Afro-Eurasia, which led up to the period under consideration here. Moreover, the Indian historian K. N. Chaudhuri refers to Braudel's ascription of a thirteenth- to fourteenth-century decline in Cambodia to ecological change, and points out that Mesopotamian irrigated agriculture was also ruined about the same time. He also asks what accounts for the case of

> Ceylon and its sudden, catastrophic demise after about AD 1236? First of all, let us note that the Sinhalese collapse was not unique. The period from the 1220s to the 1350s was one of deep crisis for many societies in Asia. . . . That near total demographic catastrophes . . . took place in every region of the Indian Ocean is not in question. . . . Were these events all coincidence? (Chaudhuri 1990a: 246–68)

Proceeding to the period under study in the present book, Linda Darling (1994: 96) in reviewing events in the Ottoman Empire and elsewhere writes that "we should take the simultaneous occurrences of these trends in such different countries as the starting point of a new agenda for research and reconceptualization. It is possible that events . . . were not just superficially similar but structurally linked."

Similarly, Niels Steensgaard observes about Eurasia as a whole:

> I find it hard to believe that the financial turmoil all over Eurasia in the sixteenth century was a coincidence, and I can find no other connecting link than the increase in bullion stocks and the imbalances attendant upon bullion flows across or crisscrossing the Eurasian continent. (Steensgaard 1990c: 20)

Moreover, Steensgaard notes that C. A. Bayly also found a remarkable "emergence of similar patterns of historiography for large parts of the eastern hemisphere, often unknown to the authors which might help point to some causative factors in this eighteenth century crisis of extra-European Empires" (Steensgaard 1990c: 22, quoting Bayly but without citation).

Most intriguingly, M. Athar Ali writes:

> Are all these phenomena mere coincidences? It seems to me straining one's sense of the plausible to assert the same fate overcame all the large Indic and Islamic world at precisely the same time, but owing to quite different (or rather miscellaneous) factors operating in the case of each of them. Even if the search should ultimately prove futile, one must see whether it is possible

to discover some common factor that caused more or less stable empires to disintegrate. (Ali 1975: 386)

Chapter 6 discusses why Ali thinks these phenomena are not coincidences and what my explanation is, which is rather different from Ali's. Mine also examines the interrelated whys and wherefores of "the Decline of the East *and* of "the Rise of the West." Before we can proceed to tackle this major problem, however, we need to construct a basis for doing so by pursuing the question and suggestions posed above by Chaudhuri, Steensgaard, Darling, and Ali. They can also usefully guide our research and analysis using the integrative horizontal macrohistory proposed by Fletcher.

Several scholars have recently made some innovative attempts in the direction of the integrative horizontal history that Fletcher called for. Below we briefly review some initiatives by Jack Goldstone (1991a, b), several students of a possible "seventeenth-century crisis," George Modelski and William Thompson on Kondratieff waves (1996), Mark Metzler (1994), and Barry Gills and myself (Frank and Gills 1993).

Doing Horizontally Integrative Macrohistory

DEMOGRAPHIC/STRUCTURAL ANALYSIS

An innovative attempt in this direction is the "demographic/structural" analysis by Goldstone (1991a). He examined near-simultaneous events in several periods of modern world history, particularly the state breakdowns or near-breakdowns in Ming China, the Ottoman Empire, and England in the 1640s. He demonstrates widespread and repeated cyclical simultaneity across Eurasia, but his demographic/structural analysis leaves little room for international rather than only "national" cyclical and other economic processes, and he emphatically rejects any worldwide monetary ones. Goldstone explains himself:

My primary conclusion is quite beautiful in its parsimony. It is that the periodic state breakdowns in Europe, China and the Middle East from 1500 to 1800 were the result of a single basic process. . . . The main trend was that population growth, in the context of relatively inflexible economic and social structures, led to changes in prices, shifts in resources, and increasing social de-

mands with which the agrarian-bureaucratic states could not successfully cope. (Goldstone 1991a: 459)

Unlike some other critics, I find Goldstone's longer-term demographic/
structural explanation persuasive or at least worthy of the most serious
attention and pursuit, even though a generalized "seventeenth-century
crisis" is more than doubtful, as argued below. My favorable review is
in Frank (1993b), and some of my critique is below. I am doubtful about
his dismissal of short-term monetary factors, which strike me as quite
compatible with and very possibly fortifying his longer-term structural/
demographic ones.

A "SEVENTEENTH-CENTURY CRISIS"?

There has been much speculation and discussion, and
some analysis, of the so-called "seventeenth-century crisis." A number
of books and chapters have been devoted to its occurrence or origin in
Europe (Hobsbawm 1954, 1960, Aston 1970, De Vries 1976, Frank
1978a, Wallerstein 1980). Still in dispute is the precise dating of the "crisis," whether and how it extended beyond the Atlantic economy, and if
so especially how it may have been related to a "Little Ice Age." For
the crisis included crop shortages and famines, disease epidemics, and
demographic declines along with economic depression and political upheaval. There is evidence for climatic, demographic, social, economic,
and political crises in many parts of Eurasia, especially in Japan, China,
Southeast Asia, Central Asia, and in the Ottoman Empire, at some—
but not always the same!—times during about three-quarters of the
seventeenth century between 1620 and 1690.

Moreover, Goldstone (1991a) has argued cogently that rapid population increase in the sixteenth century was not matched by sufficient
growth in food production and as a result generated demographic/
structural crises and political upheavals or even breakdown at least in
Ming China (1644), the Ottoman Empire, and in England (1640). In
Europe, the entire Mediterranean region declined, especially Portugal,
Spain, and Italy.

It is important to reexamine here whether the "seventeenth-century
crisis" was worldwide—including especially Asia—and really a century
or at least a half-century long. Or was the "crisis" essentially limited to
Europe (where, however, the Netherlands experienced its "golden age"
in this period) and perhaps some other regions; and how long and what

kind of crisis was there in Asia? These questions and their answers are important to our inquiry for the following reasons: Any horizontally integrative macrohistory should examine this period, not only as a significant case study, but also because it can reveal the extent to which—and what—economic forces operated all around the world simultaneously. If the crisis was really global, either a worldwide cyclical "B" down phase (in Kondratieffian terms) was at work, and/or Europe was—as many claim—already influential enough in the world economy to pull the rest of it down with itself. If the evidence does not support the case for such a crisis in Asia, the implication is that events in Europe did not yet carry such significant world economic weight and that there was no seventeenth-century *world* crisis.

Another reason why the evidence on this matter is important to our inquiry is that it will permit us in the following chapter to pursue the question of how long the "A" phase upturn lasted that started in Asia in 1400 and in 1450 in Europe. That in turn will also permit us to inquire whether or not the Gills and Frank (1992; also in Frank and Gills 1993) half-millennium-long cycles continued into the early modern period. The evidence and the argument in this regard will also play an important part in the analysis in chapter 6 about how and why "the decline of the East preceded the rise of the West," again to quote Abu-Lughod (1989: 388). Furthermore, the evidence about the existence or not of a "seventeenth-century crisis" can afford us the necessary background and context to examine the length, kind, and nature of the crises that have been identified *in* the seventeenth century. I will pay particular attention to the crisis during the couple of decades around 1640, to which we turn in the section following this one.

This question of the existence or not of a "seventeenth-century crisis" in the world or much of it has already been the subject of some examination and debate, especially in several articles in *Modern Asian Studies* (1990). The thesis of a seventeenth-century general crisis in China was launched by S. A. M. Adshead (1973: 272), who suggested that "the European crisis was in fact world wide in its repercussions, and . . . affected not only Europe, but the Islamic world and East Asia as well." Since then, several related questions have been raised and examined: Was there a *general* long-lasting crisis in the seventeenth century? The short answer seems to be no. To the extent that there was a long(er)-lasting crisis, where did it visit and is there evidence for the same in most or even many parts of the world and/or Asia? The short answer again seems to be no. Was there a shorter economic and political crisis simultaneously in several parts of the world, including Asia? The answer seems to be yes, in the 1630s and 1640s. Were these various regional and/or country crises related? The answer also seems to be yes. Can they be attributed primarily to the demographic causes stressed by Goldstone? That is dubious. Were they related to common climatic and therefore also agricultural output problems? Probably so. Were they also related to or caused by common monetary problems? That is the subject of particular dispute, and as I note below my own inclination is toward those who argue for yes.

Let us review some of the evidence. Anthony Reid (1990) argues that the region of his special expertise, Southeast Asia, definitely suffered from a "seventeenth-century crisis" and that this was also "general" for Asia. He argues that around and after mid century, Southeast Asia, exceptionally trade dependent as it was, suffered economically from lower prices for its exports, lower production, and decreased trade at Manila and elsewhere, both absolutely and relative to world trade in general. Reid perhaps makes a bit too much in Southeast Asian terms of the "crisis" in Manila, which was related to its intermediary role between Spanish America and China and Japan (of which more below). The destruction of Pegu in Burma in 1599 was rather too early to ascribe to a crisis of the mid-seventeenth century. However for east-central Java, Reid (1990: 92–95) notes especially dry conditions over the entire first seventy-five years of the seventeenth century and below normal rainfall in every year from 1645 to 1672. Drought and famine visited Burma and Indonesia in the 1630s and 1660s; and the rice-producing floodplains in Siam and Cambodia probably also were short of water. This economic depression also had negative effects on Dutch and other European traders in Southeast Asia (Reid 1990, Tarling 1992: 488–493). Reid also notes reports of declines of population in some places of European occupancy in Southeast Asia but adds that for this very reason they may not be representative.

Indeed, island Southeast Asia and the Malay Peninsula on which Reid preferentially focuses may themselves not be so representative either. In a review of Reid's book, Lieberman (1996: 802, 801) says so very explicitly: "There was no seventeenth century collapse. . . . The thesis of seventeenth century watershed seems to me to be fundamentally inapplicable to the mainland." Lieberman (1996: 800) specifically refers to "the long sixteenth century" and documents that in mainland Southeast Asia it flourishes through the eighteenth century.

Even so, Reid (1997), who collegially handed me this Lieberman critique, continues to insist on a seventeenth-century crisis for Southeast Asia in general and seems also to stick to his earlier claim that the "seventeenth-century crisis" may have been worldwide, including all of Asia, although that was disconfirmed by others writing in the same (1990) issue of the journal *Modern Asian Studies* in which Reid proposed this wider thesis.

However, the evidence from several other parts of Asia (and indeed also the Americas) does not lend much support to Reid. In the same issue of *Modern Asian Studies,* John Richards (1990) examines the Indian evidence with this very question in mind. He is emphatic that, except for the 1630s famine, there is no evidence of any such long or even short "crisis" in Mughal India. On the contrary, population, urbanization, production, productivity, government income and reserves all continued to increase as they had in previous centuries. Local, regional, interregional trade also grew. India prospered during the seventeenth century, as evidenced in the review of trade in and from India in chapter 2, as well as by the earlier discussion of the expansion of agriculture, urbanization, and manufacturing in relation to the inflow of money and the level of prices in chapter 3. All this evidence points to the same conclusion of continued economic expansion in India through the seventeenth century. Moreover, the evidence of growing overseas trade from and to India and especially *by* Indians is also overwhelming in all available sources. Since much of that Indian trade was with Southeast Asia, that seems also to contradict Reid's thesis of marked commercial decline in that region. Curiously, although Reid (1997: 4) documents a decline in four key exports from archipelago Southeast Asia after 1640, he writes that Indian "imports *must* have declined sharply after 1650, though we have figures only for the VOC's cloth imports which declined more slowly than the whole." My emphasis in Reid's sentence highlights that he has no evidence for this decline, and that the Dutch VOC decline is perfectly compatible also with the above mentioned displacement of European traders by Indian ones.

Also in the same issue of *Modern Asian Studies,* William Atwell examines the question of a "general crisis in East Asia." The short answer is that he cannot find any for the seventeenth century as a whole. However, here as in other articles to be cited below, Atwell does identify climatic problems (such as volcanic ash and cooler weather), which seem to have caused significant declines in agricultural output, especially of rice, in the 1630s and 1640s in China and Japan. Both experienced a significant worsening of economic and political conditions, including severe famine, commercial and trade declines, bankruptcies, reduced exports and lower export prices. Moreover, Atwell (1986, 1990) stresses that the short-term economic crises in China and Japan were related: they had common climatic problems; they were trade dependent on each other; and they were subject to common monetary problems. Atwell is the principal proponent of the "silver crisis" as a contributory cause of the fall of the Ming dynasty in 1644 to be examined in the next section.

However, Atwell cannot demonstrate concomitant simultaneous economic problems in Korea, which was also related to China and Japan, if only because Korea had not yet recovered from armed conflict with both several decades earlier. However in chapter 2, we did note evidence of some decline, or at least a shift, in economic activity and trade in and through Central Asia, which of course was also related to China. On the other hand, expansion in Russia did continue through the seventeenth century.

So was there a general "seventeenth-century crisis"? Fletcher (1985: 54) also posed this question. It seems that the answer is no. Also, Atwell (1990: 681) writes "in conclusion it is difficult to accept the idea that East Asia *as a region* experienced a long-term crisis during the seventeenth century." Even less so, as we noted above, is that the case for South Asia, or Russia/Siberia in North Asia, both of which undertook large-scale expansions. Steensgaard (1990b: 686, 688) also concludes that "the three essays presented here [Atwell's, Reid's, and Richards's, in the same issue of *Modern Asian Studies*], however brilliant and well-documented, do not present a firm foundation for arguing the existence of a seventeenth-century crisis in Asia. . . . They do not even convince the reader that the seventeenth-century crisis is a useful concept in the study of Asian history." On the evidence, we must agree.

There also was no generalized "seventeenth-century crisis" and decline in West Asia. Safavid rule did end in Persia in 1724, but it would be stretching things to ascribe that to a crisis in the mid-seventeenth century. The Ottoman Empire did experience problems, as analyzed for instance by Goldstone (1991a), but it survived; and as noted in earlier chapters, Huri Islamoglu-Inan (1987) and Linda Darling (1992) challenge the thesis of an Ottoman decline in the seventeenth century. On balance, so does Suraiya Faroqhi, who contributed the chapter on "Crisis and Change 1590–1699" to an economic and social history of the Ottoman Empire (Faroqhi 1994). Faroqhi takes some care to evaluate if and how the general thesis of a "seventeenth-century crisis" applies to the Ottomans and concludes that it does not. On the contrary. Textile production in and overseas trade through Bursa did decline in response to a profit squeeze (Faroqhi 1994: 454–56). However, other textile centers grew as part of increased regionalization and diversification, and such productive trading cities as Aleppo and Izmir intensified their commercial links with their respective hinterlands, which is analogous to what I found for Latin America during the same period (Frank 1978a).

> Thus it seems overly hasty to assume that around 1600 the Ottoman economy was transformed, once and for all, into an appendage of the European world economy. Rather it would seem there was a period of "economic disengagement" [lasting from the early seventeenth to the mid-eighteenth century]. . . . Certain Ottoman crafts recovered, and others . . . were newly created and thrived. . . . To put it differently, the Ottoman economy possessed potential of its own, and was not inert and defenceless. Even in the eighteenth century. . . . Assertions of global decline should be taken for what they are, unproven assumptions. (Faroqhi 1994: 525–26, 469)

Bruce McGowan's chapter in Inalcik and Quataert (1994: 710) describes "the sheer volume of fiscal innovation implemented by the Ottoman government in the eighteenth century [which] belies the myth of stagnation so popular among historians until recently."

In a chapter dedicated to the "seventeenth-century depression" in the European economy in Frank (1978a: 89–91, 94), I emphasized that there was expansion in India, that there was no "qualitative turn [in relations with Europe] different from those from the sixteenth century" in West Africa, and that there was expansion in the North Atlantic fisheries and in the North American colonies. For Latin America, I noted a decline in the production and export in silver (which since then has been called into some question) but a general regional increase in other economic activity and growth of interregional trade within Latin America.

In conclusion, there was apparently no generalized long-term "seventeenth-century crisis." It is certainly *not* true that "the European crisis was in fact worldwide in its repercussions" as suggested by Adshead (1973: 272) and reaffirmed with special reference to Asia in general by Reid (1990). In world economic and Asian terms, the regional and/or state crises were relatively localized and of only short two- or three-decade duration. Japan recovered quickly after mid century, and by the late seventeenth century so did China. More generalized declines occurred in Portugal, Spain, and Italy in Europe; but the Netherlands and then England profited from them. We will inquire what implications the continuation through the seventeenth century of the expansion in Asia had for our main argument in the following chapter. Here I wish to examine what sort of shorter crises there were in this century, in the absence of a generalized "seventeenth-century crisis."

THE 1640 SILVER CRISES

Shorter crises of two or three decades have been identified around the mid-seventeenth century, particularly in Japan and China. They seem to have had mainly climatological and monetary causes, although they may also have been part of a world economic Kondratieff "B" phase downturn, which normally lasts two to three decades.

All too often neglected has been the monetary and economic history of China, like that of Japan, not to mention Korea, in relation to their neighbors and the world economy. Or it is considered, but denied and rejected. Fifteenth-century Chinese silver production only amounted to a total of 4,000 tons (Cartier 1981: 459). Goldstone (1991a: 371–5) finds that China's trade with Europe was never more than 1 percent, and mostly less than one-third of 1 percent of China's "economy" while its import of silver from Japan was insignificant. Under the influence of additional evidence as well as Dennis Flynn, Goldstone (personal communication 1996) has somewhat revised his views on this matter.

Nonetheless, Goldstone explicitly rejects any monetary causes and even titles one of his sections on China "A Fiscal Crisis, Not a Monetary Crisis" (1991a: 371). He rejects suggestions by Atwell (1977, 1982, 1986) and Adshead (1973) that reduced silver production in and export from Spanish America and also Japan in the 1630s contributed to Ming decline. He recognizes the Ming's severe difficulties in gathering taxes and rents, and therefore in paying and outfitting its armies around 1640. But Goldstone—and Brian Molougheney and Xia Weizhong (1989) as well as Richard von Glahn (1996a), as we note below—dismiss silver supplies as a significant factor and dispute Atwell's argument that

[the] sharp decline in bullion imports . . . had disastrous consequences for the late Ming economy . . . many people were unable to pay taxes or rents, repay loans . . . [it became] impossible . . .

to adequately pay or equip military forces, Ming . . . lost control
. . . first to domestic rebels and then to the invading Manchus . . .
[which] certainly exacerbated its difficulties and helped undermine its stability. (Atwell 1982: 89, 90)

Elsewhere, Atwell writes that

Factors beyond imperial or bureaucratic control also adversely affected the late Ming economy. Not the least important of these
was the nature of the empire's monetary system. . . . Silver played
an increasingly important role in the economy. . . . With the great
influx of foreign bullion in the late sixteenth century, however,
that control [over the money supply] was lost. . . . Fluctuating
silver production in Peru, Mexico, and Japan, protectionist senti-
ments in Madrid and Edo, piracy and shipwrecks all made China's
foreign trade relations highly erratic. It was particularly capricious
during the period [1620–1644] under consideration here. Such
fluctuations had particularly serious repercussions when they coincided with unsettled weather, floods, droughts, and crop fail-
ures, which plagued China and other parts of East Asia during the
late 1630s and the early 1640s. (Atwell 1988: 589–89)

Dennis Flynn and Arturo Giraldez (1995b,c) argue that Ming finances
and rule were already weakened in the early seventeenth century by the
increase in the supply of imported silver. That reduced its market value
and therefore the value of Ming tax receipts, which were fixed in silver
terms. That may well have been the case, but it need not be taken as a
denial of the alleged further damage to Ming finances caused by a sudden decline in the supply of silver, even if the price ratios for silver/
copper and silver/grain were driven up.

Molougheney and Xia (1989: 61, 67) dispute this entire thesis. They
claim instead, referring to the second and third decades of the century,
that "the late Ming years saw this [Japanese silver] trade reach its ze-
nith" and "the nadir in the [total, including American] silver trade came
after the fall of the Ming, not before it." However, the evidence based
on their own reexamination of all identifiable Chinese silver imports
from Japan, via Manila, Taiwan, and other way stations suggests otherwise. By their own calculations, silver imports from Japan fluctuated
around 120 tons in the first half of the 1630s, rose to all-time highs of
200 tons in 1637 and 170 tons in 1639, and then dropped to an average
of 105 tons a year in the first half of the 1640s. They argue that the
observed decline in the trans-Atlantic arrival of Spanish American silver

at Seville did not signify a decline in American production, because
shipments across the Pacific, which averaged 17 percent of the total,
increased to 25 percent in the first three decades of the seventeenth
century and to more than 40 percent in the 1640s. "What was Spain's
loss was, at least in part, China's gain," say Molougheney and Xia (1989:
63).

Yet according to their table 1, the total silver remitted to Manila declined from 9 million pesos (23 tons) in the decade 1621–1630, to 7 million pesos (18 tons) in the decade 1631–40, to 4 million pesos (10 tons)
in the decade 1641–1650. "The only significant decline in trade [between
China and Manila] came in the period 1636–41" (Molougheney and Xia
1989: 64). But their rejection of the Atwell thesis and their statement
that problems for the Ming dynasty were due only to "domestic factors
rather than the vicissitudes on international bullion movements" (Molougheney and Xia 1989: 67) do not seem to be borne out by their own
data: transpacific silver declined by 13 tons (from 23 to 10 tons), and
Japanese silver declined to 105 tons in the first half of the 1640s and even
to 70 tons in 1643, the year preceding the end of the Ming. Yet Japanese
silver had been about 180 tons in the late 1630s and around 120 tons in
the early 1630s. By Reid's (1993: 27) composite estimates, total supplies
of silver from all sources, almost all of which went to China, were 150
tons annually in the 1610s, 178 tons annually in the 1620s, and 162 tons
annually in the 1630s. Then supplies declined abruptly to 89 tons a year
in the 1640s and 68 tons in the 1650s, rising again to 82 tons annually in
the 1660s (of which 40 percent however were supplied by the European
traders).

Another indication of the silver shortage may be the silver/copper-
cash ratio. In his discussion of "the market collapse and monetary insta-
bility of the years 1628–1660," Endymoin Wilkinson (1980: 30, 27–29)
stresses the very large rise in rice prices, particularly during the years of
harvest failure and famine, and the changes in the silver/copper-cash
ratio. The price of rice multiplied ten times between the 1628–1632 period and its maximum in 1642 and then fluctuated at still high levels
until declining again to two times its earlier level in 1662 and below that
by 1689, when measured in the popularly and therefore more commonly used copper-cash. At the same time, the rice price multiplied
only five times to 1642 in terms of silver taels and returned to its pre-
1630s price by 1663. As Wilkinson also emphasizes, at the same time the
copper/silver ratio gradually rose to more than double by 1642 and then
shot up to nine times its earlier ratio by 1647. Then it slowly declined

to its earlier level in 1662 and thereafter fluctuated at higher or similar levels till the 1680s.

Wilkinson, like Molougheney and Xia, attributes this decline in the silver price of copper to rampant debasement of copper, which no doubt happened. Wilkinson wrote before Atwell and the recent discussion about the silver shortage. Yet Molougheney wrote in the midst of that discussion and nonetheless still places the main brunt of the decline in the price of copper-cash to its rampant debasement (private communication 1996, citing his MA thesis). However, the equivalent two and then nine time increase in the copper price of silver may also or more so have been a manifestation of the *shortage* of silver, which is in question here. The simultaneous shortages of rice occasioned partly by weather and the small harvest were aggravated by economic, political, and social dislocation, which were also manifested in sharply falling prices of agricultural land. This situation, combined with the same shortage of silver and its increase in value relative to copper, could then also explain why the price of rice rose twice as much and stayed there longer in terms of copper than in terms of the now more valuable silver. In a word, the Chinese domestic prices of both rice and copper in terms of silver would seem to have reflected the shortage of silver, which is in question. That was so in the late 1630s, particularly so in the 1640s, and to a lesser extent still in the 1650s. Therefore I am obliged to agree with the argument like Atwell's that the supply of silver did contribute to the causes and to the consequences of the shift from Ming to Qing rule.

Additional evidence is that the Ming considered a proposal in 1643 to issue paper currency again. The proposal was rejected out of political weakness presumably coupled to fear of repeating earlier inflationary experiences, which would politically weaken them still further. In view of the continuing or growing silver shortage, their Qing successors did, however, find themselves obliged (and/or enabled) to print a limited amount of paper currency between 1650 and 1662. Then, it was again abolished (Yang 1952: 67–68) — since the supplies of silver revived?

Another empirically more informed and theoretically more sophisticated challenge to the Ming silver crisis thesis is proposed by von Glahn (1996a). Like Molougheney and Xia, he rejects both the evidence and the reasoning of a Ming silver crisis. "The volume of Japanese silver exports reached even greater heights in 1636–39, and remained high in the early 1640s, despite the restrictions and the expulsion of the Portuguese" (von Glahn 1996a: 437). He is also not persuaded that the supply via Manila, nor that via India, changed much for China so that "the data on bullion flows assembled here does not show any sharp decline in Chinese imports in the waning years of the Ming dynasty. . . . Overall, the Chinese economy did not experience any sudden diminution of silver imports during the last years of Ming rule" (von Glahn 1996a: 440).

Moreover, von Glahn also has some theoretical objections to the Ming silver crisis thesis. He argues that not the flow of silver, but its stock, is more relevant (and that it fell by only 4 percent relative to the previous century's imports). Moreover, the fall in Chinese prices preceded the decline in the flow of silver, and he also discusses the changes in the silver/copper ratio and the debasement of copper currency, already reviewed above. However, my discussion of the same also disputed the thesis about inflation in China; and von Glahn's data and argument support mine in this regard. Additionally, he argues that the silver/gold ratio declined when, in a silver scarcity, it should have risen. That could sound persuasive, except that he offers no evidence on possible changes in the supply of gold, which (as he acknowledges in a personal communication) have not been sufficiently researched.

Most curious and revealing however are von Glahn's tables, especially his table 5, in which he presents his own estimates of silver imports into China (see discussion in chapter 3). These imports, according to his admittedly conservative estimates, were 436 tons for 1631–1635; 573 tons for 1636–1640 (496 tons were from Japan); 249 tons for 1641–1645 (with 209 tons from Japan); and 186 tons for 1646–1655, after which imports again increase (von Glahn 1996a: 444). Noteworthy is that contrary to his explicit denials, von Glahn's data (just like those of Molougheney and Xia, also contrary to their denials), do show a marked decline of silver imports *by more than half* just prior to and also after the end of the Ming dynasty in 1644. That is, von Glahn's own estimates also contradict the above quoted claim that Japanese silver exports "remained high" and Chinese imports "did not decline in the waning years of the Ming dynasty." What then are we to make of the remainder of his—and the Molougheney and Xia's—argument? For my review of von Glahn, see Frank 1998b.

Moreover, Atwell (1982: 90) also notes that contemporary Chinese writers were themselves aware of this foreign silver connection. Furthermore, Japan and its rulers suffered similarly at the very same time. As in China, colder weather (perhaps the Little Ice Age again?) had generated food shortages and epidemics, and declining production of silver produced monetary and fiscal bottlenecks.

Indeed, exceptionally cold weather, increased disease, stagnating or regionally even negative population growth, trade stoppages, and problems with the money supply visited many parts of Eurasia during this period. The already weakened Ming regime fell prey to them, to economic stagnation, and to the resultant internal political rebellion and the regime's financial and military weakness to resist and then to repel the foreign Manchu invasion. In 1639 the Japanese restricted trade from Nagasaki, although Chinese trade continued and indeed replaced that of other countries. Nonetheless, Chinese traders were unable to meet their financial obligations in Manila, leading to the massacre of over 20,000 of them in 1640. Supplies of silver to China declined sharply and generated deflation and recession in South China at the same time as bad weather, locust attacks, floods, and droughts crippled agriculture elsewhere. The strapped government increased tax demands, but the now silver and cash-poor southerners defaulted. Another writer observed that

> in early 1644 arrears in army pay [had] accumulated to several million tales of silver while tax payments from the south arrived only in small parcels of several tens of thousands. The imperial granaries were now practically empty. . . . When Peking was besieged, the garrison had not been paid for five months. . . . Morale and discipline sank. . . . It was a wonder indeed that [the dynasty] survived until then. (Frederic Wakeman cited in Atwell 1988: 637)

Atwell (1986: 235) notes that the Japanese reduction in the exports of silver freed a greater part of the declining production for domestic use and that the Japanese were more successful in managing their currency system at home and abroad than the Chinese. The Japanese prohibited the export of silver, which rose in value so that now it became profitable again to export gold; but Japanese silver exports still did not cease (Ikeda 1996; see discussion in chapter 3). What Atwell and others do not say, but we can at least suspect, is that it was the continued greater availability of silver from domestic production in Japan that permitted the Japanese rulers to manage their currency better and to weather this storm, while the Ming dynasty succumbed to it.

The Mings were downed first by domestic rebellion in North China and then by conquest by the Manchus, who replaced the Ming with the Qing dynasty until 1911. But the significant intervention of the silver shortage seems inescapable—even on the evidence of those, like Molougheney and Xia and von Glahn, who deny it. As Atwell summarized, "the Ming dynasty fell, in part, because it simply did not have the funds to continue its operations" (Atwell 1986: 229). Yet even its Qing successor had to observe—in a memorial written by its viceroy of coastal Guandong in the south to the new emperor in 1647 that "trade had come to a [virtual] halt. . . . Therefore it is clear that when the people from Macao come to trade, Kwantung prospers; when they do not come, Kwantung suffers," because the Portuguese had stopped bringing silver (cited in Atwell 1986: 233). The Manila-Macao trade had been 43 tons of silver in 1630s, but Portuguese merchants stopped trading to Spanish Manila in 1642 after Portugal successfully rebelled against Spanish rule in 1640 (Atwell 1982: 87),though also in partial response to the same silver shortage, as suggested below. The tax receipts on silver exports to Manila declined by more than half between 1636 and 1640; and from then on the number of ships entering Manila from China fell from 123 to 83 in the period 1641–1645, to 58 in 1646–1650, and only 25 in 1556–1660 (Adshead 1988: 209).

The thesis of a short-term silver shortage and monetary crisis need not be incompatible with any longer-term structural/demographic and fiscal/political crisis explanation such as Goldstone (1991a) offers for the events of the 1640s in China, England, and the Ottoman Empire. On the contrary, the silver shortage and crisis may also have had similarly negative consequences in all of the above and perhaps in other regions of the world as well. Interestingly, in 1776 Adam Smith observed changes in the world silver market supply and its effects during precisely this period:

> Between 1630 and 1640, or about 1636, the effect of the discovery of the mines of America in reducing the value of silver appears to have been completed, and the value of the metal seems never to have sunk lower in proportion to that of corn than it was about that time. [Then] it seems to have risen somewhat [again] in the course of the present [eighteenth] century [when silver production again increased], and it had probably begun to do so even some time before the end of the last. (Smith 1937: 192)

That is, Adam Smith also noted that the increased supply of silver relative to the supply of other goods, especially wheat (still called "corn"), first generated an inflationary rise in their prices. However, that came to a halt in the mid 1630s, apparently because then the supply of silver declined, only to recover again after mid-century.

The shortage of silver (and gold?) seems to have had repercussions in Russia as well. The Russian czars periodically prohibited the export of silver and gold, even in the form of coin. However, these prohibitions and their repetition increased particularly during the mid-seventeenth century. Taxes now had to paid in silver and gold. Also in the attempt to increase the supply of precious metals in the 1660s, the state encouraged foreigners to bring money into Russia but set artificially low exchange rates between foreign and Russian rubles after the silver content of the latter had declined during the previous two or more decades (Burton 1993: 60–61).

Darling (1992) disputes the myth of decline in the seventeenth-century Ottoman Empire altogether and proposes the "more neutral term[s] 'decentralization' [and] 'consolidation.' " Goldstone does term the Ottoman crisis a fiscal one but denies its relation to trade, not to mention the outside supply of money, which he says scarcely declined. However, he fails to note that the Ottomans mints were forced out of business by the competition since 1580 from cheaper Spanish silver and by Persian coins. These kept the Ottoman economy going increasingly with foreign coins, so that their own mints ceased operation altogether after 1640 (Sahillioglu 1983, Brenning 1983, Chaudhuri 1978, Pamuk 1994). Fiscal crises were the order of the day in the seventeenth century. Some urban and rural economic activity stagnated if not declined (Pamuk 1994), but as we will observe below, some also moved elsewhere in Anatolia; and there was no general economic decline. It may be difficult to tell which of these "domestic" events was cause and which was effect, but both were certainly functions also of reduced inflows of silver, particularly in the 1630s.

Nonetheless, Goldstone (1991a: 367, 78–79) also disputes the silver connection with both the Ottoman crises and the English Revolution of 1640 and also dismisses trade as a significant factor. Yet, he attributes the English Revolution to three factors, the first of which was the fiscal distress of the state. The second one was intraclass conflict among members of the elite, almost all of whom were involved in commercial practices (Goldstone 1991a: 80–81). Just as elsewhere, however, the English state was in difficulties to find enough money to pay its troops in 1640. After this "revolution," commercial interests enjoyed more political weight than ever (Hill 1967: 99, 129). Moreover E. E. Rich and C. H. Wilson (1967: 439–40) stress that 1639–1640 was the first of three periods of marked price declines in Britain and elsewhere in Europe (the others were in 1645–1646 and the beginning of 1657), and they empha-

size that "the sequence of three cycles between 1640 and 1660 throughout Europe as a *whole* . . . transcend local explanations . . . [and indeed
the] overall economic rhythm . . . was certainly European, and perhaps
even encompassing the world."

Returning to Spanish silver, the precise amounts of its shipments
from the Americas to Spain have been the subject of sustained controversy. A. Garcia-Baquero Gonzales (1994: 119) reviews it once again and
also allows for unrecorded smuggling of silver. He concludes that in
the first half of the seventeenth century, the tonnage of shipping between the Americas and Spain declined by one-third and the import of
bullion by two-thirds. The decline accelerated around 1640.

Indeed, the Portuguese separation from Spanish rule in 1640 may
also have been sparked by reduced receipts of transatlantic silver shipments by Spain, and so may the revolt in Catalonia the same year. (An
archaeologist friend dug up a store of foreign coins in the Barcelona
suburb of Castelldefels, which its owner had buried between 1640 and
1643, apparently for safekeeping during these disturbances). Like the
Ming and the English, the Spanish state experienced financial difficulties to maintain sufficient armed forces, when its revenues declined first
because of the decline in the value of silver due to overproduction and
then due to the sudden shortage when American silver mines cut production and remittances in the 1630s (Flynn 1982). When confronted
with threats to its sovereignty by the Portuguese to the west and the
Catalans to the east, Madrid gave priority to the challenge from the
Catalans, who were supported by their French neighbors, which led to
the sacrifice of its dominion over Portugal. The authoritative historian
of Spain J. H. Elliot in his oft-cited article on "the Decline of Spain"
dated it "from the end of 1640 [when] Spain and Spain's international
power were visibly crumbling" (cited by Flynn and Giraldez 1995b: 33).

Also, the *Carreira da India,* as the Portuguese called their trade to
Goa, reached its "nadir" and began a "dismal" period in 1640 (Ames
1991: 17, 23). Moreover, Portugal signed its first commercial treaty in
1642. It was the first of the three forerunners (the others were in 1654
and 1667) of the Treaty of Methuen of 1703, which cemented the protection Portugal now sought and accepted—at a price—from Britain.
Portugal forced Dutch capital out of its sugar plantations in Portuguese Brazil after 1640, so the Dutch went to British Barbados, which
they converted into a sugar plantation in turn (Harlow 1926, Frank
1978a, b). The Dutch VOC exports, mostly of silver, to Asia were also
comparatively low in 1640 (Rich and Wilson 1967: 309).

As we noted above, these events on the other side of the world also had a deleterious effect on China by damaging the Portuguese traders' relations with the source of Spanish transpacific silver in Manila. On the other hand, developments in China had probably also first supported the rise of Spain and then again hastened its decline. Flynn and Giraldez (1995a, b) have repeatedly emphasized how "the rise and fall of the Spanish Empire is best viewed in the context of a sino-centered world economy." The reason is that the increasing Chinese demand for silver first raised its price and thereby Spanish fortunes but later, as the supply of silver rose excessively, again depressed the price of silver to or below its cost of production for the Spaniards. The Spanish Crown was hard hit, for even increasing arrivals of American silver generated decreasing values of silver in Spain and lowered the buying power of the Crown's tax receipts. Like the Ming at the same time and for the same reason, the Spanish state sought to counteract this decline in its revenue by demanding more from the private sector. The latter in turn was therefore doubly or triply disadvantaged by higher tax demands, lower income of its own, and then reduced production and receipts of silver, because its falling market price no longer compensated for its rising costs of production. The sudden decline in silver production around 1640 that these market forces generated then pulled the rug out from under the Spanish economy entirely.

In summary, during the "seventeenth-century crisis," the continued long "A" phase expansion in Asia was punctuated by a *world monetary crisis* culminating in the 1640s. Large-scale production of silver had led to a fall in the value of silver relative to gold. This decline in the price of silver and the inflation in terms of silver content led to a drastic drop in the profitability and thus in the production of silver for export in the producing regions of Latin America, Central Europe, Persia, and Japan. Indeed Japan finally reacted to this crisis by prohibiting any (legal) export of silver whatsoever, after having been a huge exporter during the previous period of the silver-based boom. In fact, Japan's reaction to this crisis, the famous "seclusion" policy, may also be explained in this world systemic context, that is, the economic position of being in deficit with everyone. As already noted above however, this policy of seclusion did not so much stop but rather regulate, trade—both to manage the external deficit and to favor some domestic interests against others.

Japan and some European states weathered the monetary/economic storm, perhaps thanks in no small part to their continuing sources and supplies of silver, which dried up much more for the unfortunate Ming.

Nonetheless, there also was serious disruption of some trade in East Asia due to the seclusion policy of Japan, the revolt of the Portuguese against Spain, rivalries of the Dutch and English companies, and the Qing war against the Ming base in maritime southern and coastal China—all of whose politics may be usefully reinterpreted against the background of this silver shortage monetary crisis in a world on the silver standard. In particular, it may be that devoting more attention to this monetary crisis generated by the shortage of silver can go a long way toward explaining the Japanese "political" decision to seclude themselves and to leave only one door open to the Dutch, who (unlike the Portuguese) offered Japan the possibility to export goods and not just silver. Indeed, the Chinese partial withdrawals from maritime trade should also be reanalyzed against the background of similar financial considerations. However, growth and stability returned and a newly reorganized world economy recovered from the "mini-crisis" of the mid-seventeenth century. Overall, there is still ample evidence of growth during the seventeenth century, as observed above.

This discussion began with Adshead's (1973) suggestion that the Chinese crisis and the fall of the Ming in 1644 was related to a shortage of silver. Yet whether it's true or not, it cannot support the contention of a "generalized" crisis even in China. It certainly was not like, and still less generated by, "the prolonged contraction of the European economy between 1590 and 1680" to which Adshead (1973: 272) also refers. Thus, however laudatory S. A. M. Adshead's initiative to regard China and Europe as responding to the same world-embracing forces, we cannot accept his conclusions that their paths "diverged" in the seventeenth century (Adshead 1973: 278 ff.). He argues not only that there was a general "seventeenth-century crisis," but also maintains that China and Europe responded differently, China recovering by just doing more of the same as before, and Europe by changing its institutional structure. Yet, we observed in chapters 2, 3, and 4 that China's institutional structure also adapted to and generated or at least permitted rapid economic growth in the eighteenth century. Adshead not only belittles this eighteenth-century recovery and growth that he himself recognizes in China. His Eurocentrism, which misled his analysis of the world monetary crisis, also leads him to repeat the thesis that later European growth was somehow due especially to some "exceptional" European institutions, which he thinks were formed in response to the "seventeenth-century crisis" in Europe—but not in China! Alas, that is again putting the European cart before the Asian and world economic horse. Still less can we accept the reasoning that (mis)led Adshead to this contention: "Seville was at the center of a world wide monetary system and it was the breakdown of this system which precipitated the distant Asian revolutions of the seventeenth century. . . . Evidence has been accumulating that the European crisis was in fact world wide in its repercussions" (Adshead 1973: 272). No, Seville was *not* the center of any worldwide system. Despite its monetary handle, the still marginal Europe was quite incapable of having such deep-going worldwide repercussions. Whatever repercussions money may have had—and the argument here is that they were many and deep-going—any Eurocentric perspective also handicaps and misleads the analysis and interpretation of these re-percussions—worldwide!

That was precisely the great limitation of most previous analyses of this period, which were entirely European-centered (including my own). Some analysts (including Frank 1978a), sought to analyze the seventeenth century in terms of fifty- to sixty-year long Kondratieff cycles and their two- to three-decade-long crises. However, these Kondratieff cycles were entirely based on the European or at most the Atlantic economy. I found, as already remarked above, that for instance India and Latin America (not to mention the Netherlands) experienced a simultaneous period of marked expansion. This was interpreted (or misinterpreted?) as the dependent mouse playing better while the central, or core, cat was away or busy with its own Kondratieff cyclical crisis, as proposed in my "Development of Underdevelopment" (Frank 1966) and *Capitalism and Underdevelopment in Latin America* (Frank 1967). However, the present contention, contra Frank then and Wallerstein still today, is that Europe and/or the Atlantic economy were *not* the center or core of the world economy, which rather vitiates at least part of that earlier analysis. Nonetheless, it may now be possible still—or better—to comprehend the period in the mid-seventeenth century as the manifestation of a worldwide economic Kondratieff "B" phase crisis, which also took significant monetary forms, even if there was no generalized "seventeenth-century-(long) crisis," as we appear to have found above.

KONDRATIEFF ANALYSIS

In my previous book on the 1492–1789 period, I sought to identify Kondratieff cycles beginning in the seventeenth century or earlier, albeit in what I then thought was a European-centered world

capitalist economy (Frank 1978a). Since then, Wallerstein has also organized the account of the rise and development of his European-centered
"modern world-system" increasingly in terms of Kondratieff "long" cycles. He started hesitatingly in his first volume (1974), describing the
origins of the European world-economy in the generally expansive
"long sixteenth century" from 1450 to 1640. He increasingly introduced
shorter Kondratieff-(type?) long cycles into his analysis in his second
volume (1980), on the "consolidation" from 1600 to 1750; and in his
third volume (1989), on the "second era of great expansion" from 1730
to the 1840s. Joshua Goldstein (1988) also organized his study of the
timing of great wars in terms of Kondratieff "long" cycles, which he
pursued back into the sixteenth century using the datings by Braudel
(1992) and Frank (1978a) for the early centuries.

More recently still, Modelski and Thompson (1996) have taken
worldwide Kondratieff analysis much further back, seeking to identify
about fifty-year-long cycles back to A.D. 930. That would make the
present one the nineteenth, not just the fifth Kondratieff cycle (as for
most of his followers), nor the so far last cycle of about a dozen—as for
Frank (1978a) and Goldstein (1988). Modelski and Thompson find a set
of four Kondratieff cycles in Song China between 930 and 1250. Since
then however (and this in my view is a major limitation of their work),
they see the technologically innovating motor force and world-
economic center of their Kondratieff waves as shifting to Western Europe. For them the site of the "technological innovations" driving their
nineteen Kondratieff cycles shifts from China to Europe, beginning
with the fifth one after 1190: "After Sung [Song] China, the leadership
of change shifted to Genoa and Venice before moving farther west to
Portugal and more recent global system leaders" (Modelski and
Thompson 1996; where noted, page references are to their manuscript
version—1994 ms: 225 and tables 7.2, 8.3).

Yet according to much of the evidence presented above, the world
economy and its leading centers, if any, remained in Asia until at least
1800. The resolution of this apparent contradiction may be sought at
least in part by examining the sectors in which Modelski and Thompson
identify these innovations. The first four, beginning with printing and
paper in 930, were in China. Beginning with their fifth Kondratieff cycle
(K5) in 1190, they are "in" Europe. But let us examine how European
and/or technological these innovations really were: the K5 innovation
beginning in 1190 was the Champagne fairs. Then came the Black Sea
trade, Venetian galley fleets, pepper, Guinea gold, Indian spices, Baltic/

Atlantic trade, and Asian trade, taking us through K12 to the beginning of the 1580s. Then in the seventeenth century, K13 and K14 center on "Amerasian trade (plantations) and Amerasian trade," respectively. Finally only after 1740 comes cotton and iron (though that seems a bit early, since the British cotton-technology inventions did not even start till the 1760s). In the nineteenth century, the innovations are in steam and railroads as well as steel, chemicals, and electrics; and in the twentieth century, autos, aerospace, electronics, and the information industries.

Note however, how all but two of the innovative sectors from K6 (in 1250) to K14 (from 1688 to 1740) were related to the *Asian* trade: Black Sea trade, "Venetian" galleys, pepper, spices, and "Asian trade" (specifically). The two exceptions are Guinea gold, which was to finance this trade, and Baltic/Atlantic trade. Moreover, none of them were in an industrial/manufacturing sector until K15, beginning (albeit rather too early) in 1740. It seems that Modelski and Thompson also suffer from "misplaced concreteness" in identifying "innovations" in a European "center" of the world economy. For these were no more than reflections of the long-winded European attempts to benefit from the real centers of economic activity in Asia. Modelski and Thompson (1996; 1994 ms: 217) themselves recognize that, during their K5 to K9, "for another two-three centuries, until and including the time of Columbus . . . the Chinese market still served as the magnet for world trade."

In their revised text (1996), Modelski and Thompson are even more explicit—but also contradictory:

> The K-waves beginning in the late fifteenth century were marked by their relationship to attempts to discover new routes from Europe to Asia. . . . Medieval Europe operated as a regional subsystem within a larger economic system stretching form England to China. . . . Nonetheless, we contend that four K-waves (K5–K8), centered in the trading operation of the Italian city-states (especially Genoa and Venice), maintained the continuity of the K-wave chain from its initial stimulation in Sung China to the dramatic expansion of European actors throughout the globe. . . . Yet throughout these shifts in location, the ultimate focus of leading sector trade for the European subsystem was the reordering of the flow of high value goods from Asia to Europe. (Modelski and Thompson 1996: 177, 191)

Yes indeed, but they are cutting short by at least another three centuries the powers of the Chinese and other Asian magnets and their continued attraction for Europe. As they themselves also note elsewhere, "Portugal's route to India was a graft upon the maritime trunk of that by then traditional network of long-distance trade" and "because Asian trade was a critical component of the entire Dutch network" and long remained so for the entire European one as well (Modelski and Thompson 1996; 1994 ms: 154, 113). It may be, as Modelski and Thompson (1996; 1994 ms: 97) claim, that "world powers, in their learning cycles, account for the majority of basic economic innovations." In that case, the Europeans were rather slow to learn, for the world economic and political powers still remained in Asia for at least three centuries after the Europeans arrived there! Therefore, it could be instructive to look at more Asian evidence in the "leading sectors" and "innovations" around which Modelski and Thompson center their "world" economic Kondratieffs. After all, as chapter 4 demonstrates, the alleged European technological "leadership" before the late eighteenth century is primarily located in Eurocentric mythology of the nineteenth and twentieth centuries.

Metzler (1994) also extends the search for Kondratieff cycles horizontally and argues that Japan and apparently China experienced fifty-year-long Kondratieff waves whose timing at least was the same as the "classical" European- and American-based Kondratieffs. He suggests that they may have been related systemically, or in Fletcher's terminology horizontally, across the entire world economy. This suggestion warrants far more intensive study than it has received, particularly in view of our findings above about the monetary and possible Kondratieff crisis of the 1640s. Other periods of monetary, economic, and political problems, for example from 1688 to 1690 (which may have contributed to the declines of Surat on the west coast and Masulipatam on the east coast of India) and after 1720 may bear similar study in Kondratieffian and monetary terms.

THE 1762–1790 KONDRATIEFF "B" PHASE: CRISIS AND RECESSIONS

Another downturn "B" phase analyzable in Kondratieffian terms is the period from 1762 to 1790. During that period there were several major political upheavals in France, the Netherlands, St. Dominique/Haiti, the British North American colonies and the United States of America, India, and elsewhere as well as the technological beginnings of what has been called the "industrial revolution." This period was already analyzed in European and Atlantic "world" economic terms by Frank (1978a) and Wallerstein (1989), and it is again reviewed here in a world economic context.

Although the traditional starting date for Kondratieff cycles was only 1790 at the time of my (1978a) writing, I argued that they began much earlier and examined what I regarded as a Kondratieff "B" downturn from 1762 to 1790 in Frank (1978a). Recently (Frank 1994, 1995), I compared my earlier findings about this period with those of Braudel (1992). On the one hand, Braudel claims that the *European* "world-economy is the greatest possible vibrating surface. . . . It is the world-economy at all events which creates the *uniformity* of prices over a huge area, as an arterial system distributes blood throughout a living organism" (Braudel 1992: 83). Yet on the other hand, he observes that "the influence of the world-economy centred in Europe must very soon have exceeded even the most ambitious frontiers ever attributed to it," and he goes on to muse that "the really curious thing is that the rhythms of the European conjuncture transcend the strict boundaries of their own world-economy" (Braudel 1992: 76).

Of course, we are dealing with *world* economic cycles in a *world economy*. For the difference between Braudel's and Wallerstein's "world-economy" with a hyphen and Gills' and my "world economy" without a hyphen, see Frank (1995) and Frank and Gills (1993), which also includes a response by Wallerstein. The evidence is in Braudel's book, although he does not recognize it himself. Braudel (1992: 76) reproduces a graph of the yearly fluctuations of Russian exports and its trade balance between 1742 and 1785. He does not comment other than to observe "two short lived drops in the [trade balance] surplus, in 1772 and 1782, probably as a result of arms purchases" (Braudel 1992: 463). Actually, the graph also shows a third big drop in 1762–1763, and all three coincide with a sharp drop on the graph of Russian exports, whatever may have happened to imports of arms or anything else.

However, these three short periods also fall in the same years as three world economic recessions, which Braudel (1992: 267–73) discusses at some length in another chapter devoted to Amsterdam. Yet, he makes no connection to the same periods in Russia. In still another chapter, Braudel reproduces a graph on Britain's trade balance with her North American colonies between 1745 and 1776. It shows sharp declines in British imports, and lesser ones of exports, in these same years 1760–1763 and 1772–1773 (the graph does not extend into the 1780s). But again Braudel does not look for connections either between the two graphs or between either (let alone both of them) and the recessions they reflect. This omission is all the more curious in view of the comments he does make about these recessions: About the first one, he writes that "with the currency shortage, the crisis spread, leaving a trail of bankruptcies; it reached not only Amsterdam but Berlin, Hamburg, Altona, Bremen, Leipzig, Stockholm and hit hard in London" (Braudel 1992: 269). Regarding the next recession, Braudel observes catastrophic harvests in all of Europe during 1771–1772 and famine conditions in Norway and Germany. Moreover, he goes further:

> Was this the reason for the violent crisis, aggravated possibly by the consequences of the disastrous famine which hit India in the same years 1771–72, throwing into confusion the workings of the East India Company? No doubt these were all factors, but is the real cause not once more the periodic return of a credit crisis?. . . . Contemporary observers always connected such crises to some major bankruptcy. (Braudel 1992: 268)

Finally, in the chapter on the North American colonies, Braudel refers to

> the Boston Tea Party when, on 16 December 1774, a number of rebels disguised as Indians boarded three ships owned by the [East] India Company standing at anchor in Boston harbour, and threw their cargo into the sea. But this minor incident marked the beginning of the break between the colonies—the future United States—and England. (Braudel 1992: 419)

Yet, again Braudel makes no connection between this event in America and others he analyzes elsewhere in the world for the very same years. Why does so experienced a world historian, who is exceptionally sensitive to conjunctures, not even seek such connections? At least Wallerstein (1979: 198, 228) does refer briefly to a "postwar slump" after the Seven Years War in 1763 and very much in passing to "the immediate postwar trade depression" in the 1780s after the war associated with the American Revolution. However, Wallerstein also fails to make any mention whatsoever of the intervening recession in the 1770s, which sparked the American Revolution itself.

Yet, if we do as Fletcher commends, we can see that *all* of these events and others were connected through a series of world economy/system-wide business cycles within what may have been the crisis phase of a long Kondratieff cycle, which I examined two decades ago (Frank 1978a). Summarizing briefly, the Peace of Paris in 1763 concluding the

Seven Years War was signed under the influence of a recession and long downturn, which began in 1761. From 1764 on, so were the British Sugar, Quartering, Stamp and Townsend acts, which caused so much dissatisfaction in the North American colonies, exceeded only by the prohibition against issuing bills of credit and paper money, which aggravated the deflationary conditions and hardship for debtors in the colonies. Yet the American colonists took even these in their stride, particularly during the subsequent cyclical recoveries — until another recession began in 1773. Moreover, the Bengal famine of 1770–1771 had lowered the profitability of the British East India Company. It petitioned Parliament for relief and received it in the form of the Tea Act of 1773, which granted the company the privilege to dump its tea on the American market. The Americans in turn dumped it into Boston Harbor in the "tea party" to which Braudel refers. The British reaction through the Quebec and Intolerable acts of 1774 escalated the economic conflict into political repression as well, which then rallied enough support for "the shot heard round the world" in Lexington and Concord on April 19, 1775, and the Declaration of Independence in 1776.

The recession of the 1780s brought on changes not only in British and Russian balances of trade, as is noted but partly misdiagnosed by Braudel. The same recession also had even more important repercussions in France and the new United States: it sparked the French Revolution in 1789 and led to the new American constitution. In the American Confederation, the recession of the early 1780s and the more acute economic downturn of 1785–1786 generated massive popular political movements, such as Shays's Rebellion in 1786, and both economic crises renewed and increased political support for the federalists and against the Articles of Confederation. That permitted their replacement by the American Constitution in 1787 (Frank 1978a: 206–208). On the other side of the Atlantic, the same recession led to the Batavian revolution of the mid 1780s in the Netherlands, which "has been insufficiently recognized for what it was, the first revolution on the European mainland, forerunner of the French Revolution" (Braudel 1992: 275). The same recession also sparked the French Revolution (Frank 1978a).

Moreover, the last third of the eighteenth century marked the acceleration in "the Decline" of India as well. The 1760s also spelled a sharp downward inflection in the Ottoman economy, which appears to be related to the Kondratieff crisis phase in the Atlantic economies; and the same years also marked the beginnings of economic decline in China, all of which we will observe in greater detail in chapter 6.

A MORE HORIZONTALLY INTEGRATIVE MACROHISTORY?

So to follow Fletcher (1985), we "first search for historical parallelisms (roughly contemporaneous similar developments in the world's various societies), and then determine whether they are causally interrelated." Doing so, we find that all sort of horizontally simultaneous events in world history are *not* coincidence, just as Chaudhuri (1978) suspected, but are the "interrelated historical phenomena" in an "integrative horizontal history," as Fletcher commended. Frederick Teggart (1939) had already recommended and practiced the same in his *Rome and China: A Study of Correlations in Historical Events,* which shows that doing integrative world history is possible (and Teggart and Gills and I believe also *necessary*), not only for modern but also for ancient history and even prehistory. Thus Gills and Frank (1992; also in Frank and Gills 1993) have examined simultaneous Afro-Eurasian-wide long cycles from A.D. 1700 back to 1700 B.C., and I have pursued them back to 3000 B.C. in my "Bronze Age World System Cycles" (Frank 1993a).

Such a longer historical perspective also allows us to make comparisons between different historical periods. These can afford us the opportunity to identify possible patterns of horizontally integrative history. These may reflect system "properties" such as the spatially and sectorally unequal structure and the temporally uneven process and development of the world economy/system. Wallerstein (1974) and Frank (1978a,b) among others had noted these "economic," and as Modelski and Thompson (1992) call them, "political," features in the "modern world-system" of the past five hundred years. The study of these seemingly same characteristics was extended by Gills and Frank to the "five-thousand-year world economic system" in several articles collected in Frank and Gills (1993) and is explored further by Modelski and Thompson (1996) and Christopher Chase-Dunn and Thomas Hall (1997).

A particular interest of all of the above has been the structural and temporal—possibly cyclical—systemic characteristics which give rise to "hegemonic transitions in the world system" (to use Gills's terminology). Among others, Gills and Frank (1992; also in Frank and Gills 1993) explored the significance for the world system of the thirteenth-century rise and subsequent decline of Genghis Khan's Mongols in horizontally integrative historical terms rather than only Mongolian terms. Extending that perspective comparatively, "the Rise of the West" can perhaps also be instructively regarded in analogy to that of the Mongols, as Albert Bergesen suggests (private communication 1996).

The structural similarity of the Mongols and the Europeans is that both were peoples in (semi)marginal or peripheral areas who were attracted to and made incursions into the "core" areas and economies, which were principally in East Asia and secondarily in West Asia. Indeed, China was the principal attraction and first target for both peripheral "marcher states" as Chase-Dunn and Hall (1997) call them, which tend to be the sources of world system-wide innovation. The Mongols not only attacked first China and then West Asia, but they also then set up their own Yuan dynasty in China and other Mongol states in West Asia. The Europeans' initial and continuing magnet was also "Cathay." That is what both Columbus and Magellan set out to reach by traveling westward across the Atlantic. Many generations of their followers pursued the chimera of the famous "Northwest Passage" through the North Atlantic and northern Canada (not "opened" until the advent of nuclear submarines and icebreakers), and indeed also a northeast passage from Europe through the Arctic Ocean to China. In the meantime, Europeans eventually managed to pry a semicolonial "Open Door" in some treaty ports on the China Sea, and on the way they took a colonial position in much of West and South Asia. Like the Mongols earlier, the Europeans also made derivative incursions toward Japan and Southeast Asia. The Mongols' naval enterprises were more imposing but nonetheless unsuccessful. The European naval incursions were more modest, but somewhat more successful (though only marginally so, if at all, in Japan).

Significantly in terms of the Gills and Frank analysis of world system-wide temporal long cycles, both the Mongol and the European peripheral incursions into East and West Asia were (relatively and temporarily?) successful during periods of long "B" phase economic decline in these previous economic Asian "cores." Gills and Frank (1992; also in Frank and Gills 1993) have suggested that the initial success of the Mongol invasions should be ascribed at least in part to the weakened political economic condition of their targets in East and West Asia, which were already marked by economic decline before the Mongols' arrival—as was demonstrably the case in Baghdad before its Mongol capture in 1258 (Frank 1992).

Additionally, Gills and Frank (1992) suggested that the success of Pax Mongolica turned out to be an only relatively brief "flash in the pan" despite the improved trading conditions that it offered. The un-

derlying reason, we suggested, was that these same unfavorable underlying economic conditions rendered the Mongol enterprise unsustaina-
ble and generated its breakup into smaller regional pieces. We regarded
these as more significant than the security of trade or the alleged Mongol political weakness of rival clans that were unable to rule from the
backs of horses (which incidentally the Mongols did not even try to
do). The European and Western enterprise and incursions during the
subsequent Asian downturn "B" phase seem so far to have been more
successful, thanks both to their own (and simultaneously, worldwide)
new economic departures into industrialism, although these too were
soon marked by regionalisms. The world economic/systemic positional
and cyclical significance of this innovation of and through industrialism
has been systematically overlooked or misinterpreted, as we will note
in the following chapter. Moreover from a longer historical perspective—at the time of this writing we are after all less than two centuries
past 1800—the culminating evidence on this "innovative" Western enterprise and its world economic consequences is not yet in!

In conclusion, however beautiful it may be to regard the individual
pieces of the historical mosaic, to appreciate them more fully we also
need to place them where they fit into integrative macrohistory. Failing
that, as Fletcher rightly noted, we cannot appreciate the full significance
of the "peculiarities" of particular societies or events. That must be our
guide if we wish to understand why the East "fell" and the West "rose."
Granted, it is easier said than done: the following chapter is a preliminary stab at "doing" so. There we will see that, regardless of the instruc-
tiveness or not of comparing it with the rise of the Mongols, "the Rise
of the West" must also be examined in world systemic terms. These do
suggest the emergence once again of a previously marginal region that
was able to take temporal (and temporary?) advantage of political economic decline at the Asian "core."

CHAPTER 6

Why Did the West Win (Temporarily)?

To confront world history is to confront the ultimate questions of human destiny. . . .
One must look at history, particularly world history, as the reflection of a desired
future. . . . To avoid the challenge of a global perspective is to abdicate in the face of
the historian's central task—to decipher the meaning of history. To reject world
history in a time of crisis is to renege on the historian's ultimate responsibility of
confronting society with its past in a meaningful and useful way. . . . World history
has become a pursuit of world unity.

Paul Costello (1964: 213, 8–9, 215)

This chapter poses the question *why* the West won (temporarily). It offers two answers and inquires into the possible relations
between them. One answer is that the Asians were weakened, and the
other answer is that the Europeans were strengthened. That may sound
platitudinous, but it is not if we consider what weakened Asians, what
strengthened Europeans, and what may in turn have related these two
processes. Moreover, this very question/answer combination is not
platitudinous: virtually all other contending "explanations" rest on the
supposition or assertion that Asia was and supposedly remained "traditional." They also allege that Europe first pulled itself up by its own
bootstraps to "modernize" itself and then graciously offered this "modernization" to Asians and others. According to the West and thanks to
its "demonstration effect," this offer of "civilization" and "progress"
was accepted voluntarily by some. Others had to have it imposed by
the force of colonialism and imperialism. Allegedly, other Asians, not

to mention Africans, Latin Americans, and even some Europeans (and quite a few North Americans) languish in their traditional juices.

The evidence and argument in the previous chapters show that Asians were no more "traditional" than Europeans and in fact largely far less so. Moreover as we will argue below, the Europeans did not do anything—let alone "modernize"—by themselves. That contention turns the tables on the historiography and social science of the last century or so, and indeed also on the humanities of the type "the East is East, and the West is West, and never the twain shall meet." They *did* meet, albeit not at all on the alleged Eurocentric terms, and the question is why?

This book has sought to build up, chapter by chapter, the global scaffolding that will permit the construction of at least preliminary answers derived from the structure and dynamic of the world economy as a whole. Chapter 2 outlined the productive and trade framework and regional interconnections of the global economy. Chapter 3 signaled how money went around the world circulatory system and provided the lifeblood that made the world go round. Chapter 4 examined the resulting world population and economic quantities, technological qualities, and institutional mechanisms, and noted how several regions in Asia maintained and even increased their global preponderance. Chapter 5 proposed a global marcohistory analysis, with which we can perceive how events and processes are often cyclically related around the world.

This chapter inquires whether and how the world economic advantage of Asia between 1400 and 1800 may have been turned to its own disadvantage and to the advantage instead of the West in the nineteenth and twentieth centuries. Some world economic connections and a possible mechanism that may have generated or at least permitted this interchange were explored in chapter 5: the long, expansive cycle (or "A" phase) that began in 1400 appears to have lasted into the eighteenth century but then turned into a "B" phase decline, at least for Asia. World economic cycles and especially crises generate both danger and opportunity—as the Chinese understand the word "crisis." However, these differ from one economic sector and region to another in accordance with their place and role in the world economy as a whole. So now we can use these lessons and the scaffolding from the previous chapters to inquire into the whys and wherefores of "the Decline of the East and the Rise of the West." The present chapter is organized into four main sections: (1) Is there a several-centuries-long world economic "roller coaster" cycle, whose expansive "A" phase turned into a contractive "B" phase for Asia? (2) When and how did the "Decline" of Asia manifest itself? (3) How did Europe and the West "Rise"? (4) How are this decline and rise related by the world economic structure through global and regional population, economic, and ecological dynamics?

Is There a Long-Cycle Roller Coaster?

We found in chapter 5 that, in the absence of a general "seventeenth-century crisis," the long global economic expansion lasted from 1400 in Asia into at least the mid-eighteenth century. This finding now permits us to pursue the Gills and Frank half-millennium-long cycles into early modern times. One of the initial incentives to write this book, we may recall, was to inquire about what the recognition of the existence of an old world system with its long "A/B" cycles beginning long before 1500 (Frank and Gills 1993) implies for Immanuel Wallerstein's "modern world-system" after 1500. These cycles had expansive "A" phases followed by contractive "B" phases, each of which lasted from two to three centuries. We traced, identified, and dated these cycles common to most of Afro-Eurasia since 1700 B.C. (Gills and Frank 1992; also in Frank and Gills 1993) and then back to 3000 B.C. (Frank 1993a). The question becomes whether these long cycles continued into early modern times and if so to what effect.

Without seeking to review the entire history of these long cycles again here, it may be noted that a new major period of expansion spanned the years A.D. 1000/1050 to 1250/1300. That was the period especially of the major technological, productive, commercial and general economic development under the Song dynasty in China. William McNeill (1983) regards China to have been the most important "center" of the world at that time. George Modelski and William Thompson (1996) place in China the first four of their approximately fifty-year-long Kondratieff cycles, beginning with A.D. 930. Also Wallerstein (1992: 586–8) notes that "the patterns of expansion and contraction are clearly laid out and widely accepted among those writing about the late Middle Ages and early modern times in Europe. . . . Thus 1050–1250+ was a time of expansion in Europe (the Crusades, the colonizations) . . . The 'crisis' or great contractions of 1250–1450+ include the Black Plague." Janet Abu-Lughod (1989) characterized the first century from this last phase, 1250 to 1350, as at first expansionary, but then contractionary after 1300. She did so on the basis of her analysis of a "thirteenth-century world system" in all of Afro-Eurasia. Gills and Frank (1992; also in Frank and Gills 1993) sought to review both periods as first an expansionary "A" phase until about 1250 and then a contractive "B" phase crisis until about 1450, and in the Afro-Eurasian world economy and system as a whole.

Gills and Frank (1992) dated the renewed period of "A" phase expansion as beginning about 1450, perhaps too closely following Wallerstein (1974) in his analysis of the European world-economy. We did not give adequate weight even to Ravi Palat and Wallerstein (1990), who identify the beginnings of a major expansion in India in 1400. The present review of the world economy also suggests that this expansion began in 1400, not only in India but also in Southeast Asia and probably in China.

At its marginal western end, Venetian and Genovese activities in the Black Sea and eastern Mediterranean, as well as the Genovese expansion westward through the Mediterranean and into the Atlantic, were minor parts of this world economic expansion. So were the Spanish "reconquista" on the Iberian Peninsula and all Iberian initiatives into the Atlantic. These went first to the Azores and to the Madeira and Canary islands and then around and along the shores of West Africa. This Iberian expansion laid the basis in turn for the search and discovery of a way to the prosperous and golden East Asia. The Iberians went both westward around the globe via the Atlantic and then onward via Cape Horn and Panama and/or Mexico across the Pacific, and eastward around Africa via the Cape of Good Hope. The latter would have been not only the shorter route but also the one that offered earlier and greater economic benefits from the riches of the regions bordering the Indian Ocean and the South China Sea. Only the discovery of the Americas with its golden and silver monetary riches then made the westward journey profitable. It offered the Europeans their first real opportunity to ante up in the Asian-dominated global casino. Moreover, it was initially and primarily the Asian economy that was again open for business and flourishing since 1400.

The question then becomes until when did this expansive "A" phase in the aforementioned long cycle last? When this cycle was first traced back to 1700 B.C., we really stopped at 1450 and "provisionally accepted the main outlines" of other students of cycles since then (Gills and Frank 1992; also in Frank and Gills 1993: 180).

In the revision of his test of this cycle and its phase datings on the basis of urban growth data, Andrew Bosworth (1995: 224) now writes that "it seems hasty of Gills and Frank to sound the death knell for longer term cycles . . . and embrace instead shorter Kondratieff waves (if that is in fact their position). The two phenomena . . . are not necessarily incompatible." Well, that may have been our pragmatic position de facto; but de jure we also considered that in principle the two kinds of cycles may nest within each other. That is indeed the thesis in the discussion of the "Monetary Analysis and the Crises of 1640" in chapter 5 above, even if I have not yet pursued how several Kondratieffs may nest in one long-cycle phase (but see our discussion of Modelski and Thompson in chapter 5).

But the more examined question is how long this (possible) "A" phase lasted. The answer is—to at least 1750. Bosworth also pursued a similar question with his urban growth data and concludes that they also "reinforce" the view of a longer "A" phase: for all twenty-five largest cities in the world, the fit to the long cycle is not good because of a sixteenth-century dip. However, "the relative urban hierarchy for East Asia (measuring the growth of its largest cities within the set of the 25 largest cities) is high until about 1650, after which it proceeds along with the ratio of the European/Atlantic city system. This 'tottering' lasts for more than a century" (Bosworth 1995: 221–2). In his Figure 8.4 the lines for relative urban hierarchy among East Asian and European/Atlantic cities do not cross until about 1825, when Asian economic and political power waned. London displaces Beijing as the world's largest city in 1850. As noted in chapter 4, Rhoades Murphey (1977) also puts the crossover between the decline of the East and the rise of the West at about 1815.

Therefore it again appears that this (so far last) world economic long cyclical phase of expansion lasted—at least in Asia—over three centuries, from the fifteenth through the seventeenth centuries and into at least the first part if not to the end of the eighteenth century. The evidence on the seventeenth century reviewed above also lends support to the notion of a continuation of the "long sixteenth-century" expansion from 1400/1450 throughout the seventeenth and into at least the early eighteenth century. Moreover, the major expansion of production and growth of population remained in Asia, as already noted in chapter 4, while Europe only caught up very belatedly. Both expansions were fueled by the inflow of American money brought by the Europeans. In terms of world historical reality and development, it was really (only) American money that permitted the Europeans to increase their participation in this mostly Asian-based productive expansion of the world economy. Moreover, we must conclude that the strongest and most dynamic parts of the world economy still remained in China and India.

I argue therefore that these and other major Asian economies had, and continued to have, a pattern of long cyclical economic growth reaching the upper turning point of its expansive "A" phase, then passing on to a contractive "B" phase. Moreover, these Asian economies were of course all connected to each other. Therefore, it cannot be "co-incidental" and should not be surprising that they were experiencing such expansive and contractive phases nearly simultaneously, if that is what was happening. However, these Asian economies were not only related to each other, they were all part and parcel of a single global economy, which presumably had its own long cycle of development. The argument here is that the upward "A" phase since about 1400 of such a long cycle reached its upper turning point and gave way to a succeeding long "B" phase, especially for the more central economies in Asia between 1750 and 1800. Moreover, as I argued in Frank (1978a) and again in chapter 5, the shorter Kondratieff long cycle was in a "B" phase from 1762 to 1790.

That long "A" phase of expansion that came to an end in Asia in the late eighteenth century and its subsequent (cyclical?) decline offered the still marginal West its first real opportunity to improve its relative and absolute position within the world economy and system. Only then could the West go on to achieve a (temporary?) period of dominance. The contemporary analogy is that the present world economic crisis permits the rise of what are now called the "Newly Industrializing Economies" (NIEs) in East Asia, again at the "margin" of the world economy. We may note that like these East Asian NIEs now, Europe then engaged first in import substitution (at that time in what was the "leading" industry of textiles previously imported from Asia), and increasingly also in export promotion—first to their relatively protected markets in West Africa and the Americas and then to the world market as a whole.

There are also earlier historical analogies in which some but not all marginal and peripheral "marcher states" innovatively challenged "core" economies, societies, and politics (or, empires), as Christopher Chase-Dunn and Thomas Hall (1997) argue. The previously (semi-) peripheral economies took advantage of the opportunities (and tried to avoid the dangers) generated by crises at the center/s of the world economy/system(Gills and Frank 1992; also in Frank and Gills 1993). It cannot be emphasized too much or too often that this positional change (as in musical chairs) each time owed more to the relatively sudden system-wide crisis at its center than to any long "preparation" or previously predictable "rise" of the previously (semi-)peripheral region or its newly "leading" sectors.

Thus, we are led to inquire whether the late eighteenth century may have begun a "B" phase world political economic decline in Asia to the benefit of the previously relatively marginal and now rapidly ascending Europeans. The previously identified world system cycle (Gills and Frank 1992; also in Frank and Gills 1993) implies that the simultaneous "fall" of so many important powerful states—the Ottomans, Mughals, Safavids, Qing, and Hapsburgs—would be the accompaniment of a world system crisis and "B" phase. We will speculate a bit at the end of this chapter about the historical continuation of this long cycle, whose "B" phase appears to have begun in Asia at the end of the eighteenth century. The consideration of related theoretical problems is postponed to chapter 7.

We must still pose the important historical question of just when, not to mention why, political economic declines really began in Asia and whether they were part of a long-cycle "B" phase or not. These related questions also have far-reaching theoretical and ideological implications: were these declines in the East also initiated and caused, or only accelerated—if even that—by "the Rise of the West"?

The Decline of the East Preceded the Rise of the West

This heading is borrowed from Janet Abu-Lughod's masterful *Before European Hegemony* (1989). Alas, she did not pursue the matter beyond A.D. 1350. We have seen that the "East" took several centuries more to "decline," and that the "West" did not really "rise" until very belatedly. We are able to say very little about why the Asian economies and the Ottoman, Safavid, Mughal, and Qing empires declined. Indeed, the discussion of the eighteenth century in Asia has been ambiguous and confusing:

For a considerable time now, in the historiography of Indonesia, India and the Arabic countries, the eighteenth century has been seen as a period of decline. The English saw the decline as justification for empire; the Dutch saw in the period an eclipse of the noble Company; the Arabs only regarded it as background to their modern period. In recent years this notion of decline has been criticized by historians working in each of these major regions. . . . [Some warn] about the danger of taking political fragmentation as evidence of decay. . . . [Yet] for most features of the economy the meagre evidence processed so far suggests continuity rather than sharp change. (Das Gupta and Pearson 1987: 132–3)

Nonetheless, we must follow Fletcher's admonition and look for possible systemic processes and causes in Asia's eventual "decline." Moreover, that has been my procedure for earlier periods, which has produced some significant tentative findings reported in Frank and Gills (1993) and Frank (1993a). So we should also inquire if and how the decline of the East and the rise of the West may have been systemically related.

M. Athar Ali has recently addressed the same issue. How he poses the question is worth quoting in full, although his own tentative answer seems less than satisfactory. He notes that the fall of the Mughal empire has been attributed to all manner of "internal" factors—from too much bad influence of women to institutional inadequacies that made peasant exploitation inefficient but therefore all the more severe, which generated growing nationalism. He observes that a synthesis of all relevant factors is yet to be attempted; but, before even trying, we first need to place them in "the proper context." Ali observes that

In following the scholarly discussion over the break-up of the Mughal Empire, I have been struck by the fact that the discussion should have been conducted in such insular terms. The first part of the eighteenth century did not only see the collapse of the Mughal Empire: The Safavid Empire also collapsed; the Uzbek Khanate broke into fragments; the Ottoman Empire began its career of slow, but inexorable decline. (Ali 1975: 386)

Ali goes on to suggest that it would be straining one's sense of the plausible to assert that it was coincidental for the same fate to overcome all these large regions at the same time. Therefore, also following Fletcher (1985), we should inquire whether it is possible to discover some common factor that caused these simultaneous events. Ali continues:

There is one remarkable point too, which may serve as a guideline in our search. The break-up of the empires directly precedes the impact from the armed attack of the Western colonial powers, notably Britain and Russia. But it precedes the impact with such a short interval that the question must arise whether the rise of the West was not in some ways, not yet properly understood, subverting the polity and society of the East even before Europe actually confronted the eastern states with its superior military power. It is a regrettable gap in our study of economic history of the Middle East [sic!] and India, that no general analysis has been attempted of the changes in the pattern of trade and markets of these countries, as a result of the new commerce between Europe and Asia. (Ali 1975: 386)

Ali's own attempts at a tentative answer are not satisfactory however, because of how he begins: "the major event between 1500 and 1700 was certainly the rise of Europe as the centre of world commerce" (Ali 1975: 387). The evidence amassed in this book contradicts this point of departure and obliges us to look for a different explanation. Ali goes on to suggest that European economic influence must have disrupted and weakened the Asian economies, not only relatively but also absolutely (Ali 1975: 388). This supposition is also contradicted by the evidence for the sixteenth century, especially for the seventeenth century, as well as for part of the eighteenth century, during which the Asian economies were, on the contrary, strengthened.

Then Ali argues that the supposed diversion of Asian income to Europeans and its denial to the ruling classes in Asia obliged the latter to increase agrarian exploitation to keep themselves afloat, and that "of course, spell[s] the end of the great empires" (Ali, 1975: 388). However, increased exploitation, especially of those working on the land, is usually not so much the result of declining income by those who rule them, as the result of greater and rising market opportunities to generate income for the latter from those who work the land for them. That has been the common experience in plantation and other agrarian export economies (Frank 1967). That polarizes the economy and society, making the rich richer and the poor poorer. Below, we will observe ample evidence for this in the seventeenth and eighteenth centuries in India and China as well.

In that way, economic expansion combined with polarization of income and status also resulted in atrophy in the very process that generated it. Therefore, the political stability of the Asian empires may have been undermined not so much by European competition in their econ-omies, as Ali suggests. The growing economic and political strains in Asia may instead have been generated more by the Europeans' supply of silver and by the resultant increased purchasing power, income, and demand on domestic and export markets in the world economy and especially in Asia. That presumably increasingly skewed the distribution of income, which could have led to constraints on effective demand and growing political tensions, as we will see below.

Only in the second half of the eighteenth century, especially in the last third, did trends toward decline accelerate in the Ottoman, Indian, and Chinese empires. The decline was earliest and most accelerated per-haps in Persia and then in India, with the gradual loss of competitive advantages in textiles and the reversal of bullion flows (that is, outward rather than inward) after mid-eighteenth century.

So unless it was in Safavid Persia or in Timurid and/or Bukharan Central Asia, the earliest decline seems to have occurred in India; and it is also the one for which the most studies are readily available to us. So let us start with India, and go on to examine other parts of Asia after that.

THE DECLINE IN INDIA

Historiography on India has long debated whether and to what extent especially British colonialism was responsible for famine and deindustrialization first in Bengal and then elsewhere in India. Ironically, Western-aligned and Indian nationalist observers agree that the British victory at the Battle of Plassey in Bengal in 1757 marked the most important disjuncture. Western-aligned observers tended to argue that Britain brought civilization and development to India. Some In-dian nationalist writers in the nineteenth century (reviewed by Chandra 1966) and many Soviet, Indian, and other "anti-imperialist" ones (in-cluding Frank 1978a) in the twentieth century have seen the decline of India as the result of the defeat in that battle, which led to British colonization. That began the "Rape of Bengal" by the British East India Company, the destruction of the textile industry, the zamindari (large holdings) and *ryotwari* (small holdings) structure of landownership, the "drain" of capital from India, and so on.

Without wishing to pursue this dispute here, there is nonetheless legitimate doubt about just when and where economic decline began in India and elsewhere. Those who argue that it only began after 1757, or, like Amiya Bagchi, only after 1800, or indeed really only from about 1830 as Burton Stein (1989) suggests, must confront at least some evidence that significant economic decline had already started before any of these dates. Contrary to received allegations about "stagnation" in India and elsewhere in Asia prior to the arrival of the Europeans, we observed in chapters 2, 3, and 4 and in the section on a "seventeenth-century crisis" in chapter 5 that substantial economic growth continued in India well into the eighteenth century. That is also the summary judgment of the historical evidence about eighteenth-century India by Stein (1989). In his view, however, British policy did not cause significant economic damage in India until about 1830.

Yet others have observed beginnings of economic decline in India about a century earlier. "There is a definite decline in *both* silk and cotton production in Bengal from the early 1730s" (Rila Mukherjee, private communication 1995). Mukherjee (1994) offers evidence from Kasimbazar, a major Bengali silk-producing center, where the number of merchants supplying silk to the British East India Company declined from an average of 55 merchants with investments of 17,000 rupees in the period 1733–1737 to 36 merchants with 7,000 rupees in 1748–1750. After a crisis in 1754, these merchants vanished from the factory records overnight. Procurement/supply problems had been on the increase, and the hinterland was breaking down as elsewhere in coastal India. However, Bengal was also suffering from declining demand for its silk as Chinese competition grew in Bombay and Madras. Mukherjee (1990/91) also studied Jugdia, the most important Bengali cotton-producing area. There too, matters were "coming to a crisis in the production sphere" at the same time. There were problems of procurement such as late deliveries, shortfalls in supply, deteriorating quality, sudden price hikes, and general unreliability, so that "by the mid-eighteenth century we can already foresee some of the signs of deindustrialization" under the impetus of both stronger foreign capital and weaker local mercantile organization (Mukherjee 1990/91: 128). It seems strange then that Richard Eaton's (1993) study of the Bengal frontier finds little or no economic decline, and at most a shift of economic activity from west to east toward and within Bengal before the mid-eighteenth century.

P. J. Marshall (1987: 290) also observes that "the stability of Bengal itself, which had lasted for several decades, began to crack in the 1740s. A stark picture is painted in a recent assessment. . . ." Then he quotes from K. N. Chaudhuri (1978), who refers to a "push [of] the economy of Bengal towards the brink of general collapse." Chaudhuri (1978: 308) himself goes on to refer to "the disruption of textile production. . . . "

Moreover, Chaudhuri (1978: 309, 294) observes that "the 1730s were a bad time for southern India" and that "the great Anglo-French wars of the mid-eighteenth century further dislocated trade that was already in serious difficulties; Madras suffered particularly severely." Sinnappah Arasaratnam (1986: 211), questioning whether the Coromandel trade underwent stagnation or decline, writes that especially after 1735, "there is no doubt that the region saw a downturn in economic activity and therefore in commerce."

Tapan Raychaudhuri and Irfan Habib, in volume 1 of *The Cambridge Economic History of India,* add that

> considerably more important than the decline of shipping in Bengal was the downfall of the great commercial marine of Gujarat in the early eighteenth century. Here again it is worth noting that the decline of Gujarat's maritime trade, although hastened by the growing political insecurity, had begun before the breakdown of law and order really began to bite. . . . The decline of the Mughal port of Surat and the disappearance of the fleet which was based at that port—the actual figures falling from 112 vessels in 1701 to 20 in 1750—were arguably the most important developments in the trade of the Indian Ocean during the period. (Raychaudhuri and Habib 1982: 433)

Yet, Surat in the west and Masulipatam and other Coromandel coast centers and their hinterlands to the east had declined in the early decades of the eighteenth century, as a consequence of the simultaneous weakening of the Mughals, Safavids, and Ottomans (Das Gupta and Pearson 1987:140). Europeans were able to take commercial competitive advantage of this Asian decline and of their Asian competitors' distress elsewhere as well. Marshall observes that these

> would have been difficult times for Asian ships whether the Englishman was offering his services in competition with them or not. . . . Only when their Indian counterparts were drastically weakened . . . did the English influence on western Indian trade begin to grow. . . . All Asian ships appear to have been losing ground in southeast Asia and China to British ships from Madras and Calcutta in the early eighteenth century. (Marshall 1987: 293, 292)

However, the Indian economic difficulties seem to have spread and/or deepened in the third and fourth decades of the century, and also seriously to have affected the heretofore competitively strongest regions, like Bengal. Moreover, the average annual imports (based on invoice values and sales values) from Asia by both the Dutch and British East India companies declined in the decades of the 1730s and 1740s (but recovered in the 1750s), "confirming the assumption that this was a period of marked competition in the European-Asian trade" (Steensgaard 1990d: 112–3). Chinese merchants were massacred in Dutch Batavia in 1740. It was also a time of "a general European recession in the colonial trade" (Steensgaard 1990d: 110) and a time of war—of Jenkins' Ear beginning in 1739 and of the Austrian Succession in 1740, which Walter Dorn (1963:164) characterized as "in essence a commercial one, a struggle of rival merchants" fought about overseas commerce (Frank 1978a:110). But this observation is not limited to Dorn: "The last war which was undertaken altogether on account of the colonies [was] the Spanish war of 1739," observed Adam Smith ([1776]1937: 899).

Returning to India, it does seem important to inquire further whether political problems and then European colonialism may well have come on the heels of and only accelerated an already earlier and still ongoing economic decline in various parts of India—and elsewhere. At the same time, it is also important to inquire whether, how, and to what extent such decline was related to or even in part generated by a European rise, even *before* European political/military colonial intervention in the declining region.

Arasaratnam (1995) considers this matter with regard to the Coromandel coast. Dutch colonial intervention in Southeast Asia and British efforts to profit more from the China trade simultaneously disadvantaged the Coromandel coast and its Indian merchants. Growing Dutch VOC political and commercial control in Indonesia and especially in Java and its choking effects on Malacca also cut into the long-standing Coromandel ties with Southeast Asia. These had been both bilateral and multilateral as part of the wider trading network outlined above, and both were severely damaged. The British East India Company's growing direct links with China also served to cut Coromandel out of previously important trading business. Arasaratnam summarizes some commercial changes in the early and mid-eighteenth century and "the single most decisive feature" for Coromandel, the decline in its trade with Southeast Asia:

> As far as Coromandel was concerned, European trade, in its new forms and directions, cut deep into the trade that had been traditionally carried on in that region. . . . It was this [Southeast Asian] artery that was punctured violently by the Dutch in the course of the seventeenth century. Indian trading links were cut off one by

one with the Moluccas, Macassar and the Celebes, Bantam and the north Javanese ports, [and the] west coast of Sumatra. In a series of military and naval actions, these ports and markets were shut off from competitive trading. It meant denial of a lucrative export market in textiles for the Coromandel shippers. It meant the wresting from their hands of the import trade in spices to Coromandel. And it meant the denial of mineral—gold and tin— which had formed a profitable import to India. It must be emphasized that these were achieved by brute force and not by superior commercial expertise. . . . The boom in the China trade in the second half of the eighteenth century and the consequent changes to the inter-regional trade of Asia constituted the final blow to the Coromandel trade. . . . Coromandel like Bengal, was drained of bullion to purchase Chinese exports, leading to a general shortage of capital. The Coromandel merchants had little or no role to perform in this newly emerging trade pattern. . . . The extension of direct English control over important parts of the country dispensed with their role as middlemen. . . . As the amount of power wielded by the Europeans grew, so also did [the Indian political power brokers'] dependence on it and their commitment to it. They were decidedly on the side of the European in their confrontation with the merchants and helped to undermine the interests of the merchants. Likewise they took the side of their European masters against the hinterland power and contributed to undermining the latter in the interest of the former. (Arasaratnam 1995: xiv-28, 29, 41, 40)

In summary, there is substantial evidence that economic decline in India and in particular in the Bengali textile industry had already began before the Battle of Plassey in 1757. The accompanying political disarray of the Mughals and others rendered Asians vulnerable to predatory European merchant, naval, and ultimately political power. The Europeans captured the carrying trade from the indigenous shipping and merchants in the mid-eighteenth century in Indian waters on a new scale. India was the first Asian political economic power to begin the "fall" to European hegemony.

THE DECLINE ELSEWHERE IN ASIA

The same issue arises with regard to other regions of Asia, in particular in West, Southeast, and East Asia. In the Ottoman Empire, economic expansion seems to have peaked in the late seventeenth century. The Ottoman economy became gradually weaker during the first half of the eighteenth century and decline accelerated in the last third of the century. Ottoman economic power was gradually undermined in the late eighteenth century by the ascendance of new industrial centers and the increasing commercial dominance of the Europeans. Political power began to be eclipsed by the Europeans at the turn of the eighteenth to the nineteenth centuries, following Napoleon's expedition to Egypt.

In the eighteenth century, Ottoman foreign trade as a whole stagnated and therefore declined as a share of growing world trade. In particular, trade with Europe declined, and among Europeans the French increasingly replaced the British as Ottoman trading partners. Moreover in the late eighteenth century, Ottoman exports and even domestic markets began to suffer from foreign competition and apparently from the French connection, especially with the Americas. Cheaper cotton from North American began to displace that from Anatolia, and cheaper Caribbean coffee to displace Arabian coffee exported through Cairo. Caribbean sugar invaded the domestic market. All these competing products were produced by slave labor in the Americas.

The Ottoman economic "decline" seems to have accelerated after 1760. Among the indications are the following: Migration from rural to urban areas increased. More and more agricultural land, both absolutely and relative to the total, owned by the relatively landed rich was exempted from taxes. Concomitantly, tax-farming increased on the remaining agricultural population, already poor. That increased their poverty further, contributed to driving them off the land, and made the distribution of property and income increasingly unequal. The production and export of agricultural and other raw materials increased only slowly. However their share of total exports increased rapidly, as cotton textiles and manufacturing exports decreased. Especially after 1760, the weaving and export of cotton cloth declined; and some of the foreign trade was replaced by Ottoman interregional trade. Ottoman state control weakened as the strength of its central institutions waned, and regional decentralization grew. Market-derived state revenue declined at Istanbul and several other cities. Contemporary documents quoted in Charles Issawi (1966: 30–37) also testify to increasing French and decreasing Ottoman competitiveness at one Ottoman port city after another.

The 1760s were also years of inflection and subsequent decline, according to various studies of Ottoman textile and other industries (see

Islamoglu-Inan 1987), especially by Mehmet Genc. In Aleppo, the beginnings of decline were already evident in 1750 (Masters 1988: 30 ff.).
Halil Inalcik and Donald Quataert (1994: 703) summarize: "These
trends are based on incomplete evidence, but they fit with a general
impression of faltering commercial conditions in the last decades of the
eighteenth century and the first decade of the subsequent century."
Huri Islamoglu-Inan (private communication 1996) questions even this
"decline" of the Ottoman economy in view of its partly successful competition with British textiles both at home and abroad in the mid-
nineteenth century.

What these observers do not inquire about but we may consider is
whether, how, and to what extent this Ottoman "faltering of commercial conditions" at the end of the eighteenth century was also part of the
European-Atlantic economy's Kondratieff "B" phase since 1762, which
presumably helped to reduce Ottoman markets in the West and maybe
to increase the competition from colonial slave production in the West.
Apparently, the Ottomans were not able, or at least were less able, to
benefit from the renewed "A" phase recovery at the turn of the century,
while the Europeans did. The cotton textile exports Islamoglu-Inan refers to may have derived some benefit from this recovery. However
later in the nineteenth century, the Europeans destroyed much of the
Ottoman textile industry and prevented its establishment in Egypt by
Mohammed Ali, despite his desperate efforts to do so (Issawi 1966).

In Qing China, the decline came later. In the eighteenth century,
China undoubtedly experienced economic and population growth. Its
recuperation from the crisis in the middle of the seventeenth century,
discussed in chapter 5, may have been "delayed" by the Ming/Qing succession and reorganization of the country until say 1683, when Taiwan
was reincorporated and all restrictions on trade were lifted. Then, a
veritable economic boom started in China. However, silver imports declined drastically in the 1720s and even more so at mid century, before
increasing again after 1760 and being especially high in the 1780s (Lin
1990). In 1793 Emperor Ch'ien-lung (Qianlong) wrote King George III
through the English ambassador to China the oft-quoted letter that "as
your ambassador can see for himself, we posses all things. I set no value
on objects strange or ingenious, and we have no use for your country's
manufactures. . . . There was [is] therefore no need to import the manufactures of outside barbarians in exchange for our own produce"
(Frank 1978a: 160).

Wolfram Eberhard (1977) dates the beginning of Qing Chinese internal decline to the Shantung rebellion in 1774 and the resurgence of the White Lotus Society in 1775 (the same time, we may observe, as the American Revolution and other events during the 1762–1790 Kondratieff "B" phase analyzed above). Europeans replaced Chinese traders in the China Sea only at the end of the eighteenth century; and even then the balance of trade remained heavily in China's favor (Marks 1996: 64). As is well known, it was only the British recourse to opium grown for them in India that finally reversed this situation in the nineteenth century.

Thus in China, rapid economic dislocation occurred only in the early nineteenth century, via the opium trade and its bullion drain of silver out of China, which destabilized the entire economic system. This weakening process culminated in the Opium wars and the "fall" of China. Victor Lippit's "The Development of Underdevelopment in China" (in Huang 1980) deals almost exclusively with the nineteenth century. Lippit does rather well in denying the historical or theoretical basis of most received attempts to explain China's underdevelopment. These attempts at explanations have been made in terms of "the family system" (Marion J. Levy), "pre-industrial stage theory" (A. Eckstein, John King Fairbank, L. S. Yang), and "the vicious circle of poverty" (Ragnar Nurske), none of which can account for any of China's success before 1800, nor for much of the lack of the same after 1800 (also see Lippit 1987).

However, Lippit attributes too much causative influence to the weight of Chinese bureaucracy and class structure. Indeed, as I already argued in my own contribution to C. C. Huang's book (Frank 1980), Lippit's contribution is mistitled for several reasons, only one of which is that he sees stagnation in China while its economy was still expanding before 1800. Indeed, he later rectifies this judgment himself in Lippitt (1987: 40, 42) when he recognizes "renewed economic expansion" and "thriving economic activity" between the sixteenth and eighteenth centuries. Nonetheless in both books, he attributes nineteenth-century "underdevelopment" to class-generated internal weaknesses and virtually dismisses all influences of China's position in the world economy.

Evidence of some economic decline and sociopolitical crisis can also be found in mainland Southeast Asia during the last third of the eighteenth century (Tarling 1992: 572–95). However new research by Anthony Reid (1997) and his colleagues complicate this picture. Their revisionist thesis is that "there was a distinct commercial expansion in the region from about 1760" accompanied by a decline in most indices of

Dutch VOC activity. The arrival of ships at Malacca grew from 188 in 1761 to 539 in 1785, of which 54 and 242, respectively, were captained by Malays, 55 and 170 by Chinese, and 17 and 37 by British. Almost half of these and almost all of the increase represent ships arriving from Siak, only 20 from China and about 40 from India (Reid 1997: tables 1, 2). Yet Reid also finds that Southeast Asian sugar exports reached a (temporary) peak in 1760 and that Dutch VOC imports of textiles to archipelago Southeast Asia declined from 272,000 pieces to 102,000 (Reid 1997: table 5). And Reid's comment is that "assembling the relevant data suggests that for imported textiles, as for exports, the new upturn occurred precisely in the period when documentation is most difficult at the end of the eighteenth century" (Reid 1997). These findings, and/or the lack of them, then also raise the question: was there really such an upturn precisely after 1760? Not only is the documentation scarce, but the declining Dutch VOC trade from India may reflect not only the economic decline of both (perhaps to the benefit of the British East India Company since arrivals from Indian ports remained stable between 1765 and 1785). Also arrivals from the still relatively flourishing Chinese ports tripled from 7 to 21 ships but remained quantitatively quite modest compared to the intra-Southeast Asian ones (Reid 1997: table 2). Moreover, any purported "distinct commercial expansion" in Southeast Asia would have had to go against the cyclical trend elsewhere in the world. Indeed, according to Reid's table 4, the value of average annual Southeast Asian exports of pepper, coffee, and sugar were (in thousand Spanish dollars) 864 in the 1750s; 1,236 in the 1760s, 1,043 in the 1770s, 1,076 in the 1780s, and 1,310 in the 1790s. That makes for a 50 percent increase over the fifty years from 1750 to 1800, including a 5 percent increase after 1760 (even with the absolute decline in the 1770s and 1780s)! That hardly sounds like a "distinct commercial expansion," which on further reflection seems more like a storm in a Southeast Asian teacup. So Southeast Asia as well may have remained in step with other regions.

We need more empirical confirmation of major regional and/or even pan-Asian economic decline, accompanied or followed by an inflection in the population growth rate by the mid-eighteenth century. That would place the late eighteenth- and then nineteenth-century rise of Europe to relative dominance into a rather different light and historical perspective. In that case, neither the Eurocentric European exceptionalist nor the Indo-, Sino- and other Asian nationalist interpretations of this period would be adequate. Perhaps there really *was* a long economic cycle in whose downward "B" phase one after another region and empire in Asia declined. Then, the previously rather marginal Europeans and later the North Americans were able to take advantage of this Asian cyclical "B" phase decline, like the East Asian NIEs today: it is *then* that the Europeans staked out their own claim to leadership and hegemony in the world economy—temporarily! However, not only did "the Rise of the West" follow "the Decline of the East." The two were also otherwise structurally and cyclically dependent on each other as inextricably interrelated parts of a single global economy. That is what I seek to demonstrate in the following sections.

How Did the West Rise?

So how did the West rise to win this competition—temporarily? The introduction to this book reviewed a number of received theories and answers, all of which allege one or another or a whole combination of European and by extension Western exceptionalisms. The introduction also contended that all of these theories, Marxist, Weberian, and/or whatever, are fundamentally flawed by their Eurocentrism. J. M. Blaut's (1993a) *The Colonizer's Model of the World: Geographical Diffusionism and Eurocentric History* analyzes a dozen of these answers and their flaws chapter and verse. Our first chapter cites Goody, Said, Bernal, Amin, Hodgson, Tibebu, and Lewis and Wigen, who also demystify this Eurocentrism. However, they mostly concentrate on ideological critiques of the manifest and hidden ideologies under review. Also cited is my own critique (Frank 1994, 1995) of the "modern capitalist world-economy/system" alternative proposed by Braudel and Wallerstein. But my earlier work too is limited mostly to a critique, although Frank and Gills (1993) offers an alternative world system interpretation of world history before 1500.

The historical/empirical sections of the present book demonstrate that the real world during the period from 1400 to 1800, not to mention earlier, was very different from what received theory has alleged. Eurocentric history and "classical" social theory, but also still Wallerstein's "modern world-system" suppose and/or allege European predominance, which simply did not exist. Until about 1800 the world economy was by no stretch of the imagination European-centered nor in any significant way defined or marked by any European-born (and

European-borne) "capitalism," let alone development. Still less was there any real "capitalist development" initiated, generated, diffused, or otherwise propagated or perpetrated by Europeans or the West. That occurred only by the stretch of the Eurocentric *imagination,* and even that only belatedly after the nineteenth century, as Bernal has already emphasized. A related question then is whether there had already been any "capitalist [development of] underdevelopment." For Latin America and the Caribbean, that argument (Frank 1966, 1967) can probably still stand, and perhaps for the slave trade regions of Africa as well. The argument was that in India, this process only began after the Battle of Plassey in 1757 (Frank 1975, 1978a). However, this historical review does raise some question as to what extent the Indian and other Asian decline was "imposed" by Europe, not to mention by "capitalism."

For, the data in the preceding sections have shown unequivocally that the world economy was preponderantly Asian-based. Europeans had been clamoring to attach themselves to it for centuries before Columbus and Vasco da Gama, which is what propelled them to seek some, any, and especially a golden way to do so in the first place. And yet for centuries after these European (not world!) pioneers, other Europeans still only clambered very belatedly, slowly, and marginally to attach themselves to the Asian economic train. Only in the nineteenth century did they succeed in finding a place in the locomotive.

CLIMBING UP ON ASIAN SHOULDERS

So how did the West rise? The answer, literally in a word, is that the Europeans *bought* themselves a seat, and then even a whole railway car, on the Asian train. How were any—literally—poor Europeans able to afford the price of even a third-class ticket to board the Asian economic train? Well, the Europeans somehow found and/or stole, extorted, or earned the money to do so. Again, how so?

The basic answer is two-fold, or three-fold. The most important answer is that Europeans obtained the money from the gold and silver mines they found in the Americas. The secondary answer is that they "made" more money, in the very good business first of digging up that silver—or more accurately, obliging the indigenous peoples of the Americas to dig it up for the Europeans. The Europeans also engaged in a variety of other profitable businesses they ran in—and to—the Americas. These were first and foremost the slave plantations in Brazil, the Caribbean, and the North American South; and, of course, the slave trade itself to supply and run these plantations. The Europeans employed and exploited perhaps a million workers at any one time in this profitable business, by Blaut's estimate (1993a: 195). Europeans were able to make still more money selling their own European-made products to these and other people in the Americas, products for which Europe otherwise would have found no other market, since they were not competitively salable in Asia.

The Keynesian multiplier did however operate also in Europe, first through the infusion of the American-derived money itself, and then also through the repatriation and investment in Europe of profits from the Americas, Africa, and from the "triangular"—including especially the slave—trade among them. Of course, Europe also derived profits from the aforementioned European production and export of its goods to the Americas and Africa. All these European sources of and machines for finding and making money have been alluded to in the earlier empirical sections of this book. They need not be elaborated on here, because they have already been researched and demonstrated countless times over, without however seeing some of their implications nor drawing the necessary conclusions, outlined below.

In order to avoid a tedious recounting or Marx's language of "capital dripping with blood and sweat," it should be sufficient to allude to everybody's favorite observer, Adam Smith:

Since the first discovery of America, the market for the produce of its silver mines has been growing gradually more and more extensive. First, the market of Europe has become more extensive. Since the discovery of America, the greater part of Europe has improved. England, Holland, France and Germany; even Sweden, Denmark and Russia have all advanced considerably both in agriculture and manufactures. . . . Secondly, America is itself a new market for the produce of its own silver mines; and as it advances in agriculture, industry and population . . . its demand must increase much more rapidly. The English colonies are altogether a new market. . . . The discovery of America, however made a most essential [contribution]. By opening up a new and inexhaustible market to all commodities of Europe, it gave occasion to a new division of labour and improvements of art, which, in the narrow circle of ancient commerce could never have taken place for want of a market to take off the greater part of their produce. The productive powers of labour were improved, and its produce increased in all the different countries of Europe, and together with it the real revenue and wealth of the inhabitants. . . . (Smith [1776]1937: 202, 416)

As Smith knew, it was America (in a word) that accounted for the increase in the real revenue and wealth of the inhabitants of Europe. Moreover, Smith repeatedly argues that even Poland, Hungary, and other parts of Europe that did not trade with the Americas directly, nonetheless also derived indirect benefit for their own industries from the same. Moreover of course, as Ken Pomeranz (1997) emphasizes and analyzes, the European exploitation of native, bonded labor and slave labor imported from Africa in combination with the resources of the Americas not only afforded Europe additional resources for its own consumption and investment but also lightened the pressure on scarce resources in Europe itself.

Smith also recognized Asia as being economically far more advanced and richer than Europe. "The improvements in agriculture and manufactures seem likewise to have been of very great antiquity in the provinces of Bengal in the East Indies, and in some of the eastern provinces of China. . . . Even those three countries [China, Egypt, and Indostan], the wealthiest, according to all accounts, that ever were in the world, are chiefly renowned for their superiority in agriculture and manufactures. . . . [Now, in 1776] China is a much richer country than any part of Europe" (Smith [1776]1937: 20, 348, 169).

Moreover, Smith also understood *how* the poor Europeans were able to use their new money and increased wealth to buy themselves tickets on the Asian train. Continuing with the third point in his discussion excerpted above, Smith writes:

Thirdly, the East Indies [Asia] is another market for the produce of the silver mines of America, and a market which, from the time of the discovery of those mines, has been continually taking off a greater and greater quantity of silver. . . . Upon all these accounts, the precious metals are a commodity which it always has been, and still continues to be, extremely advantageous to carry from Europe to India. There is scarce any commodity which brings a better price there [and it is even more advantageous to carry silver to China]. . . . The silver of the new continent seems in this manner to be one of the principal commodities by which the commerce between the two extremities of the old one is carried on, and it is by means of it, in great measure, that those distant parts of the world are connected with one another. . . . The trade to the

East Indies, by opening a market to the commodities of Europe, *or, what comes to the same thing, the gold and silver* which is purchased with those commodities, must necessarily tend to increase the annual production of European commodities. . . . Europe, instead of being the manufacturers and carriers for but a small part of the world . . . have now [1776] become the manufacturers for the numerous and thriving cultivators of America, and the carriers, and in some respect the manufacturers too, for almost all the different nations of Asia, Africa, and America. (Smith [1776]1937: 206, 207, 417, 591; my emphasis)

The Asian market for the Europeans was the same thing as silver, as Smith remarked, for two related reasons: One is that silver was their only means of payment. The other is that therefore the Europeans' main business was the production and trade of silver as a commodity itself. That was the main source of the profits Europeans derived from their trade both within Asia and between Asia and Europe.

Braudel declares himself "astonished," "as a historian of the Mediterranean," to find that the late eighteenth-century Red Sea trade was still the same "vital channel" in the outflow of Spanish-American silver to India and beyond as in the sixteenth century. "This influx of precious metal was vital to the movements of the most active sector of the Indian, and no doubt Chinese economy" (Braudel 1992: 491). India "had in fact been for centuries subject to a money economy, partly through her links with the Mediterranean world" (Braudel 1992: 498). "Cambay (another name for Gujarat) could only survive, it was said, by stretching out its arm to Aden and the other to Malacca" (Braudel 1992: 528). Gold and silver "were also the indispensable mechanisms which made the whole great machine function, from its peasant base to the summit of society and the business world" (Braudel 1992: 500). Braudel himself concludes that "in the end, the Europeans had to have recourse to the precious metals, particularly American silver, which was the 'open sesame' of these trades" (Braudel 1992: 217). "From the start, Spanish America had inevitably been a decisive element in world history" (Braudel 1992: 414). "Is not America . . . perhaps the true explanation of Europe's greatness?" (Braudel 1992: 387).

Precisely that is also the explanation of Blaut (1977, 1992, 1993a), who in all these regards seems to be the modern alter ego of Adam Smith. Both understand and explain the first two answers to the question of how the poor Europeans managed access to the thriving Asian market: (1) they used their American money, and (2) they used the profits of both their production/imports from and their exports to America and

Africa, and their investment of the proceeds of all of these in Europe itself.

However, the third answer alluded to above is that Europeans also used both the American silver money and their profits to *buy into* the wealth of Asia itself. As Smith noted, and all the evidence reviewed above shows, Europe used its commodities, or what comes to the same thing, the *only* commodities it could sell in Asia, that is its American gold and silver, to buy Asian products. Moreover, as also documented above, Europe used its silver purchasing power to muscle in on the intra-Asian trade, which the Europeans called "country trade." As noted above, it was the silver—and gold—trade itself that was really the main-stay of the European companies. Consider for instance this summary of Dutch VOC strategy:

> The European precious metals, the Japanese silver obtained mainly against Chinese silk and other goods, and the gold ob-tained in Taiwan mainly against Japanese silver and Indonesian pepper were invested primarily in Indian textiles. These textiles were exchanged largely for Indonesian pepper and other spices but also sent to Europe and various Asian factories. The bulk of the pepper and other spices was exported to Europe but a certain amount [was] used for investment in various Asian factories such as those in India, Persia, Taiwan and Japan. Raw silk from Persia and China also found its way to Europe. . . . The pattern of Dutch participation in intra-Asian trade was determined in part by the requirements of the trade with Japan which was by far the most important Asian source of precious metals for the Company dur-ing the seventeenth century. . . . In certain years precious metals procured in Japan were of greater value than those received at Batavia from Holland. (Prakesh 1994: 1-192, 193)

More graphical still is a frequently quoted description of Dutch trade in 1619 from VOC director Jan Pieterszon Coen himself:

> Piece goods from Gujarat we can barter for pepper and gold on the coast of Sumatra; rials and cottons from the coast [of Coro-mandel] for pepper in Bantam; sandalwood, pepper and rials we can barter for Chinese goods and Chinese gold; we can extract silver from Japan with Chinese goods; piece goods from the Cor-omandel coast in exchange for spices, other goods and gold from China; piece goods from Surat for spices; other goods and rials from Arabia for spices and various other trifles—one thing leads to another. And all of it can be done without any money from the Netherlands and with ships alone. We have the most important

spices already. What is missing then? Nothing else but ships and a little water to prime the pump. . . . (By this I mean sufficient means [money] so that the rich Asian trade may be established.) Hence, gentlemen and good administrators, there is nothing to prevent the Company from acquiring the richest trade in the world. (quoted in Steensgaard 1987: 139 and by Kindleberger 1989, who cites Steensgaard 1973 [same as 1972] but writes "sufficient money" and omits the last—and for present purposes the most significant—sentence!)

That is, Europeans sought to muscle in on *"the richest trade in the world,"* but it took the Dutch rather more than just "a little water [*meaning* money]" to pump this Asian well of treasures and capital, and of course *that* money came from the Americas. Thus, Europeans derived *more profits* from their participation in the intra-Asian "country trade" than they did from their Asian imports into Europe, even though many of the latter in turn generated further profits for them as re-exports to Africa and the Americas. So the Europeans were able to profit from the much more productive and wealthy Asian economies by participating in the intra-Asian trade; and *that* in turn they were able to do ultimately only thanks to their American silver.

Without that silver—and, secondarily, without the division of labor and profits it generated in Europe itself—the Europeans would not have had a leg, or even a single toe, to stand on with which to compete in the Asian market. Only their American money, and not any "exceptional" European "qualities," which, as Smith realized even in 1776, had not been even remotely up to Asian standards, permitted the Europeans to buy their ticket on the Asian economic train and/or to take a third-class seat on it. That is looking at this European "business" in Asia from the demand side. The concomitant supply side, emphasized by Pomeranz (1997), is of course that their American money permitted the Europeans to buy real goods, produced with real labor and resources in Asia. These goods not only increased consumption and investment beyond what it otherwise could and would have been in Europe; they also diminished the pressure on resources in Europe itself.

To refer to another analogy, their American-supplied stakes permitted the Europeans an entry into the Asian economic casino. Why were they ultimately able to prosper there? Only because of their unending, albeit fluctuating, flow of American silver and gold. That is what provided the Europeans with their one competitive advantage among their Asian competitors, for these did not have money growing on American trees. However, even with that resource and advantage, the Europeans were no more than a minor bit player at the Asian, indeed world, economic table. Yet the Europeans gambled their American stakes for all they were worth in Asia and held out there for *three* centuries. Even though the Europeans also reinvested some of their Asian earnings to buy into still more and better seats at the Asian economic table, they were able to continue doing so only because their supply of cash was being continually replenished from the Americas. Witness that even in the eighteenth century, the Europeans had nothing else to offer any Asians, for European manufactures were still not competitive. However, Smith exaggerated worldwide sales of European manufactures, unless we read his qualification of "to some extent" as meaning almost nothing.

Certainly, the Europeans had no exceptional, let alone superior, ethnic, rational, organizational, or spirit-of-capitalist advantages to offer, diffuse, or do anything else in Asia. What the Europeans may have had, as we will consider further below and in our conclusions, is some of what Alexander Gerschenkron's (1962) calls the advantages of "backwardness" afforded by their position, as Chase-Dunn and Hall (1997) also observe, at the (semi-)periphery of the world economy!

So how is it that this otherwise apparently hopeless European gamble in Asia panned out—and finally hit the jackpot? Only because while the Europeans were gathering strength from the Americas and Africa, as well as from Asia itself, Asian economies and polities were also becoming weakened during part of the eighteenth century—so much so that the paths finally crossed, as in Rhoades Murphey's (1977) diagram, at about 1815. However, in the half century before that, another— fourth—element entered into the European/Asian equation. Adam Smith is also known for arguing that colonies did not pay, even though he wrote a chapter "On Colonies" and argued primarily against colonial monopolies. Moreover, Smith wrote just before the major technological inventions and innovations of the industrial revolution in Britain and Europe. This is not the place to enter into the arguments about whether there really was such a "revolution" and whether European rates of capital accumulation really did "take off," as W. W. Rostow (1962) and others have contended.

SUPPLY AND DEMAND FOR TECHNOLOGICAL CHANGE

R. M. Hartwell, who was one of the foremost students of the industrial revolution, observed that

J. H. Clapham wrote in 1910 that "Even if . . . the history of 'the' industrial revolution is a 'thrice squeezed orange', there remains an astonishing amount of juice in it." Indeed, half a century later interest in the industrial revolution is increasing. . . . On the causes of the industrial revolution, for example, there is silence, simplicity or confusion. What was the prime mover, or what complex of movers was responsible? Agricultural revolution? Population growth? Improved technology? Increased trade? Capital accumulation? All of these have their supporters. Or must explanations be sought in noneconomic forces? Changes in religion, social structure, science, philosophy and law? . . . There seems to be little agreement. . . . The most difficult problem is to determine the extent to which this stimulus was *exogenous* (i.e., independent of the economy)—for example, an increase in demand through international trade . . . and to what extent it was *endogenous* (i.e., generated within the economy) . . . ? (Hartwell 1971: 131, 110, 115)

However, the real problem is what economy? My contention is that the key to the confusion is to be found in Hartwell's last sentence: Clapham's orange that was already thrice squeezed almost a century ago and innumerable times since then has always been regarded as only a British, European, or at most a "Western" fruit. Yet Graeme Snooks (1994:1–2) writes "we have only begun to scratch the surface of a field that needs to be ploughed long and deep . . . [and] we need to view the Industrial Revolution from an entirely different vantage point to those traditionally used." Snooks and his contributors propose several different ones, but all of them continue to search for root and cause in Europe alone, in the "dynamic quality of England (and of Western Europe generally) throughout the pre-modern period" and over the entire past millennium at that (Snooks 1994: 11, 43 ff.). So despite their "entirely different" vantage point, in all this time and even still today, no one has really even attempted a globally holistic world economic/systemic explanation of the whole orange tree that could satisfy the maxim cited from Leopold von Ranke in my opening epigraph: "There is no history but universal history—as it really was"!

The question is how and why beginning around 1800 Europe and then the United States, after long lagging behind, "suddenly" caught up and then overtook Asia economically and politically in the one world economy and system. It is important to see that this pursuit and victory was part of a competitive race in the single global economy, whose structure and operation itself generated this development. That is, a number of well-known technological and other developments and investments in new productive processes took place in (Western) Europe and then in the United States. But it simply will not do to attempt to account for these departures by looking for their roots only or even primarily in a thousand years of history only in Europe, as Snooks (1994, 1996) still proposes in his "new perspectives on the industrial revolution" or as Robert Adams (1996) does in his "inquiry into Western technology," which also examines only Europe, except when he goes back to the Iron and Bronze ages in the eastern Mediterranean and West Asia.

Yet, these technological developments of the industrial revolution should not be regarded as only European achievements. Instead, they must be understood more properly as world developments whose spatial locus moved to and through the West at that time after having long moved about the East. The relevant question is not so much what the "distinctive" European features or factors are of the industrial revolution as how and why this industrial shift took place from East to West.

We have already observed above that the answers to the reasons for this shift must be sought in both the decline of the East and in the rise of the West. The heretofore received "answers" to the "why/how?" question suffer doubly or triply. They suffer first from the misattribution of the reasons for the supposed exceptionalisms of superiority to Europe, which Blaut and others have already shown to be without any foundation in historical fact. Moreover, they suffer from looking for the reasons for the rise of Europe within Europe itself in the first place, and therefore neglecting analysis of the related decline of the (several) Easts. However, these two cases of misplaced concreteness also imply a third failure: they fail to look for the reasons of "the Rise of the West" and "the Decline of the East" in the structure and operation of the whole world economy itself. We have already observed how and why Europe was such a laggard in the economic race until well into the eighteenth century and how it improved its position by buying a ticket on the Asian train and then displacing some of its passengers, primarily through the European access to and use of American money.

The question remains, however, why and how Western Europeans and Americans then bested the Asians at their own game through recourse to the technological advances of the industrial revolution. How and why were these made then and there? A fully satisfactory answer may be still beyond us—but certainly no more than it is beyond all the erroneous ideological Eurocentric answers that others from Marx to

Weber and their latter-day followers have proffered. A world economic analysis can certainly and easily do better than that even with the still limited elements, hypotheses, and evidence offered in an only very preliminary way below.

Technological progress through the invention and application of labor-saving machinery has frequently been attributed to the profitability of the same in a high-wage economy, particularly in North America. High wages create an incentive to reduce costs of production by replacing this high-wage labor with labor-saving machinery. And wages in North America were relatively high from early on, as so many observers including Marx pointed out, because the population/land-resource ratio was low and the expanding frontier offered an escape from low-wage drudgery. Therefore, it has been argued that in the nineteenth and twentieth centuries, the incentive to invent, innovate, and use labor-saving machinery increasingly shifted across the Atlantic from Europe to America—in the world market competition to reduce costs of production and maintain or gain market share.

We can and should apply the same kind of analysis and argument to the invention, innovation, and application of labor-saving machinery during the industrial revolution in Europe. Of the increase in the British growth rate in the eighteenth century, 80 percent—and 30 percent of the total growth between 1740 and 1780—have been attributed to increased productivity alone (Inkster 1991: 67). Europeans also, even more so than Americans, were in a race and struggle in the world economy, in which they had to compete for their markets primarily with Asians. However, Europeans were also relatively high-wage/high-cost producers. That is precisely why, as we observed above, Europeans were unable to sell virtually anything to Asians, who were much more productive and competitive with much lower wage costs. How and why so? Well, because also the population/land-resource ratio was relatively higher in many parts of Asia, certainly in China and India, than it was in the more sparsely settled Europe.

Moreover, Europe also had a frontier—in the Americas and later also in Australia, as Benjamin Higgins (1991) has pointed out. Certainly during much of the nineteenth century, European emigration across the Atlantic to the Americas served to lower the population/land-resource ratio well beyond what it otherwise would have been. Thus, the lower European population and its safety-valve emigration to the Americas both served to generate incentives for labor-saving machinery in Europe far more than the Asian population/resource base did.

Adam Smith was writing just as the inventions of the industrial revolution were getting up steam; he observed at the end of his chapter on "The Wages of Labour" that

> the liberal reward of labour . . . increases the industry of the common people. The wages of labour are the encouragement of industry, which, like every other human quality, improves in proportion of the encouragement it receives. . . . where wages are high, accordingly we shall always find the workmen more active, diligent and expeditious, than where they are low. . . . the high price of provision, by diminishing the funds destined for the maintenance of servants, disposes masters rather to diminish than to increase the number of those they have. . . . [When there is an] increase in wages of labour . . . the owner of [capital] stock which employs a great number of labourers, necessarily endeavours, for his own advantage . . . to supply them with the best machinery which either he or they can think of. What takes place among the labourers in a particular workhouse, takes place, for the same reason, among those of a great society. The greater their number, the more they naturally divide themselves into different classes and subdivision of employment. More heads are occupied in inventing the most proper machinery for executing the work of each, and it is, therefore, more likely to be invented. There are many commodities, therefore, which, in consequence of these improvements, come to be produced by so much less labour than before, that the increase of its price is more than compensated by the diminution of its quantity. (Smith [1776]1937: 81, 83, 86)

In a later section on the "effects of the Progress of Improvement upon the real Price of Manufactures," Smith observes that so far in his and the preceding century the cost of production had already declined and in the future could decline most remarkably in manufactures made of coarser metals. On the other hand, he reports that in the clothing manufacture there had been "no such sensible reduction of price" (or cost of production). However, Smith does remark on three capital improvements and many smaller ones in coarse and fine woolen manufactures; but Smith does not yet in 1776 mention any such technological progress or "industrial revolution" in the cotton textile industry!

As A. E. Musson (1972) observes in the introduction to his *Science, Technology, and Economic Growth in the Eighteenth Century,*

> there seems little doubt, however, that—whatever the motives of inventors—innovators or entrepreneurs were certainly much

influenced by economic factors, such as relative prices, market possibilities, and profit prospects. Of this there is plentiful evidence in specialized historical studies of particular firms, too well known and numerous to list here. (Musson 1972: 53)

However, these relative prices and profit prospects, of course, were relative to *world* market possibilities, especially in competitive industries like textiles, which began the industrial revolution in Britain.

Indeed, Smith himself had already compared Europe, India, and China in this respect in 1776. Discussing their relative costs of transportation, he observed that in comparison to the expense of land-carriage in Europe the availability of inland navigation in China and India was already labor-saving and reduces the real and the nominal price of many manufactures.

Analogously, there was a certain rationale that chlorine bleaching of textiles, which had previously been done by exposing them to much sun, was invented and introduced where there was little sun to be had—in Britain. Similarly, its use of coal as the fuel for the industrial revolution was certainly induced and rendered economical by the growing shortage of wood for charcoal (that shortage also existed in China, but there capital was in shorter supply and coal more expensive).

Hartwell (1971: 268) observed that "there is general agreement that there was no capital shortage [in Britain] in the eighteenth century, although the implication of this admission is not always appreciated." The main implication that is not always appreciated—indeed apparently not ever and also not by Hartwell himself—is that Britain and all of these other "economies" were connected through a single worldwide division of labor and circulation of goods and money. Therefore, the competitive forces of relative demand-and-supply shortages and availabilities of labor and capital operated not just in Britain, but also worldwide. That is, the combined demand-and-supply, both-sides-of-the-coin analysis must also be extended to the single global economy as a whole. Indeed, Smith himself began to do so in his above noted comparison of labor and other costs of transportation in Europe and Asia. It is difficult to understand let alone to accept therefore that although Snooks (1996) also stresses relative factor prices, contributors like E. A. Wrigley (in Snooks 1994) limit their analysis of competition to Britain and Western Europe. Indeed, Wrigley reexamines the writings of the classical economists from Adam Smith to David Ricardo regarding the relative prices of labor, capital, land, and other natural resources; yet unlike them(for example, Ricardo's law of international comparative advantage), Wrigley's focus is on Britain alone. Snooks goes further but writes that "the Industrial Revolution emerged from a thousand years of fierce competition between a large number of small, equally matched Western European kingdoms" (Snooks 1994:15).

Yet most certainly in the textile market, which was the primary locus of the industrial revolution, Britain and Western Europe had to compete primarily with India and China, as well as West Asia. Thus, relative supply-and-demand differences generated differential regional and sectoral comparative costs and comparative advantages in relation to each other around the whole world. These structural differences could then be the basis of differential rational microeconomic labor, land, capital, and labor-saving technological responses by the various enterprises, sectors, and regions of the single global economy. The argument here is that this (and not so much "internal" European circumstances) is where we must look for the real explanation of the incentive and option for investment in and application of technological advance in some parts of the world economy. The argument is not that "internal" European circumstances were not relevant to the economic decision-making process there. It is that circumstances "internal" to Europe (or to Manchester, or to James Watt's steam-engine shop) were created by its participation in the world economy. That is, the structure and dynamic of the world economy/system itself generate the differential comparative costs, advantages, and rational responses to the same all around the world and everywhere in the world.

It is gratifying to find a the similar, albeit more limited argument, by Giovanni Arrighi:

Our thesis has been that the main historical link between the three moments of the industrial expansion [in the fourteenth, sixteenth/early seventeenth, and late eighteenth centuries] in England was integral to an ongoing financial expansion, restructuring, and reorganization of the capitalist world-economy, in which England was incorporated from the very start. Periods of financial expansion were invariably moments of intensifying competitive pressures on the governmental and business institutions of the European trade and accumulation system. Under these pressures, agro-industrial production declined in some locales and rose in others, primarily in response to the positional disadvantages and advantages of the locales in the changing structure of the world-economy. (Arrighi 1994: 209)

Indeed, except that the world economic structure and process in question was not only that of Europe but the entire world as a whole. Also noteworthy is the period, industry, and the extent of the restructuring involved: Arrighi, following Nef (1934), Wallerstein, and others, stresses centuries-long industrial "expansion" and not "revolution." In each cyclical occasion, the sectoral locus centered in textiles, which was probably the productive industry (as distinct from the financial service sector) in which competition was most rife. However, the first adjustment improved England's competitive position only relative to Flanders and the second one relative only to northern and southern Europe. Only the third adjustment managed significantly to alter Britain's competitive position worldwide. Even that required over half a century, as net textile imports to the previous competitive leader, India, did not exceed its exports until 1816.

We cannot accompany this world development here, but we may illustrate it by citing a couple of testimonies from the beginning of the eighteenth and nineteenth centuries. Reference was already made in chapter 5 to the 1703 Anglo-Portuguese Treaty of Methuen that consolidated British access to the Portuguese market, which had been opened by three prior treaties since 1642. The British statesman J. Methuen waxed loud and clear about it in December 1702: "This agreement will have this consequence in Portugal that all their own manufactures, which at this time make a vast quantity of ill cloth and dear, will be immediately laid down and totally discontinued; and the cloth or stuffs of no other nation will be able to come into competition with those of England" on the Portuguese market. His Portuguese critic Luis da Cunha agreed at least on the facts that "what the British want is to improve their manufactures, and to ruin those started in Portugal" (cited in Sideri 1970: 57, 59). And so it turned out, as related in Frank (1978a,b), which also signals the irony that a century later Ricardo would defend British industry by exemplifying his "law of comparative costs/advantage" with the exchange of British textiles for Portuguese wine!

Regarding competition in the world textile market, we may return to Braudel:

> The incentive worked the other way round—providing a stimulus to the threatened industry in Europe [by Indian exports]. England's first step was to close her own frontiers for the greater part of the eighteenth century to Indian textiles, which she re-exported to Europe and America. Then she tried to capture for

herself this profitable market—something that could only be achieved by making drastic reductions in manpower. It surely is no coincidence that the machine revolution began in the cotton industry. . . . England, held back by high domestic prices and labour costs which made her the most expensive country in Europe, could no longer cope with the competition from the French and Dutch on the markets closest to home. She was being beaten to it in the Mediterranean, in the Levant, in Italy and in Spain. . . . [but] remained ahead in Portugal, which was one of her most ancient and solid conquests . . . and in Russia. (Braudel 1992: 522, 575)

In 1776, Adam Smith observed that "the perfection of manufacturing industry, it must be remembered, depends altogether upon the division of labour . . . [which] is necessarily regulated, it has already been shown, by the extent of the market"; Smith then added in the same paragraph that "without an extensive foreign market, they could not well flourish" (Smith [1776]1937: 644). Perhaps Smith had read Matthew Boulton's 1769 letter to his partner James Watt: "It is not worth my while to manufacture [your engine] for three countries alone; but I find it very well worth my while to make it for all the world" (cited in Mokyr 1990: 245). Why then in their analysis of the factors that account for the industrial revolution do Mokyr, Snooks, and others view factor price and product competition primarily in British and at most in West European terms? By 1800, four out of seven pieces of cotton cloth produced in Britain were exported (Stearns 1993: 24); and these in turn accounted for one-fourth of all British exports—and one-half by 1850 (Braudel 1992: 572). By 1839, the Belgian Natalis Briavoinne was able to look back and observe:

> Europe was for centuries dependent on India for its most valuable products and for those of most extensive consumption: muslims, printed calicoes, nankeens, cashmeres . . . for which she could only pay in specie. . . . There was hence impoverishment for Europe. India had the advantage of less expensive and more skilled workforce. By the change brought about in the mode of fabrication . . . Indian workers cannot compete . . . [and] the balance of trade is henceforth in our favor. (cited in Wallerstein 1989: 24)

The next competitive struggle (or the struggle long ongoing but now altered) was in transportation, in which the Asian economies had also excelled. European steam-powered railroads and ships finally made far-reaching incursions on world trade only in the nineteenth century, after having failed to reduce transportation costs significantly during the three preceding centuries, as we observed in chapter 4.

The zillions of microeconomic decisions in the world market also have macroeconomic effects and causes as well. These macroeconomic relations have given rise to analyses by Marxist and other "supply-side" economists as well as by Keynesian and other "demand-side" economists. Both in turn have been combined, albeit so far rather inadequately, in attempts by L. Pasinetti (1981) and others to understand technological progress and also by Joseph Schumpeter (1939) and others to trace its long cyclical ups and downs. We cannot really assess and pursue these analyses here, other than to note how essential a real "revolution" still is in economics, which would finally achieve a double, quadruple, or indeed sextuple marriage of micro- and marcoanalysis, and also of supply-side and demand-side analysis, as well as of cyclical and "development" analysis, and finally would create an "extended family" of such economic analysis on a world economic/demographic/ecological scale. For a critical assessment and a very general indication of where and how to pursue such an economic analysis, see Frank (1991c, 1996).

What we can and must do, however, is at least to pose the question of how and where the technological advances of the industrial revolution may have been part and parcel—and therefore must also be accounted for and explained by—microeconomic options in macroeconomic contexts, and vice versa, within a pattern of Kondratieff long cycles and perhaps even longer world economic cycles.

Therefore perhaps, world economic conditions were ripe for some enterprises, sectors, and regions to improve their micro- and macropositions through measures of the "Newly Industrializing Economy" (NIE) type. Moreover, these measures could only be applied when world economic conditions became ripe for them; and these were more critical than any prior, long "preparation" by those who invoked them.

We have observed how this European noncompetitiveness in the world economy and in Asian markets in particular was counterbalanced, and even then only partly so, by the recourse Europeans had to American sources of money. Moreover, this flow and supply of money had to be constantly replenished. But even a temporary supply failure or decline in the American supply of money, as in part of the seventeenth century, a fortiori left Europeans essentially out of business in Asia. This American money-supply problem therefore generated either temporary and/or growing incentives for Europeans to compete in the world market by lowering their costs of production. The alternative would have been to be able to maintain or even increase their access to and reliance on American silver, as well as to the Asian credit that was guaranteed by this silver money. Can it be shown that after the mid-eighteenth century the availability to Europe of American money began a relative decline that threatened European market (share) penetration? That would have generated incentives for Europeans to protect and enhance their competitiveness on the world market by lowering their labor costs of production instead.

I have long since argued that the period after 1762 was a Kondratieff "B" phase in which profits declined at home and abroad for Europeans, especially from Caribbean sugar plantations and the slave trade, although the Mexican supply of silver rose again (but the Brazilian supply of gold petered out) (Frank 1978a). I have also argued that it was this Kondratieff "B" phase that generated the inventions of the industrial revolution (as well as the American and French political revolutions) in the last third of the eighteenth century. The simultaneous progressive (long cyclical?) weakening—for whatever reason—of the Asian economies and empires and the European Kondratieff "B" phase offered the typical opportunities and incentives for some previously rather marginal economies and sectors to vie for a better competitive position in the world economy. Some regions and sectors in Europe grabbed this opportunity to become in effect NIEs (like some East Asians today). They reduced their costs of production through labor-saving and energy-generating mechanization, which offered new possibilities to increase world market share—first by import substitution in European markets and then by export promotion to world markets. The higher European wages and factor costs of production supplied the opportunity and incentives to do so.

At least two other—and mutually related—circumstances offered a helping hand: One was the aforementioned economic and political difficulties of their indigenous and other competitors in some Asian markets.

However, the political economic weakening of their Asian competitors by their respective and common (cyclical?) decline also facilitated the greater European incursions in Asia. There, competitive indigenous market access, not to mention export, was also suppressed by political/military oppression. They underlay both the "Rape of Bengal," in what had been the richest region of India, as well as its extension through conquest and colonization by the British to other parts of India, and the semicolonization of China through the "open door" to European capital in the nineteenth century. These and other European colonial enterprises simultaneously opened colonial markets for industrial production and supplied capital to support British investment in its own industry. At the turn of the century, productivity in China still remained high, indeed still in the nineteenth century perhaps higher than in Japan (Inkster 1991: 233). So since China was economically still too productive and politically still too strong to be easily penetrated, the British had recourse to Indian-grown opium to force "open the door" in an attempt to take over—which despite all nineteenth-century efforts never succeeded very far.

Though we do not yet have a fully adequate "explanation" of these economic and political difficulties, the suggestion here is that it should be sought in the context of the microeconomic demand-and-supply conditions analyzed by Adam Smith for Europe and by Mark Elvin (1973) for China. But we must extend it to the world economic scale. The other circumstance, supplies and sources of capital, is discussed in the following section.

SUPPLIES AND SOURCES OF CAPITAL

The other circumstance aiding greater European incursion is their, and especially the British, supplies and sources of capital. Regarding the supply of capital, Hartwell (1971: 268) reviews the works of several experts and is very explicit: "There is general agreement that there was no capital shortage [in Britain] in the eighteenth century, although the implication of this admission is not always appreciated." One implication Hartwell discusses (citing Hill 1967) is that capital from agriculture and commerce was the result of "spectacularly large sums flow[ing] into England from abroad—from the slave trade, and, especially, from the seventeen-sixties, from organized looting of India" (Hartwell 1971: 269). This is what Marx called "primitive" accumulation of capital through colonial exploitation.

The question of whether colonies pay has given rise to a long debate. Adam Smith wrote that

the profits of a sugar-plantation in any of our West Indian colonies are generally much greater than those of any other cultivation that is known either in Europe or in America. And the profits of a tobacco plantation though inferior to those of sugar, are superior to those of corn [meaning the wheat grown in Britain]. (Smith [1776]1937: 366)

Nonetheless, like Paul Bairoch among many others, Patrick O'Brien (1982, 1990) has on several occasions dismissed any significant contribution of overseas trade and colonial exploitation to capital accumulation and industrialization in Europe. There could not have been any such, since by his calculations this trade, not to mention profits therefrom, amounted to no more than 2 percent of European GNP in the late eighteenth century. Yet he also goes on to argue that "neither quantification nor more historical scholarship will settle debates about the significance of oceanic trade for the Industrial Revolution. . . . For the history of European (and even British) industrialization the 'perspective of the world' [the reference is to Braudel's title] for Europe emerges as less significant than the 'perspective of Europe' for the world" (O'Brien 1990: 177). Alas, O'Brien and so many others could not get it more wrong. For as Braudel well put it, Europe was able to consume beyond its means and invest beyond its savings. However, it did and was able to do both primarily as a function of the structure and development of the entire world economy as a whole.

Though Bairoch, O'Brien, and others deny these foreign contributions, José Arruda again reviews the debate on colonial sources of capital and markets, and concludes that

in short, commercial investments made in the colonies, integrated into the circuit of mercantile capital and tied to the bonds of mercantile policies, substantially and strategically contributed to the economic growth of Western Europe. They opened new areas for investments—areas essential for the growth and mobility and circulation of capital. . . . THE COLONIES DID PAY. (Arruda 1991: 420, capitals in original)

Indeed, the colonies did pay. They supplied not only almost free money, but also servile labor and the cheap sugar, tobacco, timber, cotton, and other goods produced in the Americas for European consumption. Moreover, it was their American money that afforded Europeans access to the silk, cotton textiles, and spices they were able to buy from Asia and the additional money they were able to make from their participation in intra-Asian's "country trade."

Therefore, it is relevant to our present concerns to record the profits Europe derived directly from its colonies (including also from India after the Battle of Plassey) before the 1815 crossover date in European and Asian "effectiveness." Ernest Mandel (1968: 119–120) estimated the European colonial booty between 1500 and 1800 at 1,000 million gold pounds sterling, of which 100 to 150 million reached Britain from India alone between 1750 and 1800. This inflow of capital facilitated if not financed Britain's investments in the new industrial revolution, especially in steam engines and textile technology. For instance, as Eric Williams (1966: 102–3) recalled "it was the capital accumulated in the West Indies that financed Watt and the steam engine. Boulton and Watt received advances. . . . " Yet by 1800 the capital invested in steam-operated industry in all of Europe was still less than what its colonial profits had been. The most scrupulous student of the British economy for that period, Phyllis Deane (1965), detailed "six main ways in which foreign trade can have helped to precipitate the first industrial revolution" (quoted in detail in Frank 1978a: 227).

Perhaps, as Robert Denemark suggests, another "test" of whether and how much this influx of colonial capital did pay is whether that drove down the rate of interest and thereby rendered the investments cheaper and more possible in Britain and other parts of Europe. The monetary historian John Munro (private communication 1996) responded to my query that in Britain the rate of interest declined from 12 percent in the early 1690s and 8 percent after the establishment of the Bank of England in 1694 to 3 percent in 1752. By then, the rate of interest in Britain had become competitive with that on the Amsterdam money market, which had been funneling capital into Britain, where the Bank of England increasingly "managed" it.

This trend, which was only interrupted by temporary wartime increases in interest rates, is confirmed by P. G. M. Dickinson (1967: 470 and passim), who records interest rates on British public debt at 7 to 14 percent in the 1690s, 6 to 7 percent from 1707 to 1714 and 5 percent after that until the 1730s, when they declined to 3 to 4 percent and then to 3 percent by 1750. Moreover, Dickinson finds interest rates on private debt closely following that of public debt, in particular as massive Dutch funds flowed into the British market. Though much of that was managed by the Bank of England to support the public debt, some of that capital also flowed into private investment, and the public debt itself freed private capital to be invested elsewhere in the economy in turn.

British contemporaries were well aware of and welcomed this decline in interest rates and debated a myriad of domestic "English institutional" considerations to promote and extend them into the farthest reaches of the British Isles (Dickinson 1967). Adam Smith

([1776]1937:38–39) remarked that the maximum legal rate of interest was reduced in steps from 10 to 5 percent by one king and queen after another, but "they seem to have followed and not gone before the market rate of interest," which in turn he saw to be related to the demand for, and inversely related to the supply of, capital.

In addition to the Bank of England, the two other of the "three sisters," the British East India Company and the South Sea Company, also made significant contributions to the flow into and the management of the stock of capital in Britain.

All of these and other sources of capital including the Amsterdam funnel were of course derived directly from the colonies. However, these also had influences that were indirect but no less significant, for this decline in the interest price of money in London and Amsterdam was derived from their participation in the worldwide structure and operation of the global economy as a whole.

Therefore, until any and all of these domestic institutional considerations can be shown to be more important than the underlying increase in the flow and stock of capital and its world wide sources, Denmark's hypothesis seems amply confirmed. Nonetheless, having capital was only a necessary but not a sufficient reason to invest it. The mere availability of a supply of potentially investable capital, as emphasized by Hartwell, with its source in colonial exploitation in particular and in international trade in general, would not be enough to induce or account for its actual investment in the cost-reducing, labor-saving, and power-generating equipment of the industrial revolution. That required marco- and microeconomic incentives.

In a global economy, however, even such local and or sectoral microeconomic incentives anywhere were related to and indeed derived from competitive participation in the macroeconomic world economic structure and dynamic as a whole. This is my third and main argument: in that single global economy and system, "the Decline of the East" and "the Rise of the West" must have been related. The question is how?

A Global Economic Demographic Explanation

Let us review this entire process of Asian decline and European rise once again in global demographic and economic terms. Doing so suggests that paradoxically it may have been the very expansion of economic production and population in Asia in the previous centuries that militated against its continuation after 1800: previous chapters have looked at the long global economic expansion, particularly in Asia, which was fueled—but not started—by the European-supplied American money. We also noted that this expansion was even greater in Asia than in Europe. The new American money seems to have generated inflation in Europe and relatively more expansion of production, settlement, and population in Asia, as noted in chapters 3 and 4. However, the population/land-resource ratio had already been higher in Asia to begin with; and this expansion significantly increased pressure on resources in much of Asia. If the same happened less so in Europe (or as is argued below the latter had more escape valves), the global expansion may well have increased the relative and absolute population/resource gap between East and West.

A DEMOGRAPHIC ECONOMIC MODEL

The relations between population and economic growth in general and with technological development in particular have been the subject of long debate at least since Adam Smith, David Ricardo, and Thomas Malthus. Disagreement and/or uncertainty continues today among the most expert demographers and development economists. Dominick Salvatore (1988: xiii) notes for instance that conflicting conclusions still emerge from recent reports by the United Nations, the World Bank, and the Working Group on Population Growth and Economic Development of the U.S. National Research Council (1986). The latter's oft-cited report reviewed a vast literature on the subject, posed nine different summary questions, and arrived at only very tentative conclusions.

Thus, it may be vain indeed for someone as uninstructed as I to enter into the fray. For, with regard even to the explanation of the acceleration of population growth from the mid-eighteenth century onward in Europe alone, the weight of expert opinion has shifted from attributing it to a decline in mortality to an increase in fertility instead. Nonetheless the recent judgment by the eminent historian William Langer (1985: 5) is that it "can never be explained with any high degree of assurance or finality." Far more hazardous therefore is any speculation about the possible relations of population, economic, and technological growth on the scale of the world as a whole and about its regional differentiation. Indeed, as Ronald Lee (1986: 96–97) writes of his own expert modeling and analytic attempts, "can we explain the relative technological performance of Africa, China and Europe in a framework of this sort? . . . Of course there are great difficulties, perhaps even absurdities, addressing issues at such a high level of abstraction and in such generality. None the less, I believe the questions are sufficiently interesting to warrant exploration." I agree; not only are the issues interesting, but addressing them is vital for any comprehension of what really happened in the world. However, as this entire book has argued, that requires addressing the issues at an even greater—global—level of generality. Since the experts fear to tread there if only for fear of having their efforts dismissed as absurd, it falls to a foolish nonexpert to risk even more absurdity.

Lee (1986) himself reviews the "debate" between Thomas Malthus and Esther Boserup (1981), and proposes a "dynamic synthesis." Malthus, it will be recalled, argued that through the law of diminishing returns, increasing pressure on resources itself will limit the growth of population. Prior to the latter-day revival of Malthusianism, Malthus seems to have been challenged by the rapid and massive population growth in the world, made possible by repealing the law of diminishing returns through technological development, which increases the supply of resources and/or their returns. Boserup (1981), in her study of long-term trends in population and technological change, went a step further—or rather, returned to Smith, for whom population growth generated increasing returns. Boserup proposed that the growth of population and its concomitant pressure on resources can itself generate technological advance, which abolishes these decreasing returns. Lee, following F. L. Pryor and S. B. Maurer (1983), whom he credits as pioneers, seeks a "synthesis" of the Malthus thesis and the Boserup antithesis. Along the way, he constructs at least six different models of how changes or the lack of changes in population and technology might hypothetically interact.

The micro- and macroeconomic "explanation" of rapid technological change in Europe before Asia around 1800 that I propose turns out to be a variation on one of Lee's hypothetical models. My explanation is not Malthusian, which does not contemplate this technological change; and it is also not Boserupian, which attributes such technological development to rapid population growth itself. Therefore and unlike Lee's, my proposition is not a synthesis of their thesis/antithesis. Instead it is a denial of both. Indeed, my proposition is another antithesis to Boserup's, but not to Malthus. My even more "abstract and general" proposition than Lee's is that higher population growth in Asia impeded technological advance generated by and based on demand for and supply of labor-saving and power-generating machinery and that lower population growth in Europe generated the incentives for the same—in competition with Asia! One or two of Lee's "hypothetical models" contemplates such a possibility, but Lee does not seem to pursue this possibility. My reasoning is far less sophisticated than Lee's models, graphs, and equations, but my procedure may be much more realistic because I introduce three additional variables to complicate Lee's models—but eventually to simplify a real-world explanation. These three additions are (1) I put Asia, Africa, and Europe into the same globally competitive world economic bag, which is the major thesis and procedure of this book; (2) I differentiate the distributions of income, supply of labor and its price, and demand for products within economic regions, and therefore also relatively among these same regional economic parts within the competitive world economy as a whole (as per the first addition); and (3) I allow for the supply of potentially investable capital and for sources of such capital from—and indeed also its absence in or drain to—regions other than the economic region in which that capital is invested to produce labor-saving and/or energy-generating equipment and facilities.

I can briefly anticipate the resulting "dynamic," to whose plausibility Lee devotes scant attention if only because he does not give these three variables the attention they deserve in reality: around 1800, technological advance takes place in Europe, but not in Asia, which had higher population growth but also more polarization in its distribution of income and scarcity of capital. Yet it also does not take place in Africa, where the population/resource ratio was even lower than in Europe; Africa had no access to sources of investable capital from the outside, as Europe did.

A HIGH-LEVEL EQUILIBRIUM TRAP?

So let us again review this long "A" phase expansion since 1400 and suggest why and how the economies and societies of Asia and Europe may have become more differentiated. The world economic expansion since 1400 was accompanied by large increases in production, as observed in chapters 2, 3, and 4. This also permitted significant population growth in the major economies of Asia, notably since the mid-seventeenth century, as observed in chapters 2 and 4. Thus, it was the world economic expansion that produced these effects in the major core economies and societies of Asia, and it did so there more than in the more marginal Europe. For it was the more productive Asian economies that had responded "better" to the influx of new American money.

The less productive and more marginal economies of Europe, the Americas, and Africa were not able to respond as fast or as much through higher production (as we saw in chapter 4), and Europe at least experienced higher inflation instead (as noted in chapter 3). Moreover, population growth also remained low in Europe until 1750, as we saw in chapter 4. Between 1600 and 1750 the rate was only one-fourth of what it would become in the century thereafter (Livi-Bacci 1992: 68). Therefore, wages remained higher in Europe than in Asia.

In the major economies of Asia on the other hand, world and regional economic growth increased the population and productive pressure on the resource base, polarized the distribution of income, and thereby constrained effective domestic demand for mass consumer goods. The same structure and process pushed down the wage costs of production without increasing price incentives to invest capital in labor-saving or energy-generating techniques of production, as we will note below. Adam Smith ([1776]1937: 72) observed that, compared with Europe, the higher supply of labor and especially the greater poverty of laborers "of the lower ranks of people in China" depresses the wages at which they are willing to work. Moreover, Marks (1997a) suggests that in China faster growth in the production of rice and slower increases in its price than in population militated against incentives to invest in further improvements in productivity, especially through labor-saving devices. Indeed as already suggested in chapter 4, agricultural improvements in China and perhaps elsewhere in Asia (and probably also increased fertility and reduced mortality) outpaced those of Europe. "But the irony, of course, is that the subsequent growth in China's population may well have precluded the emergence of self-sustaining economic growth based on industrial development" (Marks 1997a).

Elvin quotes Smith to this effect as part of his own well-known argument (1973) about the "high-level equilibrium trap." He seeks to explain the absence of an industrial revolution in China when all the other conditions and "prerequisites" seemed to be abundant, as we observed in our review of production, trade, institutions, and technology. The essence of Elvin's thesis is that China had "gone about as fer as ya' can go" (to quote the observation about Kansas City in the musical

Oklahoma) with the agricultural, transport, and manufacturing techniques developed in the preceding centuries on the basis of abundant
human labor combined with scarce land and other resources. For instance, grazing lands were particularly scarce, because all agricultural
land is scarce with a high and growing population; however, that made
labor cheap. Therefore, low costs of transport by water and high costs
of fodder for animals made heavy reliance on human-powered transport
the rational alternative choice. For example, a 1742 reference to a water
pump argued that it could save four-fifths of the labor needed to irrigate
agricultural land. However, construction of the machine required copper, which was too expensive—indeed, literally was money sacrificed,
since circulating cash coin was made out of copper. Therefore, investment in the making of such pumps was not economical or rational.

Elvin argues that it was not any institutional or other failure to "develop" but rather precisely the opposite, rapid growth of production,
resources use, and of population based on the same, which rendered all
resources scarce—other than labor:

> Clearly the shortages of many resources grew more severe. In
> many areas there was a lack of wood for building houses and
> ships, and indeed machinery. There was a shortage of fuels . . . of
> clothing fibres . . . of draught animals. . . . Metals were in short
> supply, particularly copper . . . but also iron and silver. Above all,
> there was a shortage of good farmland: the quality of the new
> land brought under the plough in this period fell sharply. A major
> cause of these shortages was of course the continuing growth of
> population under conditions of relative technological standstill
> . . . [which] had all reached a point of sharply diminishing returns
> by the later eighteenth century. (Elvin 1973: 314)

Yet Elvin argues that it was these very same developments that

> made profitable invention more and more difficult. With falling
> surplus in agriculture, and so falling per capita income and per
> capita demand, with cheapening labor but increasingly expensive
> resources and capital[,] . . . rational strategy for peasant and mer-
> chant alike tended in the direction not so much of labor-saving
> machinery as of economizing on resources and fixed capital. . . .
> When temporary shortages arose, mercantile versatility, based on
> cheap transport, was a faster and surer remedy than the contriv-
> ance of machines. This situation may be described as a "high-level
> equilibrium trap." (Elvin 1973: 314)

Lee (1986: 124) following Boserup also suggests that China had too high a population density "to support further collective investments . . . [for a] technological breakthrough . . . China might have become caught up in a high-population, medium-technology attractive equilibrium," like Elvin's "high-level equilibrium trap" discussed above. In that trap, cheap labor due to high population, expensive resources, and scarce capital render investment in labor-saving technology neither rational nor economical. The same would have been the case in India, about which Stein (1989: 11) observes that increased elite consumption and state demands for military expenditures "placed heavier demands upon labourers, diminishing their consumption and the prospects for their very survival, especially during the later eighteenth century," as we observed above in our examination of the decline in India and elsewhere in Asia.

Tradeoffs determined by analogous demand-and-supply underlay the choices and development of fuel supplies and other sources of power. The range of their supplies may have been more locally or regionally restricted by transportation costs for their bulky raw materials, although timber had traveled long distances for millennia. However, the demand for these inputs to generate power for production was vitally affected by cost considerations, which were also derived from the worldwide competitive and/or protected market prices for products like textiles for which these fuels were inputs.

Lippit's (1987) dismissal of Elvin's argument on the grounds that Chinese surplus was high is unacceptable, because it is misplaced. Investable surplus and capital are only necessary but not sufficient conditions for their investment. I have already argued that the issue is not only whether there was an investable surplus or not, but the extent to which it was rational or not to invest it in labor-saving and power-generating technology. The Chinese did after all make huge investments in interregional canals and other infrastructure within China. Elvin argues rightly, I believe, that the Chinese were economically rational, and that that is why they then shunned some investment within a Chinese and regional/local economy-wide demand-and-supply perspective and calculations. That also strengthens my argument that, with regard especially to export industries, this economic rationality must be extended worldwide, in China and elsewhere.

That is, the same argument can and should be applied both elsewhere and worldwide. Much Asian production and export, certainly Chinese silk, was highly labor-intensive to produce under high-labor supply/low-labor cost conditions. In India also, the previous centuries of economic growth and expansion had generated analogous supply and demand relations. There also, not "stagnation" but rather its opposites—economic expansion, population growth, and even institutional change, in a word the (normal?) process of accumulation of capital—must have led to a point of diminishing returns.

The *Cambridge Economic History of India* observes that "the remarkable cheapness of labour . . . rendered labour-saving devices superfluous" in India (Raychaudhuri and Habib 1982: 295). Habib also argues elsewhere (in Roy and Bagchi 1986: 6–7) that the abundance of skilled labor and "skill-compensation" in India rendered the adoption of labor-saving devices uneconomical there (although Amiya Bagchi is cited on p. 143 of their appendix as disagreeing with this point).

So, Elvin's approach and analysis may be applied not only in China but also in Southeast Asia, India, Persia, the Ottoman Empire or wherever—and among each of these from a world economic perspective. That includes Europe. There the labor-surplus/capital-shortage argument by Elvin about China (or its application also elsewhere in Asia) is on the opposite side of the coin from the analogous labor-shortage and therefore relative capital-surplus argument that Adam Smith made for Britain and Europe and others more recently for North America.

In Europe, higher wages and higher demand, as well as the availability of capital including that flowing in from abroad, now made investment in labor-saving technology both rational and possible. The analogous argument holds for power-generating equipment. Relatively high prices for charcoal and labor in Britain provided the incentive for the accelerated switch-over to coal and mechanically powered production processes before these also became more economical in areas with even greater surpluses of labor and/or shortages of nonmechanical power, fuel, and capital to develop them. The additional argument here is that, of course, world economic market competition between Europe and China, India, and other parts of Asia rendered such labor-saving and energy-producing technology economically rational for Europeans, but not for Asians.

All this is even more the case if the distribution of income is very unequal. Then, the top of the income pyramid does not generate enough demand for production that might benefit from lower labor costs, while the low incomes at the bottom of the pyramid keep or drive down wages. So a more unequal distribution of income also militates against technological innovation in labor-saving devices and investment in power-generating processes. So what can we say about the distribution of income?

Jack Goldstone (1991a) argues that, regardless of how the use of labor is organized, population growth in agrarian societies concentrates income and wealth and lowers wages and effective demand. Yet, we have argued above that more money and higher population also reinforced each other. All of these common causes could then have undermined economic viability and political stability. Is there evidence for such a process in seventeenth- and eighteenth-century Asia? Yes!

There is indeed reason to believe that it was the very long rise in production and population itself which contributed to subsequent decline at least in the growth rates of both. Evidence from Asia suggests that its rise in production and population put pressure on the resource base and polarized both economy and society: the distribution of income became increasingly unequal.

The changing distance between rich and poor modified the "upper" end of the social pyramid. Upward mobility and conspicuous consumption, especially by merchants and speculators, was enhanced, as documented for Ming China economy and society in Timothy Brook's (1998) history, *The Confusions of Pleasure*. Lippit (1987: 90) estimates the size of the economic surplus that the gentry and others extracted to have been at least 30 percent of national income in the nineteenth century. Earlier economic boom conditions may well have elicited both absolutely and relatively higher surplus. Analogous processes have also been described in India as a result of economic expansion before its nineteenth-century decline. Indeed his attempts to compare the available evidence from India and China (and Europe) in this regard, lead Pomeranz (private communication 1996) to believe that the distribution of wealth and income was even more skewed in India than elsewhere. That increased demand from the top of the social pyramid for luxury and imported goods diverted purchasing power from the mass market for locally and regionally produced consumer goods.

At the bottom of the social pyramid some people were pushed "down and out" and marginalized altogether. A larger group of displaced peasants became low-wage workers who formed an ever bigger pool of cheap labor. Among this large and perhaps growing segment of people at the bottom of society, low income at the same time reduced their effective demand on the market for goods and increased the supply of their cheap labor to produce goods, also for export.

Regarding India, Habib (1963a: 351) explains how "the Mughal

Empire had been its own grave-digger." Its governing class got much of its great wealth through the expropriation of the surplus produced by the peasantry. Habib (1963a: 320) quotes two contemporaries who observed that seldom if ever had the contrast been greater between "the rich in their great superfluity and the utter subjection and poverty of the common people" and "the country is ruined by the necessity of defraying the enormous charges required to maintain the splendour of a numerous court, and to pay a large army for keeping the people in subjection." That must have reduced income and effective domestic mass demand and made for a low supply price of wage labor. Indeed, Habib (1963a: 324–9) testifies both to increasing exploitation over time of the peasants and to their resulting flight from the land, which increased the urban and other supply of labor, presumably at lower wages. This condition also contributed importantly to the downfall of the Mughals and their replacement by the Marahatas, who not only continued but even increased the exploitation of the peasantry. Ali (1975) also cites Habib as arguing precisely that there was intensified exploitation in agriculture and that this led to both the peasant and zamindar rebellion. (Increased earning opportunities would also increase exploitation of workers in British industry during the industrial revolution, as Friedrich Engels and Eric Hobsbawm later noted).

So how did the distribution of income in Asia compare with that in Europe and especially in Britain? Regarding China, Adam Smith ([1776]1937: 72) observed that the poverty of the poorest there was far greater than any in Europe, so that the lowest European incomes were still higher than the lowest Chinese and perhaps other Asian ones. Moreover, Smith ([1776]1937: 206) also observed that both the real wage of labor and the real quantities of the necessities for life that the laborers could purchase with their wages were lower in China and India than in most of Europe.

Nonetheless, Pomeranz (1997, private communications 1996) insists that while the distribution of income was indeed more unequal in India, in China it was more equal than in Europe. However, he also suggests that in China laborers were still able to draw on family support from the countryside for some of their subsistence, which was no longer available to urban workers in Europe, not in Britain. Pomeranz suggests that therefore workers would still have been able to manage on—and employers to pay—wages that were lower in China than in Britain or Western Europe, even if the Chinese distribution of income was not more unequal than that in Europe. So in this regard, rural family support in China could be regarded as the "functional equivalent" of a more unequal distribution of income, as in India.

More significantly however, Pomeranz's suggestion can be translated into still another one: whatever the distribution of income in China, wage goods were still relatively and maybe absolutely cheaper there than in Europe and especially in relatively high-wage Britain. That is, relative to the costs of alternative mechanical inputs and other sources of power, the availability of cheap wage goods would still have made it more economical and rational to employ more labor and less capital in China than in Britain even at similar distributions of income. However, no matter through what institutional mechanisms these cheap subsistence wage goods were or were not distributed, they could only have been made available by an agriculture that was more productive and thereby able to produce these wage goods cheaper in China than in Britain and Europe. These observations in turn confirm, or at least are consistent with, two others: Agriculture was more efficient in China, as Marks (1997a) alleges (see chapter 4). And it was relative productive efficiency in Chinese agriculture that militated against labor-saving innovation and capital-using investment elsewhere in the economy, as Elvin (1973) and I allege.

Another answer may perhaps be sought in concomitant differences in price levels. The quantity theory of money (according to which prices rise proportionately to the quantity of money) may not be foolproof. Nonetheless, the evidence is that in general, the closer the source of and therefore the availability of silver/money, the higher the level of prices; and the more distant the money source and the lower its availability, the lower the level of prices. As we have seen, Europe was certainly closer to the American mines and received a greater and earlier supply of silver than did in turn West, South, and East Asia. Can it be shown that the combination of higher wages and higher prices in Europe, not to mention North America, still left most Europeans no more or even less well off than most Asians, while still affording a greater supply of low-wage labor at the bottom of the Asian social pyramid? In that case high wage levels in Europe and low ones in Asia would also have been compatible with the less certain but probable nearly level standards of living, and the possibly even lower ones in Europe, as Bairoch, Maddison, and others suggest. That would have been particularly the case if the distribution of that income was more unequal in Asia and/or if China or even India also had the cheap wage-good "functional equivalent" suggested above. These circumstances would also have made

European goods less competitive than Asian ones in world and particularly Asian and even European markets.

Is there evidence to support, deny, or modify this proposition? Yes, there is. We have evidence both on relative population/land-resource ratios at the end of the period 1400–1800 and inferential evidence on earlier changes in the same period, based on previous rates of population growth. Moreover, we also have evidence on comparative population growth rates among major regions in the world and Eurasia, presented in chapter 4.

THE EVIDENCE: 1500–1750

So can we test this relative wage level microhypothesis and the related long-cycle macrohypothesis as part of a better world economic theory to account for the industrial revolution taking place in Europe and America and not in Asia—or Africa?

The evidence is certainly abundant, and some of it was cited above, that wages were much lower in Asia than in Europe and that for this reason European production was not competitive. Regarding relative population/land-resource ratios, Bairoch (1969: 154–5) examined ratios of population to hectares of cultivated land and projected them back to about 1800 in Asia. He found Asian ratios to have been three to four times higher, with 3.6 and 3.8 people per hectare in China and India, respectively, and only 1.1 in France and 1.5 in England in 1700 (however the ratio for Japan, albeit for 1880, was 5.0 per hectare).

Of course, data for population and its growth are sparse and uncertain, and on economic growth, not to mention their pressure on resources, even more so. However, tables 4.1 and 4.2 summarized world and regional population data from a large variety of sources, which did reveal a significant pattern. We noted that world population growth recovered after 1400 and experienced an upward inflection after 1600 and especially from the middle of the seventeenth century onward, probably for the economic and nutritional reasons outlined in chapters 2 and 4. Yet as we observed in chapter 4, from 1600 to 1750 Europe continued to account for an unchanging 18 to 19 percent of the world's population. Over the same period, the share of the world's population that lived in Asia increased from 60 to 66 percent. That is because, in the already more densely populated Asia, population grew at about 0.6 percent a year, while in Europe it grew at only 0.4 percent. According to the later figure of Livi-Bacci (1992: 68), the rate of population growth in Europe was only 0.3 percent, that is one-half or two-thirds that of Asia. As a result, according to tables 4.1 and 4.2, while from 1600 to 1750 population grew by 57 percent in Europe, it grew by 87 percent in all of Asia and by 90 percent in China and India. Moreover, the absolute increase was four times greater in Asia on its already scarcer resources, by 110 million from 1600 to 1700 and by 216 million to 1750, compared to increases of only 26 million and 51 million respectively in Europe.

Thus, the population/land-resource ratio increased more in Asia than in Europe. This difference by itself suggests that the availability of cheap labor also increased much more in Asia than in Europe. That would be all the more the case if the inequality in the distribution of income also became greater in Asia than in Europe. That was suggested above both because of the more rapid population increase itself and also because of a greater increase in production and income in Asia. In Africa, population remained stable or declined, with what effect on the distribution of income we do not know. However, we do know that unlike Europe, Africa had no significant inflow of investable capital from elsewhere and also not the same degree of competition with Asia in world markets as Europe had. Therefore, we need not expect any changed incentive to innovative labor-saving technology in Africa. Lee does not mention that reason but suggests that Africa may have been caught in a "low-level equilibrium trap" for other reasons as well.

THE 1750 INFLECTION

How and why did population change especially in the second half of the eighteenth century? Historians and demographers have noted an unexplained inflection in population growth rates beginning about 1750. Table 4.1 shows half-century world population increases of about 20 percent from 1650 to 1700 and again to 1750, but a higher 23 percent from 1750 to 1800. In Asia however, the corresponding rates were 26 percent before 1750 and only 20 percent from 1750 to 1800, and in India they dropped from 30 percent in the half century before 1750 to 20 percent in the half century after that. For this period, rather different growth rates emerge from Clark (1977), as summarized in table 4.2. World population totals increased by 24 percent in the first half century, but only by 14 percent in the second one, and then recovered to 21 percent from 1750 to 1800. In China, population growth rates were about 50 percent in the first and last half centuries but inexplicably only about 40 percent in the intervening one from 1700 to 1750. However, Clark does show a significant decline in Indian population growth rate from 33 percent in the half century before 1700 to zero in the half century after 1750 and an absolute decline of 0.5 percent from 1750 to 1800 (after the Battle of Plassey in 1757).

Other data suggest even greater relative declines of population growth in Asia and an increase in Europe. According to the estimates by Carr-Saunders (1936) that are still used by the United Nations, the world population growth rate declined from about 0.3 percent a year in the century before 1750 to 0.2 or even 0.1 percent in the half century to 1800. Most of that was due to the even more rapid decline in Asia from 0.6 percent a year to 0.13 or 0.14 percent a year between 1750 and 1800. Within Asia, the growth rate, according to more recent estimates, was 1 percent in China but only 0.1 percent in India, during its economic decline, conquest, and colonization by Britain (Nam and Gustavus 1976:11). So the eighteenth-century reversal from high to lower population growth rates in Asia emerges clearly from all of these population estimates, despite the differences among them.

In Europe on the other hand according to table 4.1, population growth accelerated from 15 percent between 1650 and 1700 to 22 percent between 1700 and 1750, to 34 percent in the half century between 1750 and 1800 and 41 percent from 1800 to 1850. In table 4.2 the growth rates for Europe are similar, rising from 17 percent in the first of these half centuries and 23 percent in the second one to 33 percent in the third one from 1750 to 1800. That is, in Europe the growth rate of population suddenly took off from the previous annual 0.3 or 0.4 percent to 1.6 percent a year for 1750–1800. The latest Livi-Bacci (1992: 68) figures for Europe are 0.15 percent from 1600 to 1750 and 0.63 percent from 1750 to 1800 (which would make them even lower relative to Asian ones in the earlier period). Notwithstanding the differences in these estimates, no one disputes that population growth rates took off in Europe, while they did not in Asia and indeed may have reversed in India. Moreover, these same trends continued and indeed accelerated in the first half of the nineteenth century.

The once proffered suggestion—that fertility rather than mortality generated this increase in population growth due to increased demand for child labor from the industrial revolution itself—is easily disconfirmed. For the population increase was not limited to newly industrializing Britain or even to northwestern Europe but was greatest in Eastern Europe and Russia. The latter's expansion into Siberia supported and funneled off its population growth, but their industrialization was generally slower than in Western Europe. As Langer (1985) suggests, we may never know exactly why population took off in Europe; but we know that it did and that in Asia it did not.

Does this evidence about the reversal of Asian and European population trends after 1750 tend to disconfirm my suggested explanation for the reversal of Asian and European fortunes and the location of the industrial revolution first in the Europe? No. Can we have it both ways? Yes.

The absolute and relative changes in population growth rates in Asia and Europe after 1750 do not necessarily detract from this explanation and perhaps even offer additional support for it. To begin with, the lower rates of population growth in Asia are a manifestation and confirmation of the decline of Asia, which is central to my explanation. Similarly, the increase in population and its growth rate in Europe are also a manifestation of the economic "Rise of Europe" and the West. Additionally however, it may be argued that under these new circumstances there indeed was a Boserup effect! Boserup (1981) herself suggests that the population/land-resource ratio in Europe did not favor technological innovation in agriculture or industry before the mid-eighteenth century. She emphasizes that European population growth offered this stimulus only after that time and that Europe had no immediately prior increase in agricultural productivity. However especially after 1800, the even faster European population increase could well also have supported innovation in labor-saving technology and less laborious and cheaper generation of power and use and handling of materials, as Boserup claims. For that to become possible however, there had to be a marked expansion of the market for European products not only at home but also abroad.

However, Europe also had to have a source of sufficient capital to make these technological investments possible and affordable, as well as the expanding market to make the investments profitable. Beginning especially after the Battle of Plassey in 1757 and from 1800 onward, these conditions were met by and in the world economy. The very decline of Asia, not to mention European colonialism, simultaneously offered Europeans the necessary increase in markets and market share as well as an additional inflow of investable capital. Moreover, emigration to the Americas made it possible to drain off much of the new surplus population from Europe. This population at the European frontier in combination with the additional new resources available in the New World then further expanded the world market for European production and exports. None of this would have been possible without the structure and conjuncture in the world economy around 1800, on which I have insisted in this book.

Another important aspect of this structure and conjuncture is examined by Pomeranz (1997). He argues that the previous long period of economic and population growth—our long "A" phase which he also finds predominant in China—exerted differential ecological demands and opportunities on the resource base among various regions in the world. By the end of the eighteenth century, according to his analysis, these ecological pressures in turn stimulated and favored the conversion to new sources of power in Britain and Western Europe, especially from coal instead of wood and through steam instead of mechanical and animal traction. This ecological/economic incentive and the demographic/economic structure and conjuncture were of course related and require further analysis in relation to each other.

CHALLENGING AND REFORMULATING THE EXPLANATION

This demographic and world marco- and microeconomic explanation of technological change around 1800 can be challenged on some empirical grounds and with some analytical reservations. However, this will also permit reformulating and strengthening the argument. The evidence and reasoning that follows builds on a tripartite e-mail discussion held between August and October 1996 among Ken Pomeranz, Jack Goldstone, and myself. It attempts to construct a stronger synthesis of our arguments that is empirically and analytically more acceptable to all of us and better defensible to the reader. The main issue is how to account for the technological change around 1800 and whether and where to invest to reduce comparative costs of production and to extend markets in terms of world market-wide competition.

1. The main challenge to the simple demand and supply hypothesis was that the technological innovations of the industrial revolution were less labor "saving" than labor "extending" and increased the productivity of both labor and capital.

2. Direct wage rates or costs may have been as high (or even higher) in some parts of China (for example, in the Yangzi Valley and the South), though probably not anywhere in India, as in some parts of Europe, especially England.

3. The distribution of income may have been similar—and not more skewed, as I contended—in China and Europe, although it probably was more unequal in India.

4. The problem of absolute, relative, and worldwide comparative wage costs—in entrepreneurial calculation as in our analysis of the same—is related also to local and regional problems of labor allocation.

5. There were some economic differences in labor allocation especially between agriculture and industry, which were related to some institutional differences. However, it is less clear to what extent these differences were underlying causes of the observed allocation of labor or whether they were only different institutional mechanisms through which the labor allocation were organized. Particularly important differences were (a) labor was bonded in India; (b) women in China were tied to the village and their labor was restricted to agriculture and domestic industry such as spinning; (c) some industrial workers in China could still draw directly on subsistence goods produced by women tied to the village and agriculture; this was less true in England, where subsistence goods often had to be acquired through the market; and (d) enclosures of more land to produce more and cheaper wool for textiles—the "sheep ate men" saying—expulsed male and female labor from the land into urban employment (and unemployment) in England and perhaps elsewhere in Europe.

6. The industrial revolution was initiated with cotton textiles, but these required both a growing "external" supply of cotton (for Europe it came from its colonies) and a "world" market for all in which everybody had to compete (except China, which still had a growing and protected domestic and regional market).

7. The industrial revolution also required and took place in the supply and production of more and cheaper energy, especially through coal and its use in making and using machinery to generate steam power, first stationary and then also mobile. The critical role of coal and its replacement of wood as a source of fuel in Britain is demonstrated by Wrigley (1994).

8. These sources of power technically and economically first required (and permitted) concentration of labor and capital in mining, transport, and production. Then they also permitted faster

and cheaper long-distance transport via steam-powered railway and shipping.

9. Investment in such "revolutionary" industrial power, equipment, organization, and the labor necessary to make them work was undertaken only where it was economically rational and possible to do so, depending on (a) labor allocation and cost alternatives; (b) location and comparative costs of other productive inputs (for example, timber/coal/animal/human sources of power and transport, as well as raw materials like cotton and iron), which were related to the geographical location of these resources and to ecological changes in their availability; (c) capital availability and alternative profitable uses; and (d) market penetration and potential.

THE RESULTING TRANSFORMATIONS IN INDIA, CHINA, EUROPE, AND THE WORLD

At the beginning of the nineteenth century these nine factors generated the following transformations in the world economy.

In India. India's competitive dominance on the world textile market was threatened despite cheap and also bonded skilled labor. Domestic supplies of cotton, food, and other wage goods continued to be ample and cheap; and productive, trade, and financial organization and transport remained relatively efficient despite suffering from increasing economic and political difficulties. However, supplies of alternative power and materials, particularly from coal and iron/steel, were relatively scarce and expensive. Therefore, Indians had little economically rational incentive to invest in innovations at this time. They were further impeded from doing so first by economic decline beginning in the second quarter of the eighteenth century or earlier; then by the (resulting?) decline in population growth and British colonialism from the third quarter of the century on; and finally from a combination of both decline and colonialism as well as the "drain" of capital from India to Britain. India switched from being a net exporter to being a net importer of cotton textiles in 1816. However, India did continue to struggle on the textile market and began again to increase textile production—by then also in factories—and exports in the last third of the nineteenth century.

In China. China still retained its world market dominance in ceramics, partially in silk, increasingly in tea, and remained substantially self-sufficient in textiles. China's balance of trade and payments surplus continued into the early nineteenth century. Therefore, China had availability and concentration of capital from both domestic and foreign sources. However, China's natural deposits of coal were distant from its possible utilization for the generation and industrial use of power, so that progressive deforestation still did not make it economical to switch fuel from wood to coal. Moreover, transport via inland canals and coastal shipping, as well as by road, remained efficient and cheap (but not from outlying coal deposits).

This economic efficiency and competitiveness on both domestic and world markets also rested on absolutely and comparatively cheap labor costs. Even if per capita income was higher than elsewhere, as Bairoch notes, and its distribution was no more unequal than elsewhere (as Pomeranz and Goldstone claim), the wage-good cost of production was low, both absolutely and relatively. Labor was abundant for agriculture and industry, and agricultural products were cheaply available for industrial workers and therefore to their employers, who could pay their workers low subsistence wages. Goldstone (1996) emphasizes the importance of one factor: women were tied to the villages and therefore remained available for (cheap) agricultural production. Pomeranz (1997) emphasizes a related factor: urban industrial workers were still able to draw for part of their subsistence on "their" villages (as in Yugoslavia during industrialization after World War II), which was produced cheaply in part by the women to whom Goldstone refers. In other words from the perspective of the entrepreneurial industrial employer and the market, wage goods were absolutely and relatively cheap because agriculture produced them efficiently and cheaply with female labor. The "institutional" distribution of cheap food to urban and other workers in industry, transport, trade, and other services was functionally equivalent to what it would also have been if the functional distribution of income had been more unequal than it was. The availability of labor was high, its supply price low, its demand for consumer goods attenuated; and there was little incentive to invest in labor-saving or alternative-energy-using production or transport. Elvin (1973) sought to summarize such circumstances in his "equilibrium trap." Even so, China still remained competitive on the world market and maintained its export surplus. As Emperor Ch'ien-lung explained to King George III of England, China had "no use for your country's manufactures."

In Western Europe. Western Europe and particularly Britain were hard put to compete especially with India and China. Europe was still dependent on India for the cotton textiles and on China for the ceramics and silks that Europe re-exported with profit to its colonies in Africa and the Americas. Moreover, Europe remained dependent on its colonies for most of the money it needed to pay for these imports, both for re-export and for its own consumption, production, and export. In the late eighteenth and early nineteenth centuries, there was a decline in the marginal if not also in the absolute inflow of precious metals and of other profits through the slave trade and plantations from the European colonies in Africa and the Americas. To recoup and even to maintain—never mind to increase—its world and domestic market share, Europeans collectively, and its entrepreneurs individually, had to attempt to increase their penetration of at least some markets, and to do so either by eliminating competition politically and militarily or undercutting it by lowering its own costs of production (or sometimes both).

Opportunity to do so knocked when the "Decline" began in India and West Asia, if not yet in China. Wage and other costs of production and transport were still uncompetitively high in Britain and elsewhere in Europe. However especially after 1750, rising incomes and declining mortality rates sharply increased the rate and amount of population growth. Moreover, the displacement of surplus labor from agriculture increased its potential supply to industry. At the same time, Britain's imposition of colonialism on India reversed its perennial capital outflow to that country. Moreover, a combination of commercial and colonial measures permitted the import of much more raw cotton to Britain and Western Europe. Deforestation and ever scarcer supplies of wood and charcoal rendered these more expensive. From the second third of the eighteenth century, first relative and then absolute declines in the cost of coal made the replacement of charcoal (and peat) by hard coal increasingly economical and then common in Britain. The Kondratieff "B" phase in the last third of the eighteenth century generated technological inventions and improvements in textile manufacturing and steam engines (first to pump water out of coal pits and then also to supply motive power to the textile industry). At the beginning of the nineteenth century, an "A" phase (the first one so identified by Kondratieff) and the Napoleonic wars generated increased investment in and the expansion of these new technologies, including transport equipment, and also led to the incorporation of ever more available but still

relatively high-cost labor into the "factory system." Production increased rapidly; real wages and income declined; and "the workshop of
the world" conquered foreign markets through "free trade." Yet even
then, British colonialism had to prohibit free trade to India and re-
sorted to the export of opium from there to force an "open door" into
China.

The Rest of the World. Most other parts of the world still
fall through the cracks of our world economic analysis. But in brief, we
can observe that most of Africa may have had population/land-resource
ratios at least as favorable to labor-saving investment as Europe. However, Africa did not have an analogous resource base (except the still
undeveloped one in Southern Africa), and far from having a capital
inflow, Africa suffered from capital outflow. The same was true of the
Caribbean. Latin America had resources and labor, but also suffered
from colonial and neocolonial capital outflow as well as specialization
in raw materials exports, while its domestic markets were captured by
European exports. West, Central, and Southeast Asia became increasingly captive markets for (if not also colonies of) Europe and its industry, to which they supplied the raw materials that they had previously
themselves processed for domestic consumption and export. In the
nineteenth century, only the European "settler colonies" in North
America, Australasia, Argentina, and Southern Africa were able to find
other places in the international division of labor, and China and Japan
were able to continue offering significant resistance. But that is another—later—story, which leads to the reemergence of East Asia in the
world economy today.

In short, changing world demographic/economic/ecological circumstances suddenly—and for most people, including Adam Smith, unex-
pectedly—made a number of related investments economically rational
and profitable: in machinery and processes that saved labor input per
unit of output, thus increasing the productivity and use of labor and its
total output; productive power generation; and in productive employment and productivity of capital. This transformation of the productive
process was initially concentrated in selected industrial, agricultural,
and service sectors in those parts of the world economy whose comparative competitive position made—and then continually remade—the
import-substituting and export-promoting measures of such Newly
Industrializing Economies both economically rational and politically

possible. Thus, this transformation was and continues to be only a temporally localized and still shifting manifestation of a world economic process, even if it is not spread uniformly around the world—as historically nothing ever has been and is unlikely to be in the foreseeable future. The suggestion is that it was not overall poverty and still less tradition or failure that handicapped Asia in the world economic competition relative to Europe around 1800. Rather, in Marxist and Schumpeterian terms, it was their very success that generated failure. For the competitive handicap of the Asian economies was generated by its previous absolute and relative success in responding to the economic incentives of the long "A" phase expansion that the inflow of American money financed, which lasted through much of the eighteenth century. That turns all received theory on its head.

PAST CONCLUSIONS AND FUTURE IMPLICATIONS

To conclude, we may summarize our findings and argument again and inquire into their implications for the future before proceeding in the next chapter to look into what all this means for social and economic theory as well as for world history—past, present, and future. The argument—and the evidence—is that world development between 1400 and 1800 reflects not Asia's weakness but its strength, and not Europe's nonexistent strength but rather its relative weakness in the global economy. For it was all these regions' joint participation and place in the single but unequally structured and unevenly changing global economy that resulted also in changes in their relative positions in the world. The common global economic expansion since 1400 benefited the Asian centers earlier and more than marginal Europe, Africa, and the Americas. However, this very economic benefit turned into a growing absolute and relative disadvantage for one Asian region after another in the late eighteenth century. Production and trade began to atrophy as growing population and income, and also their economic and social polarization, exerted pressure on resources, constrained effective demand at the bottom, and increased the availability of cheap labor in Asia more than elsewhere in the world.

Europe and then also North America (and if we wish to separate it out, also Japan at the other end of Eurasia) were able to take advantage of this pan-Asian crisis in the nineteenth and twentieth centuries. They managed to become Newly Industrializing Economies, first through import substitution and increasingly also by export promotion to and within the global world market. Yet this success, which was based on their previous marginality and relative "backwardness" in the global economy, may also prove to be relatively short-lived. These new, but perhaps also temporary, world economic centers are now experiencing absolute and relative social and economic atrophy analogous to that of the previously central Asian economies, while some of the latter seem to be recovering their economic and social impulse.

Thus, in analogy to other periods of cyclical decline and transition, the late eighteenth century was still one of competing and "shared" political economic power between the declining Asians and the rising Europeans. Only then was a new "hegemonic" order built, with European power at its center, in which a new period of industrial and economic expansion occurred, now with rapid capital accumulation in Europe itself. This nineteenth-century world hegemonic system was eventually followed by increasing intra-European rivalry and rivalry with the United States and Japan. These culminated in a general crisis and war between 1914 and 1945, leading to the construction of a new hegemonic order and renewed world economic growth under American leadership. However, the "American century" lasted only twenty years. The contemporary economic expansion in East Asia, beginning with Japan, then in the East Asian NIEs, and now apparently also in coastal China, may spell the beginnings of Asia's return to a leading role in the world economy in the future such as it held in the not so distant past.

We may speculate a bit about the continuation of this long cycle, whose "B" phase appears to have begun in Asia around 1800. From a long-term Asian and perhaps more global perspective, the ending of this long nineteenth- and twentieth-century "B" phase may have been signaled since the middle of the twentieth century by renewed political decolonization in the "Third" World, including liberation in China and Vietnam. These political events, of course, were also reflections of long-term political economic changes taking place within the West and the world it dominated, including the shift of hegemony from Western Europe to the United States.

At least two major simultaneous and related economic trends have made themselves felt from the early 1970s onward. One is the marked and still unexplained new slowdown of productivity growth throughout the West since the first major postwar recession beginning in 1973. It has also been accompanied by a decline in the average real wage and also unprecedented rampant polarization in the economy of the United States. This and the succeeding 1979–1982 recession have been wrongly attributed to the "oil shocks" of 1973 and 1979 (Frank 1980). It is notable, however, that oil exporters did pose another political economic challenge to the West and that all this economic turmoil, including "relocating" and "downsizing" its productive operations, as well as the political economic debacle in socialist Eastern Europe, have taken place within the West's long Kondratieff "B" phase since 1967.

Another simultaneous and related trend is the marked economic revival in and world impact of East Asia. It began in Japan and then in its former colonies Korea and Taiwan, but also included Hong Kong and Singapore among the first set of "four tigers." Since then, revived economic growth has been spreading also to other "tigers" or "little dragons" elsewhere in Southeast Asia and to the "big dragon" on the China coast. This is the same South (and East) China Sea region, with its diaspora of "overseas Chinese," which had been so prominent in the world economy in the previous long "A" phase from the fifteenth through the eighteenth centuries. Does that presage a renewed "A" phase there, perhaps also spreading to South and West Asia, in the twenty-first century?

Therefore, it is conceivable that the West and the East will again trade places in the global economy and in world society in the not too distant and already dimly foreseeable future. This inquiry and speculation into long cyclical downs and ups during the last seven centuries also poses a serious theoretical problem about how phases succeed each other in our long cycles. Its consideration, however, is perhaps best postponed to the discussion of cycles in our concluding, "theoretical" chapter.

These contemporary developments and future prospects demand new and better social theory to comprehend them and to offer at least some modest guide to social policy and action. It is my hope that this book's rather different historical perspective on the past can also shed more light on this present and future, which that past still helps generate and constrain. Therefore, the final chapter is devoted to drawing out the implications of this historical account of what errors our historiography and social theory should avoid and to inquiring into how it could do better.

CHAPTER 7

Historiographic Conclusions and Theoretical Implications

Macrohistorians . . . focus attention on large-scale changes in the lives of millions and hundreds of millions of persons—some of which were not noticed at all in contemporary sources. Questions asked and answered govern what the macrohistorian discovers . . . [and] give macrohistory its meaning. . . . By asking questions appropriate to the actual geographic scale of human interaction . . . real patterns from the past emerge that escape historians who interest themselves in a single part of the world. That is because different aspects of past realities emerge with a change in the scale of historical observation.

William McNeill (1996: 20–21)

It is time to draw some conclusions and suggest some implications from our study. It will be relatively easy to conclude from the evidence presented here that a number of widely held theoretical propositions, or rather suppositions, are *not* supported by the historical evidence. It will be more difficult to begin searching out the implications of this evidence for alternative theoretical propositions.

The conclusions are doubly troubling: the historical evidence against these widely held theoretical propositions is so abundant and systematic that it empirically invalidates them altogether. However, these propositions form the very basis and heart of nineteenth- and twentieth-century social theory. Therefore, the fact that these propositions are themselves quite untenable also pulls the historical and empirical rug out from under this theory itself. Thus, this "theory" turns out to be no more than Eurocentric ideology. Since this ideology has been used to "legitimate" and support colonialism and imperialism, the falsity of these propositions also exposes the Eurocentric Emperor as having no clothes. In this concluding chapter, we will strip one garment after another off this ideological emperor.

The implications are also at least double: One is that we need to fashion new social theory to which the empirical evidence is more suited. The other and related one is that we must fashion this theory at least in part inductively through the analysis of the historical evidence itself. Therefore, we also need to ask what implications the evidence may have for an alternative, more realistic social theory. However, here we can only begin to inquire into the implications for the construction of a more holistic global social theory. Those who reject either of these procedures, or both, may wish to reject them by charging that this is no more than circular reasoning. So be it.

Historiographic Conclusions: The Eurocentric Emperor Has No Clothes

THE ASIATIC MODE OF PRODUCTION

Perry Anderson (1974: 548) asked that the notion of an Asiatic Mode of Production (AMP) "be given the decent burial that it deserves." That is very decent of him, since the AMP hardly deserves even that. We need not go into the controversial and controverted history of this "concept" to see that on the evidence it never had the slightest basis in fact to begin with. I say "to begin with," because before the AMP was invented the world already knew that the real world was not that way at all. Various citations throughout this book testify to the knowledge even in Europe of the economic, political, social, and cultural advances and developments in Egypt and West, South, and East Asia. In 1776, Adam Smith testified that on all accounts China and India were ahead of Europe even in technology. Why then did he also say that China seemed not to have changed in five centuries? Of course, that was not so; but if it had been, it would mean that China was so far advanced so early on that Europe had been unable to catch up in even five centuries of its own development. In fact, China was far more developed, and as we have seen, its economy continued to expand and develop. So did that of most other parts of Asia. We have observed that, far from Asia being "stagnant," population, production, and trade expanded rapidly; and economic and financial institutions generated or at least permitted this expansion.

Therefore, Marx's description of China as a "mummy preserved in a hermetically sealed coffin . . . vegetating in the teeth of time" had absolutely no basis in fact. Nor did his idea that a supposed AMP reigned in India, Persia, Egypt, or anywhere else. That was no more than "Orientalism painted Red," as Tibebu (1990) aptly remarked. Marx's contention that "in broad outline, Asiatic, ancient, feudal, and modern bourgeois modes of production may be designated as epochs marking progress in the economic development of society" was pure ideological fiction and had no basis in fact or science (quotations from Marx are from Brook 1989: 11, 6). There never have been any such epochs, and the very idea of unilinear transitions from one "mode of production" to another, be they on a "societal" or a worldwide basis, only divert attention from the real historical process, which has been worldwide but horizontally integrative and cyclical.

Alas, "the importance of Marx's analysis of Asia is . . . that it functioned as an integral part of the process through which he constructed his theory of capitalism" (Brook 1989: 6). "The importance of Orientalism for the study of Marxism lies . . . [in] the notion that, in contrast to Western society, Islamic [and other Oriental] civilization is static and locked within its sacred customs, its formal moral code, and its religious law" (Turner 1986: 6). To that extent, Marx's entire "theory of capitalism" was vitiated both by the lack of support from the Eurocentric leg of its fables about a supposed AMP *and* by his equally Eurocentric supposition that Europe was different and that what happened there must have originated there. We have seen that no such thing really originated *in* Europe—let alone because of any supposed transition from feudalism to capitalism. The historical process was worldwide and world-encompassing—including Europe.

For another severe theoretical and empirical critique of the notion of an AMP, see Islamoglu-Inan (1987) and several of the contributors to the book she edited on the Ottoman Empire. It illustrates how slavish attempts to squeeze the evidence to fit this procrustean category, and even rebellious attempts to escape from it, handicap and contort rather than aid and extend the analysis of the contributors' own evidence. Her book also vividly illustrates how limiting not only is the category of an AMP but also that of a "capitalist mode of production" as well as Wallerstein's European-based "modern world-system" and the idea of its "incorporation" of the Ottomans or any other region in Asia, to which we return below.

EUROPEAN EXCEPTIONALISM

We must take exception to this alleged European exceptionalism on six related grounds.

First, the theses of Afro-Asian Orientalism and European exceptionalism empirically and descriptively misrepresent how Asian economies and societies performed. Not only the alleged AMP and Oriental despotism, but also the allegations about nonrational and anti-profit seeking characteristics, and other supposed pre-/non-/anti-commercial/productive/capitalist features of Asia are very much off the mark, as demonstrated by our review of Asia's participation in the world economy. In fact, Afro-Asian economic and financial development and institutions were not only up to European standards, but largely exceeded them in 1400 and continued to do so in 1750 and even in 1800.

Second, for the centuries between 1400 and at least 1700 as well as earlier, there was nothing "exceptional" about Europe, unless it was Europe's exceptionally marginal, far-off peninsular position on the map and its correspondingly minor role in the world economy. That may have afforded it some "advantage of backwardness" (Gerschenkron 1962). None of the alleged European exceptionalisms of "superiority" is borne out by historical evidence, either from Europe itself or from elsewhere, as Hodgson (1993) warned four decades ago and Blaut (1993a, 1997) unequivocally demonstrated recently. Therefore, the really critical factors in Europe's economic participation and development have also been both empirically and theoretically misrepresented by almost all received historiography and social theory from Marx and Weber to Braudel and Wallerstein. No matter what its political color or intent, their historiography and social theory—as well as that of Tawney or Toynbee, and Polanyi or Parsons and Rostow—is devoid of the historical basis from which its authors claimed to derive it. Just as Asia was not stuck-in-the-mud, so did Europe not raise itself by its own bootstraps.

Third, the comparative method itself suffers from inadequate holism and misplaced concreteness. At its worst, and Marx was among those whose analysis was so flawed, some "features" were rather arbitrarily declared to be essential (to what?) but wanting everywhere except in Europe. At best, Western observers (alas, including also some from Asia and elsewhere) compare "Western" civilizational, cultural, social, political, economic, technological, military, geographical, climatic—in a word *racial* "features"—with "Oriental" ones and find the latter wanting on this or that (Eurocentric) criterion. Among the classical writers,

Weber devoted the greatest study to the comparisons of these factors, and especially to embellishing the Marxist notions about Oriental "sacred customs, moral code, and religious law." His many followers have further embellished this comparative approach with still more peculiar features. Even if these comparisons were empirically accurate, which we have observed that most are not, they had and still have two important shortcomings: One is how to account for the allegedly significant factors that are being compared; another is the choice to compare these features or factors in the first—and last—place. Yet the choice of what features or factors to compare is based on the prior explicit or implicit decision that European characteristics are significant, distinct, and therefore worth comparing with others. We will examine these decisions and implicit choices in turn.

Fourth, the sometimes explicit supposition but mostly implicit assumption is that the institutional basis and mechanisms of production and accumulation, exchange and distribution, and their functional operation are determined by "traditional" historical inheritance and/or other local, national, or regional developments. This kind of "analysis" does not even consider the possibility that the factors under consideration were local, national, or regional *responses* to participation in a single worldwide economic system and process. Yet as we have argued and demonstrated, accumulation, production, distribution, and their institutional forms throughout Asia, Africa, Europe, and the Americas did adapt to and reflect their common interdependence. Certainly the institutional form and very lifeblood of all entrepôts like Hormuz and Malacca, and most other ports and caravan crossroads was a function of their increasing and decreasing participation in the world economy. But so were their productive and commercial hinterlands. My study of Mexican agriculture from 1520 to 1630 showed how successive institutional forms of labor recruitment and organization were local responses to world economic and cyclical exigencies (Frank 1979). In chapters 2, 3, and 4 we observed analogous institutional adaptations and development on the Bengal frontier (Eaton 1993), South China (Marks 1997a), South East Asia (Lieberman 1995), and the Ottoman Empire (Islamoglu-Inan 1987). Even related "civilizational" or "cultural" variables are not so much determinant or independent, as they are themselves derivative from and dependent on the worldwide economic structure and process. All attempts to account for or explain local, national, or regional ripple developments primarily in terms of their respective supposedly cultural or class determinants are too limited in their purview. They neglect the fundamental world economic sea change, of which the local ones often are only superficial ripples and manifestations. In short, all attempts to account for features and factors of development on the basis only or even primarily of local antecedents and in the absence of their function in the world economy/system can result only in the neglect of factors that are *essential* to any satisfactory explanation.

Therefore, my fifth objection is that even the best comparative studies violate the canon of holism, for they do not study the global whole and the world economy/system from which the factors to be compared are or may be derivative. That is, we also need to construct a holistic theory and analysis of this global economy and world system, as well as of its own operation and transformation, for these also generate and shape the institutional forms themselves. A vivid illustration that we need such a completely different approach is the issue on new approaches to European history published in 1995 in the Turkish journal *Metu*. The journal offers a "Theory of the Rise of the West" by John A. Hall and a discussion by several Turkish colleagues. Hall (1995: 231–32) admits to "more than a touch of megalomania" in being "able to offer a completely new account" of the rise of the West in which he "is going to solve Max Weber's problem in entirely different terms." He begins with his own examination of China and brief references to Islam and Hindu/Buddhist India, which he still compares unfavorably with Europe, as he had earlier (Hall 1985). Economic development allegedly was impossible in China because of the imperial state, in India because of the Hindu caste system, and under Islam because of nomadic pastoral tribalism. All allegedly lacked the unique European state and interstate system. So Hall reverts to the same old argument about European exceptionalism, except that he gives the latter a slightly new twist. One of his Turkish commentators makes "rather a defense of Mr. Hall. I think most of the counter-arguments base themselves on a certain misunderstanding" (*Metu* 1995: 251). Alas, the "counterarguments" of his Turkish colleagues do no more than take exception to some of Hall's European exceptionalism and comparisons. They themselves have no alternative explanation or even an approach to offer, least of all a holistic one that would not just compare but relate Europeans and Ottomans within a single world system. We have only just begun this task here!

Finally, studies that compare "Western" and "Oriental" societies are therefore already vitiated by their choice of the features or factors to be compared, unless that choice is itself derived from the study of the whole world economy/system to begin with. And of course it is not.

Indeed, the choice of the very features and factors to be compared is derived from focusing only on a part of the world, be that Britain, Europe, the West, or wherever. That is, the very design of the study, from Marx and Weber to Braudel and Wallerstein, suffers from the misplaced concreteness of looking for the explanandum with a magnifying glass or even a microscope but only under the European street light. The real task is first to take up a telescope to gain a holistic view of the global whole and its world economy/system. Only that can reveal what passive features, or more likely active factors, we then need to regard with greater care with a magnifying glass. To that task we turn in the discussion of implications in the second part of this chapter. But first, there are some more derivative conclusions about what *not* to do, because doing so prevents seeing history "as it really was"—in the global whole.

A EUROPEAN WORLD-SYSTEM OR A GLOBAL ECONOMY?

Contrary to the mistaken allegations of Braudel and Wallerstein among so many others, our study also leads to the inevitable conclusion that early modern history was shaped by a long since operational world economy and not just by the expansion of a European world-system. I already demonstrated elsewhere how the model and theory of Braudel and Wallerstein is contradicted by their own evidence and analysis (Frank 1994, 1995). Much more overwhelming still is the historical evidence reviewed throughout the present book: Chapter 2 shows how the worldwide division of labor was made operational through chain-linked trade relations and (im)balances. Chapter 3 shows how money was the lifeblood that went through a circulatory system all the way around the world and made the world go round. Chapter 4 shows not only that Asia was preponderant in this global economy, but also argues that its technology and economic institutions and processes were derivative from and adaptive to the world economy itself. Chapter 5 shows how common cyclical and other processes simultaneously shaped the fortunes and misfortunes of distant but interlinked economies, regions, and polities around the world. Chapter 6 seeks to analyze how the structure and transformation of these links themselves generated the related "Decline of the East" and "Rise of the West." Therefore it is only vain Eurocentrism to seek to account for or hope to explain any of these events, processes, and their relations within the framework of either "national" economies/societies or even by the expansion of only a "European world-system."

Therefore, the real world economy/system also cannot be squeezed into the procrustean structure of Wallerstein's European-centered "modern world-system," for the globe-encompassing world economy/ system did not have a single center but at most a hierarchy of centers, probably with China at the top. Therefore, it would also be difficult to establish the existence of a single-centered structure of center-periphery relations although there is evidence of such relations on intraregional and perhaps on some interregional bases. It is doubtful that there were "semi-peripheries" in Wallerstein's sense; but it has never been very clear just what that they are supposed to be.

Yet the possible countercharge that therefore there really was no such (whole) world economy/system is not acceptable. On the contrary, there clearly was a world economy/system, and indeed only one. It had a global division of labor and commercial and financial linkages, especially through the worldwide money market. Moreover, this world economy/system appears also to have had a global structure and dynamic of its own, which still bears much more study. Thus this third conclusion about the global economy is entirely consistent not only with the historical evidence but also with the first two conclusions.

1500: CONTINUITY OR BREAK?

Another and derivative but inescapable conclusion is that the alleged break before and after 1500 never took place. Historians often mark a break in "world" history in 1500 (see for example Stavarianos 1966, Reilly 1989). Even Bentley's (1996) innovative proposals to derive "periodization" in world history not just from European but from worldwide processes still marks 1500 as the beginning of the last period. Historians and social theorists of Europe, both of earlier generations as well as contemporaries, mark this same break. So do world-system theorists like Wallerstein (1974), Sanderson (1995), and Chase-Dunn and Hall (1997). The allegation that there was a sharp break around 1500 was already reflected in the opinions of both Adam Smith and Marx that 1492 and 1498 were the most important years in the history of mankind. Perhaps they were directly so for the peoples of the New World and indirectly so for those of Europe. However, Braudel (1992: 57) disputed Wallerstein's allegation of this break in Europe, where Braudel saw continuity since at least 1300 and even from 1100.

Indeed, even Wallerstein (1992) refers to the widespread agreement that an expansive long "A" phase from 1050 to 1250 was followed by a contractive "B" phase from 1250 to 1450 and then after that by still another expansive "A" phase in the "long sixteenth century" from 1450 until 1640. The evidence above, however, suggests that this long expansive phase had already begun in much of Asia by 1400—and that it lasted there until at least 1750. Wallerstein's European "long sixteenth century" probably was a belated and more temporary expression of this world economic expansion. Indeed, the voyages of Columbus and Vasco da Gama should probably be regarded as expressions of this *world* economic expansion, to which Europeans wanted to attach themselves in Asia. Therefore, the continuity across 1500 was actually far more important and is theoretically far more significant than any alleged break or new departure.

Thus I suggest that it is not appropriate or even necessary, as the common argument has it, to regard early modern and contemporary history as the result and/or as the harbinger of a significant historical break. The widespread discontinuity theses are far less a contribution, let alone a necessity, and far more an impediment to understanding the real world historical process and contemporary reality. These misleading discontinuity theses have been presented in various forms, including the "birth of capitalism," "the Rise of the West," "the incorporation of Asia into the European world-economy," not to mention the West's alleged "rationalism" and "civilizing mission." I prefer to leave for philosophical consideration by others elsewhere whether or not modern and contemporary history is a vehicle or manifestation of "progress," unilinear or otherwise.

Here, I prefer to reconsider and question the scientific validity or analytic usefulness here in Europe or there in Asia of such time-related concepts and terms as "protocapitalism" or "protoindustrialization," or for that matter such "quantitative" ones as "petty-capitalism," "semifeudalism" or "protosocialism." The endless disputations about the alleged transitions from one to another of these categories at particular but different times in any part the world is literally a blind alley which cannot possibly lead to even the faintest enlightenment. For only the study of the continuing structure and dynamic of the one and only world (system) can illuminate the hows, whys, and wherefores of the "development," "rise," or "fall" of any part of the world (system), be it in Europe, America, Africa, Asia, Oceania, and/or any part thereof.

CAPITALISM?

Of late (that is, since Marx), the "fascination," as Braudel (1982: 54) called it, with 1500 as the date of a new departure that makes a supposed break with the past is mostly a function of the allegation that it ushered in a new, previously unknown or at least never before dominant, "capitalist mode of production." That was of course the position from Marx and Sombart to Weber and Tawney, and it is still shared by their many contemporary followers. This is still the position of world-system theorists from Wallerstein (1974) and Frank (1978a) to Sanderson (1995) and Chase-Dunn and Hall (1997). Even Amin's (1991, 1993) and Blaut's (1993a, 1997) vehement critiques of Eurocentrism stop short of abandoning 1500 as the dawn of a new age of European-born (and European-borne) capitalism. All of the above Marxists, Weberians, Polanyists, world-systematizers, not to mention most "economic" and other historians, balk at pursuing the evidence and the argument to examine the sacred cow of capitalism and its allegedly peculiarly exceptional or exceptionally peculiar "mode of production."

Therefore, the mere suggestion that perhaps this conviction might or even should be open to question is already rejected as unacceptable heresy. Having already broached this heresy to little effect before (Frank 1991a,b, Frank and Gills 1993), there is little point in trying to pursue the argument further here. Suffice it to point out that the same evidence and argument that support the first four conclusions outlined above also have implications for the idea of "capitalism." These conclusions deny the AMP and European exceptionalism, but affirm a world economy and its continuity across 1500. Yet world-system theorists and Blaut accept the first two conclusions about the AMP and European exceptionalism, but reject the next two (which affirm the continuity of a global economy and deny the break in 1500). Braudel in turn also denies the break in 1500 and de facto recognizes a global economy, even if it does not fit it into his model of a "European world-economy." Yet all four of these conclusions inexorably render questionable to say the least the very concept of a "capitalist mode of production" and the supposed significance of its alleged spread from Europe to the rest of the world. Indeed, these first four conclusions question the very significance imputed to different "modes of production," of course including "feudalism" and "capitalism," not to mention any alleged "transition" between them. To begin with, these categories were derived from narrow "societal" or even national blinkers. Since then, this received conceptualization has continued to divert our attention away from the much more significant world systemic structures and processes, which themselves engendered the organizational forms that were then misleadingly termed "feudal" and "capitalist" "modes of production."

As we have observed, not only was there no unilinear "progression" from one "mode" of production to another; but all manner of relations of production were and remain widely intermingled even within any one "society," not to mention world society as a whole. Many different relations of production have "delivered" products that have been competitive on the world market. However, it has not been so much one relation or another, and still less any "mode," of production that has determined the success and failure of particular producers. Instead, competitive pressures and exigencies on the world market have been and continue to be much more determinant of the choice and adaptation of relations of production themselves.

The incessant discussions about non-, pre-, proto-, blooming-, full blown-, declining-, post-, or any other "stage" and quantity or quality of capitalism or the lack thereof have led us down the garden path and diverted us from analyzing the real world. A recent example was mentioned in chapter 1: Gates in her (1996) *China's Motor* does very well to examine the relations between commercialism and patriarchy for a thousand years. However, her continued insistence on using the categories of "the tributary and petty capitalist modes of production" and their uneasy relations handicaps instead of illuminates her analysis of the real world issues.

The review of van Zanden's "merchant capitalism" in chapter 1 also rebuts the contention that it represented a distinctive "articulation of modes of production" between "non-capitalist" modes of reproduction and use of labor "outside the system" and others inside the "world market" of the "world-economy." However, the hidden but most revealing aspect of this discussion is that, irrespective of which side of the arguments the discussants support, they all recur to these terms (quoted above) again and again. But they all use them without quotation marks, because they largely agree on the meaning and referents of what is allegedly excluded by these terms. Indeed, van Zanden and others even name several of them: slaves, peasants, those who work at home in cottage industry, in West Africa, and in East Asia (van Zanden 1997: 260). In this discussion and the related literature it refers to, all of these producers and even traders remain outside the universe of discourse in which "admittedly, the Dutch Republic became the largest staple market the world had even known"; so "Amsterdam was both the central warehouse of world commerce and the pivotal money and capital market of the European world-economy's control booth" (Lis and Soly 1997: 233, 211, 222). Of course in the real world economy, Amsterdam and the Netherlands were none of the above. But for all these discussants on the topic of "modes of production," the real world economy—of which Amsterdam was but an outpost—does not exist.

Indeed, Wallerstein's (1997: 244) intervention even stresses "let us not quibble about the unit of analysis"! But the most important issue in this whole discussion is precisely the unit of analysis, which all of the participants disregard—that is, the world economy and not their little European one. The moment we recognize that, the whole discussion about "modes of production" more than pales into insignificance and irrelevance: it becomes instead no more than a distraction from the real issue, which is the holistic analysis of the whole that all these discussants are so intent on avoiding.

Therefore, it is much better to cut (out) the Gordian knot of "capitalism" altogether. That was my argument in Frank (1991a,b), Frank and Gills (1992, 1993), and Frank (1994, 1995); and it is well put by Chaudhuri (1990a: 84) writing under the title *Asia Before Europe:* "The ceaseless quest of modern historians looking for the 'origins' and roots of capitalism is not much better than the alchemist's search for the philosopher's stone that transforms base metal into gold." Indeed, that is the case not only for the origins and roots, but the very existence and meaning of "capitalism." So, best just forget about it, and get on with our inquiry into the reality of universal history.

HEGEMONY?

The notion of European followed by Western "hegemony" over the rest of the world is implicit in most historical, social "scientific," and popularizing writing and perception. Political hegemony is explicit in much recent international relations literature, from Krasner (1983) and Keohene (1983) to Modelski and Thompson (1988, 1996). Economic hegemony is explicit in Wallerstein and his followers. I have expressed doubts about the dubious theoretical status of such hegemony before (Frank and Gills 1992, 1993; Frank 1994, 1995). The evidence presented in chapters 2, 3, and 4 is enough to lay to rest any claim to historical veracity of any such political, economic, or political economic, or indeed cultural, hegemony of a (whole) world scope by any part or even by the whole of Europe before 1800. At no time during the four centuries under review was any economy or state able to exercise any significant degree of hegemony, or even leadership, over the economy, political relations, culture, or history of the world as whole. If the world economy had any regional productive and commercial basis at all, that was in Asia and it was centered if at all in China. Europe was to all intents and purposes entirely marginal.

Still less was any part of Europe able to exercise any hegemonic power or even economic leadership in or over the world. This was certainly not possible for the Iberian Peninsula or little Portugal with one million inhabitants in the sixteenth century, nor for the small Netherlands in the seventeenth century, nor even for "Great" Britain in the eighteenth century. The very notion of such economic leadership or political power or even balance of power (as for example after the Peace of Westphalia in 1648) is itself only the effect of an optical illusion from the myopic perspective of a "European world-economy/system." It is just plain Eurocentrism. Arguably, the above-mentioned economies and/or states may have been successively relatively big fish in the small European and/or the regional Atlantic economic pond—that is, if we discount the Hapsburg, Russian, and other empires. However on the evidence, the European and even Atlantic economies, not to mention their polities, were no more than backwaters in the world economy. They did not even exercise significant technological leadership. The European states were altogether small-time players on the political checkerboard of the empires of the Ming/Qing, Mughals, Ottomans, and even the Safavids. In the face of the evidence, should we not review and revise the entire concept of "hegemony"?

THE RISE OF THE WEST AND THE INDUSTRIAL REVOLUTION

How then did the West rise, if there was nothing exceptional about it or its mode of production and it did not even entertain any hopes of hegemony before 1800? The inescapable conclusion is that there must have been some other factors at work or that some as yet unspecified circumstances let or made these factors work within them. We have seen that most efforts to address this question have heretofore suffered from misplaced concreteness, because they looked for these factors only under the European street light. Yet since the West was part and parcel of the global world economy, the West could not rise on its own or by itself. Instead, any such Western rise must have been *within* the world economy itself. Therefore, it is useless to look for the causes of this rise only or even primarily in the West or in any part of it— unless the "use" for doing so is only ideological, that is to pat oneself on the back and put all others down as incompetent.

The implication of the preceding six conclusions and the evidence from which they were derived is that the entire question of "the Rise of the West" must be reconceptualized and rephrased. The evidence suggests that the question must be addressed to the whole world economy/system itself and not just to any British, European, Western, and/ or now East Asian part of the same. I know that I will lay myself open to the charge of circular reasoning if I point out as well that the historical evidence is not compatible with any of the many singular or multiple European/Western "causes" of its rise. Yet, it is not for nothing that the industrial revolution was already a thrice-squeezed orange almost a century ago and yields still enough juice for interminable controversies—within the narrow paradigm of a British or European process or event.

Therefore in Europe, "the Rise of the West" was not a case of pulling itself up by its own bootstraps. More properly, "the Rise of the West" must be seen as occurring at that time in the world economy/system by engaging in import substitution and export promotion strategies (in the style of Newly Industrializing Economies) to climb up on the shoulders of the Asian economies. The (cyclical?) decline of Asian economies and regional hegemonies, facilitated this European climb up. The thesis of Rostow and others that there was a sudden jump in the British rate of capital accumulation has long since been disconfirmed.

The only solution is to cut the Eurocentric Gordian knot and approach the whole question from a different paradigmatic perspective. That is a fortiori the case if we consider the further controversy about whether there was even an industrial "revolution" or only an "evolution" and expansion—which was *world* economic.

EMPTY CATEGORIES
AND PROCRUSTEAN BEDS

I hope I may be permitted to add that both the evidence reviewed above and the more holistic approach invoked in analyzing it here, suggest some additional conclusions about what *not* to do. Both historiography and social theory, not to mention good common sense, have suffered far too much already from the most arcane attempts to fit the Asian evidence into the procrustean beds of received (Eurocentric) theories and models. These have, as noted above, been largely devoid of empirical content and scientific sense even in their European origins. The attempts to extend them elsewhere has been even more nefarious. Thus for instance, there have been long-winded debates about the evidence for and against the AMP, including quite recently a series of contributions by Chinese scholars edited by Brook (1989) on *The Asiatic Mode of Production in China*. Similarly, there have been incessant debates, far too many even to name, about feudalism here or there, then and now. The opposite side of the same coin was the ongoing debate about capitalism and whether it was indigenous or imported/imposed, promoted, constrained, or even eliminated in Asia by the coming of European colonialism and imperialism. We noted in chapter 2 how adherence to these empty categories and procrustean beds vitiated Soviet research on its regions in Central Asia.

Latter-day analogies are questions about whether and when the "European modern world-economy/system" incorporated, marginalized, and/or bypassed this or that part of Asia and Africa. Recently for instance, Pearson (1989) devoted an entire book to squeezing India into or yanking it out of the procrustean bed of Wallerstein's European world-economy. That leads Pearson into considerations of how that "world-economy" is or is not bounded by the trade of "necessities" and/or "luxuries" and which commodities do or do not qualify for which of these denominations. That in turn defines the boundaries of the European world-economy, what these boundaries were or were not at different times, and whether the Indian Ocean itself qualifies or not as a "world-economy" of its own. Debating the necessities/ luxuries question is a waste of time generated by a worse than useless distinction, which has already been disposed of by archaeologists such as Schneider (1977) for earlier times; for reviews see Frank and Gills (1993) and Frank (1993a). Useless also is the distinctions between world-systems and world-empires, and the attempts to squeeze parts of the real world into these categories (Frank 1993a).

Downright alarming is the question that Pearson, and also Palat and Wallerstein (1990), ask about when the "European world-economy" "incorporated" India and the Indian Ocean and its possible separate "world-economy." This question is analogous to the one about when you stopped beating your wife (the answer is "I am not married"). The whole question is literally neither here nor there, since there was no

"European world-economy" separate from an "Indian Ocean world-economy." If anything, the latter "incorporated" the former and not the other way around (Frank 1994, 1995). Pearson and others are looking under the European street light, when they should be looking for illumination in the Asian parts of the world economy. The only "answer" is to understand that Europe and Asia, and of course other parts of the world as well, had been part and parcel of the same single world economy since ages ago, and that it was their common participation in it that shaped their "separate" fortunes.

Each and all of these debates make sense only in terms of the "AMP," "feudalism/capitalism," "world-system" categories of received theories. Yet these categories themselves are not only procrustean beds. They are also useless for the analysis and understanding of world history. Their only real use has been strictly ideological. The debates they generated are analogous to those about how many angels can dance on the head of a pin. The wrong answer sometimes led to the stake and fire or the firing squad. But the "right" answer leads nowhere, at least on scientific grounds. Indeed, these categories are worse than scientifically useless, since their very use diverts us from any real analysis and understanding of world reality. The only solution is to cut the Gordian knot altogether and divest ourselves of all these useless Eurocentric categories, which only lead to arcane debates and blind us to the real historical process.

In view of my past work, of special interest to me and perhaps to many of my readers are the notions of "development," "modernization," "capitalism," and even "dependence," or call it what you will. All are procrustean and empty categories; because the original sin of Marx, Weber, and their followers was to look for the "origin," "cause," "nature," "mechanism," indeed the "essence" of it all essentially in European exceptionalism instead of in the real world economy/system. All of these allegedly essential exceptionalisms, whatever their name, were derived from the same Eurocentric perspective that, on the evidence reviewed in this book, has absolutely no foundation in historical reality—that is in "universal" history, "as it really was." They were all derived only from European/Western ethnocentrism, which was propagated around the world—West and East, North and South—as part and parcel of Western colonialism and cultural imperialism.

The Western version can be encapsulated in a selection or combination of received-theory titles, like "The Stages of Economic Growth" from "The Passing of Traditional Society" to "The Achieving Society" (Rostow 1962, Lerner 1958, McClelland 1961). "Development" by "modernization" was doing "it my way" as in the Frank Sinatra song. "Dependence" was one reaction that denied the efficacy of *that* way, only to allege that "delinking" might offer another way—to do essentially the same thing, as I only recently recognized under the title "The Underdevelopment of Development" (Frank 1991c, 1996).

The "Eastern"—and alas also the Western Marxist—version was to debate essentially the same thing under the terminology "the transition from feudalism to capitalism." That debate was even more sterile than the Western one if only because it involved (literally) interminable disputes about the categories of "capitalism" and "feudalism" and "socialism" and so on, and whether this or that local, regional, national, sectoral, or whatever piece of "reality" does or does not fit into the procrustean category. Of course, since these categories are really empty—that is, devoid of any real world meaning—these debates must be interminable until we divest ourselves of the categories themselves. This should be obvious, except that the categories themselves often prevent the debaters from seeing reality as it really was. And when they did do so, they tried to stretch, bend, and combine the categories to accommodate that reality. All manner of variations and combinations of "semifeudal," "precapitalist," "noncapitalist," and "protosocialist" "articulation of modes of production" were invented that might offer a "nonaligned," "third," or any other way to replicate or not what the West did or how it did it. (The same categories in turn constrained Marxists, "neo-Marxists," and dependency theorists to debate whether "capitalism" is or is not the "right"—or "left"—way to go.) Bergesen (1995) rightly argues that it is equally futile to stretch the procrustean category of the Euro- or Western-centric "modern capitalist world-system," and/or to try to manipulate reality to fit into the Wallersteinian procrustean bed. On the evidence reviewed here, we must agree.

This entire "how many angels can dance on the head of a pin" debate is derived from the original sin of European ethnocentrism. That was enshrined in and as social "science" by Marx, Weber, and their myriad of followers who plod the straight and narrow path of "development"— or even those who rebelled against and bolted from it. However, all their vision was—and alas mostly still remains—confined by the same Eurocentric blinkers, which prevent them from seeing the whole real world out there. Sadly and worse still, non-Westerners have imbibed and sometime choked on much of the same Eurocentric (non)"scientific" misreading of both world and their own history. That has perhaps been most dramatically visible in the debates—and persecutions—about

"Marxist" orthodoxy in Russia and its colonized Central Asia (see chapter 2), China (Maoism, the Cultural Revolution, Gang of Four, "black and white cats"), India (with its varieties of communist parties and intellectuals), the "Arab" world, Africa, and Latin America.

Not that any or all of these are devoid of their own ethnocentrism. Paradoxically, ethnocentrism itself appears to be universal and also to appear universally, or at least to be universally exacerbated by political economic crisis. It is only that most other ethnocentrisms have not lately had the same opportunities to spread, let alone to impose themselves. The Western ones have, by force of their money and arms. The Marxist ones were propagated in reaction to the former and with the support of Soviet and Chinese power. In reaction to both and to political economic crisis, Afro-, Hindu-, Islamo-, yes and also again Russo-, Sino-, and other ethnocentrisms are spreading now and offer salvation through the "Sinatra" doctrine: "Do It My Way" or "To Each His/Her Own." Many will welcome at least some of these as antidotes to the poison of Euro/Western-centrism. However, they are no remedy— unity in diversity is the only remedy!

There is no way to see what happens at a distance anywhere else in— let alone in all—the world by using a European or Chinese or any other microscopic perspective. On the contrary, any of these views is possible only with a telescopic perspective capable of encompassing the whole world and all its parts, even if the details of the latter may remain unclear from afar. Not only are all perspectives in terms of European or any other "exceptionalism" doomed to blindness. So are those using the perspective of a European-based world-economy/system (or any Sino-, Islamic-, or Afrocentric analogues thereof). The very attempt to find the "development of capitalism" or "the Rise of the West" "or the Islamic golden age" under the light shed by a European (or Chinese or Muslim) street light only blinds the onlooker.

For history and social theory therefore, the most important and neglected task is to attend to the posthumously published plea of Joseph Fletcher to do integrative "horizontal" macrohistory and analysis. His plea is a modest effort to help remedy this neglect for the early modern period from 1500 to 1800. Recall that the world-renowned historian Leopold von Ranke called for a study of history "as it really was." However, Ranke also said that "there is no history but universal history." Only world history can show how it really was. But there is no way to understand world history—or even any part of it—without abandoning the blinkers of the Eurocentric tunnel vision, which still so confine us to darkness, for there is no light at the end of that Eurocentric tunnel. The proverbial joke has it that you can't find your lost watch just because the lamppost you are looking under provides some light. In this case however, not only was the watch lost elsewhere, but the brighter light under which to find it is also elsewhere. And that is no joke.

In conclusion, what we need is a much more global, holistic world economic/systemic perspective and theory. That may permit seeing first that "the decline of the East preceded the Rise of the West," then how the two may have been related, and finally why the world economic/ systemic shift took place. The latter has been microscopically misperceived as a process that was allegedly "internal" to the West, when it should be telescopically viewed as a worldwide process. So, this catalog of eight relatively easy to draw historiographic and theoretical conclusions about which received propositions have no basis in the evidence leads to the much more difficult task of drawing implications for the construction of a theory and analysis that is or at least could be compatible with the evidence.

Theoretical Implications: Through the Global Looking Glass

If received social theory is unsatisfactory because it is based on bad Eurocentric historiography, then what? The obvious answer is to start by doing better—non-Eurocentric—history. But to do that, we seem also to need a better—more holistic—perspective, if not theory. Braudel and Wallerstein's, and Frank's (1978a), "world-economy/system" took a step in the right direction by biting off a bigger part of the whole than earlier "national" "societal" histories and theories did. However, as we have seen, they did not go nearly far enough and have themselves now become an obstacle to going further. John Voll's (1994) article on an Islamic-centered world system might seem to be a step in the right direction; however, it is only a very small step and is itself excessively ideological and confined to Muslim ideology. Afrocentrism, alas, is nothing more than ideology. Hamashita's China-centered tribute trade system (1988) might seem another step in the right direction. So is the discourse by Chaudhuri and others about an Indian Ocean world-economy and Reid's work on the Southeast Asian world. Yet, as the preceding chapters have shown, all of these welcome initiatives are still too limited because they are too limiting. All of these pieces of the jigsaw puzzle are necessary components of the whole picture. However, none of them individually nor even all of them put together can ever reveal the whole, since the whole is *more* than the sum of its parts—and shapes the parts themselves!

Only a holistic universal, global, world history—"as it really was"—can offer the historiographic basis for a better social theory. Maybe such a holistic history itself needs to be informed by elements of a more holistic alternative social theory. Both will have to deal better with the historiographic and theoretical problems broached below, which, among others, continue to be disputed.

HOLISM VS. PARTIALISM

The currently fashionable "globalization" thesis has it that the 1990s mark a new departure in this worldwide process. Grudgingly, some observers see the same since 1945 or even during the entire twentieth century, or at the very most since the nineteenth century. Yet, this book demonstrates that globalism (even more than globalization) was a fact of life since at least 1500 for the whole world, excepting a very few sparsely settled islands in the Pacific (though only for a little while). A few observers, like McNeill (1963, 1990), Hodgson (1993), Wilkinson (1987, 1993), Frank and Gills (1993), and Chase-Dunn and Hall (1997) argue that at least a Afro-Eurasian "eucumene" or "central world system" was already functioning as a single unit long before that.

So, how to regard this global whole holistically, be it before or after 1500? In previous writings (Frank and Gills 1993), I have suggested the analogy of a three-legged stool. It rests equally on ecological/economic/technological, political/military power, and social/cultural/ideological legs. The most neglected of these, also in my own work, has been the ecological component. After that, the most neglected basis has been the economic one, "economic history" notwithstanding. The political economic structure of the world economy/system requires far more study than it has received. Economic historians have neglected it altogether. Economists have mistaken it for "international" economic relations among nonexistent "national" economies. Students of international (political) relations have done what they say, that is, study relations among "nation" states as their basic building blocks. World-system analysts have confined themselves to only a small part of the real world economy/system before 1750 centered on Europe. That was something but not much more than what historians and political economists were already doing. Students of East, Southeast, South, West, not to mention Central Asia and Africa, have rarely sought to fit their regions into a wider economy. Even when they have done so, their endeavors have also been mostly European-centered. The recent exceptions are Chaudhuri (1991) and Abu-Lughod (1989), whose limitations we noted above. Therefore, lacking sufficient pioneers to follow and build on, this book has also been able take no more than a few preliminary steps to looking at the world economy as a whole. Far more work is needed, but from a really globally holistic world systemic perspective, not just from this or that regional, including the European regional, limitation. Moreover, the discussion here has itself been very limited to only the economic part of the ecological/economic/technological leg, and makes scarce mention even of the other two legs, let alone how to combine them in a global analysis.

COMMONALITY/SIMILARITY VS. SPECIFICITY/DIFFERENCES

Historians in particular, and social theorists in general, are wont to identify and stress the specific and unique particularist features of every "civilization," "culture," or "society" and their respective historical processes and events. That is the stock-in-trade of historians, especially when they are socially and economically supported and encouraged to do "national" and local history for ideological and political reasons "of state." Social scientists are supposed to devote more efforts to making generalizations. Yet much of their ideal type and comparative practice, not to mention their disciplinary divisions, lead them also to stress specificities and differences more than commonalities and similarities in the "object," and all the more so in the "subject," of their study. When pressed, most social scientists will de facto, if not also de jure, contend that differences matter more than commonalities and similarities, and that it is their job to study the former more than the latter. Otherwise, they also could not engage in their favorite "comparative" multivariate and factor analysis.

One implication of this review of early modern world history is rather the opposite: commonalities are both more common and more important even than the real differences, not to mention the many alleged differences that are not even real. Many alleged differences—"the East is East, and the West is West; and never the twain shall meet"—

are at best superficial institutional and/or "cultural" manifestations of the same essential *functional* structure and process. At worst, like this well-known quote from Rudyard Kipling, they are purely ideological fig leafs for the exercise of crass political economic colonial interests.

Even more important however, what emerges from our review of early modern world economic history is that many of the specific "differences" are themselves generated by structured interaction in a *common* world economy/system. Far from being appropriate or necessary to understanding this or that specificity here or there, differentiation then becomes an obstacle to accounting for and comprehending it. Only a holistic perspective on and from the global whole that is more than the sum of its parts can offer any adequate comprehension of any one part and how and why it differs from any other! Alas, this real-world circumstance very much limits the scientific—as distinct from the ideological—usefulness of successive local or national histories. It also poses serious limitations to time-series and cross-sectional comparative analyses, which are restricted to an arbitrarily selected, that is differentiated, process. All of these multivariate "factor" analyses, and even more so the identification of supposed specific "features" of this or that factor, violate the scientific canons of holism and therefore miss the global real-world boat. No doubt however, combining historiographic particularism and/or scientific "control" of variables with truly holistic analysis is easier said than done. Alas, hardly anyone even tries or is conscious that it should be done!

CONTINUITY VS. DISCONTINUITIES

A most particular contention about historical "particularity" is the widespread notion that the present and/or the recent past marks a discontinuous new departure. As already noted, the latest such fad is the alleged novelty of "globalization." Most particularly, this view also supposes a major historical discontinuity between medieval and modern times. There may be disputes about whether this discontinuity dates from A.D. 1100, 1300, 1500, or 1800; but there is widespread agreement that the world historical process changed radically and qualitatively thanks to "the Rise of the West"—and capitalism.

The argument here has been that historical continuity has been far more important than any and all discontinuities. The perception of a major new departure, which allegedly spells a discontinuous break in world history, is substantially (mis)informed by the Eurocentric vantage point. Once we abandon this Eurocentrism and adopt a more globally holistic world or even pan-Eurasian perspective, discontinuity is replaced by far more continuity. Or the other way around? Once we look upon the whole world more holistically, historical continuity looms much larger, especially in Asia. Indeed as suggested in the preceding chapters, the very "Rise of the West" and the renewed "Rise of the East" then appear derived from this global historical continuity.

Received theory attributes the industrial revolution and "the Rise of the West" to its alleged "exceptionality" and "superiority." The source of these alleged attributions is sought in turn in the also alleged long-standing or even primeval Western "preparation" for takeoff. This contention mistakes the place and misplaces the "concreteness" of continuity and transformation by looking for them in Europe itself. Yet the "causes" of the transformation can never be understood as long as they are examined only under the European street light, instead of seeking them under worldwide global illumination in the system as a whole.

For, the comparative and relational real-world historical evidence examined above shows that, contrary to received historiography and social theory, it was *not* the alleged prior European "development" that poised it for takeoff after 1800. That is, the rise of the West after 1800 was not really the result of the its "continuous" European preparation since the Renaissance, let alone thanks to any Greek or Judaic roots thereof. Indeed, industrialization was not even the continued outgrowth of European "proto-industrialization." The same process did not generate the same outcome in Asia and especially in China, where proto-industrialization was even more developed, as Pomeranz (1997) and Wong (1997) show to support their similar arguments that the industrial revolution was a new and distinct departure, to whose explanation we must bring other factors to bear.

The industrial revolution was an unforeseen event, which took place in a part of Europe as a result of the continuing unequal structure and uneven process in and of the world economy as a whole. That process of world development, however, also includes new departures in some of its regions and sectors that may appear discontinuous. It may indeed be the case that the industrial revolution, like the agricultural one before it, was an inflection in a continuous global development, which marks a "departure" in a vector and direction that is different from the previous one and is perhaps irreversible—short of total cataclysm, which may itself lie at the end of that vector. Thus, the systemic global structure and continuity that generated the rise of the West marked a departure in the West, which did not continue its earlier marginal position. Instead, there was a discontinuous departure of the global economy into a more industrial direction and a shift in the position of the West within the world economic system as a whole.

East Asia's rise to world economic prominence makes it all the more urgent to focus on the long historical continuity of which this process is a part. The now supposed discontinuous but really renewed rise of the East must also be seen as part and parcel of the fundamental structure and continuity in world development. Recognizing and analyzing this continuity will reveal much more than by myopically focusing on the alleged discontinuities. Perhaps it would be better to refer to two major early modern "inflections" in an essentially continuous historical process and dynamic within the same world economy and system: One was the Columbian exchange after the incorporation of the New World into the old one after 1500. The other was the "exchange" of demographic and economic productivity growth rates and perhaps of ecological pressures on resources between Asia and Europe, which generated the industrial revolution around 1800. Both, however, were only inflections generated by a process of world economic development. In both cases, Europeans were acting more as instruments than as initiators of global development.

HORIZONTAL INTEGRATION VS. VERTICAL SEPARATION

Another methodological alternative is between doing the conventional vertical history through a tunnel of time in a specific smaller or larger locality or of a particular issue (for examples, the issues of politics, culture, or women) in a specific locality and doing instead, or at least also, the globally horizontal history and analysis recommended by the Fletcher (1985, 1995). He noted with dismay that most historians "are alert to vertical continuities (the persistence of tradition, etc.) but blind to horizontal ones. . . . At 1500 I see nothing but compartmentalized histories"(Fletcher 1985: 39, 40). This methodological perspective and its blinders have been made even worse by the introduction of "area studies" in American and other universities, which produce "a microhistorical, even parochial outlook" (Fletcher 1985: 39).

If this praxis is deficient, its elevation to theoretical and methodological guideline is even worse. In my (1978a) book, I took Perry Anderson to task for writing—and doing as if—"there is no such thing as a uniform temporal medium: for the *times* of the major Absolutism . . . were, precisely, enormously diverse . . . no single temporality covers it. . . . Their dates are the same: their times are separate" (Anderson 1974: 10). That perspective and theoretical orientation and Anderson's maxim are themselves a methodological guarantee for failure to understand any of the absolutisms or anything else whose "dates are the same." I already sounded the alarm against "Anderson's apparent attempt to make historiographic virtue out of empirical necessity" in Frank (1978a). Instead I pleaded, as now repeated in chapter 5 above, that "the essential (because it is both the most necessary and the least accomplished) contribution of the historian to historical understanding is successively to relate different things and places at the same time in the historical process" (Frank 1978a: 21). That is methodologically analogous to and derivative from my maxims in the first three implications above regarding holism, commonality/similarity, and continuity.

Fletcher would make the same admonition, as cited in the epigraph to chapter 5, where he pleads for a "horizontally integrative macrohistory" of as much of the world as possible. "Its methodology is conceptually simple, if not easy to put into practice: first one searches for historical parallelism . . . and then one determines whether they are causally interrelated" (Fletcher 1985: 38). Alas, Fletcher did not live long enough to do so himself. However, Teggart (1939) had already undertaken to do so when he wrote *Rome and China: A Study of Correlations in Historical Events.* Yet even Braudel (1992), despite his exceptional sensitivity to "conjuncture," *"la longe duree,"* and "perspective of the world," failed to do so regarding the events in 1762, 1772, and 1782, as noted in chapter 5. He analyzes them in different only vertically organized chapters, even though their worldwide simultaneity stared him in the face. Or at least it would have, if only he had organized his "perspective of the world" more horizontally and less vertically.

I did so for these same "dates" (to use Anderson's terminology) in my *World Accumulation 1492–1789* (Frank 1978a) even before learning of what Teggart, Fletcher, or Braudel said and did. With the help of some additional data provided by Braudel, I proceeded further still in my critique of his book (Frank 1995) and again in chapter 5 above. It shows that, if we are only willing to look, each of the years 1762, 1772, and 1782 were marked by worldwide recessions that generated and can account for many of the economic and political events that Braudel, Wallerstein, and I observed. Yet they have occasioned countless books on the French, American, and industrial revolutions, which take no account of the cyclical instigation of these and other simultaneous events, nor of their worldwide relations.

Chapter 5 also makes some preliminary attempts to do the same for other "same times," especially around 1640. It also offers an answer to Fletcher's (1985: 54) question, "Is there a general economic recession in the seventeenth century, or not? There seems to be a parallelism here." Yet only an examination of this apparent horizontal parallelism permits an answer, and my tentative one is "No, there was no generalized 'seventeenth-century crisis'." Nonetheless, even a negative answer in this case lays the basis for the necessary horizontally integrative macro-historical study of what *did* happen, which in the seventeenth century seems to have been continued world economic growth and expansion. Of course, chapter 5 is no more than an isolated stab in the dark. What is really needed is a comprehensive, horizontally organized, global political economic macrohistory of simultaneous events, which is itself guided by the cyclical ups and downs that it should identify and analyze. Yet even before attempting that, it would be useful to pursue other more partial "horizontal" inquiries.

Fletcher himself poses several other such "parallelisms" for study in the early modern period from 1500 to 1800, including population growth, quickening tempo, growth of "regional" cities and towns, the rise of urban commercial classes (renascence), religious revival, and missionary movements (reformations), rural unrest, and decline of nomadism. Then he asks, "And other parallelisms? Are there not more? Unhappy landings" (Fletcher 1985: 56).

Some of these parallelisms have been partially addressed. Goldstone (1991a) undertook a major study of simultaneities in population growth as the basis for "demographic/structural" crises and their analysis. Wilkinson (1992, 1993), Bosworth (1995), and Chase-Dunn and Willard (1993) examined global horizontal simultaneities of urban growth to test Gills and Frank's (1992; also in Frank and Gills 1993) hypothesis about five-hundred-year-long cycles extending back long before 1500. Frank and Fuentes (1990, 1994) reviewed and found worldwide horizontal simultaneities of rural unrest as well as of various social movements (women's, peace, environment, consciousness, and so on) simultaneously in several Western countries during the nineteenth and twentieth centuries. All of these studies seem to uncover world-encompassing cyclical patterns, as do of course many studies that focus explicitly on cycles.

CYCLES VS. LINEARITY

It is frequently suggested that "Western" historiography, or at least its inclination, has gone from regarding life and history cyclically to perceiving it unilinearly and directionally through the "idea of progress." This idea was expressed by Hegel at the beginning of the nineteenth century, and it was recently reiterated by Francis Fukuyama (1989, 1992) in his work on the "end" of history. The findings about parallel horizontal simultaneities and our review of the early modern world economy imply and suggest that we would do well, however, to return to a more cyclical perspective of early modern economic history and probably of all history.

Continuity need not be linear, and horizontal integration need not be uniform. On the contrary, the continuity of a systemic structure and dynamic seems to depend on and continually reproduce nonlinearity and nonuniformity, as recently and also universally demonstrated by chaos theory and analysis in the physical and natural sciences (Gleick 1987, Prigogine 1996). To our eyes, the nonuniformity may appear as disequality, as in center-periphery or class differences and relations. (The distinction between differences only and their relational causes or consequences is emphasized by Chase-Dunn and Hall 1997.) Analogously, a continuous process can—and apparently usually does—contain periods of acceleration, deceleration, and also temporary stability, only the last of which would be represented by a flat or even straight line. That is, continuous processes also pulsate, as chaos theory and Prigogine's (1996) analysis of *The End of Certainty* also stress. However, pulsations are not indications of discontinuity in the system and process. Instead they can be manifestations of the internal structure and dynamic mechanism that maintains the system and propels its continuity itself. The question becomes whether the apparent pulsations are really in fact cycles.

Cyclical motion seems to be a universal fact of existence, life, and being, which is manifested in many or all spheres of reality. It is found in physical and cosmological, biological and evolutionary, and indeed cultural and ideational realms. Perhaps that is why there is a Society for the Study of Cycles, any and all cycles. So why should we not also expect to find cyclical history in the social world and the world economy/system—if we only look for it? At least, we should be prepared to recognize it when we see it. Aristotle observed that social life seems to be cyclical, but that people who experience the cycle phases may not be aware of doing so because the phases may be longer than their own life spans.

Early modern economic history (as well as political and social history) displays all sorts of cycles, or at least apparently quite regular fluctuations and pulsations. We have identified some of them in this study, as Frank and Gills (1993) among others have sought to do also for some earlier ones. Moreover, the evidence and the argument here are that these cycles are world-embracing and, at least in Afro-Eurasia, have existed for millennia (Frank 1993a).

The importance of these cycles, and of their recognition and analysis, is that they generate possibilities and constraints or limitations for social action, economic, political, cultural, ideological, and so on. The rising tide of an expansive "A" phase tends to lift all boats, enhance their range, and facilitate their steering and management. It also extends and encourages unifying relations among them, although it does not guarantee that some boats will not also sink at the best of times. A receding tide of a contracting "B" phase, not to mention its deepest crisis, constrains these same possibilities and imposes limitations on social action and sinks many more boats. It also tends to fractionate political economic and sociocultural "units" among and within each other. Such breakdown of previous relations may then appear to be a breakdown of the world economy/system as a whole, and at that moment might also signify or "prove" the "nonexistence" of any such system.

Yet the resultant involution or even implosion is really a function of participation in the larger world economy/system rather than of the lack of it, as it might appear from the more inward-looking and limiting perspective of that particular time and place. Therefore also, fractionating involution makes it appear that social action is more "inwardly" generated and oriented in "B" phases and more "externally" influenced in the more relational and expansive "A" phases. Yet in reality, both are a function of the structure and dynamic of the world economy/system itself. It stands to reason (rather than to crisis-generated emotion) that any awareness of the structural advantages of "A" and disadvantages of "B" phases can enhance the ability of social (and especially political) actors to manage themselves and their "society" at each of these times.

The structure and process of the world economy/system is complicated much further still by shorter cycles, insofar as they nest within longer ones. Schumpeter (1939) tried to analyze the relations among economic cycles of about three to four, ten, and fifty years' duration. However, he was far too schematic as far as he went, and he did not even consider the possibility of twenty-year-long (Kuznets 1930) cycles, not to mention Cameron's (1973) two-hundred-year-long "logistics" or

Snooks's (1996) three-hundred-year-long cycles, nor the Gills and Frank's (1992; also in Frank and Gills 1993) five-hundred-year-long cycles. The nesting of shorter cycles and their phases within longer ones complicates the identification and influences of their respective phases; but it does not mean that these cycles cannot or do not exist and matter.

On the contrary, the existence of any such cycles means that we are all in the same world economic boat at the same time and are subjected to the same forces and events at the same time. These forces themselves have their own ups and downs, which simultaneously and apparently cyclically tend to lift all boats on a rising tide at one time, and to lower them again at another. Therefore, by and large the possibilities open to "economies"—really parts of the single world economy—and to their associated polities are greater, better, and easier during upward "A"-phase "good times" than during the succeeding downward "B"-phase "bad times."

However, the Chinese meaning of "crisis" is a combination of danger and opportunity. Thus a time of crisis, especially for the previously best-placed part of the world economy/system, also opens a window of opportunity for some—not all!—more peripherally or marginally placed ones to improve their own position within the system as a whole. (For general analyses, see Frank and Gills 1993 and Chase-Dunn and Hall 1997.) We observe how this is the case with the East Asian NIEs today, as it was for West European ones two centuries ago. The analysis of this process in the nineteenth and twentieth centuries is beyond the scope of this book, which deals only with the *early* modern world economy.

However, even the above more than usually holistic review of the 1400–1800 period serves to show that we can account for and understand the subsequent "Rise of the West" only within the *world* economic/systemic scope within which it really took place. Moreover, this world systemic process included "the Decline of the East" as a conditioning factor, if not as the precondition, for "the Rise of the West," which displaced the East within the same one and only world economy/system.

This book has only begun to suggest three very preliminary world economic reasons and analyses for this "exchange": One is the hypothesis about microeconomic demand and supply for labor and capital-saving and energy-generating technology to help account for the industrial revolution that was temporarily located in parts of the West. Another is the long-cycle macroeconomic hypothesis, according to which the East "declined" as part of the structure, operation, and transformation of the world economy/system itself. The third explanation combines the other two in a demographic/economic/ecological analysis of the global and regional structure and process of world development, which helps to account for the differentiation that occurred between Asia and Europe around 1800. Pomeranz (1997) is working on a related, more ecological explanation as well.

This explanation suggests that the nineteenth and at least the first half of the twentieth centuries be considered a "B" phase for Asia. Given Asia's previous preponderance, was that a "B" phase for the world economy as well? If so, how do we accommodate the enormous expansion of productivity, production, and trade, not to mention population, which occurred in the West during this time? From a Western point of view the past two centuries appear like a long "A" phase, which at least in the West follows a long "A" phase in the East. Would this mean that one "A" phase in a previously marginal area in the West followed another one in the previously "core" area in the East? Moreover, does that "A" phase also precede still another possible "A" phase now beginning in the East, and a renewed core shift to the East as the West's time in the sun declines? That would leave us with double, and even triple or more successive "A" phases, and no worldwide "B" ones. In that case, what happened to our "long cycle"? Was it only an optical illusion?

Both the "micro" demand-and-supply hypothesis and the long-cycle "macro" one require far more testing, and presumably amendment. Moreover, they need to be systemically related to each other and to other world economic/systemic hypotheses and analyses yet to be considered or even proposed. That is, economics still needs to marry micro- and macroeconomics into a dynamic structural economic theory, and social "science" still needs to construct a real-world system theory. This social theory also requires a marriage of real micro- and macrohistory (including ecological history) to provide a real basis for the equation History = Theory for the world as a whole.

These observations also lead to the additional supposition that the very uneven cyclical process within the world economy/system itself functions as a mechanism of its own structural transformation. By analogy, we might consider how biological mutations affect the evolutionary process and the natural "system." In his *The Dynamic Society,* Snooks (1996) independently proposes a similar labor-capital-resource factor price and cyclical analysis of the industrial revolution as part of his economic interpretation of natural selection during the past two million years. As noted in chapter 6 and in my review of his book (Frank 1998a), his factor price analysis of recent developments is hampered by being limited to Western Europe. Therefore, while the focus on the "mutating" newly industrializing economy may be of paramount momentary interest, it also merits attention—much more than it receives—for its long-run significance for the world economy/system itself. On the other hand, such a cyclical "mutation" sometimes does receive inordinate historical and social scientific attention, as "the Rise of the West" has. Yet much of that attention is the result of misplaced concreteness. It reflects only the appearance that this event is uniquely self-generated, when in reality it is primarily a cyclical manifestation of the structure and process of the whole world economy/system itself. Therefore, the latter merits much more appreciation and attention, which received historiography and social theory has heretofore denied it.

In the absence of sufficient and adequate cycle analysis, it is admittedly hazardous even to speak of cycles. For any and all observed fluctuations and pulsations are not necessarily cyclical. They could be random or they could be responses to common forces "outside" the system. To have more—indeed, any—confidence that a pulsation is truly cyclical, it is necessary to demonstrate why, or at least that, the upper and lower turning points or inflection of the curve that maps these pulsations are endogenous and not only exogenous to the system. That is, not only must what goes up come down, and vice versa; but the going up itself must generate the subsequent downturn, and the going down the subsequent upturn. (For a debate on the endogeneity and/or exogeneity of Kondratieff cycle inflections, see Frank, Gordon, and Mandel 1994.) However in this regard, we are still very much in limbo, since hardly any historians even look for pulsations or cycles, and those who specialize in such "conjunctures" and even "perspective of the world" like Braudel have refrained from relating, let alone analyzing, them on a world economy/system-wide basis. Nor are demographers yet of enough help. They have not done enough even to identify possible long demographic cycles, and much less to relate them to economic ones. Global macrohistory truly has a long—and itself cyclical?—way to go.

AGENCY VS. STRUCTURE

The structure/agency problematique is age old and not likely to be resolved or even furthered here. Philosophers have long since debated about determinism vs. free will and historians about the individual in history. Does the individual make history, or does history make the individual? Marx argued that humans make their own history, but not in conditions of their choosing. This book has been an attempt to outline at least some of the underlying economic structure and transformation of early modern and therefore also of modern and contemporary world economic history. These at least condition the way in which we have and have not made our history in the past and can and cannot make it in the future.

There are two major lessons that emerge from this review of history and the conclusions drawn therefrom in the present chapter: One is that there is unity in diversity, indeed that it is the world economic/systemic unity that itself generates diversity. The other is that this unity has been continuous yet cyclical. These two structural and process conditions do influence how we can and do make our own history. Admittedly, this book still confines itself far too much to "description" and not enough to "analysis," let alone to laying bare all of the structure of the world economy/system that underlies the description of features and the relation of events.

The more we learn about the structure of these conditions, the better can we manage our "agency" within them; indeed, the better we can perhaps affect or even change these conditions. To quote Wang Gungwu's (1979: 1) takeoff on Marx's eleventh thesis on Feuerbach: "historians have only perceived the past in different ways: the point is to use it." Yes, the point is to use it, but which "it"? My point is that "it" is the one *world* history in which differences are part and parcel of its unity.

EUROPE IN A WORLD ECONOMIC NUTSHELL

Let me try to put in a nutshell what we have observed about the world economy and Europe between 1400 and 1800. Early modern and modern (and therefore presumably also future) history all have a long history of their own. Moreover, it has been a continuously common history at least throughout all of Afro-Eurasia. If there was a "new departure," it was the incorporation of the Americas and then also of Australasia into this already ongoing historical process and then worldwide system. Not only the initiative for this incorporation, but also its very causes and then the forms of its execution, had been generated by the structure and dynamic of the Afro-Eurasian historical process itself.

Afro-Eurasian history had long since been cyclical, or at least pulsating. The present millennium began with a period of system-wide political economic expansion. It was apparently centered at its far "eastern" end in Song China, but it also accelerated an accentuated reinsertion of its "western" end in Europe, which responded by going on several Crusades to plug its marginal economy more effectively into the new Afro-Eurasian dynamic. A period of pan-Afro-Eurasian political economic decline and even crisis followed in the late thirteenth and especially in the fourteenth century. Another long period of expansion began in the early fifteenth century, again in East and Southeast Asia. It soon included Central, South, and West Asia, and after the mid-fifteenth century also Africa and Europe. The "discovery" and then conquest of the Americas and the subsequent Columbian exchange were a direct result, and part and parcel, of this world economy/system-wide expansion.

So, the "long sixteenth-century" expansion in fact began in the early fifteenth century; and it continued through the seventeenth and into the eighteenth centuries. This expansion also continued to be primarily Asian-based, although it was also fueled by the new supplies of silver and gold money now brought by the Europeans from the Americas. In Asia, this expansion took the form of rapid growth of population, production, trade including imports and exports, and presumably income and consumption in China, Japan, Southeast Asia, Central Asia, India, Persia, and the Ottoman lands. Politically, the expansion was manifested and/or managed by the flourishing Chinese Ming/Qing, Japanese Tokugawa, Indian Mughal, Persian Safavid, and Turkish Ottoman regimes. The European populations and economies grew more slowly than all but the last of these Asian ones, and they did so rather differentially among each other. So did some "national" and other quite multiethnic European states, all of which were however much smaller than the large ones in Asia. The increased supply of money and/or population generated more inflation in Europe than in most of Asia, where increased production was more able to keep pace, including during the seventeenth century. In much of Europe however, economic and political growth were constrained and regionally even reversed in a major "seventeenth-century crisis," which left most of Asia unscathed. Therefore also, population growth was faster and greater in Asia than in Europe, and so continued into the eighteenth century before inflecting after 1750.

The already long existing "system" of "international" division of labor and trade widened and deepened during this expansive long "A" phase. However as usual, different productive sectors and regions were differentially situated in this "system" of accumulation, production, exchange, and consumption, which were de facto on a "silver standard." The differentiation in productivity and competitiveness that underlay the division of labor and exchange were manifest in imbalances of trade and "compensated" by flows over long distances of mostly silver specie money. Most of this silver was produced in the Americas and some also in Japan and elsewhere.

Reflecting the macroeconomic imbalances and also responding to corresponding microeconomic opportunities to make and take profit, the silver moved around the world in a predominantly eastward direction across the Atlantic and—via Europe—across the Indian Ocean, but also westward from Japan and from the Americas across the Pacific. Ultimately, the largest silver "sink" was China, whose relatively greater productivity and competitiveness acted like a magnet for the largest quantity of silver. However there as elsewhere, the incoming money generated increased effective demand and stimulated increased production and consumption and thereby supported population growth. The new supply of money failed to do so where the political economy was insufficiently flexible and expandable to permit growth of production to keep pace with the increase in the supply of money. In that case rising effective demand drove up prices in inflation, which is what happened in Europe.

Europe's disadvantaged position in the world economy was partly compensated by its privileged access to American money. On the demand side, the use of their American money—and *only* that—permitted the Europeans to enter and then increase their market share in the world market, all of whose dynamic centers were in Asia. On the supply side, access to and use of cheap—to the Europeans virtually free— money in the Americas afforded the wherewithal to acquire the supplies of real consumption and investment goods worldwide: servile labor and materials in the Americas to dig up the silver in the first place; slave labor from Africa; and from a European perspective virgin soil and climate also in the Americas. These resources were used to produce sugar, tobacco, timber for ships, and other export crops including especially cotton at low cost for European consumption. West European imports via the Baltic Sea of grain, timber, and iron from eastern and northern Europe was also paid for with American money and some textiles. And of course their American-supplied money was the only means of payment that permitted Europeans to import all those famed Asian spices, silks, cotton textiles, and other *real* goods for their own consumption and also for re-export to the Americas and Africa. Asians produced these goods and sold them to Europeans only for their American-supplied silver. That is, all these real goods that were produced by non-Europeans became cheaply, indeed nearly freely, available to Europeans because they were able to pay for them with their American-supplied money. Indeed, this silver—also produced by non-Europeans—was the *only* export good that the Europeans were able to bring to the world market.

Additionally moreover, this supply of goods produced by labor and raw materials outside of Europe also replaced and freed alternative re-sources for other uses within Europe: American sugar and Atlantic fish supplied calories and proteins for consumption for which Europe did not have to use their own farmland; Asian cotton textiles supplied clothes for which European consumers and producers did not have to use wool from European sheep, which would have eaten European grass. Otherwise, that grass would have had to be produced on still more enclosures of land for even more sheep to "eat men" in order to produce still more wool. Thus, the import of Asian textiles with Ameri-can money indirectly also permitted Europeans to produce more food and timber in Western Europe itself. Thus, West Europeans were able to use their position in the world economy both to supplement their own supplies and resources by drawing directly on those from the Americas to the west and from Eastern Europe and Asia to the east. The supply of these additional resources to Europe from the outside also freed European resources to use in its own development.

The process can be elucidated by making an interesting comparison with the second half of the twentieth century: Americans now need not even incur the small cost of getting others to dig up silver money for them. They simply print dollar bills (especially in the denomination of $100) and treasury certificates at no more cost to themselves than just the printing. Thus Americans were able to respond to the "dollar short-age" in Europe of the 1940s and in the "Third" and former "Second" worlds in the 1990s by using these paper "dollars" to buy up real raw materials and manufactures—and nuclear scientists!—for virtually nothing in the former Soviet Union and elsewhere around the world. Witness that today far more dollars circulate outside the United States than inside it; and most of its national debt, unlike that of others, is denominated in its own currency. And the United States can print at will without generating inflation at home as long as most of the dollars flow and circulate abroad. Moreover, Americans sold literally tons of treasury certificates to West Europeans and Japanese in the 1980s. Therefore additionally, Americans now continue to receive increasingly valuable Japanese yen and German marks in the 1990s in exchange for the ever more worthless American dollar debts incurred in the 1980s. That way, part of the population in the West is once again able to spend far beyond its real means and consume way beyond its own resources and production—other than of money—and to permit itself the luxury of promoting more benign "green" environmental policies that save its own ecology besides! This something-for-nothing strategy is essentially what Europe also practiced for the three centuries between 1500 and 1800. The difference is that the U.S. dollar is at least based in part on American productivity, while the European silver was only extracted from its American colonies. Of course, the later Western productivity is also derived in part from its earlier colonialism.

To return then to 1800, Europe's still productive backwardness may also have offered some of the "advantages" to catch up discussed by Gerschenkron (1962). Europe's backwardness provided the incentive and its supply of American money permitted Europeans to pursue micro- and macroeconomic advantages, which were to be had from increased European participation in the expanding Asian economies from 1500 to 1800. Of course, Europeans also took advantage of their increasing political economic relations with Africa and the Americas, including especially the "triangular" trade among all three. All of these, including of course the investment of profits derived from all of these overseas political economic relations at home, contributed to capital accumulation in Europe, or more precisely to Europe's participation in "world accumulation 1482–1789," to quote my earlier title (Frank 1978a).

Nonetheless, however much European "investment" and the Atlantic "triangle" may have contributed to Europe's participation in world accumulation, from a world economic perspective the Asian contribution was greater still. That was so for at least two reasons: To begin with, throughout this early modern period until at least 1800, productivity, production, and accumulation were greater in Asia than elsewhere in the world. Indeed it was greater in the Chinese, Indian, and other regional parts of Asia than in any other region of the world. Second, this increase in European (participation in) accumulation was possible *only* thanks to that Asian accumulation. Chapter 6 seeks to show (with the help of Adam Smith) how Europe used its American money to buy itself a ticket on the Asian economic train. Of course, in the absence of that economy or its dynamic in Asia, Europe would not have gone or gotten anywhere! That is, Europe would have remained where it already was: in world economic terms, just about nowhere; or it would have made its way only through the Atlantic "triangular" trade, which was much smaller and poorer than the Asian economies.

Finally, Europe arrived somewhere (in the world economy!) after three centuries of trying to do business in Asia. Really, however, Europeans attempted to do business in Asia even earlier than 1500; the European crusades to West Asia since the twelfth century and their fifteenth-century European excursions in search of South and East Asia were also already generated by the attractions of Asian wealth. Chapter 6 accounts for the roots of the post-1800 "Rise of the West" and "Decline of the East" in world economic and demographic terms, in which the economies of Asia played a major role. The proposed explanation has three related parts. A combination of demographic with micro- and macroeconomic analysis identifies an inflection of population and economic productivity growth rates that led to an "exchange" of places between Asia and Europe in the world economy/system between 1750 and 1850. Microeconomic analysis of worldwide supply-and-demand relations shows how they generated incentives for labor- and capital-saving and energy-producing invention, investment, and innovation, which took place in Europe. On the other hand, macroeconomic analysis of the cyclical distribution of income and derivative effective demand and supply in Asia and the world illuminated how the opportunity to do so profitably was generated by the global economy itself. The combination of these processes and of their analysis above cut the Gordian knot of Kipling's famous saying about the East and West never meeting.

Of course, the "East/West" knot was only tied, and its unraveling was boxed up, by the compartmentalization of Afro-Eurasian and world history against which Herodotus had already warned, as cited in one of our opening epigraphs: the line between West (Europe?) and East (Asia?) is purely imaginary and a Western construct. Real-world history continuously (and cyclically?) jumps and alternates across this imaginary Western/"Orientalist" division. That is what happened in the nineteenth century and promises to happen also in the twenty-first.

JIHAD VS. McWORLD IN THE ANARCHY OF THE CLASH OF CIVILIZATIONS?

However, Western historiography and social science still seek either to deny this reality of unity in diversity altogether, or to subvert and/or distort it. Pundits seek even to arouse ordinary people against unity and to use the press and other media to mobilize "us" against "them." The press has recently served as a worldwide vehicle and echo of a series of intentionally alarming pronouncements by Western pundits. Fukuyama on the "end" of history (1989, 1992) was followed by Bernard Barber on jihad vs. "McWorld" (1992, 1995), Robert Kaplan on the approaching "anarchy" (1994, 1996), and Samuel Huntington on the "clash" of civilizations (1993, 1996). Following the end of "the evil empire," all of them sound Western alarm bells against the threat of the new bogeyman, Islam—and then China. All of them do so by starting with a compartmentalized perspective on history, in which "the West is West, and the East is East." However, in their view now the two do meet on an ideologically mined battlefield in which "the West" needs to protect itself from "the rest" in general (in Huntington's terminology), and from Islamic jihad in particular. Fukuyama claims that "the end of history" has been attained through the "liberalism" of the West, but that, alas, the "East" and "South" are still marked by varieties of deplorable "traditional" "Oriental despotism." These and the hiatus between them allegedly generate "the coming anarchy in the world," as announced by Kaplan.

Although Barber detects a globalizing centripetal "McWorld" tendency, he also fears opposite and antagonistic centrifugal jihad tendencies that seek to liberate themselves through escape. Barber anticipates that in the long run McWorld will be victorious, but in the short run jihad promises to be quite troublesome. It does not occur to Barber that the fractionating jihad is itself generated by the globalizing McWorld, as it has been since time immemorial. The Bible observes that "to those who have, shall be given; and from those who have not, shall be taken" away what little they have. Moreover, both the Bible and the Qur'an are also critical of this political economic and social structure and encourage the victimized and disadvantaged to resist and redress the same. Therefore, the prospects are rather dim that Barber's McWorld globalization will soon eliminate the many forms of jihad that it itself generates.

Huntington goes even further, to deny McWorld's very existence. Instead he discovers only age-old "civilizations" (including "Latin American" and "Russian" ones) allegedly confronting each other. Since he sees no North-South economic divide and finds no more East-West cold-war battles to be fought, the future will be defined by the "clash of civilizations" instead. That is his "explanation" not only of ethnic cleansing in Bosnia, but of most strife everywhere. Therefore, this strife pits "the West against the rest," although Huntington avers that the greatest threat comes from Islam and then China—the "yellow peril" again!

These divisive ideological diatribes—it is difficult to call them anything more generous—all have their intellectual roots in ignorance or denial of a single global history. They assume the existence of innate and primeval diversity *against* unity, and they proclaim the libertarian pretensions and universalist aspirations of the exceptional, indeed exceptionalist diversity that allegedly distinguishes "The West" from "the rest." The Eurocentric social theory reviewed in this study serves as ideological "legitimation" for such divisive pronouncements and action. However, as the documentation in this book has shown, this social theory lacks all basis in historical reality and itself rests on no foundation other than Eurocentric ideology.

This ideology is being used in these new guises today when worldwide economic crisis again constrains peoples' livelihoods and accentuates their competition for even a meager livelihood around this *one* world. As a direct result, historians, archaeologists, postmodernists, and others are being increasingly pressed into service to dig up proof that "this land is—and always has been—mine" and can, therefore, be "ethnically cleansed" from, or at least "multiculturally" guarded against, all other claimants. Alas, the more people, including historians and social "scientists," are affected and constrained by worldwide forces beyond their comprehension and control, the less do they want to know about them. The faster the world spins around them or spins them around, the more do they insist on "stopping" the world: "I want to get off—and do my own thing!" The "Sinatra Doctrine" of "doing it my way" all over again.

The purpose of this book is instead to help construct an intellectual basis for accepting *diversity in unity* and celebrating *unity in diversity*. Alas, those who need it most will be the ones least interested. And those who wish to arm for the "clash of civilizations," if they even acknowledge this book, will do battle against it by invoking ever more culturalogical and civilizationist arguments. That is because the evidence presented in this book helps pull the historical rug out from under their social "science," which is little more than a mask for Eurocentric ideology of domination. And that is already being undermined by the world historical process itself—for which we can be grateful.

References

Abbeglen, James. 1958. *The Japanese Factory*. Glencoe, Ill.: The Free Press.

Abu-Lughod, Janet. 1989. *Before European Hegemony. The World System* A.D. *1250–1350*. New York: Oxford University Press.

Adams, Robert McC. 1996. *Paths of Fire: An Anthropologist's Inquiry into Western Technology*. Princeton: Princeton University Press.

Adshead, S. A. M. 1973. "The Seventeenth Century General Crisis in China." *Asian Profile* 1, no. 2 (October): 271–80.

———. 1988. *China in World History*. London: Macmillan.

———. 1993. *Central Asia in World History*. London: Macmillan.

Ali, M. Athar. 1975. "The Passing of Empire: The Mughal Case." *Modern Asian Studies* 9, 3: 385–96.

Ames, G. J. 1991. "The Carreira da India, 1668–1682: Maritime Enterprise and the Quest for Stability in Portugal's Asian Empire." *The Journal of European Economic History* 20,1 (Spring): 7–28.

Amin, Samir. 1989. *Eurocentrism*. London: Zed.

———. 1991. "The Ancient World-Systems versus the Modern World-System." *Review* 14, 3 (Summer): 349–85.

———. 1993. "The Ancient World-Systems versus the Modern Capitalist World-System." In *The World System: Five Hundred Years or Five Thousand?* edited by A. G. Frank and Barry K. Gills, 292–6. London and New York: Routledge.

———. 1996. "On Development: For Gunder Frank." In *The Underdevelopment of Development: Essays in Honor of Andre Gunder Frank,* edited by S. Chew and R.Denemark, 57–86. Thousand Oaks, Calif.: Sage.

Amin, S., G. Arrighi, A. G. Frank, and I. Wallerstein. 1982. *Dynamics of the World Economy*. New York and London: Monthly Review Press and Macmillan.

———. 1990. *Transforming the Revolution: Social Movements and the World-System*. New York: Monthly Review Press.

361

Anderson, Perry. 1974. *Lineages of the Absolutist State*. London: New Left Books.

Anisimov, Evegenii V. 1993. *The Reforms of Peter the Great. Prosperity through Coercion in Russia*. Armonk, N.Y.: M. E. Sharpe.

Arasaratnam, Sinnappah. 1986. *Merchants, Companies and the Commerce of the Coromandel Coast 1650–1740*. Delhi: Oxford University Press.

———. 1995. *Maritime Trade, Society and the European Influence in Southern Asia, 1600–1800*. Aldershot, U.K.: Variorum.

Arnold, David. 1983. *The Age of Discovery 1400–1600*. London: Methuen.

Arrighi, Giovanni. 1994. *The Long Twentieth Century. Money, Power, and the Origins of Our Time*. London and New York: Verso.

———. 1996. "The Rise of East Asia: World Systemic and Regional Aspects." *International Journal of Sociology and Social Policy* 16, no. 7/8: 6–44.

Arrighi, Giovanni, Takeshi Hamashita, and Mark Selden. 1996. "The Rise of East Asia in World Historical Perspective." Paper presented at the Planning Workshop, Fernand Braudel Center, State University of New York, Binghamton, December 6–7.

Arruda, José Jobson de Andrade. 1991. "Colonies as Mercantile Investments: The Luso-Brazilian Empire, 1500–1808." In *The Political Economy of Merchant Empires,* edited by James D. Tracy, 360–420. Cambridge: Cambridge University Press.

Asante, Molefi Kete. 1987. *The Afrocentric Idea*. Philadelphia: Temple University Press.

Aston, Trevor, ed. 1970. *Crisis in Europe, 1560–1660. Essays from Past and Present*. London: Routledge & Keagan Paul.

Aston, Trevor, and C. Philpin, eds. 1985. *The Brenner Debate. Agrarian Class Structure and Economic Development in Pre-Industrial Europe*. Cambridge: Cambridge University Press.

Attman, Artur 1981. *The Bullion Flow between Europe and the East 1000–1750*. Goteborg: Kungl. Vetenskaps- och Vitterhets-Samhallet.

———. 1986a. *American Bullion in the European World Trade 1600–1800*. Goteborg: Kungl. Vetenskaps- och Vitterhets-Samhallet.

———. 1986b. "Precious Metals and the Balance of Payments in International Trade 1500–1800." In *The Emergence of a World Economy 1500–1914*. Papers of the Ninth International Congress of Economic History, Part I: 1500–1850, edited by Wolfram Fischer, R. M. McInnis, and J. Schneider, 113–22. Wiesbaden: Steiner Verlag.

Atwell, William S. 1977. "Notes on Silver, Foreign Trade, and the Late Ming Economy." *Ch'ing-shih wen-t'i* 8, Bo. 3: 1–33.

———. 1982. "International Bullion Flows and the Chinese Economy circa 1530–1650." *Past and Present* 95: 68–90.

———. 1986. "Some Observations on the 'Seventeenth-Century Crisis' in China and Japan." *Journal of Asian Studies* 45, 2: 223–43.

———. 1988. "The T'ai-ch'ang, T'ien-ch'i, and Ch'ung-chen Reigns, 1620–1640." In *The Cambridge History of China*. Vol. 7, *The Ming Dynasty, 1368–1644*, edited by Frederick W. Mote and Denis Twitchett, 585–640. Cambridge: Cambridge University Press.

————. 1990. "A Seventeenth-Century 'General Crisis' in EastAsia?" *Modern Asian Studies* 24, no. 4: 661–82.

Austen, Ralph A. 1987. *Africa in Economic History*. Portsmouth: Heinemann.

————. 1990. "Marginalization, Stagnation, and Growth: The Trans-Saharan Caravan Trade in the Era of European Expansion, 1500–1800." In *The Rise of the Merchant Empires. Long-Distance Trade in the Early Modern World, 1350–1750*, edited by James D. Tracy, 311–50. Cambridge: Cambridge University Press.

Baechler, Jean, John A. Hall, and Michael Mann, eds. 1988. *Europe and the Rise of Capitalism*. Oxford: Basil Blackwell.

Bagchi, Amiya. 1986. "Comment." In *Technology in Ancient and Medieval India*, edited by Aniruddha Roy and S. K. Bagchi. Delhi: Sundeep Prakashan.

Bairoch, Paul. 1969. *Revolución Industrial y Subdesarrollo*. La Habana: Instituto del Libro.

————. 1974. "Geographical Structure and Trade Balance of European Foreign Trade from 1800 to 1970." *Journal of European Economic History* 3, no. 3 (Winter).

————. 1975. *The Economic Development of the Third World since 1900*. London: Methuen.

————. 1976. *Commerce exterieur et développement économique de l'Europe aux XIXeme siècle*. Paris: Mouton.

————. 1981. "The Main Trends in National Economic Disparities since the Industrial Revolution." In *Disparities in Economic Development since the Industrial Revolution*, edited by Paul Bairoch and Maurice Levy-Leboyer, 3–17. London: Macmillan.

————. 1993. *Economics and World History. Myths and Paradoxes*. Hempel Heampstead, U.K.: Harvester/Wheatsheaf.

————. 1997. *Victoires et déboires II. Histoire économique et sociale du monde du XVIe siècle à nos jours*. Paris: Gallimard.

Bairoch, Paul, and Maurice Levy-Leboyer, eds. 1981. *Disparities in Economic Development since the Industrial Revolution*. London: Macmillan.

Barber, Bernard. 1992. "Jihad vs. McWorld." *Atlantic*, no. 269: 53–63.

————. 1995. *Jihad vs. McWorld*. New York: Random House.

Barendse, Rene. 1997. "The Arabian Seas 1640–1700." Unpublished manuscript.

Barfield, Thomas. 1989. *The Perilous Frontier. Nomadic Empires and China*. Oxford: Basil Blackwell.

Barrett, Ward. 1990. "World Bullion Flows, 1450–1800." In *The Rise of the Merchant Empires. Long-Distance Trade in the Early Modern World, 1350–1750*, edited by James D. Tracy, 224–54. Cambridge: Cambridge University Press.

Bayly, C. A. 1983. *Rulers, Townsmen and Bazaars: North Indian Society in the Age of British Expansion, 1770–1870*. Cambridge: Cambridge University Press.

————. 1987. *Indian Society and the Making of the British Empire*. Cambridge: Cambridge University Press.

————. 1990. *The Raj: India and the British, 1600–1947*. London: National Portrait Gallery Publications.

Bellah, Robert. 1957. *Tokugawa Religion*. Glencoe, Ill.: The Free Press.

Benedict, Ruth. 1954. *The Chrysanthemum and the Sword.* Tokyo: Charles E. Tuttle.

Bennett, M. K. 1954. *The World's Food. A Study of the Interrelations of World Populations, National Diets, and Food Potentials.* New York: Harper.

Bentley, Jerry H. 1996. "Periodization in World History." *The American Historical Review* 101, no. 3 (June): 749–70.

Bergesen, Albert. 1982. "The Emerging Science of the World-System." *International Social Science Journal* 34: 23–36.

———. 1995. "Let's Be Frank about World History." In *Civilizations and World Systems. Studying World-Historical Change,* edited by Stephen Sanderson, 195–205. Walnut Creek, Calif.: Altamira.

Bernal, J. D. 1969. *Science in History.* Harmondsworth, England: Penguin.

Bernal, Martin. 1987. *Black Athena. The Afroasiatic Roots of Classical Civilization.* New Brunswick, N.J.: Rutgers University Press.

Blaut, J. M. 1977. "Where Was Capitalism Born?" In *Radical Geography,* edited by R. Peet, 95–110. Chicago: Maasoufa Press.

———. 1992. "Fourteen Ninety-Two." *Political Geography Quarterly* 11, no. 4 (July). Reprinted in J. M. Blaut et al., *1492. The Debate on Colonialism, Eurocentrism and History.* Trenton, N.J.: Africa World Press.

———. 1993a. *The Colonizer's Model of the World: Geographical Diffusionism and Eurocentric History.* New York and London: Guilford Press.

———. 1993b. "Mapping the March of History." Paper read at the annual meeting of the American Association of Geographers, Atlanta, Georgia, April 8.

———. 1997. "Eight Eurocentric Historians." Chap. 2 in "Decolonizing the Past: Historians and the Myth of European Superiority." Unpublished manuscript.

Boserup, Esther. 1981. *Population and Technological Change. A Study of Long-Term Trends.* Chicago: University of Chicago Press.

Boswell, Terry, and Joya Misra. 1995. "Cycles and Trends in the Early Capitalist World-Economy: An Analysis of Leading Sector Commodity Trades 1500–1600/50–1750." *Review* 18, no. 3: 459–86.

Bosworth, Andrew. 1995. "World Cities and World Economic Cycles." In *Civilizations and World Systems. Studying World-Historical Change,* edited by Stephen S. Sanderson, 206–28. Walnut Creek, Calif.: Altamira.

Boxer, C. R. 1990. *Portuguese Conquest and Commerce in Southern Asia 1500–1750.* Aldershot, U.K.: Variorum.

Braudel, Fernand. 1982. *The Wheels of Commerce.* Vol. 2 of *Civilization and Capitalism 15th–18th Century.* London: Fontana.

———. 1992. *The Perspective of the World.* Vol. 3 of *Civilization and Capitalism 15th–18th Century.* Berkeley and Los Angeles: University of California Press.

———. 1993. *A History of Civilizations.* New York: Penguin Books.

Braudel, Fernand, and Frank Spooner. 1967. "Prices in Europe from 1450 to 1750." In *The Economy of Expanding Europe in the Sixteenth and Seventeenth Centuries.* Vol. 4 of *Cambridge Economic History of Europe,* edited by E. E. Rich and C. H. Wilson, 374–480. Cambridge: Cambridge University Press.

Brenning, Joseph A. 1983. "Silver in Seventeenth-Century Surat: Monetary Circulation and the Price Revolution in Mughal India." In *Precious Metals in the Late Medieval and Early Modern Worlds,* edited by J. F. Richards, 477–93. Durham, N.C.: Carolina Academic Press.

———. 1990. "Textile Producers and Production in Late Seventeenth Century Coromandel." In *Merchants, Markets and the State in Early Modern India,* edited by Sanjay Subrahmanyam, 66–89. Delhi: Oxford University Press.

Breucr, Hans. 1972. *Columbus Was Chinese. Discoveries and Inventions of the Far East.* New York: Herder and Herder.

Brook, Timothy, ed. 1989. *The Asiatic Mode of Production in China.* Armonk, N.Y.: M. E. Sharpe.

———. 1998. *The Confusions of Pleasure. A History of Ming China (1368–1644).* Berkeley and Los Angeles: University of California Press.

Brown, Michael Barratt. 1963. *After Imperialism.* London: Heineman.

Brummett, Palmira. 1994. *Ottoman Seapower and Levantine Diplomacy in the Age of Discovery.* Albany: State University of New York Press.

Burton, Audrey. 1993. *Bukharan Trade 1558–1718.* Papers on Inner Asia No. 23. Bloomington: Indiana University Institute for Inner Asian Studies.

Cameron, Rondo. 1973. "The Logistics of European Economic Growth: A Note on Historical Periodization." *Journal of European Economic History* 2, no. 1: 145–8.

Carr-Saunders A. M. 1936. *World Population. Past Growth and Present Trends.* Oxford: Clarendon Press.

Cartier, Michel. 1981. "Les importations de métaux monétaires en Chine: Essay sur la conjoncture chinoise." *Annales* 36, no. 3 (May–June): 454–66.

Chakrabarti, Phanindra Nath. 1990. *Trans-Himalayan Trade. A Retrospect (1774–1914).* Delhi: Classics India Publications.

Chandra, Bipan. 1966. *The Rise and Growth of Economic Nationalism in India.* New Delhi: Peoples Publishing House.

Chapman, S. D. 1972. *The Cotton Industry in the Industrial Revolution.* London: Macmillan.

Chase-Dunn, Christopher, and Thomas Hall. 1997. *Rise and Demise: Comparing World-Systems.* Boulder: Westview.

Chase-Dunn, Christopher, and Alice Willard. 1993. "Systems of Cities and World-Systems: Settlement Size Hierarchies and Cycles of Political Centralization, 2000 BC–1988 AD." Paper presented at annual meeting of the International Studies Association, Acapulco, March.

Chaudhuri, K.–N. 1978. *The Trading World of Asia and the East India Company 1660–1760.* Cambridge: Cambridge University Press.

———. 1985. *Trade and Civilisation in the Indian Ocean. An Economic History from the Rise of Islam to 1750.* Cambridge: Cambridge University Press.

———. 1990a. *Asia before Europe. Economy and Civilisation of the Indian Ocean from the Rise of Islam to 1750.* Cambridge: Cambridge University Press.

———. 1990b. "Politics, Trade and the World Economy in the Age of European Expansion: Themes for Debate." In *The European Discovery of the World and Its Economic Effects on Pre-Industrial Society, 1500–1800,* edited by Hans Pohl. Papers of the Tenth International Economic History Congress. Stuttgart: Franz Steiner Verlag.

———. 1991. "Reflections on the Organizing Principle of Premodern Trade." In *The Political Economy of Merchant Empires,* edited by James D. Tracy, 421–42. Cambridge: Cambridge University Press.

———. 1994. "Markets and Traders in India during the Seventeenth and Eighteenth Centuries." In *Money and the Market in India 1100–1700,* edited by Sanjay Subrahmanyam. Delhi: Oxford University Press.

Chaudhuri, S. 1995. *From Prosperity to Decline—Eighteenth Century Bengal.* New Delhi:Manohar.

Chaunu, Pierre. 1959. *Seville et l'Atlantique (1504–1650).* Paris: S.E.V.P.E.N.

Chew, Sing. 1997. "Accumulation, Deforestation, and World Ecological Degradation 2500 B.C. to A. D. 1990." In *Advances in Human Ecology,* edited by Lee Freese. Westport,Conn.: JAI Press.

———. Forthcoming. *World Ecological Degradation 2500 BC to AD 1990.* Walnut Creek, Calif.: Altamira/Sage.

Chew, Sing, and Robert Denemark, eds. 1996. *The Underdevelopment of Development. Essays in Honor of Andre Gunder Frank.* Thousand Oaks, Calif.: Sage.

Chuan, Han-Sheng. 1969. "The Inflow of American Silver into China from the Late Ming to the Mid-Ch'ing Period." *The Journal of the Institute of Chinese Studies of the Chinese University of Hong Kong,* 2: 61–75.

———. 1981. "The Inflow of American Silver into China during the 16th–18th Centuries." In Proceedings of the Academic Sciences International Conference on Sinology, 849–53. Taipei.

———. 1995. "Estimate of Silver Imports into China from the Americas in the Ming and Ch'ing Dynasties." *Bulletin of the Institute of History and Philology,* 66, no. 3: 679–93.

Cipolla, Carlo M. 1967. *Cañones y Velas. La Primera Fase de la Expansión Europea 1400–1700.* Barcelona: Ariel.

———. 1976. *Before the Industrial Revolution. European Society and Economy, 1000–1700.* London: Methuen.

Cipolla, Carlo M., ed. 1974. *The Sixteenth and Seventeenth Centuries.* Vol. 2 of *The Fontana History of Europe.* Glasgow: Collins/Fontana.

Cizakca, Murat. 1987. "Price History and the Bursa Silk Industry: A Study in Ottoman Industrial Decline, 1550–1650." In *The Ottoman Empire and the World Economy,* edited by Huri Islamoglu-Inan. Cambridge: Cambridge University Press.

Clark, Colin. 1977. *Population Growth and Land Use.* London: Macmillan.

Coedes, G. 1968. *The Indianized States of Southeast Asia.* Edited by Walter F. Vella. Honolulu: University of Hawaii Press.

Cohen, H. Floris. 1994. *The Scientific Revolution. A Historiographic Inquiry.* Chicago: University of Chicago Press.

Costello, Paul. 1994. *World Historians and their Goals. Twentieth-Century Answers to Modernism.* De Kalb: Northern Illinois University Press.

Crombie, A. C. 1959. *Science in the Later Middle Ages and Early Modern Times: XIII–XVII Centuries.* Vol. 2 of *Medieval and Early Modern Science.* New York: Doubleday.

Crosby, Alfred W. 1972. *The Columbian Exchange. Biological and Cultural Consequences of 1492.* Westport, Conn.: Greenwood Press.

————. 1986. *Ecological Imperialism. The Biological Expansion of Europe, 900–1900.* Cambridge: Cambridge University Press.

————. 1994. *Germs, Seed and Animals. Studies in Ecological History.* Armonk, N.Y.: M. E. Sharpe.

————. 1996. "The Potato Connection." *World History Bulletin* 12, no. 1 (Winter-Spring): 1–5.

Curtin, Philip D. 1983. "Africa and the Wider Monetary World, 1250–1850." In *Precious Metals in the Late Medieval and Early Modern Worlds,* edited by J. F. Richards, 231–68. Durham, N.C.: Carolina Academic Press.

————. 1984. *Cross-Cultural Trade in World History.* Cambridge: Cambridge University Press.

Cushman, Jennifer Wayne. 1993. *Fields from the Sea. Chinese Junk Trade with Siam during the Late Eighteenth and Early Nineteenth Centuries.* Ithaca: Southeast Asia Program, Cornell University.

Darling, Linda 1992. "Revising the Ottoman Decline Paradigm." Tucson: University of Arizona. Unpublished manuscript.

————. 1994. "Ottoman Politics through British Eyes: Paul Rycaut's *The Present State of the Ottoman Empire.*" *Journal of World History* 5, no. 1: 71–96.

Das Gupta, Ashin. 1979. *Indian Merchants and the Decline of Surat: c. 1700–1750.* Wiesbaden: Steiner.

————. 1987. "The Maritime Trade of Indonesia: 1500–1800" In *India and the Indian Ocean 1500–1800,* edited by Ashin Das Gupta and M. N. Pearson, 240–75. Calcutta: Oxford University Press.

————. 1990. "Trade and Politics in 18th Century India." In *Islam and the Trade of Asia,* edited by D. S. Richards, 181–214. Oxford: Bruno Cassirer.

Das Gupta, Ashin, and M. N. Pearson, eds. 1987. *India and the Indian Ocean 1500–1800.* Calcutta: Oxford University Press.

Dawson, Raymond. 1967. *The Chinese Chameleon. An Analysis of European Conceptions of Chinese Civilization.* London: Oxford University Press.

Day, John. 1987. *The Medieval Market Economy.* Oxford: Basil Blackwell.

Deane, Phyllis. 1965. *The First Industrial Revolution.* Cambridge: Cambridge University Press.

de Ste. Croix, G. E. M. 1981. *The Class Struggle in the Ancient Greek World.* London: Duckworth.

De Vries, Jan. 1976. *The Economy of Europe in an Age of Crisis, 1600–1750.* Cambridge: Cambridge University Press.

Deyell, John. 1983. "The China Connection: Problems of Silver Supply in Medieval Bengal." In *Precious Metals in the Late Medieval and Early Modern Worlds,* edited by J. F. Richards, 207–30. Durham, N.C.: Carolina Academic Press.

Dharampal. 1971. *Indian Science and Technology in the Eighteenth Century. Some Contemporary European Accounts.* Delhi: Impex India.

Dickson, P. G. M. 1967. *The Financial Revolution in England. A Study in the Development of Public Credit 1688–1756.* London: Macmillan.

Djait, Hichen. 1985. *Europe and Islam.* Berkeley and Los Angeles: University of California Press.

Dobb, Maurice. [1946] 1963. *Studies in the Development of Capitalism*. London: Routledge & Keagan Paul.

Dorn, Walter D. 1963. *Competition for Empire, 1740–1763*. New York: Harper & Row.

Durand, John D. 1967. "The Modern Expansion of World Population." *Proceedings of the American Philosophical Society* 3, no. 3: 140–2.

———. 1974. *Historical Estimates of World Population: An Evaluation*. Philadelphia: University of Pennsylvania Population Studies Center.

Durkheim, Émile. 1965. *The Division of Labor in Society*. New York: The Free Press.

Dussel, Enrique. 1966. "Hipotesis para el Estudio de Latinoamérica en la Historia Universal." Resistencia, Chaco, Argentina. Manuscript.

Eaton, Richard N. 1993. *The Rise of Islam and the Bengal Frontier 1204–1760*. Berkeley and Los Angeles: University of California Press.

Eberhard, Wolfram. 1977. *A History of China*. Rev. ed. London: Routledge & Keagan Paul.

Elvin, Mark. 1973. *The Pattern of the Chinese Past*. Stanford: Stanford University Press.

Fairbank, John King. 1969. *Trade and Diplomacy on the China Coast*. Stanford: Stanford University Press.

Fairbank, J. K., Edwin Reischauer, and Albert M. Craig, eds. 1978. *East Asia, Tradition, and Transformation*. Boston: Houghton Mifflin.

Faroqhi, Suraiya. 1984. *Town and Townsmen of Ottoman Anatolia. Trade, Crafts and Food Production in an Urban Setting, 1520–1650*. Cambridge: Cambridge University Press.

———. 1986. *Peasants, Dervishes and Traders in the Ottoman Empire*. Aldershot, U.K.: Variorum.

———. 1987. "The Venetian Presence in the Ottoman Empire, 1600–30." In *The Ottoman Empire and the World-Economy,* edited by Huri Islamoglu-Inan. Cambridge: Cambridge University Press.

———. 1991. "The Fieldglass and the Magnifying Lens: Studies of Ottoman Crafts and Craftsmen." *The Journal of European Economic History* 20, no. 1 (Spring): 29–58.

———. 1994. "Part II Crisis and Change, 1590–1699." In *An Economic and Social History of the Ottoman Empire 1300–1914,* edited by Halil Inalcik with Donald Quataert, 411–636. Cambridge: Cambridge University Press.

Fernandez-Armesto, Felipe. 1995. *Millennium*. London: Bantam Press.

Fischer, Wolfram, R. M. McInnis, and J. Schneider, eds. 1986. *The Emergence of a World Economy 1500–1914*. Papers of the Ninth International Congress of Economic History, Part I: 1500–1850. Wiesbaden: Steiner Verlag.

Fitzpatrick, John. 1992. "The Middle Kingdom, The Middle Sea, and the Geographical Pivot of History." *Review* 15, no. 2 (Summer): 477–533.

Fletcher, Joseph. 1968. "China and Central Asia 1368–1884." In *The Chinese World Order. Traditional China's Foreign Relations,* edited by John King Fairbank. Cambridge: Harvard University Press.

———. 1985. "Integrative History: Parallels and Interconnections in the Early Modern Period, 1500–1800." *Journal of Turkish Studies* 9: (1985) 37–58. Reprinted 1995 in *Studies on Chinese and Islamic Inner Asia*, edited by Beatrice Forbes Manz. Aldershot, U.K.: Variorum.

Floor, W. W. 1988. *Commercial Conflict between Persia and the Netherlands 1712–1718*. Durham, U.K.: University of Durham Centre for Middle Eastern & Islamic Studies.

Flynn, Dennis O. 1982. "Fiscal Crisis and the Decline of Spain (Castile)." *Journal of Economic History* 42: 139–47.

———. 1984. "The 'Population Thesis' View of Inflation Versus Economics and History" and "Use and Misuse of the Quantity Theory of Money in Early Modern Historiography." In *Trierer Historische Forschungen*, edited by Hans-Hubert Anton et al., Vol. 7: 363–82, 383–417. Trier: Verlag Trierer Historische Forschungen.

———. 1986. "The Microeconomics of Silver and East-West Trade in the Early Modern Period." In *The Emergence of a World Economy 1500–1914*. Papers of the Ninth International Congress of Economic History, Part I: 1500–1850, edited by Wolfram Fischer, R. M. McInnis, and J. Schneider, 37–60. Wiesbaden: Steiner Verlag.

———. 1991. "Comparing the Tokugawa Shogunate with Hapsburg Spain: Two Silver-based Empires in a Global Setting." In *The Political Economy of Merchant Empires*, edited by James D. Tracy, 332–59. Cambridge: Cambridge University Press.

———. 1996. *World Silver and Monetary History in the 16th and 17th Centuries*. Aldershot, U.K.: Variorum.

Flynn, Dennis O., and Arturo Giraldez. 1994. "China and the Manila Galleons." In *Japanese Industrialization and the Asian Economy*, edited by A. J. H. Latham and Heita Kawakatsu, 71–90. London: Routledge.

———. 1995a. "Born with a 'Silver Spoon': The Origin of World Trade." *Journal of World History* 6, no. 2 (Fall): 201–22.

———. 1995b. "China and the Spanish Empire." Paper presented at the 55th Annual Meeting of the Economic History Association, Chicago, September 8–10.

———. 1995c. "Arbitrage, China, and World Trade in the Early Modern Period." *Journal of the Economic and Social History of the Orient* 38, no. 4: 429–48.

———. 1996. "Silk for Silver: Manila-Macao Trade in the 17th Century." *Philippine Studies*, 44 (First quarter): 52–68.

Foltz, Richard. 1996. "Central Asian Naqshbandi Connections of the Mughal Emperors." *Journal of Islamic Studies* 7, no. 2: 229–239.

———. 1997. "Central Asian in the Administration of Mughal India." *Journal of Asian History* 31, no. 2: 1–16.

Foss, Theodore Nicholas. 1986. "Chinese Silk Manufacture in Jean-Baptiste Du Halde *Description de la Chine (1735)*." In *Asia and the West. Encounters and Exchanges from the Age of Explorations. Essays in Honor of Donald F. Lach*, edited by C. K. Pullapilly and E. J. Van Kley. Notre Dame, Ind.: Cross Roads Books.

Francis, Peter, Jr. 1989. *Beads and the Bead Trade in Southeast Asia*. Lake Placid, N.Y.: Center for Bead Research.

———. 1991. "Beadmaking at Arikamedu and Beyond." *World Archaeology* 23, 1 (June): 28–43.

Frank, Andre Gunder. 1966. "The Development of Underdevelopment." *Monthly Review* 18, no. 4 (September). Reprinted in Frank 1969: 3–20.

———. 1967. *Capitalism and Underdevelopment in Latin America*. New York: Monthly Review Press.

———. 1969. *Latin America: Underdevelopment or Revolution*. New York: Monthly Review Press.

———. 1975. *On Capitalist Underdevelopment*. Bombay: Oxford University Press.

———. 1978a. *World Accumulation, 1492–1789*, New York and London: Monthly Review Press and Macmillan Press.

———. 1978b. *Dependent Accumulation and Underdevelopment*. New York and London: Monthly Review Press and Macmillan Press.

———. 1979. *Mexican Agriculture 1520–1630: Transformation of Mode of Production*. Cambridge: Cambridge University Press.

———. 1980. "Development of Underdevelopment or Underdevelopment of Development in China." In *The Development of Underdevelopment in China*, edited by C. C. Huang, 90–99. White Plains, N.Y.: M. E. Sharpe.

———. 1987. Comment on Janet Abu-Lughod's "The Shape of the World System in the Thirteenth Century." *Studies in Comparative International Development* 22, no. 4:35–37.

———. 1990a. "A Theoretical Introduction to 5,000 Years of World System History." *Review* 13, no. 2 (Spring): 155–248.

———. 1990b. "The Thirteenth Century World System: A Review Essay." *Journal of World History* 1, no. 2 (Autumn): 249–56.

———. 1991a. "A Plea for World System History." *Journal of World History* 2, no. 1 (Spring): 1–28.

———. 1991b. "Transitional Ideological Modes: Feudalism, Capitalism, Socialism." *Critique of Anthropology* 11, no. 2 (Summer): 171–88.

———. 1991c. "The Underdevelopment of Development." *Scandinavian Journal of Development Alternatives* (Special Issue) 10, no. 3 (September): 5–72.

———. 1992. *The Centrality of Central Asia*. Comparative Asian Studies No. 8. Amsterdam: VU University Press for Centre for Asian Studies Amsterdam.

———. 1993a. "Bronze Age World System Cycles." *Current Anthropology* 34, no. 4 (August–October): 383–430.

———. 1993b. The World Is Round and Wavy: Demographic Cycles & Structural Analysis in the World System. A Review Essay of Jack A. Goldstone's *Revolutions and Rebellions in the Early Modern World*." *Contention* 2 (winter): 107–124. Reprinted in *Debating Revolutions,* edited by Nikki Keddie, 200–20. New York: New York University Press, 1995.

———. 1994. "The World Economic System in Asia before European Hegemony." *The Historian* 56, no. 4 (winter): 259–76.

———. 1995. "The Modern World System Revisited: Re-reading Braudel and Wallerstein." In *Civilizations and World Systems. Studying World-Historical Change,* edited by Stephen S. Sanderson, 206–28. Walnut Creek, Calif.: Altamira.

———. 1996. "The Underdevelopment of Development." In *The Underdevelopment of Development. Essays in Honor of Andre Gunder Frank,* edited by Sing Chew and Robert Denemark, 17–56. Thousand Oaks, Calif.: Sage.

———. 1998a. "Materialistically Yours. The Dynamic Society of Graeme Snooks." *Journal of World History* 9, no. 1 (March).

———. 1998b. Review of Richard von Glahn, *Fountain of Fortune. Money and Monetary Policy in China, 1000–1700. Journal of World History* 9, no. 1 (March). Forthcoming.

Frank, A. G., and Marta Fuentes. 1990. "Civil Democracy: Social Movements in Recent World History." In *Transforming the Revolution: Social Movements and the World-System,* S. Amin, G. Arrighi, A. G. Frank, and I. Wallerstein, 139–80. New York: Monthly Review Press.

———. 1994. "On Studying the Cycles in Social Movements." In *Research in Social Movements, Conflict and Change,* edited by L. Kriesberg, M. Dobrkowski, and I. Wallimann, vol. 17: 173–96. Greenwich, Conn.: JAI Press.

Frank, A. G., and B. K. Gills, 1992. "The Five Thousand Year World System: An Introduction." *Humboldt Journal of Social Relations* 18, no. 1 (Spring): 1–79.

Frank, A. G., and B. K. Gills, eds. 1993. *The World System: Five Hundred Years or Five Thousand?* London and New York: Routledge.

Frank, A. G., David Gordon, and Ernest Mandel. 1994. "Inside Out or Outside In (The Exogeneity/Endogeneity Debate)." *Review* 17, no. 1 (Winter): 1–5.

Fukuyama, Francis. 1989. "The End of History." *National Interest* 16 (Summer): 1–18.

———. 1992. *The End of History and the Last Man.* New York: The Free Press.

Ganguli, B. N., ed. 1964. *Readings in Indian Economic History.* Bombay: Asia Publishing House.

Garcia-Baquero Gonzales, A. 1994. "Andalusia and the Crisis of the Indies Trade, 1610–1720." In *The Castilian Crisis of the Seventeenth Century,* edited by I. A. A. Thompson and Bartolome Yn Casalilla, 115–35. Cambridge: Cambridge University Press.

Gates, Hill. 1996. *China's Motor. A Thousand Years of Petty Capitalism.* Ithaca: Cornell University Press.

Genc, Mehmet. 1987. "A Study of the Feasibility of Using Eighteenth-Century Ottoman Financial Records as an Indicator of Economic Activity." In *The Ottoman Empire and the World-Economy,* edited by Huri Islamoglu-Inan, 345–73. Cambridge:Cambridge University Press.

———. 1990. "Manufacturing in the 18th Century." Paper presented at the Conference on the Ottoman Empire and the World-Economy, State University of New York, Binghamton, November 16–17.

Gernet, Jacques. 1985. *A History of China.* Cambridge: Cambridge University Press.

Gerschenkron, Alexander. 1962. *Economic Backwardness in Historical Perspective. A Book of Essays.* Cambridge: Harvard University Press, Belknap Press.

Gills, Barry K., and A. G. Frank. 1990/91. "The Cumulation of Accumulation: Theses and Research Agenda for 5000 Years of World System History." *Dialectical Anthropology* 15, no. 1 (July 1990): 19–42. Expanded version published as "5000 Years of World System History: The Cumulation of Accumulation," in *Precapitalist Core-Periphery Relations,* edited by C. Chase-Dunn and T. Hall, 67–111. Boulder: Westview Press, 1991.

———. 1992. "World System Cycles, Crises, and Hegemonial Shifts 1700 BC to 1700 AD." *Review* 15, no. 4 (Fall): 621–87.

———. 1994. "The Modern World System under Asian Hegemony. The Silver Standard World Economy 1450–1750." Newcastle: University of Newcastle Department of Politics. Unpublished manuscript.

Gleick, James. 1977. *Chaos. Making a New Science.* London and New York: Penguin Books.

Glover, Ian C. 1990. *Early Trade between India and South-East Asia. A Link in the Development of a World Trading System.* 2d rev. ed. London: University of Hull Centre for South-East Asian Studies.

———. 1991. "The Southern Silk Road: Archaeological Evidence for Early Trade between India and Southeast Asia." UNESCO Silk Roads Maritime Route Seminar, Bangkok.

Goldstein, Joshua S. 1988. *Long Cycles. Prosperity and War in the Modern Age.* New Haven: Yale University Press.

Goldstone, Jack A. 1991a. *Revolutions and Rebellions in the Early Modern World.* Berkeley and Los Angeles: University of California Press.

———. 1991b. "The Cause of Long-Waves in Early Modern Economic History." In *Research in Economic History,* edited by Joel Mokyr, Supplement 6. Greenwich, Conn.: JAI Press.

———. 1996. "Gender, Work, and Culture: Why the Industrial Revolution Came Early to England But Late to China." *Sociological Perspectives* 39, 1: 1–21.

Goody, Jack. 1996. *The East in the West.* Cambridge: Cambridge University Press.

Grant, Jonathan. 1996. "Rethinking the Ottoman 'Decline': Military Technology Diffusion in the Ottoman Empire 15th–18th Centuries." Paper presented at the World History Association meeting in Pomona, Calif., June 20–22.

Grover, B. R. 1994. "An Integrated Pattern of Commercial Life in Rural Society of North India during the Seventeenth and Eighteenth Centuries." In *Money and the Market in India 1100–1700,* edited by Sanjay Subrahmanyam. Delhi: Oxford University Press.

Habib, Irfan. 1963a. *The Agrarian System of Mughal India.* Bombay: Asia Publishing House.

———. 1963b. "The Agrarian Causes of the Fall of the Mughal Empire." *Enquiry* no. 1: 81–98; no. 2: 68–77.

———. 1969. "Potentialities of Capitalistic Development in the Economy of Mughal India." *Journal of Economic History* 29, no. 1 (March): 13–31.

———. 1980. "The Technology and Economy of Mughal India." *The Indian Economic and Social History Review* 17, no. 1 (January–March): 1–34.

———. 1987. "A System of Tri-metalism in the Age of the 'Price Revolution': Effects of the Silver Influx on the Mughal Monetary System." In *The Imperial Monetary System of Mughal India,* edited by J. F. Richards. Delhi: Oxford University Press.

————. 1990. "The Merchant Communities in Pre-Colonial India." In *The Rise of the Merchant Empires. Long-Distance Trade in the Early Modern World, 1350–1750*, edited by James D. Tracy, 371–99. Cambridge: Cambridge University Press.

Hagendorn, Jan, and Marion Johnson. 1986. *The Shell Money of the Slave Trade*. Cambridge: Cambridge University Press.

Hall, John A. 1985. *Powers and Liberties: The Causes and Consequences of the Rise of the West*. London and Oxford: Penguin with Basil Blackwell.

————. 1995. "A Theory of the Rise of the West." *Metu Studies in Development*, 22, no. 3: 231–58.

Hall, John R. 1984. "World System Holism and Colonial Brazilian Agriculture: A Critical Case Analysis." *Latin American Research Review* 19, no. 2: 43–69.

————. 1991. "The Patrimonial Dynamic in Colonial Brazil." In *Brazil and the World System*, edited by Richard Grahm, 57–88. Austin: University of Texas Press.

Hall, John Whitney, ed. 1991. *The Cambridge History of Japan*. Vol. 4, *Early Modern Japan*. Cambridge: Cambridge University Press.

Hamashita, Takeshi. 1988. "The Tribute Trade System and Modern Asia." *The Toyo Bunko*, no. 46: 7–24. Tokyo: Memoirs of the Research Department of the Toyo Bunko.

————. 1994a. "The Tribute Trade System and Modern Asia." Revised and reprinted in *Japanese Industrialization and the Asian Economy*, edited by A. J. H. Latham and Heita Kawakatsu. London and New York: Routledge.

————. 1994b. "Japan and China in the 19th and 20th Centuries." Paper presented at Ithaca, Cornell University, Summer.

Hamilton, Earl J. 1934. *American Treasure and the Price Revolution in Spain*. Cambridge: Harvard University Press.

Hanley, Susan B., and Kozo Yamamura. 1977. *Economic and Demographic Change in Preindustrial Japan 1600–1868*. Princeton: Princeton University Press.

Harlow, Vincent. 1926. *A History of Barbados: 1625–1685*. London: Clarendon Press.

Harte, N. B., ed. 1971. *The Study of Economic History: Collected Inaugural Lectures 1893–1970*. London: Frank Cass.

Hartwell, R. M. 1971. *The Industrial Revolution and Economic Growth*. London: Methuen.

Hasan, Aziza. 1994. "The Silver Currency Output of the Mughal Empire and Prices in Asia During the Sixteenth and Seventeenth Centuries." In *Money and the Market in India 1100–1700*, edited by Sanjay Subrahmanyam. Delhi: Oxford University Press.

al-Hassan, Ahmand Y., and Donald R. Hill. 1986. *Islamic Technology. An Illustrated History*. Cambridge and Paris: Cambridge University Press and UNESCO.

Hess, Andrew C. 1970. "The Evolution of the Ottoman Seaborne Empire in the Age of the Oceanic Discoveries, 1453–1525." *American Historical Review* 75, no. 7 (April): 1892–1919.

Higgins, Benjamin. 1991. *The Frontier as an Element in National and Regional*

Development. Research Report No. 10. Moncton, Canada: Université de Moncton Institute Canadien de Récherche sur le Développement Regional.

Hill, Christopher. 1967. *Reformation to Industrial Revolution. British Economy and Society 1530/1780*. London: Weidenfeld & Nicholson.

Hilton, R. H., ed. 1976. *The Transition from Feudalism to Capitalism*. London: New Left Books.

Himmelfarb, Gertrude. 1987. *The New History and the Old*. Cambridge: Harvard University Press.

Ho Chuimei. 1994. "The Ceramic Trade in Asia, 1602–82." In *Japanese Industrialization and the Asian Economy,* edited by A. J. H. Latham and Heita Kawakatsu. London and New York: Routledge.

Ho Ping-ti. 1959. *Studies on the Population of China, 1368–1953*. Cambridge: Harvard University Press.

Hobsbawm, Eric I. 1954. "The Crisis of the Seventeenth Century." *Past and Present,* nos. 5, 6.

———. 1960. "The Seventeenth Century in the Development of Capitalism." *Science and Society* 24, no. 2.

Hodgson, Marshall G. S. 1954. "Hemispheric Interregional History as an Approach to World History." UNESCO *Journal of World History/Cahiers d'Histoire Mondiale* 1, no. 3: 715–23.

———. 1958. "The Unity of Later Islamic History." UNESCO *Journal of World History/Cahiers d'Histoire Mondiale* 5, no. 4: 879–914.

———. 1974. *The Venture of Islam*. 3 vols. Chicago: University of Chicago Press.

———. 1993. *Rethinking World History*. Edited by Edmund Burke III. Cambridge: Cambridge University Press.

Holt, P. M., Ann K. S. Lambton, and Bernard Lewis, eds. 1970. *The Cambridge History of Islam*. Cambridge: Cambridge University Press.

Holtfrerich, Carl-Ludwig, ed. 1989. *Interaction in the World Economy. Perspectives from International Economic History*. London: Harvester.

Howe, Christopher. 1996. *The Origins of Japanese Trade Supremacy. Development and Technology in Asia from 1540 to the Pacific War.* London: Hurst.

Huang, C. C., ed. 1980. *The Development of Underdevelopment in China*. White Plains, N.Y.: M. E. Sharpe.

Huntington, Samuel. 1993. "The Clash of Civilizations?" *Foreign Affairs* 72 (Summer).

———. 1996. *The Clash of Civilizations and Remaking the World Order.* New York: Simon & Schuster.

Ibn Khaldun. 1969. *The Muqaddimah. An Introduction to History.* Translated from the Arabic by Franz Rosenthal, edited and abridged by N. J. Dawood. Princeton: Princeton University Press, Bollingen Series.

Ikeda, Satoshi. 1996. "The History of the Capitalist World-System vs. the History of East-Southeast Asia." *Review* 19, no. 1 (Winter): 49–78.

Inalcik, Halil. 1994. "Part I. The Ottoman State: Economy and Society, 1300–1600." In *An Economic and Social History of the Ottoman Empire 1300–1914,* edited by Halil Inalcik with Donald Quataert, 9–410. Cambridge: Cambridge University Press.

Inalcik, Halil, with Donald Quataert, eds. 1994. *An Economic and Social History of the Ottoman Empire 1300–1914*. Cambridge: Cambridge University Press.

Inkster, Ian. 1991. *Science and Technology in History. An Approach to Industrial Development*. London: Macmillan Press.

Islamoglu-Inan, Huri, ed. 1987. *The Ottoman Empire and the World-Economy*. Cambridge: Cambridge University Press.

Issawi, Charles, ed. 1966. *The Economic History of the Middle East 1800–1914. A Book of Readings*. Chicago: University of Chicago Press.

Jackson, Peter, and Laurence Lockhart, eds. 1986. *The Timurid and Safavid Periods*. Vol. 6 of *The Cambridge History of Iran*. Cambridge: Cambridge University Press.

Jones, E. L. 1981. *The European Miracle: Environments, Economies and Geopolitics in the History of Europe and Asia*. Cambridge: Cambridge University Press.

———. 1988. *Growth Recurring. Economic Change in World History*. Oxford: Clarendon Press.

Jones, Eric, Lionel Frost, and Colin White. 1993. *Coming Full Circle. An Economic History of the Pacific Rim*. Boulder: Westview Press.

Kaplan, Robert. 1994. "The Coming Anarchy." *The Atlantic Monthly*, February.

———. 1996. *The Ends of the Earth*. New York: Random House.

Keohene, R. O. 1984. *After Hegemony: Cooperation and Discord in the World Political Economy*. Princeton: Princeton University Press.

Kindleberger, Charles. 1989. *Spenders and Hoarders*. Singapore: ASEAN Economic Research Unit, Institute of Southeast Asian Studies.

Klein, Peter W. 1989. "The China Seas and the World Economy between the Sixteenth and Nineteenth Centuries: The Changing Structures of World Trade." In *Interaction in the World Economy. Perspectives from International Economic History*, edited by Carl-Ludwig Holtfrerich, 61–89. London: Harvester.

Kobata, A. 1965. "The Production and Uses of Gold and Silver in Sixteenth- and Seventeenth-Century Japan." *Economic History Review*: 245–66.

Kollman, Wolfgang. 1965. *Bevölkerung und Raum in Neuerer and Neuester Zeit* (Population and Space in Recent and Contemporary Time). Würzburg.

Krasner, S., ed. 1983. *International Regimes*. Ithaca: Cornell University Press.

Kuhn, Thomas S. 1969. "Comment." *Comparative Studies in Society and History* 11: 426–30.

———. 1970. *The Structure of Scientific Revolution*. 2d ed. Chicago: University of Chicago Press.

Kuppuram, G., and K. Kumudamani. 1990. *History of Science and Technology in India*. Delhi: Sundeep Prakashan.

Kuznets, Simon. 1930. *Secular Movements in Production and Prices*. New York: Houghton & Mifflin.

Lach, Donald F., and Edwin J. van Kley. 1965– . *Asia in the Making of Europe*. Chicago: University of Chicago Press.

Landes, David S. 1969. *The Unbound Prometheus. Technological Change and Industrial Development in Western Europe from 1750 to the Present*. Cambridge: Cambridge University Press.

Langer, William K. 1985. "Population Growth and Increasing Means of Subsistence." In *Readings on Population,* edited by David M. Herr, 2–15. Englewood Cliffs, N.J.: Prentice Hall.

Lattimore, Owen. 1962a. *Inner Asian Frontiers of China.* Boston: Beacon Press.

———. 1962b. *Studies in Frontier History: Collected Papers 1928–1958.* Oxford: Oxford University Press.

Lee, Ronald Demos. 1986. "Malthus and Boserup: A Dynamic Synthesis." In *The State of Population Theory. Forward from Malthus,* edited by David Coleman and Roger Schofield. Oxford and New York: Basil Blackwell.

Leibnitz. [1859–75] 1969. Collected Works, vol. 5. Reprint, Hildesheim, N.Y.: G. Olms.

Lenski, Gerhard, and Jean Lenski. 1982. *Human Societies.* 4th ed. New York: McGraw-Hill.

Lerner, Daniel. 1958. *The Passing of Traditional Society.* Glencoe, Ill.: The Free Press.

Lewis, Martin, W., and Karen W. Wigen. 1997. *The Myth of Continents.* Berkeley: University of California Press.

Lieberman, Victor. 1995. "An Age of Commerce in Southeast Asia? Problems of Regional Coherence—A Review Article." *Journal of Asian Studies* 54, no. 3 (August): 796–807.

Lin Man-houng. 1990. "From Sweet Potato to Silver." In *The European Discovery of the World and Its Economic Effects on Pre-Industrial Society, 1500–1800,* edited by Hans Pohl, 304–20. Papers of the Tenth International Economic History Congress. Stuttgart: Franz Steiner Verlag.

Lippit, Victor. 1980. "The Development of Underdevelopment in China." In *The Development of Underdevelopment in China,* edited by C. C. Huang, 1–78, 125–35. White Plains, N.Y.: M. E. Sharpe.

———. 1987. *The Economic Development of China.* Armonk, N.Y.: M. E. Sharpe.

Lis, Catharine, and Hugo Soly. 1997. "Different Paths of Development: Capitalism in Northern and Southern Netherlands during the Late Middle Ages and Early Modern Period." *Review* 20, no. 2 (Spring): 211–42.

Livi-Bacci, Massimo. 1992. *A Concise History of World Population.* Cambridge, Mass., and Oxford: Blackwell.

Lourido, Rui D'Avila. 1996a. "European Trade between Macao and Siam, from its Beginnings to 1663." Florence: European University Institute. Unpublished manuscript.

———. 1996b. *The Impact of the Silk Trade: Macao–Manila, from the Beginning to 1640.* Paris: UNESCO.

Ludden, David. 1990. "Agrarian Commercialism in Eighteenth Century South India." In *Merchants, Markets and the State in Early Modern India,* edited by Sanjay Subrahmanyam, 213–41. Delhi: Oxford University Press.

Ma, Laurence. 1971. "Commercial Development and Urban Change in Sung China." Ann Arbor: University of Michigan Department of Geography. Unpublished manuscript.

Mackensen, Rainer, and Heinze Wewer, eds. 1973. *Dynamik der Bevölkerungsentwicklung* (Dynamic of Population Development). München: Hanser Verlag.

MacLeod, Roy, and Deepak Kumar, eds. 1995. *Technology and the Raj. Western Technology and Technical Transfers to India, 1700–1947.* New Delhi: Sage.

Maddison, Angus. 1983. "A Comparison of Levels of GDP Per Capita in Developed and Developing Countries, 1700–1980." *Journal of Economic History* 43, no. 1 (March): 27–41.

———. 1991. *Dynamic Forces in Capitalist Development. Long-run Comparative View.* Oxford: Oxford University Press.

———. 1993. "Explaining the Economic Performance of Nations 1820–1989." Australian National University Working Papers in Economic History No. 174.

Mann, Michael. 1986. *A History of Power from the Beginning to A.D. 1760.* Vol. 1 of *The Sources of Social Power.* Cambridge: Cambridge University Press.

———. 1993. *The Rise of Classes and Nation-States, 1760–1914.* Vol. 2 of *The Sources of Social Power.* Cambridge: Cambridge University Press.

Manz, Beatrice Forbes, ed. 1995. *Studies on Chinese and Islamic Inner Asia.* Aldershot, U.K.: Variorum.

Marks, Robert B. 1996. "Commercialization Without Capitalism. Processes of Environmental Change in South China, 1550–1850." *Environmental History* 1, no. 1 (January): 56–82.

———. 1997a. *Tigers, Rice, Silk and Silt. Environment and Economy in Late Imperial South China.* New York: Cambridge University Press. Cited from manuscript.

———. 1997b. " 'It Never Used to Snow': Climatic Variability and Harvest Yields in Late Imperial South China, 1650–1850." In *Sediments of Time: Environment and Society in China,* edited by Mark Elvin and Liu Ts'ui-jung. New York: Cambridge University Press.

Marks, Robert B., and Chen Chunsheng 1995. "Price Inflation and its Social, Economic and Climatic Context in Guangdong Province, 1707–1800." *T'oung Pao,* 81: 109–52.

Marshall, P. J. 1987. "Private British Trade in the Indian Ocean before 1800." In *India and the Indian Ocean 1500–1800,* edited by Ashin Das Gupta and M. N. Pearson. Calcutta: Oxford University Press.

Masters, Bruce. 1988. *The Origins of Western Economic Dominance in the Middle East. Mercantilism and the Islamic Economy in Aleppo, 1600–1750.* New York: New York University Press.

Marx, Karl, and Friedrich Engels. 1848. *The Communist Manifesto.*

Mauro, F. 1961. "Towards an 'Intercontinental Model': European Overseas Expansion between 1500 and 1800." *The Economic History Review* (Second series) 14, no. 1: 1–17.

McClelland, David. 1961. *The Achieving Society.* Princeton: Van Nostrand.

McGowan, Bruce. 1994. "Part III. The Age of the Ayans 1699–1812." In *An Economic and Social History of the Ottoman Empire 1300–1914,* edited by Halil Inalcik with Donald Quataert, 637–758. Cambridge: Cambridge University Press.

McNeill, William. 1963. *The Rise of the West: A History of the Human Community.* Chicago: University of Chicago Press.

———. 1964. *Europe's Steppe Frontier, 1500–1800.* Chicago: University of Chicago Press.

———. 1977. *Plagues and Peoples.* New York: Doubleday, Anchor Press.

————. 1983. *The Pursuit of Power: Technology, Armed Force and Society since* AD *1000*. Oxford: Blackwell.

————. 1989. *The Age of Gunpowder Empires 1450–1800*. Washington, D.C.: American Historical Association.

————. 1990. "*The Rise of the West* After Twenty Five Years." *Journal of World History* 1, no. 1: 1–22.

————. 1996. "Acknowledgement." In *Praemium Erasmianum*. Amsterdam: Stichting Praemium Erasmianum.

Meilink-Roelofsz, M. A. P. 1962. *Asian Trade and European Influence in the Indonesian Archipelago between 1500 and about 1630*. The Hague: Martinus Nijhoff.

Menard, Russel. 1991. "Transport Costs and Long-Range Trade, 1300–1800: Was There a European 'Transport Revolution' in the Early Modern Era?" In *Political Economy of Merchant Empires,* edited by James D. Tracy, 228–75. Cambridge: Cambridge University Press.

Merton, Robert. [1938] 1970. *Science, Technology, and Society in Seventeenth Century England*. New York: Howard Fertig.

Metu Studies in Development. 1995. "New Approaches to European History." 22, no. 3.

Metzler, Mark. 1994. "Capitalist Boom, Feudal Bust: Long Waves in Economics and Politics in Pre-Industrial Japan." *Review* 17, no. 1 (winter): 57–119.

Modelski, George. 1993. "Sung China and the Rise of the Global Economy." Seattle: University of Washington Department of Political Science. Unpublished manuscript.

Modelski, George, and William Thompson. 1988. *Sea Power in Global Politics, 1494–1993*. London: Macmillan Press.

————. 1992. "Kondratieff Waves, The Evolving Global Economy, and World Politics: The Problem of Coordination." Paper presented at the N. D. Kondratieff conference, Moscow, March 17, 1992, and at the International Studies Association meeting, Atlanta, April 1–5, 1992.

————. 1996. *Leading Sectors and World Powers: The Co-Evolution of Global Economics and Politics*. Columbia: University of South Carolina Press.

Modern Asian Studies. 1990. "A Seventeenth-Century 'General Crisis' in East Asia?" 24, no. 4.

Mokyr, Joel. 1990. *The Lever of Riches. Technological Creativity and Economic Progress*. New York: Oxford University Press.

Molougheney, Brian, and Xia Weizhong. 1989. "Silver and the Fall of the Ming: A Reassessment." *Papers on Far Eastern History* 40: 51–78.

Moreland, W. H. 1936. *A Short History of India*. London: Longmans, Green.

Moseley, K. P. 1992. "Caravel and Caravan. West Africa and the World-Economies, ca. 900–1900 A.D." *Review* 15, no. 3: 523–55.

Mukherjee, Rila. 1990/91. "The French East India Company's Trade in East Bengal from 1750 to 1753: A Look at the Chandernagore Letters to Jugdia." *Indian Historical Review* 17, nos. 1–2: 122–35.

————. 1994. "The Story of Kasimbazar: Silk Merchants and Commerce in Eighteenth-Century India." *Review* 17, no. 4: 499–554.

Mukund, Kanakalatha. 1992. "Indian Textile Industry in the 17th and 18th Centuries. Structure, Organisation, Responses." *Economic and Political Weekly*, 19 September: 2057–65.

Murphey, Rhoades. 1977. *The Outsiders. Western Experience in India and China*. Ann Arbor: University of Michigan Press.

Musson, A. E. 1972. *Science, Technology and Economic Growth in the Eighteenth Century*. London: Methuen.

Nam, Charles B., and Susan O. Gustavus. 1976. *Population. The Dynamics of Demographic Change*. Boston: Houghton Mifflin.

Nasr, S. H. 1976. *Islamic Science*. World of Islam Festival.

National Research Council Working Group on Population Growth and Economic Development. 1986. *Population Growth and Economic Development: Policy Questions*. Washington, D.C.: National Academy Press.

Naylor, R. T. 1987. *Canada in the European Age*. Vancouver: Star Books.

Needham, Joseph. 1954–. *Science and Civilization in China*. Cambridge: Cambridge University Press.

———. 1964. "Science and China's Influence on the World." In *The Legacy of China*, edited by Raymond Dawson. Oxford: Clarendon Press.

———. 1981. *Science in Traditional China. A Comparative Perspective*. Hong Kong: The Chinese University Press.

Nef, John U. 1934. "The Progress of Technology and the Growth of Large-Scale Industry in Great Britain, 1540–1640." *The Economic History Review* 5, no. 1: 3–24.

Nehru, Jawaharlal. 1960. *The Discovery of India*. Edited by Robert I. Crane. New York: Doubleday, Anchor Press.

Ng Chin-Keong. 1983. *Trade and Society. The Amoy Network on the China Coast 1683–1735*. Singapore: Singapore University Press.

North, Douglass C., and Robert Paul Thomas. 1973. *The Rise of the Western World: A New Economic History*. Cambridge: Cambridge University Press.

O'Brien, Patrick. 1982. "European Economic Development: The Contribution by the Periphery." *Economic History Review* (2nd series) 35:1–18.

———. 1990. "European Industrialization: From the Voyages of Discovery to the Industrial Revolution." In *The European Discovery of the World and Its Economic Effects on Pre-Industrial Society, 1500–1800*, edited by Hans Pohl. Papers of the Tenth International Economic History Congress. Stuttgart: Franz Steiner Verlag.

———. 1997. "Intercontinental Trade and the Development of the Third World since the Industrial Revolution." *Journal of World History* 8, no. 1 (Spring): 75–134.

Oliva, L. Jay. 1969. *Russia in the Era of Peter the Great*. Englewood Cliffs, N.J.: Prentice Hall.

Pacey, Arnold. 1990. *Technology in World Civilization*. Oxford: Basil Blackwell.

Palat, Ravi Arvind, and Immanuel Wallerstein. 1990. "Of What World System Was Pre-1500 'India' a Part?" Paper presented at the International Colloquium on Merchants, Companies and Trade, Maison des Sciences de l'Homme, Paris, 30 May–2 June, 1990. Revision to be published in *Merchants, Companies and Trade*, edited by S. Chaudhuri and M. Morineau. Forthcoming.

Pamuk, Sevket. 1994. "Money in the Ottoman Empire, 1326 to 1914." In *An Economic and Social History of the Ottoman Empire 1300–1914,* edited by Halil Inalcik with Donald Quataert, 947–80. Cambridge: Cambridge University Press.

Panikkar, K. M. 1959. *Asia and Western Dominance.* London: George Allen & Unwin.

Parker, Geoffrey. 1974. "The Emergence of Modern Finance in Europe, 1500–1730." In *The Sixteenth and Seventeenth Centuries.* Vol. 2 of *The Fontana History of Europe,* edited by Carlo M. Cipolla, 527–94. Glasgow: Collins/Fontana

———. 1991. "Europe and the Wider World, 1500–1750: The Military Balance." In *The Political Economy of Merchant Empires,* edited by James D. Tracy, 161–95. Cambridge: Cambridge University Press.

Parsons, Talcott. [1937] 1949. *The Structure of Social Action.* Glencoe, Ill.: The Free Press.

———. 1951. *The Social System.* Glencoe, Ill.: The Free Press.

Pasinetti, L. 1981. *Structural Change and Economic Growth.* Cambridge: Cambridge University Press.

Pavlov, V. I. 1964. *The Indian Capitalist Class. A Historical Study.* New Delhi: Peoples Publishing House.

Pearson, M. N. 1987. *The Portuguese in India.* Cambridge: Cambridge University Press.

———. 1989. *Before Colonialism. Theories on Asian-European Relations 1500–1750.* Delhi: Oxford University Press.

Pearson, M. N., ed. 1996. *Spices in the Indian Ocean World.* Aldershot, U.K., and Brookfield, Vt.: Variorum.

Perlin, Frank. 1983. "Proto-Industrialization and Pre-Colonial South Asia." *Past and Present,* no. 98: 30–95. Also in Perlin 1994.

———. 1987. "Money-Use in Late Pre-Colonial India and the International Trade in Currency Media." In *The Imperial Monetary System of Mughal India,* edited by J. F. Richards. Delhi: Oxford University Press.

———. 1990. "Financial Institutions and Business Practices across the Euro-Asian Interface: Comparative and Structural Considerations." In *The European Discovery of the World and Its Economic Effects on Pre-Industrial Society, 1500–1800,* edited by Hans Pohl, 257–303. Papers of the Tenth International Economic History Congress. Stuttgart: Franz Steiner Verlag.

———. 1993. *'The Invisible City'. Monetary, Administrative and Popular Infrastructure in Asia and Europe 1500–1900.* Aldershot, U.K.: Variorum.

———. 1994. *Unbroken Landscape. Commodity, Category, Sign and Identity; Their Production as Myth and Knowledge from 1500.* Aldershot, U.K.: Variorum.

Pirenne, Henri. 1992. *Mohammed and Charlemagne.* New York: Barnes and Noble.

Pires, Tomas. [1517?] 1942/44. *Suma Oriental.* London: Hakluyit Society.

Pohl, Hans, ed. 1990. *The European Discovery of the World and Its Economic Effects on Pre-Industrial Society, 1500–1800.* Papers of the Tenth International Economic History Congress. Stuttgart: Franz Steiner Verlag.

Polanyi, Karl. 1957. *The Great Transformation—The Political and Economic Origins of Our Time*. Boston: Beacon Press.

Polanyi, K., C. Arensberg, and H. W. Pearson. 1957. *Trade and Markets in the Early Empires*. Glencoe, Ill.: The Free Press.

Pomeranz, Kenneth. 1997. "A New World of Growth: Markets, Ecology, Coercion, and Industrialization in Global Perspective" Unpublished manuscript.

Porter, Tony. 1995. "Innovation in Global Finance: Impact on Hegemony and Growth since 1000 AD." *Review* 18, no. 3 (Summer): 387–430.

Prakash, Om. 1983. "The Dutch East India Company in the Trade of the Indian Ocean." In *Precious Metals in the Late Medieval and Early Modern Worlds*, edited by J. F. Richards. Durham, N.C.: Carolina Academic Press.

———. 1994. *Precious Metals and Commerce*. Aldershot, U.K.: Variorum.

———. 1995. *Asia and the Pre-modern World Economy*. Leiden: International Institute for Asian Studies.

Prigogine, Ilya. 1996. *The End of Certainty: Time, Chaos, and the New Laws of Nature*. New York: The Free Press/Simon & Schuster.

Pryor, F. L., and S. B. Maurer. 1983. "On Induced Change in Precapitalist Societies."*Journal of Development Economics* 10: 325–53.

Qaisar, Ahsan Jan. 1982. *The Indian Response to European Technology and Culture (A.D. 1498–1707)*. Delhi: Oxford University Press.

Quiason, Serafin D. 1991. "The South China Trade with Spanish Philippine Colony up to 1762." Paris and Bangkok: UNESCO Integral Study of the Silk Roads: Roads of Dialogue. Unpublished manuscript.

Rahman, Abdur, ed. 1984. *Science and Technology in Indian Culture—A Historical Perspective*. New Delhi: National Institute of Science, Technology and Development Studies.

Ramaswamy, Vijaya. 1980. "Notes on the Textile Technology in Medieval India with Special Reference to the South." *The Indian Economic and Social History Review* 17, no. 2: 227–42.

———. 1985. *Textiles and Weavers in Medieval South India*. Delhi: Oxford University Press.

Raychaudhuri, Tapan, and Irfan Habib, eds. 1982. *The Cambridge Economic History of India*. Vol. 1: *c. 1220–c.1750*. Cambridge: Cambridge University Press.

Reid, Anthony. 1990. "The Seventeenth-Century Crisis in Southeast Asia." *Modern Asian Studies* 24, no. 4: 639–59.

———. 1993. *Southeast Asia in the Age of Commerce 1450–1680*. Vol. 2: *Expansion and Crisis*. New Haven: Yale University Press.

———. 1997. "A New Phase of Commercial Expansion in Southeast Asia, 1760–1850." In *The Last Stand of Autonomous States in Southeast Asia and Korea*, edited by Anthony Reid. London: Macmillan. Cited from Manuscript.

Reid, Anthony, ed. 1983. *Slavery, Bondage and Dependency in Southeast Asia*. St. Lucia, N.Y.: University of Queensland Press.

Reilly, Kevin. 1989. *The West and the World. A History of Civilization*, 2 vols. New York: Harper & Row.

Rich, E. E., and C. H. Wilson. 1967. *The Economy of Expanding Europe in the Sixteenth and Seventeenth Cenruries*. Vol. 4 of *The Cambridge Economic History of Europe*. Cambridge: Cambridge University Press.

Richards, John F. 1983. "Outflows of Precious Metals from Early India." In *Precious Metals in the Late Medieval and Early Modern Worlds,* edited by J. F. Richards. Durham, N.C.: Carolina Academic Press.

———. 1990. "The Seventeenth-Century Crisis in South Asia." *Modern Asian Studies* 24, no. 4: 625–38.

———. 1997. "Early Modern India and World History." *Journal of World History* 8, no. 2 (fall): 197–210.

Richards, John F., ed. 1987. *The Imperial Monetary System of Mughal India.* Delhi: Oxford University Press.

———. 1993. *Southeast Asia in the Early Modern Era. Trade, Power, and Belief.* Ithaca: Cornell University Press.

Rodinson, Maxime. 1970. "Le Marchand Musulman." In *Islam and the Trade of Asia,* edited by D. S. Richards, 21–36. Oxford: Bruno Cassirer.

———. 1972. *Islam et Capitalisme.* Paris: Editions du Seuil.

Ronan, Colin A. 1986. *The Shorter Science and Civilization in China. An Abridgment of Joseph Needham's Original Text.* Vol. 3. Cambridge: Cambridge University Press.

Rosenberg, Nathan, and L. E. Bridzell, Jr. 1986. *How the West Grew Rich. The Economic Transformation of the Industrial World.* New York: Basic Books.

Rossabi, Morris. 1975. *China and Inner Asia. From 1368 to the Present Day.* London: Thames and Hudson.

———. 1990. "The 'Decline' of the Central Asian Caravan Trade." In *The Rise of the Merchant Empires. Long-Distance Trade in the Early Modern World, 1350–1750,* edited by James D.Tracy. Cambridge: Cambridge University Press. Also in *Ecology and Empire. Nomads in the Cultural Evolution of the Old World,* vol. 1, edited by Gary Seaman. Los Angeles: ETHNOGRAPHICS/USC, Center for Visual Anthropology, University of Southern California Press.

Rostow, W. W. 1962. *The Stages of Economic Growth. A Non-Communist Manifesto* Cambridge: Cambridge University Press.

———. 1975. *How It All Began: Origins of the Modern Economy.* New York: McGraw-Hill.

Rowe, William T. 1984. *Hankow: Commerce and Society in a Chinese City, 1769–1889.* Stanford: Stanford University Press.

———. 1989. *Hankow: Conflict and Community in a Chinese City, 1796–1895.* Stanford: Stanford University Press.

Roy, Aniruddha, and S. K. Bagchi. 1986. *Technology in Ancient and Medieval India.* Delhi: Sundeep Prakashan.

Rozman, Gilbert, ed. 1981. *The Modernization of China.* New York: The Free Press.

Sahillioglu, Halial. 1983. "The Role of International Monetary and Metal Movements in Ottoman Monetary History 1300–1750." In *Precious Metals in the Late Medieval and Early Modern Worlds,* edited by J. F. Richards. Durham, N.C.: Carolina Academic Press.

Said, Edward. 1978. *Orientalism.* New York: Random House.

Saliba, George. 1996. "Arab Influences on the Renaissance." Paper at the Fifth Annual Conference of the World Historical Association, Pomona, Calif., June 21.

Salvatore, Dominick, ed. 1988. *World Population Trends and Their Impact on Economic Development*. New York: Greenwood Press.

Sanderson, Stephen K. 1995. *Social Transformations: A General Theory of Historical Development*. Oxford: Blackwell.

Sanderson, Stephen K., ed. 1995. *Civilizations and World Systems. Studying World-Historical Change*. Walnut Creek, Calif.: Altamira.

Sangwan, Satpal. 1995. "The Sinking Ships: Colonial Policy and the Decline of Indian Shipping, 1735–1835." In *Technology and the Raj. Western Technology and Technical Transfers to India, 1700–1947,* edited by Roy MacLeod and Deepak Kumar. New Delhi: Sage.

Schneider, Jane. 1977. "Was There a Pre-capitalist World System?" *Peasant Studies* 6, no. 1: 30–39.

Schrieke, B. 1955. *Indonesian Sociological Studies: Selected Writings of B. Schrieke.* The Hague: van Hoewe.

Schumpeter, Joseph Alois. 1939. *Business Cycles*. New York: McGraw Hill.

Schurmann, Franz, and Orville Schell. 1967. *The China Reader.* Vol. 1: *Imperial China*. New York: Vintage.

Seider, Gerald. 1995. "Social Differentiation in Rural Regions: A Political Anthropology of Accumulation and Inequality in the African Sahel." Paper presented at the American Anthropological Association meeting, Washington, D.C., November.

Shaffer, Lynda Noreen. 1989. "The Rise of the West: From Gupta India to Renaissance Europe." New York: Columbia University East Asia Institute. Unpublished manuscript.

Shapin, Steve. 1996. *Scientific Revolution*. Chicago: University of Chicago Press.

Sideri, Sandro. 1970. *Trade and Power. Informal Colonialism in Anglo-Portuguese Relations*. Rotterdam: Rotterdam University Press.

Simmel, Georg. 1955. *Conflict and the Web of Group Affiliations*. New York: The Free Press.

———. 1980. *Essays on Interpretation in Social Science*. Translated and edited by Guy Oakes. Totowa, N.J.: Roman & Littlefield.

Singer, Charles, et al., eds. 1957. *A History of Technology*. Vols. 2 and 3. Oxford: The Clarendon Press.

Sivin, N. 1982. "Why the Scientific Revolution Did Not Take Place in China— Or Didn't It?" *Explorations in the History of Science and Technology in China. Compiled in Honour of the 80th Birthday of Dr. J. Needham*. Shanghai. Also in *Chinese Science* 5: 45–66; *Transformation and Tradition in the Sciences,* edited by Everett Mendlesohn, 531–54 (Cambridge: Cambridge University Press, 1984); and *Science in Ancient China. Researches and Reflections* (Aldershot, U.K.: Variorum, 1995).

Skocpol, Theda. 1985. "Bringing the State Back In: Strategies of Analysis in Current Research." In *Bringing the State Back In,* edited by P. Evans, D. Rueschmeyer, and T. Skocpol. Cambridge: Cambridge University Press.

Sombart, Werner. 1967. *Luxury and Capitalism*. Ann Arbor: University of Michigan Press.

———. 1969. *The Jews and Modern Capitalism*. New York: B. Franklin.

Smith, Adam [1776] 1937. *The Wealth of Nations*. New York: Random House.

Smith, Alan K. 1991. *Creating a World Economy. Merchant Capital, Colonialism, and World Trade 1400–1825*. Boulder: Westview Press.

Snooks, Graeme Donald. 1996. *The Dynamic Society. Exploring the Sources of Global Change*. London and New York: Routledge.

Snooks, Graeme Donald, ed. 1994. *Was the Industrial Revolution Necessary?* London and New York: Routledge.

Stavarianos, L. S. 1966. *The World Since 1500. A Global History*. Englewood Cliffs, N.J.: Prentice-Hall.

Stearns, Peter N. 1993. *The Industrial Revolution in World History*. Boulder: Westview Press.

Steensgaard, Niels. 1972. *Carracks, Caravans and Companies: The Structural Crisis in the European-Asian Trade in the Early 17th Century*. Copenhagen: Studentlitteratur.

———. 1987. "The Indian Ocean Network and the Emerging World-Economy (c. 1550 to 1750)." In *The Indian Ocean: Explorations in History, Commerce, and Politics*, edited by S. Chandra, 125–50. New Delhi: Sage.

———. 1990a. "Before the World Grew Small. The Quest for Patterns in Early Modern World History." In *Agrarian Society in History. Essays in Honour of Magnus Morner*, edited by Mats Lundhal and Thommy Svensson. London and New York: Routledge.

———. 1990b. "The Seventeenth-Century Crisis and the Unity of Eurasian History." *Modern Asian Studies* 24, no. 4: 683–97.

———. 1990c. "Commodities, Bullion and Services in Intercontinental Transactions Before 1750." In *The European Discovery of the World and its Economic Effects on Pre-Industrial Society, 1500–1800*, edited by Hans Pohl. Papers of the Tenth International Economic History Congress. Stuttgart: Franz Steiner Verlag.

———. 1990d. "The Growth and Composition of the Long-Distance Trade of England and the Dutch Republic before 1750." In *The Rise of the Merchant Empires. Long-Distance Trade in the Early Modern World, 1350–1750*, edited by James D. Tracy, 102–52. Cambridge: Cambridge University Press.

Stein, Burton. 1989. "Eighteenth Century India: Another View." *Studies in History* (new series) 5, no. 1: 1–26.

Stein, Burton, and Sanjay Subrahmanyam. 1996. *Institutions and Economic Change in South Asia*. Delhi: Oxford University Press.

Subrahmanyam, Sanjay. 1990. *The Political Economy of Commerce. Southern India 1500–1650*. Cambridge: Cambridge University Press.

———. 1994. "Precious Metal Flows and Prices in Western and Southern Asia, 1500–1750: Some Comparative and Conjunctural Aspects." In *Money and the Market in India 1100–1700*, edited by Sanjay Subrahmanyam. Delhi: Oxford University Press.

Subrahmanyam, Sanjay, ed. 1990. *Merchants, Markets and the State in Early Modern India*. Delhi: Oxford University Press.

———. 1994. *Money and the Market in India 1100–1700*. Delhi: Oxford University Press.

Subrahmanyam, Sanjay, and C. A. Bayly. 1990. "Portfolio Capitalists and Political Economy of Early Modern India." In *Merchants, Markets and the State in Early Modern India,* edited by Sanjay Subrahmanyam, 242–65. Delhi: Oxford University Press.

Sun Laichen. 1994a. "Burmese Tributary and Trade Relations with China Between the Late Thirteenth and Eighteenth Centuries." Ann Arbor: University of Michigan Departmentof History. Unpublished manuscript.

———. 1994b. "The 18th Century Sino-Vietnam Overland Trade and Mining Industry in Northern Vietnam." Ann Arbor: University of Michigan Department of History. Unpublished manuscript.

Sunar, Ilkay. 1987. "State and Economy in the Ottoman Empire." In *The Ottoman Empire and the World-Economy,* edited by Huri Islamoglu-Inan. Cambridge: Cambridge University Press.

Tarling, Nicolas, ed. 1992. *The Cambridge History of Southeast Asia.* Vol. 1, *From Early Times to c. 1800.* Cambridge: Cambridge University Press.

Tawney, R. H. 1926. *Religion and the Rise of Capitalism.* New York: Harcourt Brace.

Teggart, Frederick. 1939. *Rome and China: A Study of Correlations in Historical Events.* Berkeley and Los Angeles: University of California Press.

TePaske, J. J. 1983. "New World Silver, Castile, and the Philippines, 1590–1800." In *Precious Metals in the Late Medieval and Early Modern Worlds,* edited by J. F. Richards. Durham, N.C.: Carolina Academic Press.

Tibebu, Teshale. 1990. "On the Question of Feudalism, Absolutism, and the Bourgeois Revolution." *Review* 13, no. 1 (Winter): 49–152.

The Times Illustrated History of the World. 1995. Edited by Geoffrey Parker. New York: Harper Collins.

Togan, Isenbike. 1990. "Inner Asian Muslim Merchants and the Closing of the Silk Route (17th and 18th Centuries)." Paper presented at UNESCO Urumqui seminar, August.

Toynbee, Arnold. 1946. *A Study of History.* (Somervell Abridgment). Oxford: Oxford University Press.

Tracy, James D., ed. 1990. *The Rise of the Merchant Empires. Long-Distance Trade in the Early Modern World, 1350–1750.* Cambridge: Cambridge University Press.

———. 1991. *The Political Economy of Merchant Empires.* Cambridge: Cambridge University Press.

Turner, Brian. 1986. *Marx and the End of Orientalism.* London: Croom Helm.

Udovitch, Abraham L. 1970. "Commercial Techniques in Early Medieval Islamic Trade." In *Islam and the Trade of Asia,* edited by D. S. Richards, 37–62. Oxford: Bruno Cassirer.

United Nations Population Division. 1951. *Population Bulletin 1.*

———. 1953. *The Determinants and Consequences of Population Trends.* New York: United Nations.

———. 1954. *The Past and Future Population of the World and its Continents.* World Population Conference Paper No. 243. New York: United Nations.

Van der Wee, Herman, and Erik Aerts, eds. 1990. *Debates and Controversies in Economic History.* Proceedings of the Tenth International Economic History Congress. Leuven: Leuven University Press.

van Leur, J. C. 1955. *Indonesian Trade and Society: Essays in Asian Social and Economic History.* The Hague and Bandung: W. van Hoeve.

van Zanden, Jan Luiten. 1997. "Do We Need a Theory of Merchant Capitalism?" *Review* 20, no. 2 (Spring): 255–68.

Viraphol, Sarasin. 1977. *Tribute and Profit: Sino-Siamese Trade 1652–1853*. Harvard East Asian Monograph 76. Cambridge: Harvard University Press.

Voll, John I. 1994. "Islam as a Special World-System." *Journal of World History* 5, no. 2: 213–26.

von Glahn, Richard. 1996a. "Myth and Reality of China's Seventeenth Century Monetary Crisis." *The Journal of Economic History* 56, no. 2 (June): 429–54.

———. 1996b. *Fountain of Fortune: Money and Monetary Policy in China, 1000 to 1700*. Berkeley and Los Angeles: University of California Press.

Wakeman, Frederic E. 1986. "China and the Seventeenth-Century Crisis." *Late Imperial China* 7, no. 1 (June): 1–23.

Wallerstein, Immanuel. 1974. *The Modern World-System*. Vol. 1, *Capitalist Agriculture and the Origins of the European World-Economy in the Sixteenth Century*. New York: Academic Books.

———. 1980. *The Modern World-System*. Vol. 2, *Mercantilism and the Consolidation of the European World-Economy, 1600–1750*. New York: Academic Press.

———. 1989. *The Modern World-System*. Vol. 3, *The Second Era of Great Expansion of the Capitalist World-Economy 1730–1840s*. New York: Academic Press.

———. 1991. "World System versus World-Systems: A Critique." *Critique of Anthropology* 11, no. 2.

———. 1992. "The West, Capitalism, and the Modern World-System." *Review* 15, no. 4 (Fall): 561–619.

———. 1993. "World System versus World-Systems. A Critique." In *The World System:Five Hundred Years or Five Thousand?* edited by A. G. Frank and Barry K. Gills,292–96. London and New York: Routledge.

———. 1995. "Hold the Tiller Firm: On Method and the Unit of Analysis." In *Civilizations and World Systems. Studying World-Historical Change,* edited by Stephen K. Sanderson, 239–47. Walnut Creek, Calif.: Altamira.

———. 1996a. "Underdevelopment and Its Remedies." In *The Underdevelopment of Development: Essays in Honor of Andre Gunder Frank,* edited by Sing Chew and Robert Denemark, 355–64. Thousand Oaks, Calif.: Sage.

———. 1996b. *Open the Social Sciences*. Report of the Gulbenkian Commission on the Restructuring of the Social Sciences. Stanford: Stanford University Press.

———. 1997. "Merchant, Dutch, or Historical Capitalism?" *Review* 20, no. 2 (Spring):243–54.

Wang Gungwu. 1979. "Introduction: The Study of the Southeast Asian Past." In *Perceptions of the Past in Southeast Asia,* edited by Anthony Reid and David Narr. Singapore: Heinemann.

———. 1990. "Merchants without Empire: The Hokkien Sjourning Communities." In *The Rise of the Merchant Empires. Long-Distance Trade in the Early Modern World, 1350–1750,* edited by James D. Tracy, 400–422. Cambridge: Cambridge University Press.

Weber, Max. 1950. *General Economic History*. Glencoe, Ill.: The Free Press.

———. 1958. *The Protestant Ethic and the Spirit of Capitalism*. New York: Charles Scribner's Sons.

Weinerman, Eli. 1993. "The Polemics between Moscow and Central Asians on the Decline of Central Asia and Tsarist Russia's Role in the History of the Region." *The Slavonic and East European Review,* 71, no. 3 (July): 428–81.

White, Lynn, Jr. 1962. *Medieval Technology and Social Change.* New York: Oxford University Press.

Whitmore, John K. 1983. "Vietnam and the Monetary Flow of Eastern Asia, Thirteenth to Eighteenth Centuries." In *Precious Metals in the Late Medieval and Early Modern Worlds,* edited by J. F. Richards. Durham, N.C.: Carolina Academic Press.

Willcox, Walter F. 1931. *International Migrations.* Vol. 2. New York: National Bureau of Economic Research.

————. 1940. *Studies in American Demography.* Ithaca: Cornell University Press.

Wills, John E., Jr. 1993. "Maritime Asia, 1500–1800: The Interactive Emergence of European Domination." *American Historical Review* February: 83–105.

Wilkinson, David. 1987. "Central Civilization." *Comparative Civilizations Review* (Fall): 31–59.

————. 1993. "Civilizations, Cores, World Economies, and Oikumenes." In *The World System: Five Hundred Years or Five Thousand?* edited by A. G. Frank and B. K. Gills. London and New York: Routledge.

Wilkinson, Endymion Porter. 1980. *Studies in Chinese Price History.* New York and London: Garland.

Wittfogel, Karl. 1957. *Oriental Despotism: A Comparative Study of Total Power.* New Haven: Yale University Press.

Wolf, Eric. 1982. *Europe and the People Without History.* Berkeley and Los Angeles: University of California Press.

Wong, R. Bin. 1997. *China Transformed: Historical Change and the Limits of European Experience.* Ithaca: Cornell University Press.

Wrigley, E. A. 1994. "The Classical Economists, the Stationary State, and the Industrial Revolution." In *Was the Industrial Revolution Necessary?* edited by Graeme Donald Snooks, 27–42. London and New York: Routledge.

Yamamura, Kozo, and Tetsuo Kamiki. 1983. "Silver Mines and Sung Coins—A Monetary History of Medieval and Modern Japan in International Perspective." In *Precious Metals in the Late Medieval and Early Modern Worlds,* edited by J. F. Richards. Durham, N.C.: Carolina Academic Press.

Yan Chen. 1991. "The Cultural Relations Between China, the Philippines and Spanish America Through the Maritime Silk Route." Paris and Bangkok: UNESCO Integral Study of the Silk Roads: Roads of Dialogue. Unpublished manuscript.

Yang Lien-sheng. 1952. *Money and Credit in China. A Short History.* Cambridge: Harvard University Press.

Zeitlin, Irving M. 1994. *Ideology and the Development of Sociological Theory.* 5th ed. Englewood Cliffs, N.J.: Prentice Hall.

Index

Abbas I (1588–1629), Shah, 81, 83
Abbeglen, James, 18
Abu-Lughod, Janet, xxi, xxiii, 31, 228–29, 232, 341; *Before European Hegemony: The World System A.D. 1250–1350,* xix, 56–57, 264–65; "Decline of the East" preceding "Rise of the West," 57, 264; on institutions, 212–13, 218, 219; and Southeast Asia, 93; "thirteenth-century world system," xix, xxii, 56–57, 128–29, 260–61
Acapulco, trade, 91, 116, 144
Aceh, 81, 100; Indian trade, 91; Muslims to, 100; population, 97; port city, 84; shipping tonnages, 100
Adams, Robert, 190–91, 285
Aden: credit, 151; trade, 62, 78, 84
Adshead, S. A. M., 121, 232, 236, 237, 247–48
"Afrasia," 2–3
Africa, xxiv, 3, 64–74; Afrocentrism, 339; "capitalist underdevelopment," 277; carved up (1884), 33; colonial, 33, 316, 317; "Columbian exchange" and, 60; cowrie shells, 73, 136–37; da Gama voyage around (1498), xviii, 53, 57–58; East, 66, 72, 73, 84, 130; in Eurocentric histories, 3, 24; expansion, 353; expatriate merchants from, 99; gold, 67, 72, 73, 84, 127, 139, 150; Indian trade, 88, 91; Marx on, 14; "Marxism" in, 338; new maritime trade, 72; Ottomans and, 80; population (1500–1800), 71–72, 171; popula-

tion/resource ratios, 300, 309, 317; production (1750), 173; protocapitalism pre-1492, 21–22; silver, 149; slave trade, 71, 72–73, 127, 136–37, 316; Southwest, 72; trade around Cape, 56, 119, 141, 261; trade within, 72–73; urbanization of Muslim North (sixteenth-century), 12; West, 72–73, 84, 136, 137, 150, 236, 261, 263, 331. *See also* Afro-Asia; Afro-Eurasia; South Africa
Afro-Asia, 8, 16, 22, 31, 130, 324
Afrocentrism, 8, 339
Afro-Eurasia, 2–3, 8, 23, 27, 32; and Chinese tribute system, 115; "Columbian exchange," 59–61; common history throughout, 352–57; gold-silver market, 131–32; money and credit, 55–56; regions, 56, 64–70, 128–29; single global economy rooted in, 43, 52–53, 340; temporal dynamics, 228–29, 255, 260–61, 348; trade, 63, 64–71
After Imperialism (Brown), xviii
Age of Gunpowder Empires 1450–1800 (McNeill), 195
agency, vs. structure, 351–52
agriculture, 55, 60, 63, 79; Americas, 60, 70, 112; Chinese, 60, 108–12, 127, 161–62, 203, 220–22, 234, 301–2, 307; deforestation and, 55, 63, 111, 159–60; drill plow, 203; Indian, 159, 175, 203, 306; irrigation, 15, 16, 203; Japanese, 106–7, 173, 234; labor, 174, 277–78, 312, 315; Mexi-